Reading W. G. Sebald

Studies in German Literature, Linguistics, and Culture

Reading W. G. Sebald

Adventure and Disobedience

Deane Blackler

CAMDEN HOUSE

Rochester, New York

First published 2007
by Camden House

Camden House is an imprint of Boydell & Brewer Inc.
668 Mt. Hope Avenue, Rochester, NY 14620, USA
www.camden-house.com
and of Boydell & Brewer Limited
PO Box 9, Woodbridge, Suffolk IP12 3DF, UK
www.boydellandbrewer.com

ISBN-13: 978–1–57113–351–9
ISBN-10: 1–57113–351–8

Library of Congress Cataloging-in-Publication Data

Blackler, Deane, 1952–
    Reading W. G. Sebald: adventure and disobedience / Deane Blackler.
        p. cm. — (Studies in German literature, linguistics, and culture)
    Includes bibliographical references and index.
    ISBN-13: 978–1–57113–351–9 (hardcover: alk. paper)
    ISBN-10: 1–57113–351–8 (hardcover: alk. paper)
        1. Sebald, Winfried Georg, 1944–2001.   2. German prose literature —
    20th century — History and criticism.   I. Title.   II. Series.

PT2681.E18Z55 2007
833′.914—dc22

                                                                2007009395

A catalogue record for this title is available from the British Library.

This publication is printed on acid-free paper.
Printed in the United States of America.

We live in our own souls as in an unmapped region.

Edith Wharton, *The Touchstone*, 1900

Contents

Preface

THIS BOOK ARGUES THAT Sebald's unusual and idiosyncratic prose fiction, which privileges the use of language and the imagination, engages the reader in ways that encourage "disobedience," licensing the reader, as it were, to step outside the elided or effaced textual boundaries into her own empirical otherness, and to bring into what Rupert Sheldrake describes as the contiguity of morphic fields that generative and transactional connectivity that is a form of dialogism and an antidote to the essential human condition of isolation or loneliness. Plato's invention of the philosophical dialogue, growing out of the need for an interrogative other to ask the questions that Plato could explore, underpins the transactional nature of the dialogue between the reader and the text, the author and the text, which reflects this need for critical engagement, a condition brought to a kind of crisis in an age where the collapse of the old illusions and meta-narratives (in Jean-François Lyotard's estimate) has engendered a state of anxiety about our lack of future manifest in our preoccupation with the past and its consoling sense of identity, as Peter Conrad avers.

In the introduction I begin by sketching the circumstances in which I came to Sebald, mapping some of the ways in which we can be engaged by this fascinating writer, whose unusual books and idiosyncratic approach to writing caused such a stir in the popular media when they first appeared.

In chapter 1, I map the life of the man and the emerging profile of the writer as he was constructing himself in the production of his texts. I deal with some of the biographical details of Max Sebald that were made available in interviews over the comparatively short period of time between the first translation into English in 1996 and his death in 2001. A full-length biography is, at the time of this writing, still forthcoming. I also consider the emergence of the writer, both creative and academic, and the language choices he had made.

In chapter 2, I engage with the task of establishing a critical position from which to forge a set of keys with which to unlock some of the writing that has produced a seductive and intriguing reading problematic or "reception dilemma" (Hoesterey's term). Employing aspects of the palimpsest-effect of Sebald's own writing, I have argued that it can be read by a postmodern, skeptical, contestatory, and disobedient reader as an intriguing new kind of fiction that cannot be contained by the conventional notion of the novel and yet, in the tradition of prose fiction, affords that thoughtful and imaginative reader serious play.

In chapter 3, I argue that three aspects of Sebald's practice manifest in the four works of prose fiction, his use of a writerly narrator figure, the insertion of black-and-white photographs into the text, and his construction of place as poetic space confirm the fictional nature of his literary enterprise and produce a disobedient reader. In stage 1 I argue that the Sebaldian narrator is a constructed figure through which the texts are mediated and not the author himself, as in nonfiction discourses such as travel writing or memoirs or the essay. In stage 2 I argue that Sebald's use of photographs is not illustrative or evidential so much as images appropriated within a fictional context and therefore part of the deceptive exercise of beguiling the reader, and more particularly, of engaging the disobedient reader's capacity for thought and imagination. In stage 3 I argue that the construction of place in Sebald's work constructs a textual space within which the narrator's subject is able to remember, think, and imagine, and with which the reader can then engage collaboratively to produce an unbounded textual imaginary.

Finally, this book contends that Sebald's prose fiction represents a new way of writing about experience, of describing our engagement with the world, of constructing in the metaphorical language of literary discourse an imaginative and thoughtful resonance which accommodates the possibility of mystery that escapes the rational systems and institutions and conventions we construct to impose a sense of meaning on our experience of the world. Sebald's engagement with the patterns discernible in the coincidences and contiguities of one kind and another suggests that his primary position is one of wonder rather than the melancholy one he ironizes in the lighter caricature of the ubiquitous writerly narrator figure constructed in his own image. Above all, Sebald's poetics foreground the disobedient, adventurous reader in whose subjective, interrogatory, and imaginative response the creative connectedness of our being in the world takes on a moral resonance, one which valorizes reading as the educative means by which we might become more civilized, less predisposed to our natural tendency to destruction, able to resist unthinking obedience to institutional imperative.

As much as he dwells on the appalling litany of destruction and catastrophe that is the human story, Sebald considers also the beauty and diversity of the natural world and the human capacity for feeling, for sensation, for critical thought, for imagination in what we create. His prose style is highly crafted, considered with the meticulous attention of a poet and the scrupulous conscience of a man whose deep humanity is afflicted by the "luggage he carries" (Zeeman 1998), his German background and his literary task of "restitution" (Sebald 2005), which his prose fiction then situates within a broader cosmography.

A scholarly, sensitive, and private man, profoundly reflective and wittily imaginative, Sebald has left behind books that will come to be seen as offering a bridge of hope from a century scarred by persecution, folly, and a paralyzing sense of anxiety about the future into a more humane, modest, attentive way of living and being in the world reflected in the lives of the writers and painters he admired and loved, and whose traces are caught in the butterfly net woven by his own connecting or networked texts, which celebrate our common humanity, *multa membra corpus unum*, many parts of one body.

Notes Toward an Itinerary

I always try to write *pour ceux qui savent lire*.
— Max Sebald to Arthur Williams

You need that tension between documentary evidence and questioning in the reader's mind: "Can it really have been so?"

To read with vigilance is to question authority.
— Max Sebald and Maya Jaggi, *The Guardian*, London
22 September 2001

A traveller's chief aim should be to make men wiser and better, and to improve their minds by the bad as well as good example of what they deliver concerning foreign places.
— Jonathan Swift, *Gulliver's Travels*

SEBALD WROTE A BRIEF ESSAY on Vladimir Nabokov, "Dream Textures" (Sebald [1996] 2005: 146–55), which distills an understanding of the poetic rhythms of Nabokov's prose, the finest instance of which, in Sebald's assessment, is drawn from his memoir, *Speak, Memory*. In this essay Sebald observed: "Nabokov repeatedly tried, as he himself has said, to cast a little light into the darkness lying on both sides of our life, and thus to illuminate our incomprehensible existence" (147). We can reflect what Sebald admired in the Russian writer back to what we admire in Sebald's own prose.

In Sebaldian poetics the business of writing, that Proustian memorializing activity, is a means of arresting time, of slowing down to walking pace our inevitable movement toward death, to reclaim as writers and as readers, in the numinous intensity of some transcendental experience, the illusion that Kafka also described, where we "seem to stand on the threshold of the revelation of an absolute truth." It was the arduous creation in language of something beautiful that "releases the ideas that are shut inside our heads" held in the gravitational field of our subjective consciousness out into the "universe" as the art of literature that was, I believe, the matrix of Sebald's own fictional poetics, a writing enterprise whose ambition was to refocus the art of reading at the end of the ever-accelerating twentieth century, and to do so writing in the language the world had reason to "forget," his native German, the language he was to use to make us mindful.

The passage from Nabokov's *Speak, Memory* that Sebald quotes as his "finest" was originally written in Russian. I do not know whether Sebald read it in its English translation or in its German one, but I can be fairly certain that he did not read it in the Russian original. Those of us who read Sebald in translation might also, as Sebald does of Nabokov, express our admiration for his prose which balances, like Nabokov's, its montages of *kinesis* and *stasis*, that *bricolage* that memory resolves into the vivid imagery of painterliness, with its "touch of the surreal" (152), its "touch of humour" (154), and above all, its "*claritas*" (151) in the four works of prose fiction regarded as his major achievement.

Our position as readers is to disobey the coordinates of our own present reality and to pursue the adventure of reading which takes us out of our spatial and temporal moment into "another realm," one created by the writing of another. Perhaps this too is "a tiny spiritual movement which releases the ideas that are shut inside our heads" (152) into the curiously hallowed space of mind in which the writer and the reader are demarcated, the self and the other, in a dialogical space of encounter, an imagined and imaginative space which is mapped by the text itself, that *salle des pas perdus* framed by the art of carefully wrought prose, in which our historical selves take flight, set off on some *vagabondage*, an adventure which disobeys the coordinates of our predestined journey, a different itinerary.

Acknowledgments

THERE ARE MANY PEOPLE whose support, encouragement and assistance, both direct and indirect, have been intrinsic to the completion of this project. Not all of them can be named here, although their presence haunts these pages.

I thank Professor Lucy Frost (University of Tasmania) for her astute and sensitive companionship during the greater part of this journey, Professor Mark McCulloh (Davidson College, North Carolina) and Associate Professor Gail Jones (University of Western Australia) for their enthusiastic encouragement, Gordon Turner (formerly of the University of East Anglia) for threading a connection between Norwich and Hobart with his generous conversations, Jim Walker (Boydell & Brewer) for his professional advice and support, Dr. Ulrich von Buelow and Chris Korner (Deutsches Literaturarchiv Marbach) for copies of Sebald's photographs, the Wylie Agency in New York for permission to use excerpts from Sebald's texts, the collegial community of the School of English, Journalism & European Languages at the University of Tasmania, and my patient friends and family who shared in this adventure in all sorts of places, particularly Stuart, with whom I often conversed on the road and who never abandoned hope.

D. B.
Melbourne, Australia
March 2007

Introduction: A Pre-amble

> Paradigmatically postmodern writers are often operating on linguistic borderlines.
>
> — Sebald to James Atlas, 1999

> . . . an Opportunity of employing that wonderful Sagacity, of which he is Master, by filling up these vacant Spaces of Time with his own Conjectures; for which Purpose, we have taken Care to qualify him in the preceding Pages.
>
> — Henry Fielding on the reader, *Tom Jones*, 1749

Generic Coordinates

THE EVOLUTION OF European literary prose fiction out of classical and vernacular epic poetry and romances which privilege imagination has become a familiar story. Ian Watt and other scholars begin with Miguel de Cervantes's *Don Quixote* (1605, first translation into English 1612). It is the tale of a picaro who is plunged into a melancholy state by reading fiction. His cure entails setting out on a journey — accompanied by his steady companion — and engaging sober philosophical questions about the nature of reality, not least his own. Cervantes, a voracious reader, created a Menippean dialogical text full of incongruities and self-reflexive ironies, which was purportedly a factual tale written in Arabic and discovered in a Spanish marketplace. Jorge Luis Borges appropriated it in his postmodern fashion. Bakhtin reminds us that history shows that fiction lends itself to the *carnivalesque* or the ludic. In one sense at least it is intrinsically ludic. The distinctions between art and nature, artifice and the real, as well as imagination and historical fact, have become less distinct in various individual practices, even as they underpin Cervantes's own text and the history of the European novel. In our own period the rise of fiction which draws in very explicit ways on historical events or persons has caused not a little debate about the distinction between historical and fictional discourses.

After Cervantes, the novel continued to evolve, reaching a narrative apogee in the realist novels of the nineteenth century. It changed again as language was increasingly foregrounded, as one kind of fiction evolved even more into metafiction of the kind Sterne had practiced in *Tristram Shandy*, and as visual culture became a dominant medium for imaginative and reflective self-expression.

Sebald's relationship with the literary might well be described as post-modern and appropriative. Contemporary Austrian and Swiss writers attracted his critical interest, and Sebald was also interested in the technical innovations of Alexander Kluge and New German Cinema as well as the photographic hyperrrealism of the paintings of his friend Jan Peter Tripp and the European paintings he alludes to in his own books. He draws upon the classical authors he encountered during his years at the Gymnasium in Oberstdorf, the German and French writers he studied while at university in Germany, Switzerland and England, and the writers from the broader European and British traditions that he read deeply in throughout his adult life. Sebald's embrace of a variety of media that he has allowed to shape and influence the form of his texts as well as the development of his style is concomitant with his desire to give voice to something that would otherwise remain silent. It is not just an expression of a second-generation German sense of guilt about the European tragedy of the twentieth century or bafflement at the human capacity for destruction; it is also an expression of the subjectivity that is Winfried Georg Maximilian Sebald (1944–2001), the richly cultivated mind and very human voice which is articulated in texts which he described always as "prose books," just "writing" in a postmodern sense, eschewing the generic category of "novel."

Sebald's texts elicit what I term a "disobedient reader," namely, a reader who exercises his or her own imagination in a manner typical of postmodern reading that blurs the boundaries of traditional academic literary discourse and other kinds of writing, and engages historical referents and other references in imaginative and poetic ways, making creative links for him or herself. This term, the "disobedient reader," will be expanded on as the arguments in the book unfold.

Kluge's theory of montage, the "cut" which "opens up a space for the spectator to enact her or his own imagination" (Langford 2003) might illuminate how the Sebaldian reader can be likened to the spectator of Kluge's cinematic practice, both enacting their own imaginations in the spaces afforded by these kinds of texts. In this way the Sebaldian reader is active rather than passive, operating in the spaces that Sebald, like Kluge, has opened up for that imaginative and intellectual response to occur by resisting the linearity of narrative, the causality of plot, the theatrical artifice of characterization and so on, rather than being confined in a prescriptive or proscriptive role created by the directive author/auteur. His text displaces that authority in such a way that the reader, like Kluge's spectator, has an imaginative and collaborative constructing role to play, not one determined by an authoritarian *auteur* or author and shaped rigidly by the form of the text.

The notion of a disobedient reader resulted, in part, from speculation about reading the apostle Luke's account of the Annunciation story independently from the conventional interpretation mandated by the church in the broadest sense, as the historical foundation of its discourse. We are used to reading this narrative and to seeing it expressed visually so often that it seems to resist interrogation or contestation. Thus we seem to accept it as documentation of a prior historic reality, either because we accept it as a literal record of an historical event or because it has become so embedded in our cultural memory that it has acquired that status over time, not least because, if we are believers, we have made that imaginative leap of faith which itself sets reason to one side. By bringing a degree of postmodern skepticism to our reading of that portion of text, believers or not, stripping away from it the authority of the institution which has preserved it (the Church), we can read the text as literary — that is, as something constructed in human language that in poetic terms is unstable (in T. S. Eliot's poetic sense), something that resonates unexpectedly and offers up meanings in the reader's mind beyond the literal denotation of fact or event that can be proved by evidential means.

Luke claims historical veracity or authenticity for his narrative in the four-verse preface to his Gospel modeled on classical rhetoric, and proceeds to tell a poetically charged story which confronts our very notion of reality. In part this is what faith in a transcendent reality invites us to do. This embedded contestation requires the reader "to question the authenticity" of the narrative at his or her own peril: believe or die, believe and be saved, question and suffer the consequences. If a greater number of God-fearing Christians in Germany had perhaps been less obedient, less passive, or more prepared to interrogate and contest the authority of the "authorized" or "standard version" of the truth about the Jews and other "enemies of the state," then who knows what changes might have been rung? If more members of the Bomber Command, or the Allied civilian populations, had questioned the morality of the annihilating strikes against the inhabitants of Dresden and Hamburg and the authority of those who gave the orders, like the lightning strikes against London and Coventry, would lives have been saved and horrors and destruction of cities averted?

Our capacity to question, and to engage in dialogue with one another, to be "disobedient" to what we construe as authority, or the "Authorized Version" (a translation and therefore interpretation after all), our capacity to see for ourselves, is one safeguard at least against passively allowing what Sebald calls the "litany of destruction" that is human history to keep repeating itself in a way that he construes as our "genetic flaw," our predisposition to destruction. His writing is an artist's response to that horrific history: the creation of something beautiful, and something that has the potential to change us for the better if we "know how to read." Is it coincidence that we can hear in that private note of Sebald to Williams, "For those who know how to read," the echo of another Gospel, Mark's recording of Christ's saying "Let those who have ears to hear, let them hear?"

I am grateful to Jonathan Long for the suggestion that led me to reconsider Kluge's links with Sebald in my formulation of the "disobedient reader," and it led me to the Australian academic Michelle Langford who notes Fassbinder's understanding of Kluge's iconoclasm. "One of his chief aims [is] to call every kind of institution into question, particularly those of the state — if I interpret half way correctly — and if his work is not indeed even more radical, that is, designed to prove that basically Alexander Kluge is interested in the destruction of every type of institution" (2003).

I do not mean to suggest that Sebald was as radical as Fassbinder suggests Kluge is; however, we might surmise that Sebald's rejection of the institutional conventions concerning the novel draws a little on Kluge's theory and practice of montage and fantasy. Langford observes:

> Kluge's theories of the cinema are founded on the conception that mainstream narrative cinema — not only Hollywood, but also importantly, "Papa's Kino" (the post-war German cinema denounced in the *Oberhausen* manifesto) — works by a process of closing off the ability for the spectator to engage their imaginative faculties while watching a film. Kluge does not simply take for granted the notion of spectator as passive observer. For him, under the right circumstances — that is, those circumstances created by the right kind of film — the spectator can assume a much more active role during the screening of a film.
>
> Kluge aspires consciously in his various roles as filmmaker, theorist, and activist to develop new modes of constructing films that will in turn provide the spectator with new and more active ways of engaging with such films; ways of activating the spectator's own capacity to make connections between vastly disparate images. (2003)

In his 1982 essay "Between History and Natural History: On the Literary History of Total Destruction" (Bell's translation was published in 2005), Sebald refers to Nossack's "documentary tone," and writes of the "culture of contingency that breaks the mould of the culture of the novel," as well as "the mutation in mankind that makes the author an anachronistic figure," and "the wide distance between the subject and object of the narrative process" (77). These are qualities reflected in Sebald's own works in his adventurous determination to shake off the generic conventions of the novel's form to the extent that he does while continuing to assert the literary qualities of fictional poetics, not least in providing the reader with an imaginatively rich collaborative experience by extending an invitation to an unusual reading adventure in an unfamiliar textual space.

Sebald quotes Nossack who notes, "we come from a fairy tale and shall return to a fairy tale again" (78). This is one of Nossack's observations about the timeless beauty of the natural landscape that he made from the periphery of Hamburg just prior to witnessing its destruction. "Collective catastrophe marks the point where history threatens to revert to natural history." We are doomed, predisposed by our genes to a cyclical repetition

of catastrophe. Nossack "breaks out of the novel form that owes its allegiance to bourgeois concepts" (89) by focusing on our capacity for delu-
sion, as exemplified by the consoling stories we tell to deceive ourselves.
These are not the stories Sebald wants to tell, so he destabilizes the reader's
perception of the boundary between fiction and nonfiction and puts the
imaginative and intellectual responsibility on the reader by focusing on the
opportunity for asking, "Can it really have been so?" In Sebald's work, this
positioning of the reader as interrogatory is both political and moral. The
reader's imagination is not to be exercised in some bourgeois escapist fantasy, but in a profoundly disturbing way that unsettles our complacency
and our passivity.

Sebald goes on here to trace the narrative shift toward documentation
in the "West German" tradition (89) and focuses on how Kluge "resists
the temptation to integrate that is perpetuated in traditional literary forms
by presenting the preliminary collection and organization of textual and
pictorial material, both historical and fictional, straight from the author's
notebooks, less to make any claim for the work than as an example of his
literary method" (84–85). Sebald's literary enterprise is also resistant to
the artifice of integration, but not because he imitates Kluge. He appropriates Kluge's method, itself derived from Eisenstein, to his own metafictional purpose. While Eisenstein's dialectical notion of montage, "what is
juxtaposed is not phenomena but chains of associations connected with the
given phenomena for the given audience" (Leyda and Voynow, 17), Kluge,
in contrast to Eisenstein's Soviet ideology of shaping the audience's
response, wanted to liberate its imaginative potential. Thus, eliciting the
reader's own subjectivity without seeking to direct it in an authoritarian
way, he engages that reader as an individual subject so that he or she
becomes a dialogical partner in the text's construction. As such, that reader
is free to be disobedient, that is, capable of imaginative and intellectual
envol and *vagabondage* of his or her own (these are Julia Kristeva's terms),
allowing the text thereby to have a life and shape beyond the author's
thinking and imagining in the reader's collaboratively constructing mind.

Sebald explains: "If this procedure undermines the traditional idea of
a creative writer bringing order to the discrepancies in the wide field of
reality by arranging them in his own version, that does not invalidate his
subjective involvement and commitment, the point of departure for all
imaginative effort" (85). Written in 1982, these words resonate for us now
as indicative of what was to become Sebald's assertion of the individual
subject. By foregrounding the "point of departure for all imaginative
effort," Sebald creates the space where "human beings can actually think,"
rather than merely "drawing their own self-image" from literary productions which he quotes Stanislaw Lem as deploring because they deny the
reader's free will or responsibility, just as he deplores thinking machines or
laboratory rats (90). This "subjective involvement and commitment" is

what Sebald elicits in his disobedient and adventurous reader, activating the integrity of the individual, that site of creativity, knowledge and imagination in Sebald's sense of the man alone in a room writing — or reading, as a prelude to acting for the good, remembering the past in an authentic and truthful way.

Sebald makes it very clear that "Kluge reminds us all the time, and in every nuance of his complex linguistic montages, that merely maintaining a critical dialectic between past and present can lead to a learning process which is not fated in advance to come to a 'mortal conclusion'" (93). Sebald had recognized in the early 1980s that "Kluge's way of providing his documentary material with vectors through his presentation of it transfers what he quotes into the context of our own present." He cites Andrew Bowie to explain that "history is no longer the past but also the present in which the reader must act" (95). Those who remember or take on "the risk of remembering" (87) are the ethical and moral custodians of civilization; we try to preserve and learn from the fragments we keep within the orbit of our consciousness.

Sebald, like Kluge, makes the past both coeval with and the matrix of the present through the medium of the narrator's memory in his fiction. Our relationship with the past is determined by our capacity to engage with it gladly, as in our celebration of its rich cultural legacy to us, as in our admiration of the landscape and environment we have been good stewards of, but also in our capacity to be affrighted by the "traces of destruction" for which we are responsible, those things which are our burden in the present and which haunt us, leaching the life from us just as it is leached from the Sebaldian narrative spectres wandering in some field of asphodel in his fictional spaces.

Sebald's text generates a discourse with the reader so that a critical and creative space can evolve and enable a dialogical encounter between the "I" of the nameless narrators of Sebald's constructed fiction, which is and is not the "I" of the author or the ontological Sebald, and the "I" of the reading subject.

> Rather than putting these fragments together with a final "ideal meaning" in mind, Kluge places the emphasis on the role of the spectator in the production of meaning. The looser the logical connection, or wider the gap between consecutive images, the more space is left for the spectator to activate her or his own *Phantasie*. Kluge is therefore, not interested in "conquering the spectator" or directing them toward a predetermined series of associations, as was the case with Eisenstein's dialectical approach, but his theory of montage is interested in involving the spectator in the production of meaning, effectively making them "co-producers" of the film. (Langford 2003)

Readerly disobedience entails a sense of adventure. It is experienced when Sebald frees the reader from the protocols of reading in a conventional or passive way that is subject to the authority of the text. This focus on the reader's subjective and imaginative capacity to construct the text is post-modern. It is applicable to both the viewer who stands before a painting in a gallery and to the spectator in the cinema.

According to Langford, "Kluge believes that the aesthetic and polit-ical possibilities of cinema should and can be based on subjective modes of experience" (2003). Similarly, Sebald relies on the reader's creativity and ability to make connections between fragments:

> This is what Kluge calls the "film in the mind of the spectator," a capac-ity which he believes has existed for thousands of years, long before the technological invention of cinema. Kluge writes: "film takes recourse to the spontaneous workings of the imaginative faculty which has existed for tens of thousands of years." This capacity to make connections is an abil-ity to edit together images and experiences into something meaningful, to see the hidden correspondences between diverse things, a capacity that is not unlike Walter Benjamin's notion of "involuntary memory." Montage, for Kluge, which is certainly not equivalent to the editing of the filmstrip, occurs between the film and the spectator, and within the spectator's own mind. (Langford 2003)

This "film in the mind of the spectator" is the way in which a film, or a work of fiction like Sebald's, becomes imbricated within that "film in the mind" of the spectator — that is, his or her consciousness. This is the repository of photographs, images, snatches of sound and dialogue, fra-grances and tastes, the instances of ideas waiting for triggers and connec-tions, that vast collection, in short, of what we store in our mind and of which our individual consciousness is composed — the raw material of our thought and imagination. The "ability to make connections," to "edit together" to "make something meaningful," to "see the hidden corre-spondences between diverse things" that is "montage" for Kluge is in fact both Benjamin's appropriation of Proust's appropriation of Henri Bergson's idea of involuntary memory, and Sebald's means of composition which also engages the mind of his reader. It is an extraordinarily adven-turous synergy because it allows for the unexpectedness of disobedience, of the creativity of the mind's imagining. For Proust there was some pat-tern of connectedness or design behind our lives that we glimpsed from time to time, and for which we yearned all our lives. For Sebald the con-nection between his mind and that of others, mediated through the liter-ary language of his texts, is the moral connectedness whose lack leads to destruction.

In his book *Loiterature* (1999), Ross Chambers observes that "the reading relation is regularly cited as one that questions rigid distinctions of subject and object, self and other, and substitutes for them a relation of split. The text-reader relation is one of mutual dependence: discourse becomes text, that is meaningful, only by virtue of its being read, but the reading subject is the site of a self-recognition that is mediated by the otherness of a text" (273–74).

Chambers goes on to discuss the way in which reading itself "can be described as the production of (just such) a split between an *énoncé* and an *énonciation*," that is, what it "says" is not what it "means in, in context, as *énonciation*" (275). This is another space in which the reader's imagination is given subjective space to construct. Reading too is essentially a rupture, an interruption of space between the author's determination of language in the past and the future of possibilities that the reader, and a multiplicity of readers, opens up. This is the dialogism embedded in all texts, and the hope of the "radiant possibility" of *claritas* (Sebald's term) that the writer creates in the arduous labor of crafting language. In this paradigm the reader is always disobedient and adventurous, because that "split" — foregrounded in Sebald's writing — emancipates the reader from adherence to narrative protocols which solicit obedience, even in the reading of postmodern texts which challenge the reader to question diegetic playfulness not just in a prescriptive theater of mimesis but in memoir, essay, and history too, and in fiction which presents itself as non-fiction, or at least as more documentary than we are accustomed to expect.

Mapping

Since I began this project, W. G. Sebald's prose fiction has won an international readership and his celebrated work is enjoyed both in its original German and also in translation. This study evolved out of an engagement with Sebald's texts in their English translations and I make no claim to German-language scholarship. I am interested in Sebald as a writer of literary fiction, rather than specifically as a German writer. While I accept Arthur Williams's observation that "the multi-layered precision of his language is inevitably at its richest and sharpest in the original German" (*The Literary Encyclopedia, 24 April, 2002, The Literary Dictionary Company*), the experience of Sebald in translation is so rich and rewarding that it also merits consideration.

Some of the early critical writing on Sebald available in English argues that his writing is particularly reflective of German culture and Germans during the twentieth century. As many have remarked, the Holocaust is a spectral presence that haunts Sebald's books. After all, Sebald was born in the second generation of postwar Germany, retained his German passport and taught and wrote about German literature, theater, and film. Moreover, he wrote nearly all his academic and literary texts in German. In many ways, Sebald's works helped restore and demonstrated the capacity of the German language to create aesthetic beauty, in the way that Klopstock (whom Sebald quotes in *After Nature*) wanted German to be regarded as we regard Latin and Greek, capable of expressing literary verities at the core of our humanity. It is not always noted that Sebald did this work in England, where he had placed himself in voluntary exile at the age of twenty-two, more or less permanently. In the anglophone world, Susan Sontag, James Wood, Peter Craven, Anita Brookner, John Banville, and J. M. Coetzee drew critical attention to this curious writer who had seemingly sprung from nowhere. He was a middle-aged German academic from a provincial English university, whose critical work in German on Austrian and Swiss writers was unlikely to have been read by many outside the academy.

A few readers of German poetry, however, had read the long poem, *Nach der Natur* (*After Nature*), which focused on the lives of an artist, a scientist/theologian, and the poet as writer. There was also the strange prose text, *Schwindel. Gefühle* (*Vertigo*) with bizarrely comic images. The first book was published by the small press, Greno. Although Greno Verlag is relatively small, Sebald's works were published in a series known as "Die Andere Bibliothek," which was selected by Hans Magnus Enzensberger and received attention even before it moved to Eichborn Verlag in 1989. *Schwindel. Gefühle* was published by Eichborn but it was *The Emigrants* (*Die Ausgewanderten*), a collection of four loosely related stories with black-and-white photographs, which appeared in English first and launched W. G. Sebald into the wider public view. The anglophone world quickly embraced him as a very accomplished writer and *The Emigrants* appeared on reading lists in universities and schools in places as culturally diverse as South Africa, Australia, Canada, and the United States, where the various waves of European diaspora had been received.

The impressive writing in *The Emigrants* that was evidenced by the autobiographical and essayistic elements and the dualism of personal and academic voices developed out of the writing in *After Nature* and *Vertigo*. Germanists have identified specific elements in Sebald's early writing that invoke cultural discourses such as survivor-victim pathologies, Freud's theories of the uncanny and of desire, German guilt about the persecution and genocide of Jewry, the suffering of the German civilian population, the autobiographical turn in German writing, and the narrative of war in Europe in the twentieth century. Anglophone readers have responded differently to these topics. The unspeakable horror precipitated by a system of destruction perpetrated by one of the most civilized of nations reflected a pessimism that focused on a heart of darkness in mankind that Sebald draws explicitly from Joseph Conrad's 1901 novella as prophetic of mankind's continuing capacity for barbarism under the guise of civilization, as well as historically documenting colonial destructiveness and exploitation in both *The Rings of Saturn* and *Austerlitz*, along with a hope for salvation or redemption. Moving forward or away from that past is considered curiously affirming.

Readers of the English translations tend to find that they voice a profound and wide-ranging understanding of human experience rather than a specifically German expression of cultural and social anxieties and pathologies. For many, the Germanness was mediated by the elegant translations of Hulse, Bell, and Hamburger as a vector for a universal perspective. Sebald is preoccupied with human nature, literary language, memory, the past and the nature of history, trauma, the use of photographs, and a catholic allusiveness to a shared cultural archive that was cosmopolitan rather than national, human rather than German. He seems to suggest that the crimes committed throughout history are a matter of a failure to acknowledge the humanity of the other.

Writing on Sebald has reflected both the culturally specific reading of Sebald and the situation of his writing within a universal literary context. Sebald was keen to question institutional orthodoxy of various kinds and was also concerned about the beauty created by human intellect and imagination. We know that Sebald read and valued Sontag's book on photography (Sheppard 2005), while Sontag herself thought that Sebald dared to voice the unutterable in oblique, masterly, and unusual literary ways. Sontag states explicitly that she does not consider him a post-Holocaust writer (2002, 41) and contends that Sebald's writing belongs among the literary giants to be revered and remembered because his vision is generous and profound. Her claim is framed as a rhetorical question and intended, perhaps, to assemble a broad spectrum of readers. Sontag observes that "the awareness of the solitary narrator is the true protagonist of Sebald's books" (2002, 45). It is the articulated consciousness of the *promeneur solitaire* (Rousseau's solitary walker; 44) that invites a dialogical relationship with the reader. The gesture is mediated by a highly allusive and self-consciously literary use of language, and is inflected, in my view, by a more subtle form of irony and self-reflexivity than Sontag perhaps allows (41). It is one that elicits an awareness of the solitary reader.

Sebald deliberately destabilizes that reader and thwarts the nostalgic romantic and realist desires for identification with the text. There is some ordered and benign Nature that refuses the postmodern desire for, in Sontag's slightly contemptuous phrase, "undermining or undignified self-consciousness or irony" (41). By deliberately thwarting the contemporary demand for the *hic et nunc* (Williams 2002, 2006), the instant gratification of the moment in the moment, Sebald promotes the cultural value of reading as our connection with the minds of the past and the legacy on which we might build in the present for the future without recourse to sermonizing about it. There is in this something of the educator.

Sebald doesn't offer conventional consolation or solace in the form of some benign transcendental order that is beyond our view but to which we might aspire. McCulloh and others suggest that Sebald's texts are ultimately too complex, too unsettling, or too destabilizing for the reader to provide consolation, or a sense of being at home in the world. Sebald relentlessly returns our attention to the discomfort, the unsettledness, the sense of self and the world as fragmented, as well as the gap between the way things seem and the way they are. Our condition is transient, and we transform fleeting experiences into words and pictures with metaphors of construction and architecture that define space; however, the mind, as the realm of thought and imagination, remains a mysterious space where we might catch a glimpse of our real being and its creative and destructive potential. His texts also create that space.

Sebald's wily self-reflexiveness is even more audacious than Sontag asserts. Perhaps she avoids the issue in order to ensure that readers take responsibility for their reading. It is not a question of forcing readers to obey or to be obediently disobedient, since the *gravitas* of Sebald's text is ironized from time to time through a Menippean excess of melancholic lifelessness. Rather, the text emancipates readers from the tyranny of that conventional authority and makes them responsible. Sebald creates uncertainty in his texts that each reader must confront in the journey of reading. The reader becomes responsible for the trajectory of her thought and imagination as it arises out of that engagement. Reading Sebald cultivates and enriches the subject through the connection that evolves. It becomes a matter of education, of civilization and, as Williams observes, the "integrity of the individual" (2002). Sebald's poetics posit consciousness as a place where one is "at home" but also wandering, unable to map the space in which one dwells because there is no godlike perspective of its beginning and its end.

Writers including Cynthia Ozick (United States writer and critic), Randolph Stow (Australian writer, long-time resident in the UK), Brian Castro (Australian novelist), Ali Smith (in the United Kingdom), Delia Falconer (Australian novelist and critic), Michael Ondaatje (Sri Lankan-born writer who lives in Canada), Nicholas Shakespeare (British writer who divides his time between the UK and Tasmania), and J. M. Coetzee (South African Nobel-Prize-winning novelist, now an Australian citizen) have reviewed Sebald's books, expressing curiosity about and admiration for the form of his writing as well as his complex poetics. They are readers who approach Sebald with different understandings of what constitutes a literary text that can't be described, or categorized, as a novel.

Anita Brookner, celebrated London-born novelist and critic of long standing with Polish-Jewish forebears, emphasizes the German and Jewish elements in Sebald's texts, but she too underscores the poetics of fiction, Sebald's curious style, his use of photographs, his peculiar narrators, and the question of whether his writing is fact or fiction. How is one to read the books by W. G. Sebald? Writers like Brookner, who asks this question more than once, are interested in writing that invites engagement with a cosmopolitan and a metaphysical notion of civilization in a different way.

There is in these sorts of review a sense of curiosity and a desire to explore this complex textuality. How Sebaldian this kind of response to his work seems, opting for rhizomatic digression of an ever-enrichening kind rather than linear rhetorical assertion to appropriate and confine, to argue a particular position for his books within a specific discourse. It was uncannily appropriate for Sebald who, while eschewing the theoretical discourse of Gilles Deleuze (Richard Sheppard comments on the absence of specifically theoretical books in Sebald's library), nonetheless employs this idea of rhizomatic digression as a creative process, instanced by his dog's following the trail of some scent or other, and this we see echoed again in exploratory and respectful reviews such as Brookner's.

Like Thomas Hurd writing on *Othello*, though, D. J. Enright didn't get it quite right when he reviewed *The Rings of Saturn* as an unmediated travel story. Other writers such as Alain de Botton and Peter Robb also failed to consider the possibility of fiction. There is at least one famous precedent: Mandeville's story was accepted for centuries as travel writing when in fact it was shown later to be a work of the imagination. Germanists like Arthur Williams, Rüdiger Görner, Mark McCulloh, and Jonathan Long, as well as comparativists and English scholars like Lilian Furst and Anne Whitehead, however, were quick to recognize that Sebald's poetics demand attention as fiction.

Sebald creates *une salle des pas perdus* in his writing. It is a textual space, as is each of his texts. This architectural term is used to designate the vast hall in a railway station between the tracks' departures and the entrances into the stations, such as those employed by Sebald in *Austerlitz*. This is the space, too, between the signifier and the signified, to use Derrida's terms, but one might also employ Chambers's "split" between *énoncé* and *énonciation*, or Kluge's notion of the "cut" in montage in film and spectator that allows for the reader's *Phantasie*. This space is constructed for the reader's consciousness to play in by the architecture of Sebald's elegant prose. It is a space where the "ontological flicker" (McHale) of the author and the (author's hoped-for) presence of the reader are given the opportunity to encounter one another through dialogical engagement in the reader's contingency as they pass one another in this fleeting encounter that is the text, a space where the echoes of "lost footsteps" are the traces of people who have passed. In a memorializing textuality like Sebald's, this is a central notion, just as the solitary traveler "hears" and "sees" everywhere, if he has ears to hear and eyes to see, the traces of who, and what, is now no more.

Although readers do not always agree with one another about the many ways to read Sebald, and this is but one, a Sebaldian discourse emerges and the rich complexities of his texts can continue to be articulated and explored, not flattened into a simple consensus, even a *consensus fidelium*. Reading, for "those who know how to read," is an unashamedly elitist view of a particular kind of literary fiction, and, after all, what Sebald confided to at least one academic colleague he was writing to provide (Williams 2005).

Companion Voices

The premise of my exploration is that Sebald's artful use of gestures drawn variously from mimetic and modernist fiction is supplemented by archival material, intertextual excursions, and a curious deployment of photographs. These gestures and his writing in the first person challenge the reader to resist the referentiality in his writing which they actually invite and to explore the imaginative, poetic aspects of his writing that liberate the reader's sense of disobedience and adventure, the reader's thought and imagination.

Sebald plays a game with the reader that is different from the lexical and stylistic exhibitionist game-playing that Sontag deplores for privileging surface over substance (2001, 41). This is the "game-of-hide-and-seek" that he alludes to in his interview with Maya Jaggi (2001a) in which the author does his best to "hide" his presence in the text from the reader, and the reader does his or her best (as Wayne C. Booth writes, 1961) to "seek" the author's voice. One instance of this game is Italo Calvino's iterative beginnings in *If On a Winter's Night a Traveller.* Calvino's repetitious playfulness, the beginnings of ten different novels which foreground the reader's experience of reading itself, can be seen to some extent at the beginning of each of Sebald's works of fiction. Each starts with his familiar *incipit* which indexes time and place and the narrator's voice. The use of photographs, the narrative voice, and the translation of indexed place into poetic space are recurrent strategies, as will be discussed in subsequent chapters. This repetition with variation offers a new beginning, as do Calvino's, in the choices that a reader makes in the construction of "his" text but also the choices the author or narrator has made too. Calvino's fiction foregrounds the reader's collaborative responsibility in constructing the reading experience of the text very explicitly; Sebald's approach is much more subtle, and to some extent is concealed under the guise of what seems documentary — the first-person narrator who is Sebald-like and appropriates historical referents, the documentation of the photographs, and the carefully indexed places.

Sebald is unusual in sustaining an implicit and ironic link to reader-response theory, as in Hans Robert Jauss's notion of a "horizon of expectation" as well as Wolfgang Iser's concept of the "implied reader" (built on Roman Ingarden's phenomenology of the reader). Though the tenor of Sebald's relationship to theory seems somewhat ironic (as I shall discuss later) and he condemned those critical practices which he felt colonized or even violated a writer's creative work, his foregrounded engagement and apparent disengagement of the reader are so important to his poetics that they must be considered as a way of privileging the act of reading itself.

Sebald ironizes, and not without a touch of black comedy or the absurd, the idea of a shared "horizon of expectation" by emphasizing that this is in actuality the inevitability of death, and the uncertainty of the existence of or the nature of what lies beyond that very real boundary, even though he describes it as more "porous" than we might suppose. Consequently, the idea of the "implied reader" is a ghostly presence in the space of the text, that *salle des pas perdus*, just as the "dead author" is (Barthes's concept).

This position is unsatisfactory for readers seeking hermeneutic or indeed mimetic certainty, but for those who, like Sebald, admire the resistance of Kafka's enigmatic texts to interpretation and, for that matter, a mysterious Lucan gospel, this is a tantalizing poetics of fiction at a time when the reader as imaginative subject is at issue. McHale identifies foregrounding the practice of fiction as an important, even central, characteristic of postmodernism. However, in Sebald's case, it is also tied to traditionally modernist and Romantic elements related to his desire to renew a moral and even a sacralized dimension in literary fiction that in his view has been eroded by the careless commodification culture of the twentieth century less interested in the "moral backbone" of literature or the idea of "*campo santo*" — hallowedness or reverence or transcendence of any kind at all that is dependent on "slowness" (Calvino's term in *Six Memos for the Next Millennium*), such as a walking traveler or pilgrim experiences, on contemplation, on thought and imagination and the particular creativity they can give rise to.

In the conversation with James Atlas cited above, Sebald describes himself as "paradigmatically postmodern." While the pompous phrase is probably ironic in Sebald's self-reflexive use of it here, even in translation his prose is exceptionally elegant and evocative of the stylistic *longueurs* of a more gracious age. It foregrounds consciousness in a way that allows for meaningful comparisons with Shakespeare's soliloquies, especially in *Hamlet* where, as Frank Kermode and Stephen Greenblatt have recently written, the inauguration of the modern subject occurs; with the Romantic poetry, with its Christian and classical meldedness, of Friedrich Hölderlin, who is mysteriously and appropriately lyrically evoked in the Hamburger section of *The Rings of Saturn* and whose creativity ends sadly in decades of madness, and that of William Wordsworth, in whose poems such as "Michael" the sense of moral and divine presence in the natural world seems to suggest an engagement with Sebald's own attitude to nature; with Vladimir Nabokov's painterly prose, where the gloved hand of the servant lighting the lamp at Vyra or the appearance of his father's figure in the framed space of the upper window are intensely contingent moments of the remembered past with the vividness of a painting which the spectator also constructs imaginatively; and with Franz Kafka's enigmatic and resistant parables encoding the hidden subject of Kafka himself. Then too

Sebald writes in a way that explicitly engages the impression of nonfiction or a documentary account of his perceptions and experiences, but the reader comes to realize it can be as playful as Laurence Sterne or Miguel Cervantes in its protestations of authenticity or veracity, so that a different kind of authenticity emerges in the reader's imaginative engagement and collaborative constructing of subjective response that is deeply authentic in a way that no external authority can prescribe. This is, as Roland Barthes predicted, the birth of the reader that was to follow the death of the author — surely another of Sebald's embedded and illuminating writerly jokes.

The overt claims in Sebald's fiction to historicity and the invocation of a prior reality in his narrator's voices put him in curious proximity with the writer of Luke's Gospel, who claims authority on just those grounds (the "eyewitnesses" — or in a linguistic twist, the "I-witness," that Anglo-Saxon *witan*, to know, the "many who believed these things to be true") or with Homer, who also conflated historically verifiable events with remembrances and oral testimony and with flights of fancy, including the appearance of the interventionist god in a small cloud, just as Sebald's narrators' pathologized sense of reality evokes comparisons with a writer like Franz Kafka, whom he so admired and whose writing was so disconcertingly and imaginatively prophetic of the horror that lay ahead.

From the Edge of the World

My curiosity in Sebald was piqued by an article about contemporary writing by Peter Craven in an Australian newspaper where he briefly mentions *The Rings of Saturn* as a curious book and includes a photograph of the writer of whom I had never heard. He was dressed in a white, open-necked shirt, sitting on a garden seat on a luminous summer day, staring directly, albeit somewhat quizzically, at the camera lens, with pages on his lap. A bookshop in Hobart, Tasmania had placed the book under travel and not fiction where I first looked, and I was intrigued. Here possibly was a dilemma in reception that might entail interesting questions about the nature of fiction at the end of the twentieth century, the fiction that Italo Calvino had written about so hopefully in his unfinished *Six Memos for the Next Millennium* (1992) and that Jonathan Culler had wanted reasserted as the primary discourse of the literary (2000). Later, I learned that Sebald also expressed his concern that his books were difficult for publishers to categorize and risked being classified as travel books; it was not difficult to suspect that there was some wryness, even some playfulness, in this remark.

My study began while Sebald was still alive and before a critical industry around him had evolved, so I had to rely on newspaper and journal articles, interview transcripts and a few early essays. I developed a reading practice to come to terms with the complexity of what I considered rich, poetic, fictional texts. Some early reviewers, however, suggested that they were essentially nonfiction texts or that they were so historically embedded that they could be read as cultural or social essayistic documents and not examples of fiction. Other readers privileged the historicity Sebald invokes and how he reflects the vexed predicament of a German born in 1944 who gradually learns about the horrors of German twentieth-century history. I wanted to see whether one might respond differently. Admittedly, it was initially an intuitive response that offered a sense of adventure into the unknown, susceptible to charges of succumbing to a subjective impulse; however, the writing instilled in me a renewed awareness of the capacity of literary fiction at the end of the millennium to engage the reader's imagination and thoughtfulness.

This power to unsettle or destabilize is an aspect of art that goads the audience to act or change one's behavior (cf. Horace's *utile*) with beauty that can console or redeem (cf. Horace's *dulce*) In this case, it was perhaps the German language that was being redeemed along with its capacity to create something sublime and enduring. If one were to consider foundational texts of literature and literary criticism with which to compare Sebald's texts — Sontag explicitly invokes Longinus' term, the "sublime," for the imaginative transport of the reader in her acclamation of Sebald's literary accomplishment — then one must consider something that not only reflects the sociohistorical context of his writing but also its specific engagement with the art of fiction and poetics. In *Six Memos for the Next Millennium* (1992), Italo Calvino suggests, like Jonathan Culler (2000), that the art of the literary could be renewed in exciting ways at the end of the twentieth century and the beginning of the twenty-first. Was this, in the former instance, the challenge that Sebald had set himself in his fiction? For one reader, at the world's edge, it seemed that this might be so, and part of it entailed the eliciting of a reader who was being encouraged to be as disobedient and as adventurous as the author himself seemed to be in the production of his texts.

* * *

I found myself thinking about the vexed ways in which sacred Christian scriptures, those foundation stories which danced on the cusp of historicity and poetic *mythos*, were read inside and outside an institution. This might include the academy, which had had little to say about Sebald at that point, but as a starting point, part of the discourse of the Christian Church, which seemed to be some kind of marginal presence in Sebald, led me to thinking about the way in which language, and the reader, operated in this kind of hybrid textuality of god-narrative that polarized readers and readings: historically true, literally true, fundamentally true, imaginatively true, poetically true, or just fancifully spinning to shore up our need to believe in some kind of order or meaning? How were we to read Sebald?

If some were reading him from the perspective of fiction and some were reading him from the perspective of history, then this was part of a problematic reception. How were we to read his books when he was foregrounding the readerly contract itself in an interrogatory way? Why subvert the reader, unsettle or destabilize him or her so consistently? How were we to play what seemed to be a particularly serious Sebaldian game, encoding something essentially enigmatic, and invoking both that "flickering" self of the reader and the author in some kind of dialogue mediated by the language of a literary text? What did it mean to "question the authority" of what we read anyway? To read?

The reader, that curious entity in Sebald, was being licensed by the reading problematic his books presented to pursue a solitary subjective itinerary, sometimes at the narrator's side, at others heading off into little side-trips as an *excursus* into the kind of thought and imagination I suspected Sebald saw as the corollary to his own position as writer: alone in his room, unable to harm anyone, that mysterious entity the thinking and imaginative subject weaving lapidary sentences into patterns. That in itself was a displacement for a more active engagement with the world.

The rich vitality of human experience seems unavailable in these strangely etiolated texts. It is as though the reader's consciousness is invited to wander through fields of asphodel, that classical limbo in some quasi-afterlife, where death becomes a landscape and where there is no future. There are voices, cadenzas of memory reinscribing fragments of the past. This realm of living death is only occasionally lightened with sardonic irony and humor that suggest the presence of an author or the historical person behind the author. It is seductively beautiful, but perhaps only in the way that Keats's knight-at-arms is seduced in "La Belle Dame Sans Merci." As it does in Tennyson's "The Lady of Shalott," art keeps the writer and the reader apart from life, suspended in some *salle des pas perdus*, arrested in a *stasis* whose immediate corollary is death.

Sebald intimates death everywhere; the knowledge of both its imminence and immanence is both a frightful cosmic joke, our *noir* condition, and a fate no one can escape. To my mind, there is a distinct possibility that Sebald's notions of trauma, witness, home, and destruction function both on a sociohistorical level, the way many read him as speaking the consequence of being born a German in 1944 and the wider experience of so many Europeans, and others in the anglophone world, in the twentieth century, and on metaphoric and metonymic planes. Our condition as homeless in the world, transients condemned to a journey's end that we cannot know or understand, our being wired for destruction as it were, is reflected in the form of Sebald's texts, where the part — or fragment, like a photograph or some other trace of what was alive in the world — must suffice for the now absent whole. In this way Sebald's texts, like Proust's great novel, like Nabokov's memoir, like his own use of Pisanello's painting and the Verona garden where Goethe spent time, all speak as fragments of something whole that is no longer available. This is the image in the epigraph to *The Rings of Saturn*, too.

The fragmented, traumatized, and disrupted narrative of a particular historical reality can code the metaphysical discourse in his texts more authentically because we live in a condition of uncertainty; our memories and minds are filled with incomplete fragments and traces of experience and knowledge, our desire for certainty tempts us to integrate and make whole, provide closure and confirmation, and any attempt, aesthetic or otherwise, which presents the human condition as other is, in Sebald's term, inauthentic. The *kinesis* of the urgent forward movement that is our lives is interrupted by moments of *stasis* where the fragment, some distraction or some digression, some rupture or "cut" or space, makes us stop or slow down momentarily for the purpose of reflection, of contemplation and imagination. Sebald's books combine the freeze-frame of the photograph as a still point, a rupture of an enigmatic kind, with the voice-over of the narrator playing as the film in the reader's mind responding to Sebald's literary language spools.

A Digressive Itinerary: The Sebaldian Reader

> I'm also interested in the energizing or generative qualities of gaps and blanks . . .
> — Wolfgang Iser to Richard van Oort, 1998

While considering whether Luke's story of the Annunciation contains something problematic for a reader at the end of the twentieth century, I continued to reflect that it might resonate with a reading practice for W. G. Sebald's prose fiction, emboldened by Sebald's own embrace of unlikely juxtapositions. I went back to the Greek text of Luke to see if I could find the rift between the explicit claim to historical authority in the preface and the imaginative leap subsequently required of the reader to accept both the poetic and mystical details of archangel's appearance, the Annunciation, and "Mariam's" initial perturbation and ultimate acquiescence in the narrative as true in the language of the text.

The salient questions concern how the reader's position is created by Luke's text and why the reader must make an imaginative leap of his or her own. As with Luke's gospel story, I was clear in my own mind that Sebald's fiction is presented as nonfiction that segues into enigmatic fiction. As Robert Alter points out (2003), Biblical exegesis is the wellspring of literary criticism and it seemed an interesting, possibly adventurous and disobedient, way to proceed. But reading Sebald has less to do with the exegetical industry and its interpretation of texts in a manner that Alter deplores, as did Sebald in a different context, and is instead more involved with questions about the way in which the text relates to the reader, or the reader relates to the text.

My own reading in literary studies suggested that Sebald's prose texts can be considered self-consciously fictional in their foregrounding of fictionality and the ironic appropriation and transformation of historical reality, so that the reader is actually being challenged to read them as nonfiction rather than accepting them as such. This too is part of the game where Sebald puts the reader on his or her mettle as reader, actively engaged rather than passively acquiescent. They were also fictional in the sense that the non-fictional presentation of their fictionality had a very real connectedness with texts that had sought ways of saying things that could not otherwise be said, as Luke's sacralized metaphors did and as much poetry does, and for that matter as painting or even film might.

Furthermore, Sebald's secular poetics of death implicate the reader in the act of reading as well as shaping his writing. The curious metaphysical preoccupations in Sebald's texts demand interpretation, just as the *différance* of the static images in the kinetic verbal text seems to invite the reader's interrogation. Unlike Luke of course, Sebald can be playful and ironic in a way that might confuse the reader. He leavens the ur-earnestness of a moral writer, German notwithstanding, with that touch of British eccentricity that he found so endearing. Gracie Irlam in *The Emigrants* and his own quixotic sense of wit and humor in the whimsy of many of the photographs (although not all) are only two instances of the appropriation of a sense of the comic that might also be evocative of the Irish Samuel Beckett's plays, very unlike the French intellectualism of the language in which some of them were written, which combine these two antithetical elements so successfully in a theatre of the absurd. The German moral seriousness in Sebald is counterbalanced by his acquired British sense of the wryly comic.

Sebald's characterization of his writing as "paradigmatically postmodern" (Atlas 1999) does not mean that the presentation of elements of nonfiction or documentary writing is mere play. It is, in fact, morally serious writing, concerned with memory, death, the enigma of human self-destructiveness, and how we understand ourselves and our condition; however, it requires the reader to make an imaginative leap, to see that the thin silk veil Sebald draws over his camera lens, as it were, blurs the picture slightly and presents nostalgically, enhanced by his anachronistic syntax, our contingent moment, a present in which the past is always there.

There seems to be a connection between the resonance of the essentially mysterious Lucan text and Sebald's audacious funambulism that keeps the reader suspended between the twin poles of the referential and the poetic, a linguistic tension that in Sebald's metaphor of Nabokov's butterfly net made out of the language of prose and creative connectedness, both allusiveness and dialogism between reader and text, seeks to catch those fleeting epiphanies that are our lives and whose fragments continue to exist in the contemplative and imaginative space of the subjective consciousness and the aesthetic objects we make. These are the nets used, texts of all kinds finally, to catch those fleeting epiphanies of subjective consciousness, the moments of *claritas*, that shed some light on who we are or what our lives are.

Sontag's use of the term sublime proclaims a postmodern reader who does not engage in reading that is passive and consoling; rather, a reader who seeks to be discomfited, destabilized, and confronted by the very fact of her belatedness, Freud's "Nachträglichkeit," the act of reading itself: always retrospective, always a moment of rupture or arrest, a space in which the reader's imagination is solicited in Sebald to be creatively collaborative.

Sebald uses the first-person narrator, black-and-white photographs, and a reconstruction of a particular place to provide some sense of historicity. He foregrounds his use of language with some subtlety and hints at an artfulness more appropriate to fiction. Sebald's texts cannot be accommodated, or read, under the rubrics of travel writing, autobiography, sociology, or even the essay in the tradition of Montaigne, Bacon or Browne. Sebald's texts are above all literary fiction, read as literary works even if they are presented as works of nonfiction.

The early reception of Sebald's prose fiction in many early reviews responded to what a cultural critic like Ingeborg Hoesterey later calls "the reading dilemma" that it presented, in a cultural studies sense as much as literary one (Hoesterey 2001). In four prose-fiction texts, Sebald's narrators were monologists in the tradition of Hamlet's inauguration of the self as subject, perhaps influenced by Beckett's disaffected, possibly traumatized, monological characters, as evidenced by the exclusive interiority that is voiced in a text that seems syntactically and lexically anachronistic and does not pander to a narratee with a conventional narrative contract (cf. Ross Chambers's and Gérard Genette's notions of these). Of course these narrators cannot be confused or conflated with the W. G. Sebald who held a chair in European Literature at the University of East Anglia, since these are works of fiction and the narrative voices in them are not Professor Max Sebald's, or W. G. Sebald's for that matter. This is the effect of the thin silk veil, or scrim, again.

Sebald's books are self-conscious of their literary heritage. They share something with the first four verses of Luke, in that they clearly establish the paradoxical subjective authority of the eyewitness while simultaneously destabilizing the discourse. Luke's Annunciation ruptures both the form and content of the narrative with an apparition that operates in bodily form and as a spiritual entity. The historical narrative, documented and evidenced, also contains the mysterious and inexplicable rendered as metaphor: the angel Gabriel and its message from God. This is the intrusion of the fantastic into the world of a Jewish girl, Mary, and into the story that documents the foundation of the Christian faith. The disobedient postmodern reader of the Lucan text disregards the prescribed literal reading and experiences the adventure that the text engenders. Kristeva terms it *"le vagabondage de l'imagination et l'envol de la pensée"* (2000), this marvelous reading adventure which enables us to take flight and set forth disobediently from our *hic et nunc*, our *terminus ad quem* fate.

The institutional conventions of textual authority entail that the reader surrenders largely passively to the discourse in the act of reading itself, no matter what interrogation might occur later. Sebald's texts invite an interrogatory or contestatory approach even as we read. It does not seem improbable that Sebald constructed texts that emancipate the reader from the tyranny of textual authority and valorize the imagination of both the author and the reader. By foregrounding the linguistic constructedness of his texts, he calls forth the reader that Roland Barthes claimed some time ago (1979) would succeed the author, as "a wayward subjective creature."

In *Six Walks in the Fictional Woods* (1995), Umberto Eco formulates the notion of an "obedient reader" as one whom the author desires and who obeys the protocols embedded in the text in order to play (meaningfully) in the discursive space the author has created. For comparison, Luke summons the reader's belief in his claims that follow from the documented historicity of his text and his own authority as writer. Sebald does the opposite by summoning the reader's disbelief and by problematizing the protocols and undermining the authority of the text by confusing the narrator with the author and by providing illustrative images that resist reading. It is difficult to read the verbal texts as a narrative because they defy the form and function of a story. They oppose the stereotype of vacuously playful postmodern textuality (Long and Whitehead, introductory essay, 2004). This too is adventurous and disobedient. My formulation of the "disobedient reader" is therefore predicated on the author's own adventurousness, and disobedience, in allowing the reader's imagination to share in the collaborative construction of his text by abrogating his own position of authority. If the reader is audacious enough to disregard the claims to historicity that Sebald and Luke make as the primary focus of these texts, then he or she can read the texts as poetic, as fiction, as writing in the liberating postmodern sense of borderlessness.

The reader of Sebald's prose fiction can expect surprise on the reading journey because, like Benjamin's use of Klee's painting, "Angelus Novus," as the "Angel of History," the reader travels into the future of the text while facing only the past in the retrospective narration of the various narrators. Fittingly therefore in a *noir* sense, the narrators are for the most part melancholic and obsessed with death (the future) even while contemplating, willfully it might seem, the remnants of the (dead) past (cf. Richard Sheppard's brilliant formulation, Sebald's *"mors* code"). This too is some kind of writerly joke, this temporal collapse into the *stasis* of what is in effect the contingent reading space: timeless and spaceless, a metaphor with considerable resonance in a poetics of death that desires eternal life. It is a metafictional conceit of seventeenth-century metaphysical proportion in the English tradition of Browne and Donne.

If the future can be, as Sebald fears the present is, desacralized, no longer affording the dream of redemption or salvation, then the subjective consciousness, and its capacity to think, read, and write, to enter imaginatively and contemplatively into the space of a Sebaldian text, that *salle des pas perdus*, is possibly our only salvation in a fast, prosaic modern world which has little time or space for either. Obviously, Sebald's prose has no more than a tenuous link with ancient Gospel scripture; however, by means of interrogating authority a unique reader can be formulated, a reader who resists the institutional prescriptions of reading, a postmodern one who is creatively subjective. These were the kinds of readers who, sitting in their own rooms engaged in the creative act of reading, might, like his or her dialogical companion the text which is also partly the mind of the writer W. G. Sebald, refrain from harming other people. This modest hope had great appeal, it seemed, for many readers of Sebald at the end of the twentieth century.

Transatlantic Side-Trip

Wolfgang Iser observes that in modern theories of art and literature, "the work of art . . . is always viewed in relation to its interaction with its context and its recipient. Hence the human subject, and the various human faculties upon which art begins to work, must always be taken into consideration. The work of art is never independent of these faculties, which it activates and mobilises into a possible reformulation of our knowledge" (2006, 9). While making the argument for a theory of the interpretation of texts that is applicable across the humanities, Iser observes that after the nineteenth century "theory provided an ever-expanding exhibition of art's multifariousness" and "became a means of preventing and unraveling the confusion created by impressionistic criticism" (3). By drawing on Lessing's distinction between the temporal verbal and the spatial pictorial arts, Iser shows that the verbal arts are privileged because they "spurred the imagination" and that theories "serve as tools for charting the human imagination, which is after all the last resort that human beings have for sustaining themselves" (9). Sebald too privileges the human capacity of imagination.

Despite the difficulty and, in some real sense, the undesirability of translating Sebald's complex and idiosyncratic practice into theory, it is possible to theorize, building on the earlier groundwork, the adventurous and disobedient reader with the aid of Iser's reception theory and in particular his essay on Dewey's *Art as Experience*. Iser focuses on the effect of literature on the reader. His major works include readings of Shakespeare and Samuel Beckett, both important to Sebald, as discussed earlier.

Iser was strongly influenced by his teacher, the philosopher Hans-Georg Gadamer, and his colleague Roman Ingarden. Iser wrote *The Implied Reader* (1972) and *The Act of Reading: A Theory of Aesthetic Response* (1976) not long after arriving at the University of Constance, texts that are considered Iser's most important contributions to the development of aesthetic response theory. This last asserts that the dialogical interaction between the reader and the text is what creates meaning, which in turn consists of the aesthetic effect that the text has on the reader. This is also the effect Sontag's use of the term sublime registers.

This dialogical space refers to the "implied reader" that privileges the imaginative capacity of the reader to construct meaning. This ability reflects the adventure and disobedience inherent in the role of the reader, which can travel beyond the textual boundary and resist the authority of the text by recognizing its otherness.

In *The Fictive and the Imaginary* (1993), Iser argues that the subject is constructed imaginatively because it is not ontologically available to the mind. Fiction can play an important role in that construction process. Iser remarked in an interview with Richard van Oort in 1998 that "Bacon once said that fictions provide a 'shadow of satisfaction to the mind of man in those points wherein the nature of things doth deny it.'" Iser goes on to cite the edict uttered by Beckett's Malone, "live or invent." He considers the conundrum as a question where "either we live — but then we don't know what it is to live — or we want to know what it is to live." In the same interview, Iser explains that

> there is a continual interaction between the conscious element which is prevalent in fiction and the imaginary potential which that conscious element stimulates in order to effect something . . . literature . . . assembles items which can be identified from the world in which we find ourselves, and it combines them in such a way that they point to something beyond this familiarity. Literature is structured in such a way that something beyond our ordinary reach is charted and thus incorporated into our lives. (1998)

Iser insists that the historically contextualized reader responses concern "how a piece of literature impacts on its implied readers and elicits a response" (57). He adds that "a theory of aesthetic response has its roots in the text; an aesthetics of reception arises from a history of readers' judgments" (57). It is important to note how Iser privileges the foregrounded text over the *consensus fidelium* of the interpretive community and emphasizes the dialogical connection between the reader and the text. Similarly,

Sebald's poetics both foreground and problematize this connection in all his fictional works, just as the possibility of transcending our own subjectivity is gestured at in a note of hope or salvation.

In a remark that has particular resonance for Sebald, Iser asserts that "we are sure that we are born and that we shall die, but we have neither experience nor knowledge of either of them. Frank Kermode has once cited the Greek physician Alkmaeon who earned Aristotle's approval by stating that human beings must die because they cannot bring beginning and end together."

Iser continues to explain that "in this mutual mirroring of the mutually exclusive, a world beyond the world in which we live is created, a possible world emerges" (van Oort 1998). For Iser, the essential duality of fiction generates possible worlds and the reader slips into their multiplicity of possibilities. Here, Iser does not refer to the implied reader, but rather the real reader who produces meaning through the process of reading. I argue that the particular reader elicited by Sebald's texts is uniquely endowed with interrogatory and contestatory abilities because of his or her position in the ruptured spaces of his text, the possibility of an imagined future becoming thus the reader's domain.

Iser asserts that when the author's intention was replaced by "the impact that a piece of literature has on its intended recipient" as an index of meaning, the "focus switched from what a text means to what it does" (2006, 60). Since Sebald deliberately attempts to unsettle, disquiet, or even to trick the reader, he denies or undermines the idea of the author's intent as the vehicle of meaning and thus invites concurrence with Iser's theoretical formulation of the reader.

In an essay on Roman Ingarden, Iser remarks that "the linguistic signs themselves do not invoke the fictional nature of literature, but shared conventions do. Among the most obvious and most durable of such conventions are literary genres, which have provided a wide variety of contractual terms between author and reader. Even such recent inventions as the non-fiction novel reveal the same contractual function, since they must invoke the convention before renouncing it in order to highlight the fact that the text is not discourse but 'staged discourse' " (18–19).

We might be tempted to collapse Sebald's books into the category of "non-fiction novel" except that "staged discourse" is inappropriate here. Sebald's own desire for authenticity results in a poetics that is closer to Kluge's idea of refusing the artifice of synthesis and encouraging the spectator, or the reader, to perform that part of the reading process on his or her own terms, as the imaginative and creative collaborator or dialogical partner.

Sebald creates a certain belatedness in his texts by using a narrative *incipit*. There he typically invests the apparent autobiographical first person with such detailed apparent authenticity (much like Kafka's careful seeming-verimilitude) that the reader is quickly deluded into concluding that the author is speaking without the mediation of a fictional construct at all. Iser asserts that "reception theory focuses primarily on two points of intersection: the interface between text and context, and that between text and reader" (60). Iser's second dyad, the interface between text and reader, receives less attention in the writing on Sebald to date. However, some recent writing such as the essays in Long and Whitehead's book (2004), Whitehead's *Trauma Fiction* (2004), and articles by Summers-Bremner (2005), Sheppard (2005), McCulloh (2003) and Williams (2000) do consider Sebald's artful and ironic literary gamesmanship. Time will tell as to how strong this strand in Sebaldian discourse becomes.

This study focuses on how three dominant features in Sebald's poetics impact on the reader and elicit a willingness to disobey certain conventions as well as embrace the contemplative and imaginative adventure this affords. Sebald's position as a writer mirrors the disobedient reader's and displays a similar sense of adventure for traveling into the unknown with hope for redemption and for embracing the unexpected and the unknown.

Iser uses Laurence Sterne's subversion of John Locke's system of empiricism and his "association of ideas" in the subject as the basis of human knowledge in *Tristram Shandy* to show that human knowledge is essentially arbitrary, as Sebald also suggests through the single-voicedness of his texts. According to Iser, literature privileges the reader as the subject, who cannot be contained, who is by nature therefore disobedient. Sebald's texts engage the reader's capacity for intellectual and imaginative disobedience even more particularly than Tristram Shandy's enclosed world.

Iser quotes Virginia Woolf's account of how Jane Austen "stimulates us to supply what is not there" (64). This summoning of the reader's mind, thought, and imagination, is similar to what painters term "lost and found edges" (I thank Pamela Turner for pointing this out to me) so that the viewer supplies what is missing in the painting in order to complete what is only suggested by the juxtaposition of tone or color. Unlike in Austen's prose or in conventional, representational paintings, the "space" between the reader and Sebald's text is much greater, both writers and artists of such works trusting nevertheless to their audience's imaginative capacity.

In contrast to Iser's account of *Tristram Shandy*, there is no fictitious reader in Sebald's works. The reader in Sebald's texts is unmistakably real, even though she occupies a space that Sebald creates by emancipating her from the tyrannical expectations of convention, just as he or she is emancipated from the tyranny of contingency. Iser's notion of "the productive matrix" helps to explain how the "same literary text can mean different things to different people at different times" (68), a notion of a postmodern reader who is unstable and unpredictable, full of imaginative surprises, in short, adventurous and disobedient. Furthermore, it is the veritable fulcrum in reception theory of the dialogical encounter between the writer's production of the text and the reader's reception of it.

Iser's discussion of John Dewey's *Art as Experience* emphasizes Dewey's notion that the work of art is not merely the work itself but instead includes the experience of the work by the viewer or reader. "On the one hand the work of art triggers an aesthetic experience in the perceiver, and on the other this very experience allows us to grasp what the work consists of — namely, a range of diversified experiences" (150). Sebald ironizes precisely this aesthetic response in *Vertigo*. Using T. S. Eliot's montage of allusions and intertextual fragments in *The Waste Land*, Iser demonstrates how Dewey's notion of an aesthetic experience works in this text. The reader must discern relationships through the imaginative response to the patterns it creates. Sebald also offers the reader the space and the contemplative silence shaped by language to construct her own aesthetic experience. Sebald differs from Eliot in the control that he maintains in the pattern of love in "The Fire Sermon" that Iser cites. Sebald loosens his patterns so that they can proceed in different directions, according to the reader's own sense of adventure. Here, Sebald's example is better understood using Lévi-Strauss's notion of bricolage, which is less determined and more random in its appropriativeness than the more authoritarian, modernist idea of montage, not quite like Kluge's notion which emphasizes the "cut" or the space between the sequences. Iser writes that Eliot "orchestrates" the reader's reception as an interventionist; Sebald, instead, refrains from directing the the reader. His is a bolder, emancipatory poetics, less hieratic and authoritarian than those of his Modernist predecessor.

The Road Ahead

Since his untimely death from a heart attack which caused a car crash in December 2001, Sebald's profile has grown considerably in the English-speaking world. Mark McCulloh wrote the first full-length monograph in English, *Understanding W. G. Sebald* (2003). Later that year, the papers presented at the Institute of Germanic Studies in London on the occasion of the "W. G. Sebald Memorial Day" in London in January 2003 were published in a volume edited by Rüdiger Görner (2003). The first collections of critical essays on Sebald's writing in English are *W. G. Sebald — A Critical Companion*, which was edited by J. J. Long and Anne Whitehead (2004) and *Reading W. G. Sebald: History, Memory, Trauma*, edited by Scott Denham and Mark R. McCulloh (2006). Curiously, as previously mentioned, although Sebald lived and worked as an academic in England for more than thirty years, he wrote his major works in German. His friend and colleague at the University of East Anglia, Gordon Turner, observed that in spite of Sebald's excellent command of English, he was exceedingly humble, reticent to write in English owing to his own exacting linguistic standards (Turner, private conversation, North Carolina 2003). Still, Sebald never considered his German untranslatable. Anthea Bell attests (2003, 13) that he relished the task of translation. Indeed, he established the British Centre for Literary Translation in 1989 in order to ensure that non-English literature reaches a wider audience now that English dominates global commerce. Sebald's critical and academic work mostly concerns writers from Austria and Switzerland, whose works are not widely read because of their language. A sign of literary language being of profound importance for Sebald is evident in his particularly close collaboration with the translators of his books, Michael Hulse, Anthea Bell, and Michael Hamburger.

It is especially interesting that Sebald's writing attracted so much interest at a time when literary discourse appeared to have been both appropriated and marginalized within cultural studies. This is the spirit in which both Calvino and Culler wrote about this, as discussed earlier, and theirs are by no means lone voices. In 1836 Wilhelm von Humboldt wrote that "language . . . is perpetually and at every moment something transitory . . . Language itself is not a work (*ergon*), but an activity" (Cupitt 1998, 110). This idea is germane to Sebald's self-reflexive enterprise. Not only does Sebald seem to express the fear that the unique tradition of knowledge in the humanities is disappearing — something that was certainly informed by his experience teaching — but he also embeds many arcane references to challenge his readers, often serio-comically, to perform some research. It is part of Sebald's transgressive nature that is not didactic, but nonetheless didactic in tenor. Similarly, he embeds theoretical jokes such as his inclusion of photographs that beg the question of realism. It also follows that his referential fiction and stylized prose prompt the reader to consider whether that art form is endangered at the end of the second millennium. If we were to apply Jonathan Culler's hope that the literary will be revivified in literature itself, and not just in the other discourses which have appropriated it (although Culler does not refer to Sebald), Sebald's practice of fiction does indeed appear "to reground the literary in literature" (2000, 290). Sebald's writing might also be considered part of an act of redemption: of the German language, of literary values, of the imagination, of the human in its best creative sense, of the capacity for moral behavior, of our relation with the natural world. Still, in these curious works, Sebald also establishes a narrative that gives postmodern literary discourse pause to reconsider fiction, and its poetic potential, as art, offering truth that "only the imagination or the heart can verify" (Craven 2005). One might imagine that Calvino (now dead) or Culler (still living) would concur.

Sebald's "hypotactic" syntax (as he it himself described it, Silverblatt 2001) resonates more in a literary register of the ninetenth century than that of the twentieth. This is the practice of weaving the prose patterns in a vertical way as well as paratactically. Hypotactic sentences with one main clause and chains of subordinate clauses and phrases suspend the reader's sense of the present. As in Proust's diegetic prose, contemplation, reverie, remembering are facilitated. Paratactic sentences, on the other hand, with their coordinate clauses, hold actions or notions loosely together without ordering them hierarchically. Whereas hypotaxis privileges continuity, parataxis creates a discontinuous and juxtapositional effect. Sebald's insertion of photographs, for instance, is part of his use of a paratactical rhetoric.

Eric Santner's essay "Paratactic Composition in Hölderlin's 'Hälfte des Lebens'" (1985), gives an interesting account of this effect, citing an earlier essay by Adorno and an interpretation by Michael Hamburger. Parataxis, Santner writes, enables the text of this poem to enact a process of resistance to the very narrative project to which the other poems in the collection appear to be dedicated. "'Narrative vigilance' [Santner's own term] in general signifies the compulsion to watch over experience by 'narrativization,' to tether the concrete particulars of experience to the 'deep structure' of a narrative signification'" (166). The formal texture of the poetry, with its narrative pretensions, is shown to be subverted by the imagist sensibility that informs it. This has great resonance with Sebald's writing.

> Once he had descended from the pinnacle of the grand narrative of redemption, Hölderlin was threatened with the danger of becoming "ein einsam Wild." Without the view from above — a standpoint which can be sustained only with the utmost vigilance — the way the poet comports himself to the things of the world becomes quite different; no longer above the arena of historical experience, he enters into it, surrounded now on all sides . . . No longer authorized to narrate the grand myth of redemption, he must choose a more modest task: discovering relations, correspondences, constellations of meaning within the field of history, amidst the "millionfold hydra of the empirical world" [Goethe in Santner's translation], and finally within language itself. He has entered into the play of relations which is always — or so it seems in the modern period — a game of chance. (171)

Hypotaxis is a narrative rhetorical device engaging temporal continuity to an unknown end; parataxis is the vector of digressive and imagistic writing that slows time down to a temporary arrest. What a net to catch those butterfly photographs in!

There is a witty self-reflexiveness in Sebald's attempt to restore the same kind of pleasure that Theodor W. Adorno ascribes, as Drew Turner pointed out to me, to the art of traveling in *Minima Moralia*:

Rampant technology eliminates luxury, but not by declaring privilege a human right; rather it does so by both raising the general standard of living and cutting off the possibility of fulfilment. The express train that in three nights and two days hurtles across the continent is a miracle, but travelling in it has nothing of the faded splendour of the *train bleu*. What made up the voluptuousness of travel, beginning with the goodbye-waving through the open window, the solicitude of amiable accepters of tips, the ceremonial of mealtimes, the constant feeling of receiving favours that take nothing from anyone else, has passed away, together with the elegant people who were wont to promenade along the platforms before the departure, and who will by now be sought in vain even in foyers of the most prestigious hotels. That the steps of railway carriages have to be retracted intimates to the passengers of even the most expensive express that he must obey the company's terse regulations like a prisoner. Certainly, the company gives him the exactly calculated value of his fare, but this includes nothing that research has not proved an average demand. Who, aware of such conditions, could depart on impulse on a voyage with his mistress as once from Paris to Nice? (119)

Sebald refused the aid of a computer as an expeditious writing machine, preferring the older technology of the pencil, and deliberately practiced a luxurious stylistic anachronicity in order to to conjure the past and countervail the unappealing aspects of the present by providing the consoling memory of beauty (Silverblatt 2001). While his distaste for modernity is clear, Sebald's double-edged sword of memory, however, resurrects both beauty and horror. According to Sebald, style connects to lost beauty that is retrievable or redeemable in a Proustian or Nabokovian discourse, that is, through memory. Furst maintains that there is a "disconcerting contingency" for the reader (2003) in a momentary illusion where time stops, or decelerates to the point that it seems to stop. This is the enchantment of reading and Sebald's texts restore the pleasure of a particular kind of reading. Robert Alter has written about it in *The Pleasure of Reading in an Ideological Age* but Sebald has written the books that provide the pleasure and they do so by recalling the patterns of the past, the shared past of a common identity that will be irretrievably lost unless it is memorialized in enduring forms.

Nabokov's recollection of his first love, in *Speak, Memory*, also reproduces this spiraling pattern of the past in a brilliant image of the dissolution of arcing, circular patterns that trace the segue from the material observation in the present to the specter of memory and the subject's revenant-haunted consciousness.

Colette was back in Paris by the time we stopped there for a day before we continued our homeward journey; and there in a fawn park under a cold blue sky, I saw her (by arrangement between our mentors, I believe) for the last time. She carried a hoop and a short stick to drive it with, and everything about her was extremely proper and stylish in an autumnal, Parisian, *tenue-de-ville-pour-fillettes* way. She took from her governess and slipped into my brother's hand a farewell present, a box of sugar-coated almonds, meant, I knew, solely, for me; and instantly, she was off, tap-tapping her glinting hoop through light and shade, around and around a fountain choked with dead leaves, near which I stood. The leaves mingle in my memory with the leather of her shoes and gloves, and there was, I remember, some detail in her attire (perhaps a ribbon on her Scottish cap, or the pattern of her stockings) that reminded me then of the rainbow spiral in a glass marble. I still seem to be holding that wisp of iridescence, not knowing exactly where to fit it, while she runs with her hoop ever faster around me and finally dissolves among the slender shadows cast on the graveled path by the interlaced arches of its low looped fence. (119)

Sebald also reproduces sharply focused moments from memories of the past and leaves traces in his own unique, spiraling prose, which engages memory as that which enriches and disquiets. The visual quality of Nabokov's filmic sequence as it fades into and out of view as memory does, the patterns blurring together, is a marvelous instance of the way *stasis* and *kinesis*, the past and the present, the dead and the living moment, can be conjured into the mind's imagination. This is an intrinsic and sustained element in Sebald's poetics, as we will see.

Still, it is inaccurate to suggest that Sebald is merely interested in poet-ics and aesthetics. On more than one occasion, he refers to "the moral backbone of literature — that whole question of memory" (Jaggi 2001a). He explained that "if a story is aesthetically right, then it is probably also morally right. You cannot really translate one to one from reality. If you try to do that, in order to get at a truth value through writing, you have to falsify and lie. And that is one of the moral quandaries of the whole busi-ness" (Green 2000). This matter is inevitably related to the vexed question of his German identity as well as to his criticism of the silence in German literature about the war. It is the focus of the lectures he delivered in 1997 at the University of Zurich, which were published in English as *On the Natural History of Destruction* (2003). His writing always has some moral resonance, but the tenor evokes Terence's dictum *nihil humanum a me alienum puto* ("I consider that nothing human is foreign to me") rather than particular political or ideological positions.

The question concerning German cultural amnesia is connected with other issues of association and memory complicit in considering the history of humanity as a litany of destruction and horror. "My compatriots" is the sardonic phrase he uses (Silverblatt 2001) to describe those in some way asso-ciated in the world's memory with the unspeakable horror, Arthur Koestler's *abor*, of the crimes against humanity that scar the middle of the twentieth century, just as Sebald wants us to be horrified by the systematic bombing campaign directed by Arthur Harris for the Allies. Sebald places the "con-soling patterns" of beauty as a promise of redemption and change in oppo-sition to the horror so that the literary becomes a site of possibility, just as individuals of any nationality, Solly Zuckerman, for instance, whose title for his unwritten article for *Horizon* Sebald used ("The Natural History of Destruction"), are rendered language-less (unable to write, like Austerlitz) when confronted by the horror and destruction of which mankind is capable. Aporia — is its silence the moral decorum Sebald seeks to utter?

Sebald's oblique prose shapes the haunted silence of the unutterable in a way that makes the reader reflect and think critically and creatively. Even in its sonorous English translations, his language affords the reader an aesthetic experience that indicates imaginative possibilities. The Sebaldian reader is "forced to see" in the manner that Guido Almansi scrutinizes art (Almansi 1975) and to think and to imagine by "seeing" in the way that John Berger writes that photographs make us (Berger 1972). Seeing can reduce one to silence, a consequence of trauma, as we saw with Zuckerman, as is also the case with Austerlitz, and the coded silence represented by the photographs in Sebald's books. Bearing witness includes bearing the burden of memory. Knowing, we are more politically and morally alert to the possibility and the desirability of change, of taking action that will prevent further calamity, destruction, or catastrophe.

In a literary context, the reader is forced to read reflexively — an active aesthetic engagement with literature that foregrounds the language practice of literary style, with its resistant and self-reflexive textuality. We do not "salivate" at the apples in a still life; we "look" at them, in a self-conscious looking that reconstructs them as apples. This is the creative response of the disobediently subjective reader, our Kristevan *envol de la pensée, vagabondage de l'imagination* (1998). Sebald's prose solicits our looking, our reading, in a similar way.

Lest we identify the authorial Sebald with the constructed Sebald-like narrator, a dangerously false mapping of fictional narrative, Sebald's oneiric melancholy tone, seductive as it is, is very often subverted by its own excess, undercut by a play of humorous irony that distances the reader from the lugubrious narrator by means of a playful intertextuality or some self-reflexive theorizing, just as the phantoms of the past, momentarily resurrected by the instantiations of memory represented by the annunciatory photographs which are intercalated in his fictions, arrest the temporal movement of the narrative of the verbal text. These moments of *stasis* afford the reader the space in which the reader's imagination can be active.

Like that silk filter over a camera lens, these distancing devices recall to the reader in a very deliberate way that he or she is reading constructed fiction, however sharply focused, however powerfully suggested the referentiality of the detail. In fact the hyperreal presentation, through foregrounding, of the apparent non-fictionality of the discourse ironizes the truth claims of the fiction in a way that shifts the *locus* of what critics like Whitehead (2004a) call an "ethics of reading" to an imaginative or poetic site that is located in the reader's response. That referentiality, heightened by Sebald's poetics of a foregrounded use of literary language and the walking/reading pace in which it unfolds in the reader's own journey, embodies, like a photograph, the aspirational illusion of permanence, but it captures too, like a photograph, the strange intensity of the lived present, and its transience.

In Sebald's fictional practice, like Proust's, the consoling illusion of arrested time, like the inscription of memory in place, offers a kind of redemption from uncertainty, from the oblivion of the future, in the vertiginous gaze into the spiraling perspective of the past located within each subject's sense of self, described by Proust in exactly those terms in the final pages of *A la recherche du temps perdu* (Proust 1972, 473). What Lilian Furst calls Sebald's "disconcerting contingency" (2003) is the self-reflexive provision of the reading experience itself, of the intimate dialogical intersectedness between the reading subject and the alterity of the text, that intense and ephemeral sense of what Miroslav Holub calls the three-second duration of the consciousness of the present moment (1990, 2). Reading Sebald is to be mindful of reading itself. In that contingent space between the past and the future, conscious awareness, and Sebaldian reading, is suspended.

Sebald's fictional strategies undermine the conventional position of the reader as passive and encourage him or her to be disobedient, to interrogate the construction of the text and to assume collaborative, imaginative authority in the reading adventure.

One Particular Station —
W. G. Sebald: A Critical Companion

The essays collected in *W. G. Sebald: A Critical Companion*, edited by J. J. Long and Anne Whitehead (2004), and Richard Sheppard's long review of it which contains his own take on Sebald's poetics (December, 2005), are among the more substantial recent contributions to scholarship on Sebald in English which warrant some brief comment here. [Note: These essays were published after I had completed my initial study. Similarly, the essays *W. G. Sebald: History — Memory — Trauma*, published late in 2006, based on the papers given in North Carolina at the Davidson Symposium in 2003, edited by Scott Denham and Mark McCulloh (Walter de Gruyter) are not referenced here.] Long and Whitehead organize twelve essays in three sections entitled "Landscape and Nature," "Travel and Walking," and "Haunting, Trauma, and Memory." There is also an additional essay by Martin Swales, "Theoretical Reflections on the Work of W. G. Sebald," and a poem by George Szirtes. This arrangement reflects the editors' view that "Sebald's work is situated at the confluence of numerous discourses, contexts, and debates" (5) and the twelve essays indicate the breadth of Sebald's concerns without positioning him in any one particular discourse.

Whitehead's monograph, *Trauma Fiction* (2004), however, uses the concept of trauma fiction to inscribe Sebald into a subgenre of postmodern fiction based on Cathy Caruth's Freudian theory of trauma. Whitehead reads the representation of trauma in formalist terms that are characterized by disruption and fragmentation. She argues that Sebald's fiction should be read as witnessing trauma, which demands an "ethics of reading" that implicates the reader. Whitehead contends that Sebald is not able to reconcile the "problems of identification and generalisation" that his fiction prompts and he cannot "provide the reader with any means of departure or working through" (139). Thus the reader is condemned to an iterative acting out of trauma with "no way of coming to terms with the traumatic experiences which they represent" (138).

Richard Sheppard presents his review of the Long and Whitehead collection of essays as "a series of responses" to the essays that allows him to present his own reading in the manner of a Sebaldian digression. He makes a compelling, three-part argument. First, he posits that Sebald is an academic and critic who strives to improve the understanding of his literary writing. Second, he asserts that "a diachronic understanding of the way Sebald's mind develops from 1963 onwards can help us appreciate more fully the central concerns of his literary work." Finally, he maintains that readers should approach Sebald's narratives and interviews with "benign scepticism" (2005).

Swales's brief piece "Theoretical Reflections" identifies the intermedial state between "a high degree of literariness" and "documentary solidity and authenticity" (23) as the central paradox of Sebald's poetics. Swales considers Sebald's "omnipresent mental landscape" (26) to be equally critical and creative, which provides the reader with a postmodern view of writing as writing. Swales argues that Sebald's Germanness is intrinsic to the construction of the subject in his fiction. He claims that German literary history exhibits less concern for this question than European literature that emphasizes the "specificity of human experience" or the "psychological" concept of the subject, as well as English literature that emphasizes the "social experience" or the sociohistorical context of the subject (24). Swales maintains that Sebald was "steeped in" German novels from the middle of the eighteenth century that evince an "intense inwardness" and play a central role in Sebald's prose.

Massimo Leone is a semiotician and he cites Eco's 1979 work when distinguishing between the reader's conventional affective engagement in narrative fiction and "the strategies of semantic isolation, alienation and dismantling which constantly frustrate the reader's ingenuous and naïve longing for an effortless and transparent textual coherence" that serves as a counterpoint (89). Leone writes that he is "resisting Sebald's literary charisma and trying to describe and understand the textual devices through which it is built" (90). He tries not to forget the pleasure of that "literary charisma" when trying to better understand "how and why his travelogues trigger the desire to travel with him" (90). Leone adds "that one can easily perceive the meaningfulness of Sebald's works, but one cannot as easily describe or explain it" (91). Leone helps to understand how "the lexicological precision of Sebald's prose produces a maieutic effect: it helps reality to come into existence" (97). This mysterious transubstantiation of Sebald's poetic practice is difficult to discern and easy to misapprehend. Even reading "vigilantly" (Sebald to Jaggi 2001) can be very destabilizing, because the contestable and questionable constructedness of one's self becomes apparent.

John Beck's essay provides sensitive insights into *The Rings of Saturn*, which many consider to be Sebald's most poetic work. Beck writes that "the book is about the erosion of confidence in the power of representation to record a knowable world adequately and thereby control it" (75). It is the same problem for Jacques Austerlitz in the later book. Beck's general view is that the book "is sceptical about representational truth-claims, stable viewpoints, and the authority of rational argumentation" (76). Sebald's writing resists linear logic and systematic rational discourse; nevertheless, he creates compelling arguments with his associations and intuitive leaps that are all part of "the complex power of reading and writing defended and exemplified" by his text (77).

Richard Sheppard focusses this Janus-duality in Sebald, the one face serious, disciplined about stylistic and linguistic perfection, mindful of the horrors of human suffering and the evil which causes them and of the mystery of his own consciousness, the other reflecting the comic and ironic, even Menippean, carnival spirit of a man whose lively wit and humor became, according to Sheppard (2005), gradually eroded by the self-imposed work ethic of the "two prisons" of writing and working in the academy, and perhaps the melancholy which both plagued and drove him. It must have been a regime of work which seems Dickensian, and which may have been, as it was for Dickens too, at least a factor in Sebald's early death. Michael Hamburger makes some allusion to this in his brief tribute in *Unrecounted* (2005).

If Sheppard is right about Sebald's underlining, in his own copy, of Lévi-Strauss's idea of *bricolage* as an aleatory way of producing art that could still be "auratic" (424), then we might conclude that for Sebald writing was above all the art of literature, words that could be powerful enough to change people, or change the way people saw themselves, each other, and the world, an essentially imaginative power. Sebald's statement "I just want to write good prose" (Atlas, 1999) masks a hugely ambitious, and almost self-destructive commitment to a moral task, to bring about a shift in people's perceptions for the common good, or perhaps for something akin to another Southern German's position (now Benedict XVI), Cardinal Ratzinger's sense of "justice" as a "right engagement with the world" (December 7, 1965).

As Sheppard observes, the Long and Whitehead essays open up the Sebaldian discourse in very rich ways, but we might give the last word here to Sebald, in the words that Sheppard quotes him writing on Kafka in "Kafka Goes to the Movies": " 'The smooth surface of Kafka's work has remained an enigma in spite of what his interpreters have managed to dredge from its depths. It has preserved its integrity against the advances of criticism' " (Sheppard 43).

A Couple of Brief Stations

Two important pieces by Richard Crownshaw and Eluned Summers-Bremner also need to be considered, not least because they contribute to the diversity of perspectives and positions that Sebald's work encourages. Richard Crownshaw's article was first delivered as a paper at a conference in Manitoba and then published in *Mosaic*. In "Reconsidering Postmemory: Photography, the Archive, and Post-Holocaust Memory in W. G. Sebald's *Austerlitz*," he "scrutinises the theory, practice, and ethics of postmemory." Like Long and Anne Fuchs, he employs Marianne Hirsch's notion of postmemory to interrogate the "potential for adoption to turn into appropriation" in Sebald's works whereby a writer identifies with the memories of another. Crownshaw quotes Hirsch here on the need to "resist annihilating the difference between self and other, the otherness of the other." In his reading of *Austerlitz*, Crownshaw claims that "memory work" is "inevitably subjective." He glosses the Benjaminian use of photographs, "in which the traumatic loss of the past, irreplaceable by its photographic representation (or supplement), intrudes upon the present." He enlists Eduardo Cadava to explain that "the photograph cannot be relied upon to form the disruptive content of the futural archive, holding it open, for it relies on the subjectivity of its beholder to animate this disruption." The animation solicits the reader's creative imagination.

Eluned Summers-Bremner's essay, "Reading, Walking, Mourning: W. G. Sebald's Peripatetic Fictions" considers the psychological affect of Sebald's fictions on the reader. She observes that

> the apparent mundaneity of the journeys undertaken in the books is of another kind. It speaks to the dynamic configuration of traces of just passed moments that make up our own subjectivities, and which narrative conventions more often encourage us to reverse and replace in order to register them substantively in developmental or *Bildungsroman* mode, in a kind of working denial as the means of imaginative progress.

Using Lacanian terminology, she develops her argument further.

> I am less interested in the range of nameable emotions readers agree are part of the experience of digesting the books than in the peculiar way the

narratives involve and implicate the reader. In its Lacanian aspects, my argument does not attempt to apply psychoanalysis to literature but to demonstrate the supremely literary qualities of Sebald's view of history, which he shares with Lacan, and as a result of which the reader becomes imbricated with the ongoing and reverberative impact of past events.

Summers-Bremner underscores the sharp distinction between mourning and melancholy and explores how they impinge on the reader, rather than the affect on the narrator that Whitehead examines in *Trauma Fiction*.

> Trauma as a relation is also at issue for the reader of Sebald's works to the extent that they consistently problematize the reading relationship while making it inexplicably compelling. As an event that annihilates the experiential frameworks of space and time through which we are usually kept from being too much for ourselves to cope with, trauma is elaborated in Sebald's works through the alterations and dislocations of readerly perspective performed by memory, visual and architectural technologies old and new, and walking.

Whitehead constructs reading as an experiential site of trauma. This is partly right, but the reader's sense of the narrator's traumatized state is actually shaped by the disjunctive nature of the form of Sebald's texts. The reader cannot simply identify with or share empathetically in this state of trauma, because the narrator is only ever a voice. Mimetic wholeness is withheld, and whether or not that reflects the narrator's traumatized or pathologized state in that the language of the text seems to be the expressedness of the narrator is of no consequence to a reader for whom imaginative projection into the state of this "person" is withheld. In Sebald's view of history the gap or lack which signifies trauma is a trauma which both the author and the reader have in common but do not necessarily use as a means of communication or encounter, of arriving at a mutual understanding or the expression of compassion, as Summers-Bremner observes:

> Where Lacan's accounts of reading and writing subjectivity meet Sebald's praxis of summoning narrative emotion is at the point where human response must acknowledge the trauma of its already having been written by the wishes and dreams that gave rise to it, especially those of others, and the dual responsibility and impossibility of accommodating these alien origins within one's own space and time, of simultaneously living and telling one's own story.

Arguing that Sebald's belatedness (Freud's *Nachträglichkeit*) registers the temporal space or delay that signifies one effect of trauma which Sebald's narrator and characters in *The Emigrants* manifest, their isolation or lostness, Summers-Bremner adds that his uncanny spatialization reinforces this destabilized and destabilizing effect on the reader.

It is in their rendering of space as profoundly uncanny, as irreducible to a logic of the temporal ordering of events such that space is disregarded and is mere backdrop for action or character, that Sebald's texts are literally catastrophic. . . . Space in Sebald is substantial, phenomenal, it compresses and expands, harbors dreads and anxious feelings and refuses to be flattenened and externalized in the way a consciously purposeful narrative journey might require. But it cannot readily be internalized as a sense of containment or support for self-consolidation either. . . . it is space that animates and exceeds the arbitrariness of temporal ordering, but in a manner the more disturbing because of the way temporal ordering usually domesticates or makes space safe, in narrative, while simultaneously relying upon and all but excluding it (in this respect, Sebald's fictions may also be described as versions of the contemporary Gothic).

Moving toward a poetics of fiction that incorporates Sebald's use of visual elements, Summers-Bremner notes that

In Sebald the reading subject finds, as Lacan too would have it, "itself in its very effacement, in its own modern graveyard" (Copjec 1994, xi), as it encounters precisely the moment of its founding which it can never recognize, where the empty place its arrival transmuted into life is shadowed by both its former and eventual end (the world before we were in it, and the world as it will unthinkingly survive us). This place of simultaneously specific and universal lostness is the readerly version of Stendhal's recognition that history is not only battle scenes and bleached bones, which are indeed universal, the endlessly recurring stuff of history, but the placement of himself at the scene of his own end "alone with himself, like one meeting his doom" (*Vertigo*, 18). This is a crisis of existential space, its marker a vertiginous confusion.

This is precisely the destabilizing and disconcerting effect that Sebald has on his reader. The reader realizes that she is also implicated in the inevitable historical narrative (death) which underscores the very nature of fiction, as well as its end.

In this sense, the text is already the graveyard of the author (as Barthes asserted) and possibly the graveyard of the reader as well, when it is recognized that it is the site where he or she was inaugurated and where he or she must return. Summers-Bremner continues that books "affectively inaugurate a new kind of post-traumatic reader." Sebald focuses on the belatedness of the human condition and the memorializing tendency within it. Summer-Bremner observes that "we all experience instead a sense of incommensurability between life as it is lived and its narrative properties or meaning." This is surely Sebald's focus, on the *Nachträglichkeit* that is our human condition. "Like the analyst, Sebald provides the holding framework in which we are required to feel our complicity with this ex-centric element, our unavoidable relationship with death." This is the epicenter of Sebaldian poetics: our being made ever mindful, as readers, of being in a *salle des pas perdus*, the intense and brief interval in time and space between arrival and departure.

Pour ceux qui savent lire?

The dominant of postmodernist fiction is ontological. . . . (it) engages and foregrounds questions such as "which world is this?"; "what is to be done in it?"; "which of my selves is to do it?" (McHale 1992)

Applying Brian McHale's notion of the "dominant paradigm" of postmodernism that "engages and foregrounds ontological questions" to Sebald's texts brings the question of both our own being and a foregrounded reader into relief. Sebald's self-description as "paradigmatically postmodern" (Atlas 1999) seems ironic in light of his narrators' paralysing and pathological melancholy. Writerliness itself is foregrounded as a therapeutic solution to this chronic condition in which the reader must, to avoid being appropriated by it, preserve his or her alterity, just as the author may well do by means of the detachment of irony in his own writing practice.

Sebald's texts unsettle his reader most in these fictional works without a clear future when they imply, "what is to be done?" However, unlike Benjamin's angel of history, being blown backward into the future by the wreckage of history, the reader is able to step out of the discourse that determines this past to address Sebald's most pressing question, "how are we to change?" If the past is a litany of destruction, then the nature of the postmodern in Sebald, as Sheppard in part articulates (2005), is to find a way back beyond the horror of the twentieth century, not to some golden age (for there is none in Sebald), but perhaps also a place beyond that circumscribed by Hölderlin's poem "Hälfte des Lebens," in Santner's observation, where "Nature, finally, has been displaced by artifacts of culture, and what is more, by a culture in a state of decay" (Santner, 167).

Faced with the etiolation and the melancholy of Sebald's texts, the reader is nudged into an ethics of reading that pivots on inquiry and disputation as an alternative to appalling victim-hood. To engage in more thought and imagination, both reflectively and prospectively, to pose questions that delay, that slow down to walking pace the ways in which we engage, authentically, with ourselves, the world, and with each other seem to be part of the protocols of the Sebaldian itinerary.

Sebald is determined to create the possibility of finding or constructing meaning where meaning is supposedly unavailable, namely, "our incomprehensible existence" (Sebald 2005, 147). This effort contributes to the restoration of the literary experience as imaginative and redemptively creative that Eco and Culler have adumbrated as we will see.

Another Turn in the Road:
Sebaldian Postmodernism

the chaff ground out in the mills of academia . . .
                                    — *Kafka Goes to the Movies*

Sebald's contempt for "plodding studies," "manufacturers of literary theory," "secondary works inspired . . . by the theories of existentialism, the-
ology, psychoanalysis, structuralism, poststructuralism, reception aesthetics
or system criticism," "the mills of academia," and "exegists" is by now
familiar. Therefore, one should perhaps use real caution in applying the
idea of the postmodern to Sebald and his works since he certainly prefers
that his writing receives the "conscientious and patient work" of "editors
and factual commentators," writing "unpretentiously" about any theoretical positioning. Still, he confesses that he too is not "entirely innocent of
the fatal inclination to speculate about meanings" (2005, 154–55). In his
second book on postmodernism (1992) Brian McHale sought to interrogate his own misleading authority in writing about the same subject in his
first book (1987) and observed that "there is a delicate balance to be maintained between advocating a particular version of constructed reality and
entertaining a plurality of versions" (1992, 1–2). He wanted to embrace
Alan Thiher's notion that "postmodernism has become a counter in our
language games" (1992, 1) in order to acknowledge that postmodernism
exists discursively, but later he wants to focus on the idea that postmodernism is "a plurality of constructions" (3). This theoretical *mise-en-abyme*
is, nonetheless, more useful for considering Sebald as a postmodern writer,
as many do (for instance, Furst, Williams, McCulloh, Long, Whitehead).

McHale advocates beginning with the text and working back to the
theory in order to minimize the risk of institutionalizing the text, since the
pursuit of an institutional discourse, a *consensus fidelium*, sublimates the individual reader and precludes the imaginative generation of the text's future.
By advocating that we approach the work as a reader open to the text,
McHale concludes: "Postmodernist fiction is . . . fiction whose formal
strategies implicitly raise issues of the mode of being of fictional worlds and
their inhabitants" (147).

1: Encounter with Disobedience

This Reader's Adventure

> The creativity of the reader grows as the institution that controlled it
> declines.
> — Michel de Certeau, *The Practice of Everyday Life*

THE READER, POST ROLAND BARTHES AND OTHERS, is no longer quiescent, that obedient, passive creature subject to the explicit and implicit tyrannies of the text and its author, the text and its narrator(s). I shall be more essayist than theorist, the kind of transgression which has no place in a scholarly monograph, a kind of disobedience, blurring the boundaries between orthodoxy or convention and imaginative or creative license, that errant "I," that restless traveler, that ambulant, writerly voice.

In 1995 in early December, when the academic and school year was slowing down in its bright, warm Australian way with the promise of liberty voiced in the staccato sweep of sprinklers elongating summer days and nights and the shrill antiphonal music of cicadas and crickets, all those still mornings holding their breath and warm night air of long evenings sighing heavy with the fragrance of some giant cream magnolia somewhere, the small pale stars of native daphne already scattering across footpaths and nature strips browning, I found myself sitting at the end of one afternoon, tired and empty after a long stint of work, on a hard, cedar cathedral pew in Melbourne.

The place was packed — some sixteen hundred people, and six hundred pairs of small black school shoes clattering across the narthex, through the rood screen and up the tesselated floor of the nave aisle, the sound rising into the clerestory as small figures took their places in the crossing. A giant navy and white insect with a thousand eyes and one voice — modern children, ancient words. A rumor of words echoed up into the empty air. The child reading from the elevated pulpit was about eleven, her blonde hair a golden nimbus under the arc light, her diction precise and clear, neither mannered nor nervous. I cannot now recall whether she read from the prophet Isaiah or from the Gospel according to St Luke or perhaps St John, but I remember that as she finished her reading in which she, or possibly one of the other children who also read whom I cannot now recall in any particular or detailed way, narrated the Virgin Mary's conception of the child who became the Messiah, an elegant man whom I did not know, dressed in a dark suit and sitting in the pew behind me, spoke, well above a whisper, to someone whom I presumed at the time was his wife, although

I did not turn to look at her, saying, "That's some story." I was amused and, on reflection, slightly irritated.

Amused that he was bold enough to speak his mind, postmodern, secular, and contestatory, I was irritated that this man had voiced his view loudly enough for those of us adjacent to him to hear his skeptical voice. It was an intrusion into the moment that the child's reading had created, with the reading of verses both familiar and strange, suddenly both at once for one of his neighbors, and perhaps simply just strange for him. Of course he was right: it was "some story," on a number of reckonings. It had lasted nearly two thousand years of telling, not a bad run, and so many people read it or heard it read at least once a year all over the world in so many languages that the idea of calculating without surrendering to vertigo was dizzying in itself. It was, in his more than slightly ironic tone, "some story."

Whatever the language spell was that the child's reading had cast, that timeless and spaceless moment in the echoing space of hallowedness, whatever incantatory or exhortatory effect that ritual reading had had, or might have had, whatever the power of those words had been or might have been, one thing was absolutely certain: it had been routed, for those who had had ears to hear, by the disruptive intrusion of the other voice. He had collapsed the mysterious conjunction of the reading and listening, to the thinking and imagining, to the eidetic here and now, to the precisely indexed moment. He had ascribed to the story the status of historical referentiality, of documented reality, and had done so by denying it its *poiesis*, its power as metaphoric utterance. Space had been diminished, reduced to place.

It seemed a very literal rejection. He had denied that language itself could speak, expressing the view that language had to speak something "real" in Barthes's sense (1977), and the something was to his mind if not a patent absurdity, "some story," then at the very least a tall order — especially, and this seemed to be his assumption, if one were asked to believe it. He was, in short, closing down the rich indeterminacy of the poetry in the language in favor of the referentiality of prior reality, historically recorded and textually documented. Then, ruminating, I reflected that he had been led to this observation by the same language that I had heard, and that his contestation of the "scriptural economy" (de Certeau 1984, 58) was an expression, perhaps unconscious, of de Certeau's problematizing of "the ways in which reading is suppressed or standardised" (Ahearne 165).

Did the child suspect any of this yet, I wondered, or had she simply, at ten or eleven, accepted the mystery of the syllables, the cadence of the prose rhythm, the phrasing and the emphases, the strange seeming resonance of it all, some glimpse even of what Walter Benjamin called the aura of a work of art? Was the man embarrassed, or merely dismissive of this ritual reading in the Christian tradition, irked by his attendance at what was surely, in late twentieth-century Australia (that most secular of societies in this period of late modernity) a quaint, anachronistic observance smacking of cultural desuetude?

I never saw the man again, but the child who read and the man who spoke embodied part of a dialogue that had been going on in my mind for some time between the vexed division of sacred and secular literature, between the ritual reading of texts that were preserved in institutional formaldehyde and the reading of texts that kept slipping clear, resisting their static preservation and yet being preserved in more dynamic ways, redeemed and resurrected in the ongoing conversation of critical discourse. Of course, that too seemed in some ways to be engulfed by the tsunami of cultural studies, that proliferation of competing discourses of signification, those racks of lenses through which we could read texts, that secular metanarrative in which, as Jonathan Culler had pointed out, the literary had triumphed by informing every discourse in the humanities only to be at risk now of being leached, like a productive matrix, of its own energy and vitality. This was to be the beginning.

Authorized Versions and Disobedient Reading

What in fact was, I reflected, this reading? Was there an adult equivalent to the child's acceptance of the sonorous mystery of language that embraced both ends of the admittedly artificial reading spectrum, the literalists and the non-literalists? Or had two thousand years of hermeneutic scholarship, the business of interpreting the coded utterances of the Holy Ghost, the God-narratives which had given rise to literary studies in the first place, and the various waves of reading fashion of typology and form criticism and the like by those "certified interpreters" of the Bible (Ahearne 165) marginalized the pew-sitting listeners to the outer circle of the inner sanctuary after all?

I wondered if it really mattered anyway in an increasingly secularized society, even though it seemed that death, or the threat of death, on an individual or collective scale, still had the power to draw people into sacred spaces for ritual purposes, spaces where language was still used to shape a response to the incomprehensible, the mysterious, even the absurd (our mortality), in metaphor, in language that was, after all, essentially, perhaps even intrinsically, poetic. This seemed like a quest for alterity, a desire to step into a space where the other, or the Divine Other, could be encountered as truly heterological, an uncanny and adventurous alternative to contingent anxiety, uncertainty, even fear. This seemed to be desire for poetry and mystery rather than literal or historical determinism. In this sacralization, in this focusing of the power of the literary to say what could not otherwise be said, Sebald's own poetic enterprise nudged itself forward.

In Australia, where there were clear divisions, at least in the Anglican Church, between those who read the Bible as the literal testament of the Divine Word and those who read it as a library of hallowed but constructed texts, a polarization loosely aligned with different brands of churchmanship, there was food for thought for someone whose own secular training in reading literary texts favored an interrogatory method of reading predicated on the assumption that a text was a polysemous matter, a site of exploration. De Certeau, a former Jesuit, had observed that "as the institution weakens, there appears the reciprocity between the text and its readers, previously hidden by the institution" (Ahearne 249). As the institution of the literary weakened, it seemed that the "reciprocity between the text and its readers" was being foregrounded in a postmodern way — in Sebald's own writing, his creative not his academic writing. In Culler's formulation the institution now in decline was the academic discipline of the literary, and with it, perhaps, the domain of the imagination, held hostage by our complicit cultural desire for some literal truth.

Centuries of Biblical hermeneutics and commentary, including the Judaic reading practice of the Torah and the Talmud, had given rise to literary studies. This specific act of reading was an "occulted" one (Ahearne 166). What did that mean for our engagement with these texts, and other kinds of texts, in the new millennium? De Certeau had written, "the story of humankind's tracks through its own texts remains in large measure unknown" (1984, 246). This then was a travel story too, or at least de Certeau's lexicon suggested so. It was time to retrace my own steps to look at some small section of a very familiar text, to experiment by defamiliarizing myself with it by grappling with it in the original, or a version that was closer to the original text than the finely nuanced clarity of the twentieth-century New Revised Standard Version of the Bible or the seductive sonorities of the seventeenth-century-committee King James Bible.

Language which presents as history is as susceptible as language which presents as poetry to being read both obediently and disobediently. Reading obediently is to read Luke as a historian whose text is validated through reference to external authority. Reading disobediently is to read Luke's text as language-constructed, open to multiple readings through textual analysis. The distinction is one of reading practice, not of faith, as Sir Frank Kermode had pointed out to Dame Helen Gardner (1982, 87–102). As Robert Scholes puts it: "To read the biblical text as literary, rather than sacred, would be to recognize its complexity and to open it to criticism, thus giving readers the freedom to accept or reject the values they have discovered there" (238–39). The disobedient reader, who may be more generally a "believer," is faced with making decisions *as a reader*. Reading Sebald beckons the reader down a similar path: making decisions as a reader simply cannot be avoided.

In the ancient text, the problem occurs when the parallel stories of angelic annunciation are recounted by Luke, following his elegant Greek preface. Four carefully formulated verses, composed of one long sentence, are written on a template of classical Greek rhetoric, in the tradition A. J. Minnis describes which establishes the authority of the writer of a text as *auctor* (1988, 102). This is the Syrian Greek Luke, a Gentile born in Antioch and called "beloved physician" by Paul (*Corinthians* 4.14), who introduces the story he is about to narrate in *Luke-Acts* (Cadbury 1999) as documented historical truth. Immediately he has established that writerly authority, and the documented historicity of his text, that preface segues into a pair of parallel mystical fables mediated in part by the reported voice of an archangel. The gospel according to Luke begins as follows in The New Revised Standard Version (1989) of The Holy Bible:

> Since many have undertaken to set down an orderly account of the events that have been fulfilled among us, just as they were handed on to us by those who from the beginning were eyewitnesses and servants of the word, I too decided, after investigating everything carefully from the very first, to write an orderly account for you, most excellent Theophilus, so that you may know the truth concerning the things about which you have been instructed. (52)

επειδηπερ (since), the Greek word with which this passage opens, is a rhetorical word, not the narrative one εγενετο (it happened that), with which the fifth verse and the beginning of the narrative section proper begins. This seemed to braid two discourses together, a rhetorical one and a narrative one.

This elegantly written piece of rhetoric whose "magisterial shaping and pacing" (Drury 419) is designed to persuade the reader that what was to follow was incontrovertibly non-fiction, historical truth, is grounded in eyewitness testaments and shared cultural belief. The stories that followed, about Zacharias in the inner temple and the young Jewish girl Mariam, were also carefully contextualized by historically authentic detail: temporal index (the reign of Herod of Judea), genealogies (Elisabeth's father's family and Joseph's father's family), the priestly order of Abijah, the rites of the temple, a town in Galilee called Nazareth which, unlike Emmaus, did actually exist. All very historicized until we get to verse 11, and the appearance to Zacharias: "Then there appeared to him an angel of the Lord, standing at the right side of the altar of incense" (NRSV 52). The archangel Gabriel appears to Mary (or Mariam) a few verses on, although we are not told where, and says, "Greetings, favored one! The Lord is with you." Here the precise indexing of place and historical persons is interwoven with the mysterious, the enigmatic, the mystical, in other words with alterity, a de Certeau heterology.

This textuality the Catholic Sebald from provincial Southern Germany had imbibed in his youth (*Campo Santo*, 196). Luke's textual rupture, marked by the shift in register from the conventional rhetorical claim to authority based on documented historicity to the narrative incorporation of the fantastic or fabulous, requires of the reader a leap of faith that draws its energy from the human capacity for imagination. It was possible that Sebald's own poetics, like Pierre Bonnard's painting for instance, drew our attention to the "tension between appearance and effacement" itself (Philippe Dagen, "Bonnard, en grand et autrement," *Le Monde*, 2 February 2006, 26, *my translation*), to the point of juxtaposition where the act of memory retrieves the appearance of the real and at the same time destabilizes us by showing us that it is a chimera — that very site where we "see" memory and imagination expressed in us as readers, as spectators.

Curiously, in no other book in the New Testament, including the other three Gospels, is there any reference to these Annunciation stories, the appearances of the archangel Gabriel to Zacharias and to Mary. They appear only in Luke's Gospel. John Drury observed, "Neither Mark nor Matthew, the previous narrators whose work he builds into his own, enjoyed such calm literary self-confidence and self-consciousness. It is something new" (1987, 418). These stories, one of which inaugurates the Christian narrative and is therefore foundation discourse, have attracted remarkably little commentary. Luke's singular story of the Annunciation to Mary, the most painted image in Western art according to John Ruskin in *Modern Painters* (259), contained in the first section of his Gospel, has somehow slipped past really sustained scrutiny. I felt emboldened. It was the kind of boldness that Sebald elicits in his interrogatory reader.

Luke has made a clear distinction, both in diction and style, between the preface, which asserts the historicity of the text to the reader (in this case a man called Theophilus, to a suspicious, possibly disobedient reader) and the narrative proper, which employs simpler diction, a very direct style, a different voice and a much more colloquial address. For a vigilant and contestatory reader, this is fascinating. The preface establishes an authorial commitment to the validation of historical truth claims in the narrative to follow, using a classical Greek literary tradition that would persist for centuries in all kinds of secular scriptural economies, as Minnis discusses (1988). The narrative itself is a mystical and poetically self-conscious one, alive to the impact it will have on the reader.

This is the discourse, this blend of the historical, as Dawsey points out (104), and Cadbury confirms (65), and which Frank Kermode described thus: "The gospels sound like history, and that they do so is the consequence of an extraordinary rhetorical feat" (1979, 113). This is what underpins and confirms the *magisterium*. This is what gives authority to the institution of the church. One part of it is couched in the claims of documented historicity; the other is an extraordinary literary narrative of an intensely imaginative and poetic kind. In the Lucan Annunciation narrative the precise indexing of place and historical persons is interwoven with the mysterious, the enigmatic, the mystical, with alterity, a de Certeau heterology.

Fra Angelico painted the Annunciation twice in the San Lorenzo monastery in Florence, at the public entrance at the top of Michelangelo's staircase and in a monk's cell. The first is a detailed rich fresco, suited to the public gaze, the other a more ascetically rendered one, for private contemplation, meditation and prayer. Unlike Zacharaias' angelic encounter, Mary's, in Fra Angelico's second rendering in particular, is a deeply private, interiorized moment. The first fresco is, like Leonardo's painting of the same moment, depicted as occurring in a particular place; the second smaller one, whose figures are very like those in the first, is painted as though it occurs in the poetic space of the subject, firstly of Mary, and then of the spectator, so that the subject of each becomes, curiously and strangely, indistinguishable in the act of silent meditation, of contemplation.

Seen for the first time in the closed interior space of the cell, the second fresco strikes the viewer, having seen the first painting at the top of the stairs, as a destabilizing experience. One has the curious sense of being inside a contemplative moment, as though that monk's cell is less a place than a poetic space. To be inside the contemplative moments out of which and within which his narrators "write" the texts is, as we shall see, a Sebaldian reader's experience.

The first part of the Gospel of St Luke might seem a curious textual fragment to invoke in a book whose focus is W. G. Sebald's late twentieth and early twenty-first century prose fiction, but this ancient paradigm of Luke's parallel annunciation stories (Luke 1: 1–38) suggests itself as offering the dualism of an obedient reading of them as historical and a disobedient reading of them as literary. The disobedient reader walks in an ambulatory of desire, between the tension of truth-seeking documentation and the poetic leap into imagination.

The displaced or decentered authority of Sebald's prose which, as Macfarlane points out, draws attention to the way in which "writing disturbs the hive of the imagination" (2003, 38), elicits the disobedient reader, calling him or her into being. The shocking rupture of the divine into the human, the metaphysical presence of something "other," the angel representing The Divine, in Beckett's terms, The Unnameable, which destabilizes our certainty about ourselves and the material world which seems to be our home, offers a point of intersectedness, of association with Sebald driven by a readerly, contemplative and imaginative response rather than a conventional reading logic, the causal narrative logic of E. M. Forster's "and then."

With this institutionalized discourse about angelic messengers and their intrusion of alterity into the historical world of time and place experienced by a subject enslaved to entropy and death, in its institutionalization of ritual remembrance of the promise of redemption from temporal abjection,

Sebald's secular literary enterprise has some contiguity. With its chronic sense of "never feeling at home anywhere in the world," its spectral voices and their disclosures, its preoccupation with the relentless passage of time, with the redemptive power of memory and its inscription in place, its capacity to translate represented place into poetic space, the variety of all those painted Annunciations, and the tantalizing glimpses of the self-reflexive constructedness of literary language to say what could not otherwise be said, Sebald's *promeneur solitaire* and cinematic *montage* poetics, complete with spectral voice-over (as in Patrick Keiller's British films of the 1990s, *London* and *Robertson in Space*), a restless search for the place in which one's being is at home (Malpas 2005), offer some point of encounter, not least because, as in Keiller, consciousness is all.

Sebald was interested in metaphysics, in what he referred to as the "metaphysical lining of reality" (2004, 88), what Jeff Malpas has called the thinking that arrests being (2006). Metaphysics underpins ancient Hebrew literature and the early Christian writings that succeeded it. For Sebald it was an explicit engagement with the mysterious aspects of human experience, expressed in his admiration for the lucidity of the writing of scientists (at the expense of the writers of contemporary fiction) in their presentation of very dense ideas (Silverblatt 2001) and in his distaste for the "grinding wheels" of conventional fiction, still predominantly realist even in some of its modern and postmodern formulations.

The doctrine of redemption and salvation is fundamentally a literary construct (cf. Kermode, 1979, 117), and underpins a metanarrative that we do not, for the most part and for interesting reasons, interrogate in literary terms. Rather than positioning the reader to suspend his or her disbelief, in Coleridge's sense of the poetic — accepting the metatrope of literary constructedness as the essential illusion of the fiction-reading contract — Sebald provokes the reader to suspend belief, destabilizing the reading contract by inverting it, presenting as documented nonfiction what is in fact a literary construction. So foregrounded is his method that the reader is compelled into disobedience, into contestation and interrogation as an index of his or her readerly identity, of self, of being in the world. Sebald's essay on Tripp's pictures ("As Day and Night, Chalk and Cheese," 2004, 79–94) is the *locus classicus* of his own statement of poetics.

In Ross Chambers's sense, following Barthes's notion of a *scriptible* text which makes the reader one of its producers, this seemed to be the kind of narrative practice, like a disobedient reading of Luke, which invited "the necessarily *dual* input" of the text and reader into "the communicative event" (14). In Sebald's case, the disobedient reader's transgression of the textual boundary, eliding that boundary in some places altogether, was both invited and in some respects compelled. Reading Luke's text obediently, from within the *consensus fidelium* authorized by the certified interpreters or according to the authority of the Christian Church, now ebbing in the West, is possibly the less adventurous alternative to ranging disobediently outside institutional readings to renegotiate a revitalized engagement with the language of the text as its interrogatory reader. In this way the text retains its vitality, not merely preserved in the memory of mankind as something ritually intoned.

Chambers's notion that "the 'literary' . . . is not a characteristic of the texts *as such* but that it is a contextual phenomenon" (24) goes some way toward accounting for the shift in the reading of Luke, both in the polarization of current churchmanship, at least in Australia, between literal fundamentalism and liberal practices, and in my own disobedient appropriation of it as reader. In the light of what Chambers called the "alienation" of the literary (13), Sebald had taken on that very decentring, that alterity of the literary, as part of his enterprise and ironized it in the form that he gave it.

Sebald's fiction strips back the conventional "mechanisms" of the novel, its plot and its characters, what might seem part of the bones of narrative, and substitutes for them the "authority" of what seems to be nonfiction, only to playfully subvert it by exposing its constructedness and foregrounding the unstable writerly subject, in turn destabilizing the reader and positioning him or her to assume authority for him/herself, privileging that very engagement between the reader and the text's language, the temporal act of reading itself. This too seemed to suggest that what Chambers names the "situationally self-referential" quality of the literary (25) liberated Luke's text from its institutional dignity, so that I, for one, might play in its space as disobedient reader, opening a pathway into Sebald's textual landscape, that linguistic topology which is also the place of the subject, and which, at first sight, resisted being identified as literary, but gradually revealed itself to be paradigmatically so in its very resistance. As reader, I would also have to be crafty myself (Robert Scholes's term), resistant (de Certeau's formulation), and disobedient.

The postmodern practice of foregrounding the readerliness of the reader and the writerliness of the text was a part of the postmodern paradigm (Atlas 1999) that Sebald could comfortably occupy. The God-author was absent, as in Joyce and Flaubert, hidden behind the text. In Luke's case the God-narrative, and the narrator, who seemed to be the author, was exposed as an artful construction after all, someone made in the author's likeness. The reader's response in Sebald is destabilized because his or her engagement cannot encounter a stable mimetic alterity; the coordinates in Sebald's prose are the patterns of thought, observation, contemplation, association, in short the subject, represented by the syntactical patterns of his prose, no reassuringly historical individual.

Luke's task, by contrast, is to find the solid ground of certainty for the reader in translating the fearsome, vertiginous subjectivity in Zacharaias's and Mary's encounters with alterity — the one witnessed by the crowd outside the temple, the other only able to be witnessed by a corpus of believers formed by the transmission of oral testimony — into a scriptural economy, into the simple, colloquial prose in which Luke documents the historicity of what he, with others, believes is the incarnation of God, conceived by the Holy Spirit and born as Mary's child, the Messiah: an ambitious textual task.

Obedient readings of Luke's story were perpetuated in the institution of ritual liturgical readings which shaped private devotional ones, but its many painted representations suggested that there was some place for play, both for the artist and for the spectator. Mary's clothes, for instance, place her in a Renaissance setting more often than a Middle Eastern one; she more often resembles an aristocratic European lady of considerable means than she does a humble Jewess from Judaea. For that matter the incarnation of the Divine Word, that seraphic androgyne Gabriel, looks more often like an irresistibly beautiful postpubescent *putto* wearing the elegant textiles of Western Europe, red stockings on the accompanying angel notwithstanding (*Annunciazione di Filippo Lippi*, 1437–41, in Cappella Martelli, Florence), than the embodied Word of God. The narrative of the text confirmed for believers and obedient readers what they may have wanted to hear: that redemption from sin, and salvation from death, was the gift of the grace of faith. The artists who depicted this exercised their imaginations by locating the past in their own, and the viewers', actuality.

Sebald has an interest in uncertainty because it is authentic, what Lyotard construes as a skepticism that makes us mistrust totalizing metanarratives, favoring the intimacy of personal voice in micronarrative. Sebald's interest lies in part in what he calls "metaphysics" (Cuomo 2001), that science of the uncertain, which permeates his writing and which intrudes, irrationally, into the world in which we live. Sebald, buried from an ancient Norman church according to the rites of the Church of England having lived in a former rectory just outside a great Cathedral city, is interested in his writing in the ways in which "decent prose" (Atlas 1999) traces, in the patterns of its syntax, the otherwise unutterable space in which we live, to which our thought takes flight and in which our imagination wanders.

The picture on Sebald's parents' bedroom wall, reproduced in the essays in *On the Natural History of Destruction* (73), is that of Christ in the Garden of Gethsemane, abandoned to face a destiny of suffering and death alone. This picture, bought by his parents just before their wedding in 1936 in Bamberg when his father was "transport sergeant in the cavalry regiment" (74), is perhaps the *locus* of his own deeply destabilized sense of his German background, a site opening into the "jumble" (74) of the abyss of time. It is an image of great complexity, especially in the context of his memory and the photograph of his devout parents' bedroom wall. Its purchase as a mutual pre-wedding gift by a couple of ordinary Germans from a provincial place whose son will become a major writer preoccupied by metaphysical possibility and the mystery of the human was something that Sebald himself called to our attention.

By scrutinizing the Greek text and dealing with the task of translation, I could see more readily how some of the provisionality of translation revealed the intrinsic valency of language and its constructions, which in turn affected my reading of the text, so familiar to a more obedient reader, as less stable than the authorized English versions suggested it was. The attributes of reliable authority are lined up by Luke in his preface in a tight phalanx of rhetoric. πολλοι επεχειρησαν — "many people have put their hands to it" (my translation, as in the sections that follow). αναταξασθαι διηγησιν περι των πεπληροφορημενων εν ἡμιν πραγματων — "to order in their proper sequence the account of what has been completed/accomplished/fulfilled and things which we all firmly believe are true." The narrative task of history is the "proper" sequencing of the past, which includes a collective or shared notion of authenticity or truth of actual deeds. καθως παρεδοσαν απ' αρχης — "as having been handed down from the beginning." Luke confirms a sense of continuing tradition that confers additional authority. ʽοι αυτοπται ʽυπηρεται γενομενοι του λογου — "the eyewitnesses who were humble servants of the word." Luke's identification of his sources here includes the strongest historical authority, eyewitnesses, a claim of authority that will become sharper, and more necessary, in the Annunciation narratives that follow, and these eyewitnesses are also "laborers" or "humble servants," people who seek no privilege or advantage for themselves in the transmission of their stories, but have become servants of the "word" (the plural, λογοι, means history, chronicle, authentic narrative) identifying their task as the duty of storytelling, of disseminating story in the metonymy of "word"; εδοξε καμοι — "it seemed to me": this is Luke inserting the self-reflexive subject. παρηκολουθηκοτι ανωθεν πασιν αριβως — "having attended closely to everything and with a sense of overview, from the very first." Luke is invoking his own authority, with the adverb αριβως — "exactly, accurately, precisely" — suggesting that in the smallest detail, both in the narration and in the ordering or arrangement of his narratives, he stands accountable, absolutely reliable. This is historical discourse taking on an almost scientific notion of exactitude, a verifiability inflected with the voice of the author.

Later on in verse 29, where the narrative of the Gospel has begun, Mary is, when the archangel appears to her, "much perplexed by his words and ponder[s] what sort of greeting this might be" (NRSV). Mary's reaction to this angelic encounter, which has fascinated artists for centuries, is more complex in the Greek than the NRSV translation quite suggests: Η δε ιδουσα διεταραχθη επι τω λογω αυτου, και διελογιζετο ποταπος ειη ο ασπασμος ουτος. (She, having seen, was thrown into great confusion by what he said and she turned over in her mind from where this affection/ embrace might be.)

The meditative response can be read in different ways, fearfully and passively obedient, or signaling potential resistance. Mary's angelic encounter, unlike Zacharaias's earlier more public one, is a deeply private, interiorized moment. Fra Angelico's fresco at the top of the staircase is, like Leonardo's painting of the same moment, depicted as occurring in a particular place and setting; the second smaller one in the monk's cell, whose figures are very like those in the first, is painted as though it occurs in the poetic space of the subject, firstly of Mary, and then of the spectator, so that the subject of each becomes, curiously and strangely, indistinguishable in the act of silent meditation, of contemplation. The Greek text catches, as do many paintings, the dread of the moment and Marian interrogation. The NRSV smoothes that away into something more doctrinally satisfactory.

By alienating the text, creating a readerly *Verfremdungseffekt*, that Brechtian alienation of the audience, I could enjoy a perspective across that space of detachment in which I was able to construct my own reading, triggering that readerly "flight of thought" and "wandering imagination" (Kristeva) that revitalized my engagement with that text as its reader. What follows in this book is a reflection of that experience, an encounter with a language-constructed reality that claimed historicity, a scrupulous historical perspective, for something that had engaged the author's imagination, as it would the reader's.

The angelic voice behind me in the pew that early evening, in that twilight of the raven, had provided me with one of the keys to the writing of someone else, a writer of fiction presenting as nonfiction in the last decade of the twentieth century, which posed Hoesterey's "reception dilemma" (2001, 93). We might read the texts of a certain W. G. Sebald, that presenter of what seems to be unmediated nonfiction ironized by a quasi-autobiographical, constructed narrator, modeled on a template of authority, in ways that are suggested in the chapters that follow.

That mediating angelic voice had suggested, obliquely, that it was difficult to distinguish between the voices: God's and Gabriel's, Sebald's and the Sebaldian narrator, except by close textual scrutiny, except by locating the difference between Luke's first four verses and the rest of the chapter's narrative, except by registering Sebald's use of the subjunctive of indirect or reported speech in the German original, and the tendency to the elision of that in the English translations. In Sebald's case the confusion is artful, as he would realize most fully in his most melancholy text, *Austerlitz*; in Luke's case I was happy to leave it at the point of de Certeau's mystic story (1992), unutterable mystery expressed in the only way possible — through the metaphor of *fabula*, Gabriel's painted red

Renaissance hose and those many faces of Mary, some potentially disobedient, notwithstanding.

Presenting fiction as nonfiction in such a bold way and then ironizing reading protocols and subverting the reader's position suggested a high level of ludic interaction for a disobedient reader, also a little jaded perhaps by what Sebald, as writer, called "that tiresome *Realismusfrage*" (Silverblatt 2001) persisting in narrative practice, and avid for something new. An adventurous and disobedient reader could be invited to play, subjectively, in the spaces which had opened up, making links and connections and patterns by exercising his or her imagination, playing across that tension between the appearance of what was being represented and its dissolution into oblivion.

What Hoesterey calls the "creative appropriation of the past, the imaginative theft of the past," in her designation "a critical and intellectual operation of the contemporary consciousness" (68), is wedded in Sebald to the intrinsic subversiveness of art which must "provide for a discourse of difference and resistance" (119). In Sebaldian poetics the reconstructed story of the past, in which are juxtaposed those fragments of recorded or documented fact, the silent spaces (like Kluge's cuts), and the narrated fictions to which those fragments have given rise, is a "discourse of difference and resistance" because of that disobedient and adventurous reader. That reader, that imaginative and thoughtful reader, is invited to be a proactive reader because Sebaldian fiction, like Alexander Kluge's films in Langford's excellent formulation, "place[s] the emphasis on the role of the spectator in the production of meaning" (2003).

2: From W to the Norwich–London Road

The smell

of my writing paper
    puts me in mind
of the woodshavings
in my grandfather's
    coffin
    — "The smell," W. G. Sebald and Tess Jaray, *For Years Now*, 2001

I do think that we largely delude ourselves with the knowledge that we
think we possess, that we make it up as we go along, that we make it
fit our desires and anxieties and that we invent a straight line of a trail
in order to calm ourselves down.
    — Sebald to James Wood, New York, July 1997

Our brains, after all,
are always at work on some quivers
of self-organization, however faint,
and it is from this that an order
arises, in places beautiful
and comforting, though more cruel, too,
than the previous state of ignorance.
    — Sebald, "Dark Night Sallies Forth," from *After Nature*

Tracking Max: Winfried Georg Maximilian "Max" Sebald (1944–2001)

THIS STORY, A DOCUMENTED FRAGMENT, begins in a village in a remote
corner of southern Germany and concludes in Norfolk on the main
road leading from Norwich to London.

The writer W. G. Sebald was born in the Bavarian village of Wertach
"at the back of a valley" (Sebald 2002, 86) in the mountains of the Allgäu
in Southern Germany to Rosa, née Engelhofer, and Georg Sebald
(McCulloh 2003, xv). In Sebald's own words, "Wertach was a village of
about a thousand inhabitants, in a valley covered in snow for five months
a year. It was a silent place" (Jaggi 2001b). He was born on 18 May 1944,
Ascension Day, the feast that commemorates the completion of the Jesus pilgrimage from the appearance of the archangel Gabriel to Mary, with the message from God that she will conceive and bear a son who will be the Son of

God — The Messiah, the Savior of the World, The Anointed One (the "Christos"). The ironic resonance of that ubiquitous Sebaldian date, which appears in his last text without any gloss like an eloquently silent annunciation (Sebald 2001b, 415), reflects the inauguration of the Christian narrative by a "messenger" (Jaggi 2001a) — a moment handed down in textual tradition to mark the birth and also the death of God's Messiah, both mortal and immortal, a metaphysical disclosure promising redemption from death, a principal preoccupation of Sebald's oeuvre. The historical fact of Sebald's own birth is therefore inextricably connected with mystery, as he mischievously and obliquely reminds us in his reference to the date's significance in each of his texts, and this nexus of historical determinism and the irreducible sense of the mysterious which subverts, destabilizes, and reflects the porosity of boundaries between the observed and the imagined, the living and the dead, the present and the past, will become a dominant motif in the pattern of Sebald's extraordinary and generically transgressive prose.

Sebald's father Georg, a locksmith (Alvarez 2001), came from an "intensely Catholic" (Lubow 2001) glassmaking family whose values reflected the small, conservative and insular rural community in the forests of the foothills of the Bavarian alps. Sebald's mother, Rosa, was the daughter of a country policeman in Wertach (Jaggi 2001a). The shape of Sebald's life was to be marked both by a distinct rupture from this background — geographically, nationally, and professionally — and by the disruptive annunciations of the past that haunted the contingent moments embodied in his lyrical use of language, mediated by and reconstructed through memory: Sebald's own memorializing subjectivity and his often arcane and carefully researched appropriations from the collective memory of the European cultural archive (Green 1999).

In the circumstance of being born German near the end of the Second World War, Sebald's continuing use of the German language in his own writing voiced the past's silent haunting in the present. In his subversion of what he often referred to as the national character of Teutonic earnestness reflected in his own inherited predisposition to a "saturnine temperament" (Zeeman 1998), he exercised an idiosyncratic, playful wit reinforced by a delight in British eccentricity that expresses itself in his use of irony, that ludic spirit which insinuates itself into the plangent melancholy of his contemplative narrative voice. Sebald weaves a kind of postmodern texture of the most confronting tragedy with the interpolation of comic leaven. Greek and Shakespearean drama did the same. At no time though does Sebald allow this ironic and comic dimension to erode the moral seriousness of his enterprise, what he calls "the moral backbone of literature" (Lubow 2001). On the contrary, his saccadic flashes of black humor, playful wit, or mordantly ironic allusion create in a finely judged, often exquisitely calibrated way a comic foregrounding in the reader's carefully scrutinizing perspective; this in turn provides a sense of distance from which his readers can "peer into the depths" (Sebald in "Wie Tag und Nacht," 1998b) in the memories of the past, the "long perspectives" the English poet Philip Larkin says "Open at each instant of our lives. / They link us to our losses" (from "Reference Back," 106). Sebald's exquisitely poised aesthetic, that balancing on the tension between "*apparition et effacement*" (Dagen 2006), is a poetically complex vision, one not easily reducible to discussion as narrative let alone as signifying practice, as McCulloh, among others, points out (24).

Born Winfried Georg Maximilian, Sebald was known later as Max to his friends and colleagues ("because he loathed the Germanic mythological pomposity of Winfried," Alvarez 2001). Sebald had discovered, like many of his generation growing up in rural parts of Germany, the history of his own country's immediate past through indirect means, thanks to the "conspiracy of silence about the war" (Homberger 2001). He described his childhood as ordinary: "I never thought much about anything at all. I had a penchant for reading, but otherwise I was the same as everybody else — skiing and all the rest of it" (Atlas 1999). In his case the silence about the war was broken only in his adolescence, through the viewing of a film about the liberation of the concentration camp at Belsen one afternoon at school in Oberstdorf when he was sixteen, after which, Sebald related, there was "no discussion" (Homberger 2001).

In the economic slump after the defeat of Germany in the First World War, Sebald's father, unemployed in 1939, joined the Wehrmacht, "the Weimar One Hundred Thousand Man Army" (Atlas 1999), as a result of which the family fortunes continued to improve during the rise of the Third Reich (Homberger 2001). Captured and put in a French prison camp, Georg Sebald had been absent for the first three years of his son's life, until 1947. By the end of the war he had risen to the rank of captain. Sebald, the eldest of four children with three sisters (Jaggi 2001a), was in other respects shielded from the realities of war by his youth and by the accident of his birthplace, a beautiful rural valley in the foothills of alpine Germany near the Swiss border, a marginal part of Germany close to the borders with Switzerland, Austria and France. Nonetheless, the college for the Nazi elite, the Sonthofen Ordensburg, was in the nearby market town whose name the college bore. Sebald's mother, Rosa, as he relates biblically in terms reminiscent of Mary's journey, but also of Lot and his wife, in his poem *After Nature*, was pregnant with him when she was prevented from traveling home to Wertach through Nuremberg, and turning to look, she saw Nuremberg burning after the Allied airstrikes, a bombing raid which would most likely have set off from the airfields in East Anglia. Less than thirty years later Sebald would make East Anglia his home. These are coincidences and contiguities in his own life that would later be reflected in his poetics, and in his ambivalent relationship with his cultural origin.

Sebald recounts that he was taken to Munich when he was three, and that his first impression of a city as being a place of ruin never really left him. Later in the story based on one of his primary-school teachers, the one-part Jew and three-parts Aryan Paul Bereyter in *The Emigrants*, Sebald draws on another retrospective glimpse into the silent and pervasive presence of the traumatic legacy of unspoken horror, whose geographic, national and familial proximity to Sebald's childhood would subsequently be embodied in his construction of what Delia Falconer calls the "neurasthenic" narrator of his fictional texts (2001a), what Sebald would later describe as an "authentic" narrator, someone whose hypersensitive perspective was known to the reader, who recounted only what he himself saw and heard (Lubow 2001), in his case a narrator who reflected the ruins, the trauma, the suffering, but also a consoling engagement with the beauty of the natural world and with art that offered a glimpse of man's capacity to create rather than destroy. The shadows cast by the Third Reich, by the Second World War, and by the emerging story of the Holocaust would come to haunt Sebald's prose, particularly in the etiolated quality of the narrative voice, but they do not in themselves comprise the scope, or sole focus, of Sebald's writing. Sebald's preoccupations concern even larger, less historically determined questions about the nature of the human, in his own term, its "oddness," the term reflecting his tendency to laconic *litote*. In Sebald's writing in each of his texts the resonant and unfathomable mystery at the core of human experience is irreducible, inexplicable, and his writing invests the scrupulously rendered *quidditas* of observed and contemplated detail with a luminous quality, a curious evocation of the phenomenon of epiphany that makes reading him such an unsettling experience and which engages the subjectivity of the reader in such an explicit way, much as a painting can.

We see this, early on, in the first part of the triptych poem, *After Nature*, in section IV, where Sebald is describing a painting in the Chicago Art Institute that the scholar Zülch believes is a self-portrait of the young Matthias Grünewald. Sebald's ekphrastic account segues into a mysterious conjunction or juxtaposition of absence and presence, of life's concrete details recorded and art's imaginative transmutation of them:

> . . . The small maple panel shows a scarcely twenty-year-old at the window of a narrow room. Behind him, on a shelf not quite in perspective, pots of paint, a crayon, a seashell and a precious Venetian glass filled with a translucent essence. In one hand the painter holds a finely carved knife of bone with which to trim the drawing pen before continuing work on a female nude that lies in front of him next to an inkwell. Through the window on his left a landscape with mountain and valley and the curved line of a path is visible. This last, Zülch philosophizes, is the way into the world, and no one took it other than the man, vanished without trace, to whom his research is devoted and whose art he thinks he can recognize in the anonymous picture. (2002, 17–18)

Sebald spent a good deal of the childhood he described as "idyllic" in his maternal grandfather's company, "practically by my grandad's side" (Alvarez 2001) — "his hiking companion and confidant" (Lubow 2001). He seems never really to have developed a close relationship with his father, who, after the war during which he was taken prisoner, "was a clerk in an office until the fifties" (Atlas 1999) "in a neighbouring village" (Alvarez 2001). Georg Sebald rejoined the reconstituted German army in 1955, spending further periods of time away from the family home.

The death of Sebald's grandfather, Josef Engelhofer, "an exceptionally kind man" (Jaggi 2001a), in 1956 had a lasting effect. "As a boy I felt protected. His death when I was 12 wasn't something I ever quite got over. It brought an early awareness of mortality and that the other side of life is something horrendously empty" (Jaggi 2001b). This event appears to be a significant part of the inauguration of a preoccupation in his writing, "some would call it an obsession" (Wood 1998), with death, what Richard Sheppard calls Sebald's "*mors* code." "My interest in the departed, which has been fairly constant, comes from that moment of losing someone you couldn't really afford to lose. I broke out in a skin disease right after his death, which lasted for years" (Lubow 2001). In his adult life Sebald kept a photograph of his grandfather on his desk in his office at UEA (Gordon Turner, remark made at Davidson Symposium, 2003). "He died when I was 12 and this huge hole entered my universe. It's now 45 years hence, and I still miss the man" (Alvarez 2001). The pathology of Sebald's narrators begins here. We should not position Sebald as a writer characterized by the autobiographical turn in German fiction but rather construct his narrator as a figure whose very voice articulates the imprisoning narcissism of the modern subject by representing it as disengaged, as exiled, as posthumous. This is a voice unable to free itself from the anxieties attached to its individual history, unable to accept its absorption into the collective history of mankind.

When he was five, Sebald saw in his father's photograph album a photograph of a fellow soldier who had died in a motor accident, lying dead with his eyes open and surrounded by flowers. In Sebald's telling, this was another instance of his growing consciousness of human subjection to natural destiny and to historical accident: "I had a hunch that this is where it all began — a great disaster that had occurred which I knew nothing about" (Lubow 2001). There is an ambiguity here: is this the fact of death itself, the child's awareness of his own mortal fate, or was it his first intimation about his country's immediate past and its complicit role in the destruction of Jewry and of Europe? That the historical events which shape us are the history of our (self-)destruction? The soldier's death was an accident — perhaps the irony of this absurd death and the paradox of seeming life ("eyes open") are even more telling here than soldierliness. Sebald's awareness of death, of chance, and of the irreversible impact of historical events in the past was, in his telling, shaped early. The inexplicable mystery at the heart of things is coded here in a five-year-old's perception becoming a memory that shapes the adult's poetics.

Sebald revealed to Lubow that both his father and grandfather were depressive types, the source perhaps of his own melancholy. Sebald contextualized this by adding that he only ever saw his father read one book, recounting that it was a book given to him "just at the beginning of the ecological movement, with a name like *The End of the Planet*. And my father was bowled over by it. I saw him underlining every sentence of it — with a ruler, naturally — saying 'Ja, ja'" (Lubow 2001). This anecdote captures Sebald's subversive wit, his capacity for sardonic mockery and, perhaps, his strategy for dealing with his own temperament: reading, writing, and comic irony so sharp in his prose that it can often be barely discernible. In an earlier interview Sebald again referred to his father: "He retired early as one does in that profession (the army), and has done nothing for the last forty years but read the newspaper and comment on the headlines. He has a critical bent of mind, and very pronounced opinions about the issues of the day" (Atlas 1999). When Atlas asked Sebald about his father's opinion of his son's work, Sebald replied, "He took a certain interest when there was public attention; then he seemed to be jolly pleased about it" (Atlas 1999).

Sebald began his undergraduate degree in German literature at the University of Freiburg, where he met Ute, the fellow student who became his wife subsequently in 1967 (Lubow 2001). While Sebald was an undergraduate student at Freiburg in 1965, the Auschwitz trials were taking place in Frankfurt (Homberger 2001): "It gave me an understanding of the real dimensions for the first time: the defendants were the kind of people I had known as neighbors — postmasters or railway workers — whereas the witnesses were people I'd never come across — Jewish people from Brooklyn or Sydney. They were a myth of the past" (Jaggi 2001a).

Sebald's disaffection with the teaching in the early sixties of what he was to describe as a "culture of xenophobia," ideas with a residual Nazi tenor (Wood 1998), by the senior academic staff ("dissembling old fascists," Sebald to Green 1999) in the German department at Freiburg where Martin Heidegger was Rector (where, as he relished in the telling, one of Sebald's papers was annotated "This is not a cabaret, this is a German literature seminar" [Lubow 2001]), had resulted in Sebald's transferring to the University of Fribourg in the French-speaking canton of Switzerland to finish his degree. This gave him, as McCulloh points out, "a lifelong devotion to French literature" (xvi), a strong intertextual presence in Sebald's later writing.

This move, geographical and cultural, signaled the first decisive step away from his German national identity, a link which he explicitly regretted on several occasions, both in references embedded in his texts and in interviews. We read in *Vertigo*, when the narrator lies awake in his hotel room because of the noise that the German tourists below are making, "How I wished during those sleepless hours that I belonged to a different nation, or, better still, to none at all" (93–94), and in *The Emigrants*, "I felt increasingly that the mental impoverishment and lack of memory that marked the Germans, and the efficiency with which they had cleaned everything up, were beginning to affect my head and my nerves" (as Schwartz notes in Clark et al. 2002).

When offered a position in creative writing at the University of Hamburg in 1998, Sebald told James Atlas, "I did not want to be drawn into the German culture industry. I do feel uncomfortable in Germany. It feels like a cold country" (Atlas 1999). In an interview with Arthur Lubow in 2001, Sebald said that one of the principal reasons that he had left Germany was that he "found it agreeable not to hear current German spoken all around me" (Lubow in Clark et al. 2002). In one of his last interviews, held in England in 2001 in the year he died, Sebald joked that, in his chronic condition of homelessness in the world, his "ideal station is a hotel in Switzerland" (Jaggi 2001a), an implicit and ironic reference to Nabokov, who lived in the Grand Palace Hotel in Montreux in his final years. He had fantasized with Lubow a little earlier about retiring to rented accommodation somewhere in Northern France, "to Combray" (Lubow 2001), which, although Lubow does not comment, does not exist outside Proust's novel but is based on the village of Illiers, a name now, rather arrestingly, hyphenated on French maps as Illiers-Combray.

Sebald, whose command of English was "rudimentary" when he finished his undergraduate degree (McCulloh xvi), went to England in 1966 as a language assistant. "That I ended up in Manchester was again rather a fluke. I knew hardly any English at the time, and I had no idea what England was like" (Wood 1998, 94). "I scarcely spoke English, and coming from a backwoods I found it difficult to adapt" (Jaggi 2001a). In conversation with Christopher Bigsby at Norwich, Sebald had said: "I decided to go to Manchester because in Freiburg I had come across an English guest professor for whom I did some quite decent work. He was my only contact in this country and it was through him that I found my first teaching post in Manchester" (Bigsby 2001). Happenstance had led Sebald to the city "Disraeli called . . . / the most wonderful city of modern times, / a celestial Jerusalem" (*After Nature*, 95), its industry Hebrew in tenor, as Disraeli was.

Sebald lived there for a year while undertaking a Master's degree at the University of Manchester, researching the writing of Carl Sternheim, a playwright born in Leipzig in 1878 to a Protestant mother and a Jewish father, and who died in Brussels in 1942. Sternheim's sharply satirical farces were banned by the Nazis. This was a telling choice of writer and topic. The owner of an outstanding contemporary art collection,

Sternheim also owned a work by Albrecht Altdorfer, a richly imaginative, nature-loving German painter important to Sebald, particularly in *After Nature* where he writes about *The Battle of Alexander at Issus* (1529) hanging in the Alte Pinakothek in Munich, with its depiction of historic events within a cosmic discourse and the diminution of the human scale of the figures in it.

Manchester, Sebald's first English "station," is the highly industrialized city where many Jews had settled after escaping from Europe and where there had been an established Jewish population prior to that. This is where Sebald situates the painter Max Aurach (German)/Ferber (English translation) in *The Emigrants*, the artist based on Frank Auerbach, who actually lives in Camden Town in London and many of whose works hang in the Tate. It was the city where, as he discovered later, the Viennese philosopher Ludwig Wittgenstein had lived for a time when he first came to England from Austria as an engineering student, and where the writer Elias Canetti had lived, like Sebald, in Palatine Road, coincidences that he found suggestive, even prophetic. Sebald described himself as completely unprepared for Manchester, and for England. In the conversation with Bigsby conducted under the auspices of the Arthur Miller Centre at the University of East Anglia, Sebald remarked:

> I knew very little about England. I had practically no English — at school I had done Latin and Greek. English wasn't on the curriculum for me. And I certainly had no idea of the history or the culture of this country, or of its topography. I knew nothing about the north/south divide or any of the other great English myths. Nor had I ever lived in a large city before. In Germany and Switzerland I had lived in idyllic, beautiful towns. I had no concept of what an industrial wasteland was because I hadn't seen that kind of degradation before. I arrived at Ringway airport and as I drove into town in a taxi I could not believe my eyes. I thought I had arrived on another planet and it took me a long time to get used to it. The experience cast me into a considerable depression which lasted until Christmas. (Bigsby 2001)

In 1968 Sebald returned to Europe and for a year taught at an elementary school in St Gallen, Switzerland, as Wittgenstein had done before him, but in 1969 he was back in Manchester teaching German literature. In 1970 he was appointed to a lectureship in German at the University of East Anglia. When Bigsby asked why he had decided to stay in England, Sebald pointed out that there were considerable advantages for "aspiring young scholars" that to him were "out of the ordinary" (Bigsby 2001). Sebald listed them as "a heated office," the ability to "go to the library at any time and pretty much all the books that I wanted [be] there," "a salary which was paid in what were then quite valuable pounds sterling . . . I could, for the first time, buy an aeroplane ticket and even put money aside" (Bigsby 2001). These material benefits were reinforced by Sebald's observation that "you gradually got to know the people and you found out that these British were a strange race but extremely nice. They left you alone most of the time but if you needed them they would be there in a very generous way. At the university there wasn't anything that resembled an authoritarian structure. For someone who had grown up in a system of this sort and who, by nature, has something perhaps of an anarchist streak, this really felt like freedom" (Bigsby 2001).

In 1975 he was granted leave of absence, an "unusual" concession which was the result of "the perspicacity of our German Professor" (Gordon Turner, private communication 2004). Although "perfectly happy at UEA" and with no desire to teach in a German university, Sebald had wanted to explore "in the 'spirit of the grass being greener' . . . the possibility of making a career in the propagation of the German culture in its widest sense" (Turner 2004) at the Goethe Institute in Munich. This points up the ambivalence Sebald seems to have felt about his Germanness, his conflicted sense of national belonging. According to Turner, Sebald had got to know fellow Germans in Manchester who were members of staff at the Goethe Institute there, and "had been quite attracted to the work and the possibility of living abroad that the job of Director entailed" (Turner 2004). His return to UEA after a year was determined by his discovery that "he was neither fulfilled by the DAF (Deutsch als Fremdsprache) teaching which he was required to do . . . nor by the bureaucratic mentality expected of top administrators" (Turner 2004). Turner recognized too the irony of this decision, noting that "by the late 70s it was to become clear that Germanistik [German Studies in the original literature-based sense] was showing the first signs of its subsequent terminal decline" (Turner 2004). The contemporary vigor of Germanistik in relation to Sebald's work, and to other contemporary writers, is indicative perhaps of something like a revival.

Returning to UEA with a firmer and clearer sense of "where his career should take him" (Turner 2004), and in order to consolidate his credentials, Sebald wrote a doctoral thesis on Alfred Döblin, the modernist novelist and essayist born in 1878. This too was a choice of writer and topic with repercussions in Sebald's later writing. Döblin had completed a medical degree at the University of Freiburg in 1905, another similarity, specializing later in psychiatry. His best-known novel Berlin Alexanderplatz (1929) uses an unconventional interior monologue narration reflecting James Joyce's use of it in Ulysses (1922), a book much admired by Döblin, who wrote on it in an essay published in 1928, praising Joyce for discarding the narrative conventions of what he called "the old flat fabulation" (Liukkonen 2004). Döblin rejected "one-dimensional linear plots and character" as "non-essential" (Liukkonen 2004). This too would resonate later in Sebald's own practice. Berlin Alexanderplatz provides, as Joyce does of Dublin in Ulysses, a scrupulously documentary description of

Berlin, and Döblin's last novel, *Hamlet* (1956), uses the montage technique he had employed in *Berlin Alexanderplatz* nearly thirty years earlier.
Döblin wrote: "art is individual, anarchistic, but accumulation of facts and
details is also important to the modern epic," and in an essay published in
1936, entitled "The Historical Novel and Us," Döblin wrote that every
novel was "essentially historical" and also "the modern-day fairy-tale"
(Liukkonen 2004).

It is difficult not to think here of those *Märchen* moments, those fairy-
tale fabulations, like the scene in the Jewish cemetery in the East End of
London in *Austerlitz*, the turbanned porter with the broom in Liverpool
Street station, also in *Austerlitz*, Coleridge's Ancient Mariner's barque in
The Rings of Saturn, Dante appearing on Gonzagastrasse in *Vertigo*, the
daughters of the night at their loom in *The Emigrants*, not least that filmic
technique of *montage* and the scrupulous rendering of facts that Sebald
shares with the subject of his doctoral project and which he has adapted in
his own way for his own writerly purposes. This thesis was published in
1980 as *Der Mythus der Zerstörung im Werk Döblins* ("The Myth of
Destruction in Döblin's Work"). It is not yet available in English.

His academic career was progressing and Sebald would remain at the
University of East Anglia for the rest of his life, teaching there mostly in
the School of Modern Languages and European History, with the exception of "a short break when he returned to Switzerland" (Williams 2000,
100; unless, as he seems to have done, Williams has confused the year in
1968 spent in St Gallen with the year spent in Munich in 1975), until the
School of Modern Languages and European History was rationalized, the
staff reassigned (see below) and he found himself in the School of English
and American Studies. In 1986, very quietly (Gordon Turner, private communication 2004), Sebald had completed a dissertation and submitted it
formally to the University of Hamburg for the award of a *Doktor phil.habil.*,
the second professional doctorate required for teaching in German universities. According to his friend Turner, Sebald had "continuing misgivings
about neoconservative Germanist professors in Germany" and was therefore unlikely to have "ever seriously considered applying for a post at a
German university but it was one way of advancing his career in the UK"
(Turner 2004).

Proposed for and appointed to a personal chair as Professor of
European Literature at UEA in 1987, the year after he had been awarded
this second doctorate by the University of Hamburg, Sebald continued
teaching as a Germanist particularly interested in the German-language literature of Austria and Switzerland, what he called the marginal German-
speaking world. His colleague Jo Catling described him as a "Kafka
scholar," a photograph of whom he had posted on the door to his room
at UEA (Catling 2003, 19). Sebald taught a unit on the films of the
Weimar Republic (Sebald's webpage at UEA, accessed 2001), an interest

that is reflected in his references to Fritz Lang's films in his fiction, as well as to the much more recent ones of Werner Herzog, and which inform his own technique, what we might call, after Jeff Malpas, writing about place and experience, "juxtaposition" and "displacement" (1999, 168). Another academic colleague at UEA, Eric Homberger, in his reflection, describes Sebald's lectures as "sardonic and challenging," possessing "the same dry wit, and feel for irony, which enlivened his conversation" (Homberger 2001), qualities that other colleagues, Jo Catling, Clive Scott, and Gordon Turner, also attest to (Catling in Görner 19, Clive Scott Obituary 2002, Turner Presentation, The Third Occasional Davidson Symposium on German Studies, Davidson College 2003).

In the 1980s and 1990s the University of East Anglia changed as a result of cost-cutting measures. Sebald was transferred to the School of English and American Studies and also, with one other Germanist colleague, to the newly constituted School of Language, Linguistic and Translation Studies, which, in Gordon Turner's estimate "was the beginning of the sharp demise of language teaching at UEA" (2004). According to Turner,

> . . . with Max and the colleagues in English and American Studies the German Sector now, very uncomfortably, straddled both schools of study [EAS and LLT]. All the language and linguistics teaching was provided by LLT with the ever-diminishing provision for pure German Literature teaching (e.g. no more than 3–5 individuals of a total of 40+ students in any one year majoring in Lit) covered by Max and colleague. Their input to German-language teaching thus reduced (Max had taught some language classes until the move), they were subject to the pressure of putting on classes in "European" (meaning Comparative and including English) Literature. (2004)

Sebald was under increasing pressure to teach in the Creative Writing Program, which had been established earlier at UEA in 1970 by Sir Angus Wilson and Professor Malcolm Bradbury, the head of which, since 1995 when Sebald taught within it, having succeeded Bradbury, was the Poet Laureate, Andrew Motion. According to his friend and colleague Turner, Sebald felt uncomfortable as a teacher in the new roles he was expected to fulfill, particularly aware of the anomaly of a German speaker and writer working in an English-language discipline where he felt he was in no position to be correcting and guiding the English prose of student writers (Turner, private communication 2003). In the face of declining numbers of language students, a nationwide phenomenon, it was also a question of professional employment. Sebald had told Toby Green in an interview, "what is happening at the moment is a very critical mutation in our collective figurations. Here in the university I can see how people who were once meant to be critical thinkers are being deautonomized and strapped into networks where they slave away at pointless tasks, while all the time

people become less able to use their own language properly" (1999).
These concerns are major ones in his own writing, not least in the artful
production of a creative reader who is disobedient, encouraged to resist
the apparent authority of the text, together with his own exacting standards of language use and the development of his style.

Arthur Williams describes these standards as "his scrupulous aesthetics
and his principled humanity," which bring "identifiable individuals . . . within
the range of his own and our empathy, and, therefore, within the realm of our
sense of responsibility" (2002, 2006). Richard Evans at Cambridge observed
in his tribute to Sebald that "the decline of the study of European languages
and literatures in Britain, and the growing bureaucratization of university life,
led him to take up creative writing toward the end of the 1980s" (2002).
Williams adds that what Sebald did was to center the "dignity of the individual," and that he "revisited the past in order to enhance our understanding
of the present in the hope of a better future" (2002, 2006).

During his presentation at Davidson College, Turner commented:
"Max was always diffident in English; he never wanted to write in English.
He would always ask someone like me to check his official letters" (2003).
Listening to Sebald in interview, whether on radio or on television
(Silverblatt 2001 and Zeeman 1998), one hears his soft Bavarian accent
very lightly intincting what amounts in every respect to a highly sophisticated use of the English language. It is perhaps a reflection of Sebald's own
professionally and aesthetically exacting standards of "proper" language use
that he was "diffident in English" (Turner, Davidson Presentation 2003).
"I teach in English" (Baker 2001) is after all, in the ephemeral discourse of
oral language, not the same language act as the permanently available
record of writing, something of which Sebald as a literary scholar who was
employing the trope of a speaking voice committing other people's fiction
to permanence in a written text in his imaginative fiction, was clearly mindful. Someone who acquires at school, as Sebald had done, the knowledge
of Latin and Greek, has a foundation experience, if they choose to retain it,
in that curious phenomenon: the capacity of language to demand absolute
precision and a high degree of sensitivity (much valued by Sebald) from a
translator, together with its fearful tendency to movement and entropy. In
T. S. Eliot's words, this is the tendency to "slip, slide, perish, / Decay with
imprecision, will not stay in place, / Will not stay still" (from "Burnt
Norton V," *Four Quartets*, 1968, 17), to stray into the perilous and anar-
chic freedom of disobedience, escaping from the writer's, or translator's,
authority and control. The deep precision of language crafting that kept
Sebald in his study with his face to the wall (Sheppard 2005) as he polished
his German sentences to stylistic perfection is that solitary obsession that
obeys a different authority, one that Sebald recalls out of the past.

Ironically, however, Sebald's growing unease with his role as a teacher
of creative writing was paralleled by his own shift from academic critic to

creative writer. Until the late 1980s, Sebald's published work had consisted entirely of critical writing on German, Austrian and Swiss literature, some of it on well-known writers like Kafka, some of it on less well-known figures, in an English-language sense, like Gottfried Keller and Adalbert Stifter. He also wrote about writers with some profile on the English-language literary scene, Robert Walser and Thomas Bernhard most prominent among them, and was interested in the work of Elias Canetti, a writer who had not received the attention he deserved for many years because of the language of production. Sebald edited one collection of essays in English on German radical theater, a legacy of his work on Sternheim and evidence of his continuing interest in the power of the voice and the theatrical monologue, to be reflected also in his own writing.

Sebald had written a novel while he was in Manchester in 1967, which had been rejected by the publisher to whom he offered it (Tabbart 2003), but in 1988, more than twenty years later, Sebald published, in German, with an offbeat German press, Greno, his first nonacademic work: a long three-part prose poem he called *Nach der Natur — Ein Elementargedicht*, "From Life — an Elemental Poem." It would be published posthumously fifteen years later in English in the translation he had collaborated on with his friend, the poet Michael Hamburger, under the title *After Nature* (2002), the long interval reflecting perhaps the diminished market for an esoteric work of poetry from an unknown writer. In 1990 Sebald published, again in German and in Germany, his first nonacademic work of prose fiction, *Schwindel. Gefühle*, followed by two more in 1993 and 1995, *Die Ausgewanderten* and *Die Ringe des Saturn*. In 1996 his first work translated into English, *The Emigrants*, appeared in Britain, the United States, and Australia, in the poet Michael Hulse's collaborative translation.

In 1989, the year after *Nach der Natur* was published, and two years after his appointment to a personal chair, Sebald established the British Centre for Literary Translation, based at UEA and linked with the British Council, whose annual St Jerome Lecture in London would be renamed the NESTA Sebald Lecture in his honor and memory in 2003. Susan Sontag, who had so eloquently promoted Sebald's writing in its English translations, was invited to deliver the lecture in 2002, the year after his death. Tariq Ali gave it in 2003; in 2004 Carlos Fuentes delivered it and in 2005 Germaine Greer was invited to do so. Gordon Turner remarked that "Max believed in the propagation of literatures other than English in the English-speaking world" (Presentation, Davidson College 2003). A way of getting out of teaching in someone else's creative-writing program was to develop this new institute for translation, in which he would feel more comfortable as an academic.

The language of production is itself, interestingly then, less important as some kind of specific cultural statement or designed to rouse a national "agenbite of inwit" (James Joyce's phrase describing conscience) than as the least troublesome means to a more global sense of literary production, a desire inscribed also in Sebald's founding of the Centre for Translation to give writers whose language of production might otherwise have denied them a larger literary readership and therefore a more sizeable market, dominated as it is in the contemporary global context by what is the *lingua franca* of the new millennium — the hegemonic language of English, an anxiety for Sebald. "There are many reasons why German texts don't really get noticed in the Anglo-Saxon world. There is a natural gradient out of English, which is such a dominant language, into all other minor languages. German certainly is rapidly beginning to acquire the status of a minor language, together with Italian and French . . . Whilst the English had a very highly developed translation culture in the nineteenth century when people like Coleridge and so on were very closely liaised with the German culture, that has largely fallen by the wayside, for historical reasons not least" (Wood 2002, 94).

Nonetheless the Centre for Literary Translation didn't bring in the student numbers, and as an academic Sebald still had to teach, which meant that he couldn't avoid the postgraduate Creative Writing program. Sebald's being asked to teach it had, according to Turner, continued to make him feel distinctly uncomfortable, and he reiterated keenly the view that it was "ridiculous" that he, as a non-native English speaker, should be advising postgraduate writing students in the program which had launched successful writers like Ian McEwan, Kazuo Ishiguro, and Tracy Chevalier, and a generation of newer writers including Ben Rice and Trezza Azzopardi.

The students enrolled in this program were generally taught by a core of people on staff, including Sebald, together with visiting teachers who were established writers, drawn usually from the British and American literary worlds. It must have been an interesting dynamic for a disobedient, a slightly disaffected academic. Increasingly, according to Turner, Sebald was looking to develop a way of living by writing outside the academy, not teaching creative writing within it. In the interview with Maria Alvarez (2001), he had revealed that he had "three years left to teach," turning sixty in 2004, an age sadly that he did not reach.

In the final decade of his life, as Sebald struggled through his academic workload, his new career as a writer took off. In 1997 he was invited as an academic critic to deliver a series of lectures at the University of Zurich, the "Lectures on Poetics." When these were reported and subsequently published in German in 1999 as *Luftkrieg und Literatur* and in English in 2003 in Anthea Bell's translation *On the Natural History of Destruction* (on which Sebald had been working at the time of his death), there was considerable response to Sebald's criticism of postwar German writers for failing, in his view, to confront the consequences of the Second World War in cultural productions in the decades following 1945. This especially focused on the silence that hung over the suffering of the

German people after 600,000 civilians were killed in the Allied bombing raids on the cities of Germany, the "question of why German writers would not or could not describe the destruction of the German cities as millions experienced it" (78). Further on in his "postscript" (69) to these lectures Sebald wrote, "I think that even in their incomplete form they cast some light on the way in which memory (individual, collective and cultural) deals with experiences exceeding what is tolerable" (79). He referred too to the "largely unwritten social history of the corruption of the Germans" and observed that "the combination of fantastic delusions on the one hand and an upright way of life on the other is typical of the particular fault line that ran through the German mind during the first half of the twentieth century" (100). This reflects his position as both a critic of Germany and an academic critic of German literature in the second half of the twentieth century, and also as a writer whose vision of the human is complex: "Such is the dark backward and abysm of time. Everything lies all jumbled up in it, and when you look down you feel dizzy and afraid" (74). This sentence layers references to both Shakespeare (*The Tempest*; 1.2.56–57) and Proust (Vol. XII, 473).

1997 was also the year in which Sebald was interviewed, for the first time in such depth in English, by the critic and writer James Wood of *The New Republic*. This magazine is based in Washington, and the interview was published in the Canadian journal *Brick* the following year (and republished in 2002).

In the last three years of his life, this unassuming, middle-aged academic found himself an international writing star. In 1998, the English translation of his third prose work, *The Rings of Saturn*, was published, followed in 1999 by a translation of *Vertigo*, his first prose work in German. By this time Sebald was developing a considerable profile on the international literary stage and a large number of reviews had appeared, particularly in Britain and the United States. His work had been awarded a number of prestigious literary prizes in Germany, including the Feder-Malchow Prize for lyric poetry for *Nach der Natur* (1991), the Berliner Literaturpreis, the Brobowski Medal and the Preis der Literatur Nord for *Die Ausgewanderten* (1994), the Mörike Prize and the Heinrich Böll Prize for *Die Ringe des Saturn* (1997), and the Heinrich Heine Prize and The Literary Prize of the City of Bremen for *Austerlitz* (2001) (McCulloh xxiii–iv and Long and Whitehead xi–xii). The prizes in the English-language world were slower to come: the Wingate Prize for Fiction (1997) (Long and Whitehead xi) and the *Los Angeles Times* Best Fiction Book Prize (1998) (McCulloh xxiv) were awarded to *The Rings of Saturn* and *The Independent* Foreign Fiction Prize (U.K.) (shared with Anthea Bell as translator) and the National Book Critics Circle Award (U.S.) were awarded posthumously for *Austerlitz* in 2002 (McCulloh xxiv).

One or two of the early reviewers of his first work in English translation, *The Emigrants*, were acquainted with the other texts, not yet translated, and aware of Sebald's literary profile in Germany as a highly individual contemporary writer living and working as an academic in England. It is a matter of some irony that while the Germans recognized Sebald in this public way, in the English-speaking world where he enjoyed such remarkable acclaim, fewer prizes had been forthcoming. He needed perhaps a well-placed literary agent to promote his work in a more proactive way. As remarked earlier, McCulloh observed this from the perspective of variable cultural reception: "Ironically, despite numerous literary prizes in his homeland, he seems to have struck a chord with English-speaking readers to a greater extent than with his fellow Germans" (25). McCulloh speculated that, having lived away for so long and "having absorbed so many different literatures," Sebald was less German than contemporary German readers (25); Sebald had described himself as a European writer on several occasions.

In 1998 the Dutch television literary program, *Kamer met Uitzicht*, had recorded a twenty-minute interview conducted by Michael Zeeman with Sebald in Amsterdam in English, and in 1999 James Atlas published a very detailed interview he had conducted with Sebald in Norwich in *The Paris Review*. Sebald was beginning to be profiled, in depth, as a significant European contemporary writer in the English-speaking world of letters.

Under the auspices of The National Endowment for Science, Technology and the Arts set up by an Act of Parliament in Britain in 1998, which uses "the interest on a National Lottery endowment to pioneer ways of supporting and promoting talent, innovation and creativity" (NESTA website), Sebald was awarded a NESTA grant, under the category of "Global Reach and Relevance," from May 2000. This grant, of £73,000 over four years, would free him from teaching to write for six months each year (Catling 2002), together with the opportunity to develop, under the provisions of the NESTA program, an association with a suitable colleague/mentor. Sebald, who had thrown the letter of award into the wastepaper basket in the mistaken belief that it was from Nestlé, the Swiss-based multinational company, greeted the opportunity afforded by his wife's retrieval of the letter with gratitude and the expression of relief that this would afford him the opportunity perhaps to extricate himself eventually from academic teaching altogether (Gordon Turner, private conversation, 2003). The "scholarship" provided by the NESTA Foundation was a godsend, as it was going to enable Max to teach just one semester a year, with the resultant funding allowing him to concentrate on his writing for the other half of the year. In the event he was able to avail himself of one year's worth of the scholarship. "The plan was to continue with this one semester on / one semester off until the academic year 2004/2005 when he would have negotiated early retirement" (Turner, private communication 2004). In his conversation with Christopher Bigsby, Sebald had observed that "in German institutions there is a great deal of intrigue and one-upmanship, a vice which is now beginning to grow in British universities also" (2001).

Sebald's paired NESTA mentor was Richard J. Evans, Professor of Modern History at Cambridge, with whose support Sebald had begun researching the project of his next book (Evans 2002). This was not a surprising association, given Sebald's preoccupation with arcane aspects of the past in his texts, and his declaration in an earlier interview that he did not read contemporary fiction, adding that his particular reading preference was actually the writing of scientists, for the precision and exactness of their use of language, their ability to make complex subjects accessible (Sebald to Silverblatt 2001). A fragment of this last and uncompleted project which begins in Corsica, about the effect of World War One on the lives of two women and constructed more in the manner of *The Rings of Saturn* than *Austerlitz*, was published in its original German under the Italian title *Campo Santo* (2003) — this translates as *"Hallowed Ground."* This has appeared, since this project was written, in Anthea Bell's translation under the original title of *Campo Santo* (2005), together with a selection of Sebald's critical essays written over a period of twenty years. The deeply engaged essays on Nabokov and Kafka and the artist Tripp are particularly revealing for those interested in Sebald's poetics, as is the first draft of his Zurich lectures, "Between History and Natural History," with its reflection on "the ruined civilization" and on Alexander Kluge's "subjective involvement and commitment, the point of departure for all imaginative effort" (85), together with the coruscating observation, drawn from Stanislaus Lem, that wonders if "human beings can actually think or are merely simulating that activity" (95). This too would lay the foundation for a poetics in which a reader is elicited who is positioned by the stylistic and narrative strategies employed to think for him or herself, "actually think" and make "imaginative effort" through "subjective involvement and commitment." Neither of these activities, were fostered by the "plodding studies" of "the general run of German critics" or "the manufacturers of literary theory" (158). As Sheppard observed, there were no books on literary theory among Sebald's effects passed over to the Marbach archive (2005). For Sebald it was the writers, poets and artists who "tried . . . to illuminate our incomprehensible existence" (Sebald 2005, 147), as in his estimation Kafka and Nabokov did.

Arthur Lubow had noted, in an interview with Sebald in 2001, that "in two years he would (be able) to step down with a full pension from his position teaching literature at the University of East Anglia" (Lubow in Clark et al. 2002). It was this cruelly unfulfilled promise of Sebald's opportunity to write full time that added such terrible irony to his fate.

On 15 February 2001, Sebald spoke about and read in German from his newly published book, *Austerlitz*, to the German Studies Group at Gonville and Caius College, Cambridge. Later that same year *Austerlitz* was also published in English. Sebald had changed his German and English publishers following the suicide of his German publisher, and had engaged

Andrew Wylie, who had been alerted to Sebald by Susan Sontag's enthusiasm (Alvarez 2001), as his literary agent. In the same year a volume of short poems in English appeared, together with graphics by a young British artist, Tess Jaray, *For Years Now*. There was virtually no critical response to this slight volume, perhaps in the light of the overwhelming publicity given to the publication of the far more substantial work, *Austerlitz*.

Sebald was interviewed on television in New York by Joe Cuomo after he had given a reading at Queens College, City University of New York, and was interviewed in London by Maya Jaggi for *The Guardian* after he had given a reading from *Austerlitz* in both German and English with Anthea Bell at South Bank. There was considerable and prominent publicity surrounding the release of *Austerlitz*, and some of it, including profiles of Sebald as a writer, was published a matter of months, and in one case a few days, before news of the traffic accident in Norfolk was reported, firstly in the British press and within hours internationally.

Sebald died at the age of 57, driving his twenty-eight-year-old daughter Anna home along the Norwich-to-London road. The sad irony of his premature death seemed to his readership a Sebaldian ending, a life that had ended in weirdly literary terms, like a bad fairy tale — shockingly unexpectedly. The coroner's report, recording a verdict of accidental death, showed that Sebald had died from multiple injuries, but that he had had a serious heart condition of which "he may have been unaware." The haunting reference in *Austerlitz* (375) to an inherited weak heart that he puts into the mouth of Jacques Austerlitz suggests otherwise. A witness driving behind the tanker into whose path Sebald had swerved while negotiating a bend in the road observed that "Professor Sebald had his head back and "was making no attempt to steer the car'" (Jury 2002). Sebald's daughter Anna, though injured, recovered.

Sebald was buried "within walking distance of his house" in a very simple and very private ceremony according to the rites of the Church of England following a service in a "little Norman Church which had been Catholic before it became Anglican" (Hamburger 2003, 9). The grief and shock of his colleagues are caught in Clive Scott's resonant inversion of the temporal and utterly apt Sebaldian phrasing: "It is a painful thing that, in remembering Max, one also, urgently, wants to remember his future" (Clive Scott 2002). In a moving German tribute, Franz Loquai, who had edited and published some of Sebald's earlier poems, remarked on Sebald's habit of concluding telephone conversations with him by saying, "Adieu," a form of mutual blessing as farewell, "as though this conversation could have been the last. And indeed, as it transpired, one of them turned out to be the last" (Loquai 2002 — my translation).

Sebald's friends and colleagues were, in 2003, planning a memorial in tribute to him: stone seats set in a circular formation in a clearing within a pretty copse in an area where he enjoyed walking in the countryside outside Norwich (private communication, Turner 2003), a fitting memorial for a habitual walker, in the best English Romantic tradition, someone born to hiking in the foothills below the Bavarian Alps and who valued opportunities for thought and contemplation afforded by that engagement with landscape and the natural world.

When Sebald's friend, the Swiss painter Jan Peter Tripp, who now lives in Alsace, read some of Sebald's last poems, on death, at Sebald's house after the burial, his friend Michael Hamburger described the poems as employing "allusion, ellipsis and sardonic understatement" (9). He added: "It is this humour, along with the sharp, loving eye for seemingly trivial minutiae so unusually combined with a visionary panoptic momentum, which opened this collector of existential extremities to a wider British readership . . . His last resting place, therefore, accords as well as any other that could have been chosen with Max's peripatetic writings and the magnanimous imagination, sympathies, affinities and curiosities from which they sprang. The unceremoniousness and privacy of his exit was in keeping with this . . . There was so much he knew at which he only hinted . . ." (9–10). Sebald's final "home" is the hallowed ground of a Norman Church in the English landscape, where he was buried according to the "new rite" within an ancient tradition: a fitting palimpsest for his body as his soul "set out on its final journey" (*The Rings of Saturn*, 296) to some other space.

Andrew Motion wrote a personally evocative poem in memory of his colleague and fellow writer, "After Nature and so on — In Memory of W. G. Sebald," which was published in the national newspaper, *The Australian*, in June 2002. Part of it reads:

> it would be so like you to be here
>
> twinkling behind your sad specs,
> smoothing your sleek walrus down
>
> to bring a *diminution of disorder*
> after a whole morning of listening
>
> to questions no one on earth can answer.
> But then you always were a past-
>
> master at taking the weight,
> and later, knowing the best response
>
> must be *to arm ourselves with patience*,
> sliding away to worry it through and over.

Motion catches Sebald's playful doubleness in "twinkling behind your sad specs" and the affectionate observation of the habitual gesture, the amusing personal detail, "smoothing your sleek walrus down," catching exactly Max Sebald's expression, that blend of melancholy and wit. The sardonic allitera-tive irony of German *Ordnung* in that Teutonic polysyllabic phrase requiring careful articulation, "diminution of disorder," and the pun on "morning of listening," catches the attributes of his person reflected in the style and form of his writing. The apparent banality of the colloquial phrase "no one on earth" suggests both metaphysical engagement with mystery and Sebald's passion for and solitary engagement with the natural world. The rhetorical emphasis of the punning *enjambement* of the endline caesura, "past-/master at taking the weight," with its intertextual tribute appropriated from Auden's "Musée des Beaux Arts," is both mock heroic, a reflection of Sebald's own self-deprecation, and a literary aesthetic tribute to a "master" whose preoc-cupation was with profound questions. Motion catches what must have been another habit: "sliding away" from discussion or conversation, to contem-plate in solitude. In his title, his beginning, the Poet Laureate fuses and focuses his colleague's idiosyncratic and witty engagement with the mystery of death, "After Nature and so on," that typically German phrase "*und so weiter*," here enunciated as that foregone conclusion about the end, as a paradoxical, poetic and postmodern certainty about a future. ". . . through and over" sounds very much like passage across, out to something like *envol* and *vagabondage*. Motion's line connects, for us, with Sebald's suggestion that "behind the illusions of the surface a dread-inspiring depth is concealed. It is the metaphysical lining of reality, so to speak" (2004, 87–88).

Tracing W. G. Sebald: Writer

> There was a vogue of documentary writing in Germany in the 70s which opened my eyes. It's an important literary invention, but it's considered an artless form. I was trying to write something saturated with material but carefully wrought, where the art manifests itself in a discreet, not too pompous fashion . . . as a writer you are an accom-plished liar . . . a game of hide-and-seek with the reader. . .
> — Sebald to Maya Jaggi, *The Guardian*,
> London, September 22, 2001

> The fictional aspect lies in the making, not in the substance.
> — Sebald at South Bank, London, September 2001,
> reported by Boyd Tonkin, *The Independent*, 6 October 2001

> *Es ist ein Prosabuch unbestimmter Art*
> [It is a prose work of an indeterminate kind; my translation]
> — Sebald on *Austerlitz* to Martin Doerry and
> Volker Hage of *Der Spiegel*, Norwich, November 2001

After news of Sebald's death had reached his readership, several reflections on his career as a writer began to appear in obituaries and tributes. In the obituary he wrote for NESTA, Professor Richard J. Evans, the Cambridge historian who was Sebald's NESTA mentor, wrote: "The writer W. G. ('Max') Sebald . . . had gained a worldwide reputation for the unique and inimitable blend of fact and fiction . . . Beneath the surface of Max's subtle and sinuous prose there is a melancholy that gradually works its way through, so that the overall effect is far more profound and disturbing than might at casual first reading seem to be the case . . . I am convinced that the book Max was writing when he died would have been his greatest yet. His death is a tragedy for literature . . ." (Evans 2002).

Mark R. McCulloh at Davidson College in North Carolina, who had begun writing what was to be the first monograph on Sebald's texts — *Understanding W. G. Sebald* (Columbia: University of South Carolina Press, 2003), had invited Sebald in 2000 to attend the first major academic conference to be held on his work. Having been telephoned by one of Sebald's colleagues the day after the accident, McCulloh remarked, "I think he'll probably be recognized in the future as one of the greatest writers of postwar German literature . . . He's one of the most remarkable and original writers of the last decade of the twentieth century. He wrote his four major works of fiction relatively late in life, and critics and general readers alike have commented that the books are unlike anything they've previously encountered" (reported in the prepublicity for The Third Occasional Davidson Symposium on German Studies, Davidson News & Events, 7 March 2003).

Susan Sontag, writing that "The loss feels unbearable," added, "He had an exemplary sense of vocation, full of scruples and self doubts. The work is recklessly literary . . . several kinds of moral seriousness, luminousness of description, and purity of motive. He was one who demonstrates that literature can be, literally, indispensable. He was one by whom literature continues to live" (Sontag in Clark et al. 2002). Ali Smith in her tribute observed that Sebald's next project involved "a study of the blatantly colourful cine home-movies SS officers took of their families over the waryears" (Smith 2002, 60).

The Guardian obituary entitled "Winfried Georg Maximilian Sebald — Writer," written by Eric Homberger and syndicated in Melbourne's *The Age*, concluded with the following observation: "Sebald became a writer who enriched the culture of Europe. The loss to literature and to his friends and family is unspeakable." Homberger wrote, "Scorning the Holocaust 'industry' . . . Sebald disliked feel-good sentimental portrayals of terrible events — such as Thomas Keneally's *Schindler's List* [*sic*: the title of Keneally's novel, as distinct from Steven Spielberg's film, is *Schindler's Ark*] . . . He wanted to find a literary form responsive to the echoes of human tragedy which spread out, across generations and nations, yet which began in his childhood . . . He was reluctant to call his books 'novels,' because he had little interest in the way contemporary writers seemed to find all meaning in personal relationships, and out of a comic but heart-felt disdain for the 'grinding noises' which heavily plotted novels demanded . . . the clumsy machinery . . . which Sebald mocked" (Homberger 2001).

In a brief but lyrical obituary published in *Die Zeit*, Rolf Vollmann turned Sebald's death into an elegant metonymy of death with a typically Sebaldian oblique classical allusion to the myth of Theseus and the Athenian sacrifices to Minos: "senseless deaths swelling like the heavy waves of the sea which keep the broken black sail of melancholy in ceaseless motion" (Vollmann 2001 — my translation). To his English-language readership Sebald had appeared like a comet, with a dazzling trajectory both brilliant and brief, his distinctive voice and idiosyncratic fiction recognized as having made a significant original contribution to literary culture.

The University of London's Institute of Germanic Studies held "The W. G. Sebald Memorial Day" on 31 January 2003 and published the papers presented at that occasion under the title *The Anatomist of Melancholy — Essays in Memory of W. G. Sebald*. In his introductory remarks Professor Rüdiger Görner, Head of the Institute, described "friends, fellow-writers and critics" as "united in their grief and conviction that literature had lost one of its truly exceptional protagonists" (7). He added: "The day . . . turned out to be infinitely more than an academic occasion. It developed into a manifestation of people's highly informed appreciation of, if not love for, Sebald's oeuvre and what it continues to stand for: the sovereignty of literary imagination" (7).

Max Sebald's unpublished novel of 1967, according to his student roommate Reinbert Tabbart who both read it and observed Sebald's reaction to its rejection by the publisher, reflected Sebald's characteristic skill of enlivening his conversation with "stories which were part comic, part melancholy, but always sharply vivid" (my translation — "teils witzigen, teils melancholischen, immer aber anschaulichen Erzählungen" 21). These are the characteristic qualities which we now recognize and value in the books that were published later and which were accepted for publication.

Twenty-one years passed between the rejection of Sebald's first novel and the publication in German of his first creative work. As Reinbert Tabbart commented in his *Akzente* tribute to Sebald, "Max had to wait a long time'" (April 2001). In 1988, Sebald's three-part prose poem, *Nach der Natur: Ein Elementargedicht*, was published in German, followed by the four works of prose fiction in German and a volume of short poems in English, in the space of thirteen years between 1988 and 2001. This period overlaps that in which the prose works were also published in English, in translations on which Sebald was a close collaborator, between 1996 and 2002, an astonishingly short six years given the intensity of the work of translation. Five of these were published in Sebald's lifetime and the sixth (he had revised nearly all the final version of *Nach der Natur* with

Michael Hamburger) (Hamburger 9) was released just a few months after his death. This represents a prodigious amount of work.

Nach der Natur is a three-part prose poem — the subtitle of which in German, not used in the English translation, is "an Elemental Poem" — with epigraphs from the poetry of Dante, Klopstock, and Virgil and section titles that read as incomplete lines of poetry scanning to different rhythms. Each part tells the stories of three southern Germans: the Renaissance painter Matthias Grünewald, the eighteenth-century theologian-turned-expeditionary scientist Georg Wilhelm Steller, and Sebald himself — the artist, the scientist, and the writer (Görner constructs them slightly differently, suggesting "historian" rather than writer, 77).

Schwindel. Gefühle, the first prose fiction work, was published in 1990 by Eichborn. This comprised four curiously linked narratives that considered writers, first Beyle-Stendhal, then the narrator abroad, then Kafka, then the narrator traveling home, in time and space from the Napoleonic campaign in Italy to Austria, back to Italy, to his childhood home in Germany and then returning to England, traveling home to Norwich by train in a narrative present striated by a terrifying dream. Two sections are narrated in the third person, two in the first. *Schwindel* is both "dizziness" and "sleight of hand," and the vertiginous response is the affective *Gefühle* — "feeling," the dizzy feeling of being swindled or deceived, as well as the dizziness of looking back into the jumble of the past in the abyss of time. This alludes to both the narrator's state of mind and the author's ludic engagement of the reader. Throughout this book, unlike *After Nature* (the German edition of *Nach der Natur* included a photograph which was not reproduced in the English version), inserted black-and-white photographs appear for the first time, some reproducing Beyle's sketches, some of curious items like pizzeria bills and entry tickets, some of places and scenes, some strangely indeterminate in their focus. It was an idiosyncratic and puzzling début in prose, a kind of self-reflexive writerly apprenticeship served on the road to adventure.

This book was followed by *Die Ausgewanderten* in 1993, Sebald's second work of prose fiction. It too consisted of four sections, this time four loosely linked stories, related again by a quasi-autobiographical narrator curiously like the one encountered in *Schwindel. Gefühle*. The first of the stories had appeared by itself in *Manuskripte* (vol. 100, 1988, 150–58) under the title "Verzehret das letzte die Erinnerung nicht?" The stories recount the narrator's perceptions of the lives of a retired surgeon, the Jewish Lithuanian husband of the landlady of the flat the narrator and his new wife "Clara" leased in "Prior's Gate," a large house in a village outside Norwich; a German primary-school teacher, one-quarter Jewish, who had taught the narrator in his home village in southwest Germany; the narrator's *émigré* great-uncle Ambros, a hotel worker turned valet-companion to the disturbed son of a wealthy New York Jewish family; and a German artist who, having migrated to England and losing his parents in the deportation of Jews to the death camps in Europe, lived a very modest life, painting for decades in his studio down by the Manchester docks, where the narrator meets and befriends him, prior to his public recognition. Sebald uses black-and-white photographs throughout this book too, and the connective threads between these stories include, particularly, depression and suicide, the different forms of the damaged, marginal existences lived by these people, the story of the narrator's own life, "ausgewandert" (having emigrated), woven obliquely through the accounts of the others. These are spectral lives recounted by a narrator who, prey to the melancholy that afflicts those whose stories he tells in a grey tone, avoids death or illness through the therapy of writing.

In 1995, two years later, *Die Ringe des Saturn* was published, the third fictional work to appear in German, with the subtitle *Eine englische Wallfahrt*. It is a series of meditations and anecdotes recounted by a bedridden narrator, based on recalled stories and observations linked to the East Anglian countryside of Suffolk, through which he had walked a year before he was confined to hospital in Norwich in a state of paralysis. The principal preoccupation of these meditations, constructed like discursive essays on the template of Sir Thomas Browne, is concerned with aspects of death and loss and various memorializing practices, woven into prose that is often intensely evocative. The linking between the ten sections is more explicitly achieved by the itinerary constructed by the narrator's voice, marked by the places he stops at, a kind of quincunx traced on the topography of Suffolk, meditating on details which he observes, both in the external landscape and in the geography of his mind as he travels through Suffolk, narrating to himself while lying immobilized on a hospital bed in Norwich the journey he had undertaken a year earlier, and then a year after that, writing up his memories into a text. Like the earlier ones, it too contains a number of black-and-white photographs, by now a Sebaldian hallmark.

In 1996 the first English translation of Sebald's creative writing appeared in Great Britain — *The Emigrants* (translated by Michael Hulse), the American edition following in 1997 (McCulloh xxiv). For most English-language readers, Sebald was both an unknown person and an entirely new kind of writer. The following year, in 1997, four of Sebald's poems appeared in a German publication edited by Franz Loquai, *W. G. Sebald*: "In Bamberg," "Am 9. Juni," "Neunzig Jahre später," and "Ein Walzertraum" (McCulloh 175), not yet available in English.

In 1998 Hulse's translation of *The Rings of Saturn* was published, and in 1999 *Vertigo* appeared, translated from *Schwindel. Gefühle* (by Michael Hulse again). In English-language domains this set of three of books consolidated Sebald's arrival on the literary scene. In 2000 two poems in English were published in an English journal, *Pretext 2* — "I remember" and "October Heat Wave," marking, as McCulloh points out, "Sebald's poetic debut in English" (175).

The German edition of *Austerlitz* was released in February 2001, and the English translation (by Anthea Bell) in October of the same year. A work of nearly four hundred pages, one seamless paragraph long in each of its four sections, it too incorporated black-and-white photographs. It recounted the association between an anonymous narrator, a German academic who lives in the north of England and travels on occasion to Europe, and an architectural historian based in London at the Courtauld Institute, Jacques Austerlitz, a Jewish *Kindertransport* child from Prague brought up from the age of five in Wales by a Methodist minister and his childless English wife, who rename him Dafydd Elias. The friendship between the narrator and the historian, for so it becomes, spans more than thirty years, deepening over time. It is constituted here as a series of recalled conversations that are represented as directly reported monologues, the most extended of which comprise Austerlitz's life story, his discovery of his real name, the loss of everyone meaningful to him, and his spiral into deep loneliness. In retirement Austerlitz pursues knowledge of the fates of his parents, in Prague and Paris, in Czechoslovakia and Belgium, and the narrator is delegated the task of writing Austerlitz's bleak story because Austerlitz, linguistically and psychologically paralysed, is unable to do so.

Six poems in German were published in *Akzente* (April 2001) (McCulloh 175). In 2001 *For Years Now*, the collection of very short poems written in English and printed facing Tess Jaray's graphics, was also published. *After Nature*, the translation by Michael Hamburger of *Nach der Natur*, was available at the end of 2001, although the release of copies was delayed following Sebald's death until 2002.

In 2003, a collection of poems written in German together with Jan Peter Tripp's very finely rendered, almost photographic drawings of faces focusing on eyes was published in a beautifully presented, elegiac edition with a grey cloth cover and Tripp's drawing of Sebald edge-inserted under a transparent plastic jacket, a horizontal, landscape-formatted A4 rectangle printed with the title *Unerzählt*. This was published in English late in 2004 as *Unrecounted*. The unfinished fragment in German of Sebald's last work, published in *Akzente* as *Campo Santo* (2003), was translated into English and published in 2005, together with Sven Meyer's selection of several of Sebald's essays drawn from different collections.

Sebald's critical books in German have mostly not yet been translated into English, except for those seminal essays, so revealing of Sebald's writerly mind, that Meyer had chosen for *Campo Santo*. The other exception is the Zurich Lectures of 1997, *Luftkrieg und Literatur*, published posthumously in English in 2003 in Anthea Bell's translation, *On the Natural History of Destruction*. There are seven critical works in all, published between 1969 and 1999. When asked by James Atlas in 1999 why he began to write at forty-five, Sebald replied, "I had quite a demanding job. There was never time to write" (Atlas 1999). It is an interesting response, and a suggestive one.

Sebald's academic theses were both published: his Master's thesis, *Carl Sternheim: Kritiker und Opfer der Wilhelminischen Ära* — "Carl Sternheim: Critic and Victim of the Wilhelminian Era," described by McCulloh as one of the "early products of Sebald's fascination with 'problematic' writers" and "whose works Sebald associates with fascist ideology, a charge that proved controversial in critical circles" (McCulloh xxiii and 176), in 1969, and in 1980, his doctoral thesis on Döblin, *Der Mythus der Zerstörung im Werk Alfred Döblins* — "The Myth of Destruction in the Work of Alfred Döblin."

In 1985 ten critical articles on Austrian literature were published in Vienna under the title *Die Beschreibung des Unglücks: Zur österreichischen Literatur von Stifter bis Handke* — "The Description of Melancholy: Austrian Literature from Stifter to Handke" (McCulloh xxiii). McCulloh argues that "his thesis [is] that 'depressive' or melancholy writing represents an attempt to resist the power of depression, rather than (acquiesce) to it" (176). Sebald then published, in 1988, a series of essays in English which he edited on "the major figures of 'radical theater' in Germany, Switzerland, and Austria," including Achternbusch, Braun, Müller and Strauss: *A Radical Stage: Theatre in Germany in the 1970s and 1980s* (McCulloh xxiii).

In 1991 another volume of criticism was published in Austria: *Unheimliche Heimat: Essays zur österreichischen Literatur*, "Alien Homeland," exploring the "sociological factors that have influenced and shaped the works of Postl, Kafka, Roth, Broch, and Handke" (McCulloh 176). This emphasis on "never feeling at home anywhere" (Jaggi 2001a) was clearly of academic interest to Sebald before he began to pursue it in his creative writing.

In 1998 *Logis in einem Landhaus* was published, a collection of five essays on literary figures — Rousseau, Keller, Hebel, Walser, and Mörike — together with one essay on Sebald's friend, the Swiss painter Jan Peter Tripp. This set of essays, even less like academic essays than the earlier volumes, also included black-and-white photographs of the writers and the painter being discussed, of places and paintings that were alluded to in the essays. Williams also observed that Sebald's essays "are no heavy *ex cathedra* disquisitions, but, perhaps closer to the English tradition, lessons in sensitivity of perception and elegance of expression" (2002, 2006).

Sebald's Zurich lectures were published in Germany in 1999 as *Luftkrieg und Literatur*, together with his comment on the avalanche of responses he received to these lectures, a third postscript chapter, and, only in the English-language editions, three additional essays on the writers Alfred Andersch, Peter Weiss, and Jean Améry. Anthea Bell's translation,

On the Natural History of Destruction, was published in 2003, an excerpt of which appeared in *The New Yorker* (November 2002), and drew letters from readers who saw Sebald's allusions to the suffering of German civilians as opening old wounds, depicting Germans as innocent victims and distorting the history of the rise of the Third Reich, rather than as a criticism of the silence of postwar German literature, its failure to deal with the cultural impact on Germany of the massive Allied bombing campaigns of the Second World War (McCulloh xxiv). These lectures in their English translation were widely reviewed in Australia, the United States, and Britain, perhaps even more than the four problematic works of fiction.

The texts for which Sebald will be remembered and which position him as a major European writer at the end of the twentieth century and at the beginning of the twenty-first are those whose prose fiction pushes out the generic envelope of the novel with its innovative form, refreshing the nature of its textuality and sharpening its engagement of the imaginative and reflective reader as a collaborative authority.

Language Choices

Like Conrad and like Nabokov, Sebald had emigrated to and subsequently settled and worked in an English-speaking nation. Like Nabokov, he lectured in English to academic student audiences. Sebald's academic writing being in German (with the exception of the edited book of essays on theater) was one thing, for that was his professional domain as a teacher and critic. His creative writing, though, was another. He elected to write in German, with the exception of a small number of poems.

Gordon Turner observed, "Max was a private person. He was never keen to read from his works in English. There were only three appearances in Britain. He read from *The Emigrants* at UEA in Norwich, from *The Rings of Saturn* with A. S. Byatt — which he found excruciating, retelling it in an amusing series of anecdotes — and in September 2001, with Anthea Bell, he read from *Austerlitz* in German, after which he took questions from the floor. In October and November 2001, he visited the United States, mainly the West Coast, prior to the upcoming marriage of his daughter" (Turner, Davidson College, 2003). Sebald read from *Austerlitz* in English when in conversation with Joe Cuomo at Queens College, in New York.

In the August 2001 interview with Arthur Lubow, Sebald had commented with characteristic asperity, "The contemporary language is usually hideous, but in German it's especially nauseating." He named "nineteenth-century German prose" as an influence, "if there is any," on his style, adding later that eighteenth- or nineteenth-century "discursive prose in English essays" was interesting to him (Silverblatt 2001). In another interview in the same year he remarked that the time might well come in the future when he grew sufficiently unconfident with German, after such a long time away from Germany: "I have lived in this country far longer than in Bavaria, but reading in English I become self-conscious about having a funny accent. Unlike Conrad or Nabokov, I didn't have circumstances which would have coerced me out of my native tongue altogether. But the time may come when my German resources begin to shrink. It is a sore point because you do have advantages if you have access to more than one language" (Jaggi 2001b). Lubow had remarked that "Mr. Sebald . . . sprinkles his fluent English with many French words but no German ones" (Lubow 2001), perhaps a sensitive response to his American interviewer, or perhaps a matter of cultivated habit. Interestingly Sebald chose to be interviewed in English by the German-speaking Dutch interviewer Michael Zeeman in a program broadcast in Holland with Dutch subtitles (1998).

Sebald's establishment of the British Centre for Literary Translation was a means of keeping faith with his professional commitment to the teaching of foreign languages and literatures, not least German as the source of his own livelihood, in an English-language environment, as an antidote to the linguistic hegemony of English as well as a way of ensuring that linguistically "marginalized" or decentered writers were enabled, through translation, to access a wider readership and all that that might entail. Hölderlin's (mentioned in the Michael Hamburger section of *The Rings of Saturn*) and Klopstock's (mentioned in *After Nature* and from whose poem, "Die Verwandelten," the title of *Die Ringe des Saturn* is derived, Görner 77) ambitions for German as a literary language on a par with Greek and Latin, for instance, seem not to be entirely irrelevant here. It might be seen that Sebald was both keeping something of that cultural/linguistic dream alive in his own German writing and a second dream, of justice or equity for marginal writers who did not write in English, giving them a more centered voice.

The resurrection or redemption of German as a literary language, never actually voiced so specifically by the essentially modest Sebald, is therefore a real possibility, not so unexpected from someone who had spent his professional life teaching, and devoted to, both language and literature. Part of the ambivalence of Sebald's attitude to Germany is constituted in his own ongoing demonstration that German still had the capacity to produce beautiful literary prose, that literary German, in his own postmodern appropriation of nineteenth-century syntax and diction, could be restored to the forefront of the stage of literary production. He seems to have achieved just that, but it is also one which his English-language readership has embraced, on his terms, as supranational.

Then there is his habit of using phrases or words in languages other than German in his texts that are, even in works translated from the

German, often not translated from the original French, Italian, Welsh, or Czech. This is a characteristic signaling of the residual respect that Sebald has as a linguist for the unique integrity of different languages, preserving the individuality of their forms and thus the astonishing variety of the human capacity for language, that most intrinsically human property.

Deeply sensitive to language in a poetic sense (as Görner points out, 75–80), Sebald was also anxious about his estrangement from contemporary German as a result of having lived in England for so long. He observed that it was no longer possible, for instance, for him to write dialogue in German that would not sound old-fashioned. One way to avoid solecisms was to write a German which could not be mistaken as contemporary — this was an intriguing solution to his German-language problem, which had aesthetic repercussions.

What Catling calls his "characteristic modesty" (Catling 2003, 19) is perhaps only part of what lies behind Sebald's decision to write in an old-fashioned and hypersubordinated German, as is his characteristic distaste for the "modern world," a technophobia manifest in his declining the university's offer of a computer (see also Sheppard, 2005), avoiding mobile phones and answering machines, together with his loathing of soulless architecture and shopping malls. Commenting on the degradation of language in one interview, Sebald mocked the German word for mobile phone (*ein Handi*) as an obscenity. Turner commented, in his Davidson College presentation, on Sebald's "exquisite handwriting" executed with a dip pen and black ink, on his habit of keeping a "huge box of pencils" and his using "all the bits of pencil" — his "cocking a snook at technology" (2003).

Sebald's deliberately anachronistic prose style echoes in its very form his work's preoccupation with some of the consoling beauty of the past, including the poetic language of German literary culture. In some deeply resonant way, Sebald writes in German because his "German-ness" informs his being-in-the-world. As he said to Michael Zeeman, ". . . where you were born . . . is the primal landscape which determines you . . . the more your future horizon shrinks, the more prominent . . . your place of origin becomes in your mind . . . the past is what we carry with us" (1998). The older he became, as in Hölderlin's "Hälfte des Lebens" perhaps, the more Sebald felt the proximity of his German origins in the second half of his own span.

Given the rupture that German history in the twentieth century represented in terms of suddenly making the historical perspective of German cultural production unacceptable, its language too was rebarbative to many. Vikram Seth, who had learned German in England for his entrance to Cambridge, commented in a presentation on his book *Two Lives* at the University of Melbourne in March, 2006, in which he writes about the effect of events on his German Jewish great-aunt and Indian great-uncle in Berlin in the thirties, that he found reading his great-aunt's letters in

German had produced in him a deep antipathy for the language itself — some seven decades after the letters were written.

Sebald's decision to write in German carries, whether Sebald intended this or not, an elegiac resurrection of the sonorousness of German literary syntax and style as practiced before the damage to the regard for German culture and its language in the modern world was inflicted by Germans themselves. To forget the past was foolish, and dishonest; to remember it was tragic. The past could not be redeemed, but it was also, surprisingly, culturally beautiful. Writing in German was to recognize that there could be no escape from the past: "I've still got it in my backpack and I can't just put it down" (Zeeman 1998). To write in German was "An Attempt at Restitution" (Sebald 2005, 206).

Sebald's exile was not just geographical; it was also the condition of writing in the language of Germany in the foreign country he chose to live in. "A lot of people do not perceive the patterns of the past . . . only those with a certain education . . . it's part of your make-up . . . it will determine where you will end up" (Zeeman 1998). Quoting Lichtenberg, Sebald observed that "you have to go away for a while if you want to write in your own language" (Zeeman 1998) — to end up in East Anglia, the beginning of his own life (in 1944) having been inextricably bound up with the destruction of Germany, writing in German, seemed part of a pattern to someone who gave great weight to coincidence. "Only in literature can there be an attempt at restitution over and above the mere recital of facts and over and above scholarship" (Sebald 2005: 215).

One of Sebald's translators, Anthea Bell, disagreed with the deferential position he adopted toward his own language competence, saying that in her view "the long sentence winding its way through many subordinate clauses suited him" and adding that "to the practicing translator of German it is almost with a shock, if an agreeable one, that one rediscovers the pleasures of the subordinate clause and the long sentence" (Bell 12).

These linguistic and syntactical characteristics become for the reader of the elegant English translations also a matter of style, one that recalls the elegance of prose writers from Thomas Browne in the seventeenth century to Virginia Woolf in the first half of the twentieth, the bleak humor of Beckett, the Romantic poetry of Wordsworth and Coleridge, as much it may otherwise recall Goethe or Theodor Fontane or other German writers in translation for those who cannot read German, or the French writers Sebald so admired (McCulloh xvi).

Bell described the pleasure of working on two translations with Sebald as "very intensive indeed" (*The Anatomist of Melancholy*, 2003, 12). "Max took a deep and close interest in the translations of his works" (13), "working mainly by correspondence" (14) in "his elegant handwriting" (17). Recounting that Sebald had mentioned to her that he had been reading Edmund Gosse's *Father and Son* while working on the Welsh naturalist section in *Austerlitz*, Bell observed, "It was a pleasure to work with an author whose own knowledge of English was so good" (15). Further on she remarks, "So wide was Max's knowledge of English that I was disproportionately pleased when I could introduce him to anything he didn't know already" (15). Collaborative translation was clearly something that Sebald took very seriously indeed. His English translations bear that out, and Michael Hamburger remarks that the copy of *Austerlitz* in English that Sebald presented to his (Hamburger's) wife contained inked amendments (Sebald 2004, 1–2).

By 2001, the year when *Austerlitz* was published in both German and English, the highly enthusiastic reception of his work in English, building on his growing reputation as a writer of unusual and enigmatically beautiful books, was also being enhanced by the machinery of the powerful publishers of his English translations, Random House/Hamish Hamilton/Penguin, and his literary agent, Andrew Wylie, alerted to Sebald by Sontag's acclamation (Alvarez 2001).

When I began my own exploration, Sebald was still alive and *Austerlitz* had not been published in English. There was little critical material on Sebald's writing in English. Now in 2006 there are over a hundred Sebald citations on the MLA Index; one critical monograph has appeared (Mark R. McCulloh); a memorial collection of essays has been published in association with the German Institute at the University of London (edited by Professor Rüdiger Görner); one collection of critical essays has appeared in Britain and the United States in August 2004 (edited by J. J. Long and Anne Whitehead); the collection of papers from The Third Occasional Davidson Symposium on German Studies, entitled *W. G. Sebald: History — Memory — Trauma* and edited by Scott Denham and Mark McCulloh, appeared in late 2006; and a biography is being written.

Before Sebald had come to the attention of the academy, the first English-language reviews of *The Emigrants* had registered the unusual form and the complexity of Sebald's writing. Philip Brady, reviewing it for *The Times Literary Supplement* (12 July 1996), had read Sebald in German and could position this first English translation in the context of the other three published works. He drew a comparison between Siegfried Kracauer's 1927 essay on photography and Sebald's use of photographs "as narrative material," observing astutely that "where records fail . . . imagination takes over."

Randolph Stow took issue with the publisher's description of *The Rings of Saturn* as "fiction" in his review in *The Times Literary Supplement* (31 July 1998). He deliberated over Sebald's theme as "ruin," over his use of photographs, but summed up by declaring that here was "a voice of memorable originality." Curiously Stow commented on things that he found odd that Sebald didn't mention (Conrad's descriptions of the men at Lowestoft or Edward FitzGerald's "Posh" or the "ancient vegetation of Staverton Thicks" or Dickens's use of Blundeston as David Copperfield's childhood home with the frightful Murdstones). This is exactly the invitation to the reader that Arthur Williams was to sense (1998, 101) and what this study is arguing constitutes the invitation to disobedience, to transgress the textual boundaries into one's own contemplative and imaginative subject, precisely as Stow has done here in his review.

In Australia Peter Craven asserted that Sebald's "decadent books" inhabited "the ruins of our late moment in the history of literature where the merest glint of prose style is likely to be mistaken for the toll and grandeur of the imagination and all its silver bells" but that his "are ringed with the fire of the Word" *Heat* (1999, 212–24). When *Austerlitz* came out in 2001, by which time the general consensus in reviews in English was that Sebald, in the words of A. S. Byatt, was "one of the most important writers of our time" (*The New Statesman*, October 15, 2001), Anita Brookner described it as "ancient European writing. Its strangeness so convincing that one is obliged to recognise the truly phenomenal configuration of the author's mind" (*The Spectator*, October 6, 2001).

The Academy Begins to Speak

The first critical article in English from the academy appeared in 1998. Arthur Williams, Professor of German at the University of Bradford, wrote an article about three German contemporary writers, Bernd-Dieter Hüge, Reiner Kunze, and Sebald. The article is comparative and the Sebald focus is on *The Emigrants*, but Williams takes pains over adumbrating what he calls "Sebald's compositional principles," including Sebald's "incorporation of insights gained from contemporary literary theory, reception theory, and the visual arts" (101). He also alludes to "Sebald's irresistible involvement of his reader in his project. He does this by addressing the reader directly . . . and indirectly, and by playfully interweaving levels of the real and the unreal, the authentic and the counterfeit" (101). He observed that "Sebald's fugally polyphonic text has much about it that is "carnivalesque" in the Bakhtininan sense, uniting many voices artfully in the shared discourse of a people" (106). Referring to Sebald's "new historicism," Williams observed nonetheless that "so complex is Sebald's text . . . that anything approaching a complete exegesis of it would be presumptuous" (107). "Elusive First Person Plural," the title of Williams's article, was published in the book whose series he edits, in a volume called *Whose Story? German-Language Literature Today* (1998, 85–113).

In Williams's eyes Sebald was a highly sophisticated writer of fiction who developed an intriguing relationship with his reader, his "Fahrgast' " or "traveling companion" [my translation](110), drawing in a number of complex ways on literary tradition: "Sebald constantly problematizes his sources, thus highlighting his authorial role in interpreting them" (111).

In 1999 Ernestine Schlant, Professor of German and Comparative Literature at Montclair State University, published her book *The Language of Silence* with Routledge. She named Sebald as one of a number of German writers engaged with the "silence" about the Holocaust, thus contextualizing his writing specifically within a German cultural context and inscribing him into the discourse of Holocaust studies (224–34). This positioning was a dominant thread in several of the reviews and articles that were appearing in periodicals and journals, especially in the United States. Schlant concluded: "Sebald's text is steeped in images of the Holocaust and a language of mourning and melancholy so pervasive that it applies even when the text speaks of other events and times" (234).

Arthur Williams's second article, "W. G. Sebald: A Holistic Approach to Borders, Texts and Perspectives," was published in 2000 in *German-Language Literature Today: International and Popular?* (99–118). McCulloh, in his subsequent study regarded this essay as "the most comprehensive study of Sebald's aesthetics to date" (149). Its focus is on Sebald's practice as a "post-modern" writer, without pinning down exactly what kind of postmodernism might be operating here, and he describes Sebald as "Europe's great painterly writer" and "a committed teacher" (99). Williams took the view that "Sebald's work seeks neither to conquer nor to relativize the German past; it is rather an engagement with and an acceptance of a past whose imprint we need to throw off if we are to invest in a new approach to the future of our planet . . . His view of the world is holistic" (99). Like McCulloh, Williams saw in Sebald a desire to return to a more comforting world view in some Edenic, prelapsarian order that seems, now, somehow discordant with Sebald's more troubled, and troubling, image of the human predicament.

Williams saw Sebald also in the great European tradition of thinkers as well as "Europe's great painterly writer" (99). His insight into Sebald's troubled Germanness is worth quoting in detail:

> If Germany is largely absent as a direct subject of Sebald's work, it is an incontrovertible subliminal presence; the Holocaust is present almost throughout as a palimpsest. . . . when there is direct reference to Germany, and this is most particularly the case in *Die Ausgewanderten*, there is an immediate association with ugliness and antisocial behaviour. We are brought face to face with "die hässlichen Deutschen" [the hateful and ugly Germans — my translation]. There is a certain anti-German element about Sebald's work . . . Sebald's work, then, is characterized by a self-imposed exile from a Germany he seems not particularly to like, but which, perhaps for this reason, is a constant nagging presence in his self-reflection. (103)

Williams sees this "conundrum" as underpinning Sebald's "search for perspective and orientation." He goes on to say that "the geographical peregrinations in Sebald's creative work are also associated with travel through time and with fluent transitions across genres and media" (103). He sees Sebald's writing as concerned with the big picture, with "civilization" (103). Observing that even Sebald's publishers could not classify *The Rings of Saturn*, Williams added further on that "There is an underlying and unifying belief here in the power of literature to open up horizons and keep hope alive" (107). Sebald's belief in the power of education, and reading, to civilize underpins his enterprise, even as he records the trauma of our decivilizing, self-destructive impulse to destroy the cities that we have created.

In 2001 Stefanie Harris, a German scholar from Northwestern University, published a paper on *The Emigrants* in English in *German Quarterly*, the journal of the American Association of Teachers of German (available in an (unpaginated) online version). She began with the problem of the photograph at the beginning of the text, seeking to locate its context, and describing it as resisting "intelligibility." Her emphasis is on what she calls "traumatic memory," traced in both Freud and Benjamin, and she links that to Sebald's use of photographs (what Benjamin regarded as the "paradigmatic medium of modernity") in the text by referring to Siegfried Kracauer's theories in an essay published in 1927, "Die Photographie" (as Brady had done, op.cit.) in which he argues that "photographs are ghostly." Her essay concludes with her invocation of John Berger and Jean Mohr's view, and she uses them elsewhere in the essay to claim, like Barthes and Sontag, that photographs "arrest" time, "arrest" interpretation and in so doing "announce our own death," that photographs and text are supplements in an enterprise which seeks to rescue the "past from the lagoons of oblivion." Citing Freud's definition of trauma in *Jenseits des Lustprinzips* as "a breach between mind and memory," Harris asserts that "trauma acts as an interruption of meaningfulness in that the event is never given psychic meaning through incorporation into narrative memory." She concludes that the "final long descriptive passage of Sebald's work is an ekphrasis of one ghostly image that is described in detail but never reproduced for us" (which, as she says, recalls the Winter Garden photograph "at the heart of Roland Barthes's own book"), that of Barthes's mother in *Camera Lucida*.

A book by Christopher Woodward called *In Ruins* was published in Britain in 2001. This quirky, essayistic work considers our relationship with the past through our engagement with the fragments that survive around us. Drawing a distinction between the archaeologist, for whom the fragments of the past are "parts of a jigsaw, or clues to a puzzle to which there is only one answer, as in a science laboratory," and the artist, "to [whom] any answer which is imaginative is correct" (30), Woodward makes sustained reference later in his book to the section in *The Rings of Saturn* where the narrator arrives at Orford Ness, privileging Sebald's writing as the art of the imagination.

In 2002 Joanna Scott, writer and Professor of English at the University of Rochester, wrote a detailed article published in the journal *Salmagundi* (Summer 2002), available online. She observed Sebald's remaining "so vividly, precisely mysterious." Scott positioned *Austerlitz* within the domain of fiction, asserting that Sebald is "a daring writer," although she remarked that *Vertigo* and *The Rings of Saturn* "lack . . . the full imaginative leap from meditation into fiction," nonetheless designating Sebald as "one of the great writers of our time." She wrote: "he makes the visual world vividly strange and new. He furthers the potential of language to render the mind's complexities." Invoking Samuel Beckett again, as she had in her title ("Why crawl at all?"), Scott asked, "why write fiction instead of history?" She answered, "Writers — and readers — are nervous about the paradoxical nature of fiction, its serious play, its true deceptions," concluding that "Sebald suggests that whatever purpose imaginative art has in our difficult world, its mystery is to be respected." The "magic" of the imagination, and the "importance . . . of mystery," were for Scott what Sebald's writing had particularly reasserted in the contemporary literary scene.

This was not the angle that Andreas Huyssen, Villard Professor of German and Comparative Literature at Columbia University, took in writing about Sebald's writing but he did take up some of Woodward's refrain. Huyssen published *Present Pasts — Urban Palimpsests and The Politics of Memory* in 2003, in a series called *Cultural Memory in the Present*, edited by Mieke Bal and Hent de Vries (Stanford University Press). The German epigraph in his book is taken from *Austerlitz*: "Even now, when I try to remember . . . the darkness does not lift but becomes yet heavier as I think how little we can hold in mind, how everything is constantly lapsing into oblivion with every extinguished life, how the world is draining itself, in that the history of countless places and objects which themselves have no power of memory is never heard, never described, never passed on" (30–31 of the English translation, 2001). He devoted much of the focus of the ninth chapter in his book to Sebald, where his particular focus was the Zurich Lectures, *On the Natural History of Destruction*. In passing, Huyssen made reference to Sebald's "narrative style and use of language" in *The Emigrants*, slower paced and nineteenth century, as strategies which "clash in estranging ways with the psychic catastrophes that make up the content of the stories" (150). In Huyssen's estimate Sebald was mainly reinscribing trauma into literature, writing out of the "overbearing memory culture of the nineties," but he ended his own book on an interestingly open-ended suggestion: that Sebald's writing, "this literary high-wire act," might well be "something of a new beginning" (157).

In January of the same year (2003) J. J. Long, from the University of Durham, published an article in *Modern Language Review* which considered "History, Narrative and Photography in *Die Ausgewanderten.*" Long, a Germanist, argued, using Marianne Hirsch's theory of postmemory and C. S. Pierce, that *The Emigrants* revealed Sebald to be a generically hybrid writer drawing on historical archives and employing photographs in ways that engage in an aestheticized memory discourse which compensates for the "disruptions" of historical process. Long would later be one of the editors of the first collection of critical essays in English (with Anne Whitehead, 2004).

Early in the same year (March 2003) Mark R. McCulloh, Professor of German at Davidson College, published the first full-length critical monograph on Sebald in English, *Understanding W. G. Sebald*, in an American series that introduces readers to "Modern European and Latin American Literature" (University of South Carolina Press). As he himself notes, he came to Sebald in English through the recommendation of *The Rings of Saturn* by a friend, by way of James Atlas's 1999 article in *The Paris Review* (McCulloh xiii). McCulloh's sensitively nuanced book profiles Sebald as a writer of "novels," although Sebald himself rejected that term, preferring the less determinate "Prosabuch unbestimmter Art" (Doerry 2001, 228). McCulloh constructs Sebald as a writer of fiction, and, writing about each text in some detail, he contextualizes Sebald's writing as a "blend of fact, fiction, allusion and recall" that he calls "Sebald's Literary Monism" (vi), seeing Sebald's poetics as a self-reflexive expression of creativity itself, a means by which what was fragmented is made whole.

McCulloh's conclusion is that Sebald focuses ultimately on "writing itself" (McCulloh 2003: xxi): "where Sebald always ends up, contemplating the writer and writing" (139). This self-referential dimension in Sebald that McCulloh identifies and stresses consistently in his study, together with Williams's observation about the engagement of the reader ("Sebald's irresistible involvement of his reader in his project" 1998, 101), galvanize my argument that Sebald's positioning of the reader as disobedient reinstates the imaginative potential of a narrative practice which is, with its deliberately subversive and destabilizing strategies, both playfully postmodern and morally engaged. As Williams observed in his later essay, "[Sebald] never forces his view on his reader; his aesthetics places his reader in a position to empathize and to think for herself or himself about the new associations and significations he has placed on offer" (2000, 105). Sebald's death-haunted poetics of rupture, it seemed to me, created a destabilized reader, a more confronting grimness, and, occasionally, an ironic playfulness.

McCulloh was responsible for an invitation being extended to Sebald to attend the first academic symposium on his work. This was to be The

Third Davidson Occasional Symposium on German Studies, hosted by the Department of German and Russian at Davidson College in North Carolina. It transpired, tragically, that Sebald would not make it. His death in December 2001 did not, however, cause these plans to be abandoned. *W. G. Sebald: Works & Influences* was held from 13–16 March 2003, participants coming from Europe, Britain, Canada, Israel, Australia and many parts of the United States. The majority of papers presented were given by Germanists, many of whom naturally enough appropriated Sebald as a German writer and inscribed him into that specific cultural context. This augured a possible tension between those coming to Sebald as a writer whose books had won considerable acclaim in their English translations and those for whom he was, essentially, a German writer preoccupied with his particular take on German political and cultural history.

Interestingly this was not the case in all instances, nor was it the case in the two keynote addresses, the McGaw Lectures, given by Professor Lilian Furst and Professor Peter Fritzsche, or indeed in the "Gala Presentation: Sebald in His Own Words" by Sebald's friend, Gordon Turner. The two keynote speakers represented the disciplines of Comparative Literature and of History, itself an interesting decision on the part of those responsible for the organization of the Symposium (Professor McCulloh and his colleague at Davidson, Professor Scott Denham). Professor Lilian Furst, the Marcel Bataillon Professor of Comparative Literature at the University of North Carolina at Chapel Hill, an eminent scholar renowned for her work on European Romanticism and Realism, spoke on "Realism, Photography, and Degrees of Uncertainty," describing Sebald as a writer of postmodernist narratives whose playful subversion of certainty ran counter to the principally mimetic tradition of the European novel, and who used photographs as a means to further disconcert the reader. Her positioning of Sebald was literary in a formalist sense, using a reader-oriented methodology to explicate some of Sebald's narrative strategies, particularly his subversion of mimetic realism and the "creation of uncertainty." Furst's emphasis on Sebald's thematic preoccupation with memory and his postmodern "ambivalence and dualism" constructed him as a writer of fiction from a formalist perspective. Referencing Flaubert's use of realism, the "effects of the real," in *Un Coeur Simple*, she contrasted it with the irony in the agricultural fair scene in *Madame Bovary*, which "affords a glimpse of the narrator's feelings," to show the shift in Flaubert between a purely representational realism and a subversive voice that invites a particular response, subverting the realist narrative, something Sebald shares. Drawing a distinction between the "basic conventions of realism conformed to in *The Emigrants* and *Austerlitz*, where realism has gone wild," Furst asserted that in Sebald the "narrative's strategy is to breed uncertainty." Using Diderot's *Jacques Le Fataliste* ("where everyone repeats what everyone says"), Furst asserted that Sebald shares that "doctrine of fatalism exposed by a distancing satirical irony," adding that Sebald's habitual use of the phrase "*sagte er*" ("he said"), to which one might want also to add his use of the German subjunctive in the originals to designate indirect speech, is part of that distancing irony. For Furst, a *Kindertransport* child herself, Sebald was first and foremost a writer of fiction, not a postwar German writer of historical fiction. The distinction meant that for her, the daughter of parents who had had to flee their home in Europe, Sebald was a writer of imaginative fiction whose books were of interest to a literary scholar, not a German writer voicing the silence of the postwar era.

The second McGaw Lecture, delivered by Peter Fritzsche, Chair of the Department of History at the University of Illinois, "Sebald's Twentieth-Century Histories," positioned Sebald as a writer whose "aestheticization of history" reflected a notion of history as "testimonies of loss written on the open road, accounting for displacement by the witnesses of history, the exiles," the "secret histories of pain and loss," a "sonorous invocation of history" as a means of enchanting the present which in turn depends on these "stories of the past." The "lustre of the past" in Sebald's writing, Fritzsche asserted, is set in opposition to the "disenchantment," "the blandness of the present," offering a "bewitching" alternative to the "melancholy" and "disintegration of the present." This broad and aestheticized view of history, as the way in which we employ the stories of the past to enchant the present, also embraces, according to Fritzsche, our complicit "desire for the history of catastrophe," to "hear the whispers lost irretrievably in the past," a "gravity" which might be offering a means of reversing the violence of the human story. In our "invention" of history, Fritzsche suggested, we privilege some things but others get lost. For Fritzsche, Sebald's textuality inverts some of those hierarchies of preservation and loss. This resonates with Sebald's NESTA mentor, Evans, an academic historian, who had in particular noted that Sebald's research interests pursued the very oddities that most "professional historians omitted" from their own writing (Evans 2002).

In Gordon Turner's presentation, "Sebald in His Own Words," the focus centered Sebald again as a literary figure rather than situating him in a specifically historical or cultural context. Extracts were played from sound recordings of Sebald reading in English and German from *The Emigrants* and *Austerlitz*, from Sebald's twenty-minute televised Dutch interview conducted in English in Amsterdam by Michael Zeeman (*Kamer met Uitzicht* 1998), and from a brief recording of the interview with Maya Jaggi in London in September 2001. The audiovisual part of the presentation concluded with a short film of Sebald reading in 1990 from *Vertigo*. The film was shot inside the picturesque little Bavarian chapel at Krummenbach mentioned in the book. Sebald sits in a pew under the Stations of the Cross, and then moves to a bench outside the chapel in a beautiful alpine setting.

Whiteout

Sebald's creative writing was first published in German by Greno, based in Nordlingen, a provincial town. The first English translations came from The Harvill Press in Britain and New Directions Books in the United States (McCulloh 175), both prestigious publishers. Sebald's second German publisher at Eichborn in Frankfurt, as has already been mentioned, was found dead in the snow after apparently drinking vast amounts of alcohol (Clark et al. 2002). This unfortunate turn of events effected a change to the much bigger house of Carl Hanser Verlag, with offices in Munich and Vienna, and a consequent change of Sebald's publishers in English to the very large and very powerful house of Hamish Hamilton/Penguin in Britain and Random House in the United States. Andrew Wylie, arguably the most prominent literary agent of the day, based in New York, took Sebald on after Susan Sontag's rapturously enthusiastic endorsement of his writing (Alvarez 2001). He was, too, negotiating the project of Sebald's biography (Turner, private communication 2004). According to Maria Alvarez, the Penguin contract, with Wylie as agent, was for £175,000 and "Random House in America allegedly paid a great deal more" (Alvarez 2001).

These changes brought the powerful machinery of major publishing houses to bear, including the efficient international distribution of the English translation of *Austerlitz* and the vigorous marketing of the hardback edition in the months leading up to Christmas following its release in October 2001. Prominently displayed in Australian bookshops, for instance, the appealing sepia-toned photograph of the small, fair boy in the fairy-tale page's costume lent immediate market appeal to the dust jacket.

Then suddenly Sebald was dead. Up until the last twelve months of his life he had been teaching full time in a British university, and this remarkable volume of writing he produced, including the collaboration on the translations, represented an astonishing industriousness. It is reasonable to suggest that the intensive, arduous labor which reflected Sebald's obsessive determination to construct a second career for himself as a writer contributed to his death. Sheppard in his essay is quite explicit about this and goes so far as to suggest that there was an element of self-destructiveness about it (2005). The abrupt ending to his literary career seemed incredible.

"I don't consider myself a writer," Sebald said in an interview with Arthur Lubow in August 2001, four months before he died. "It's like someone who builds a model of the Eiffel Tower out of matchsticks. It's devotional work. Obsessive." This revealing remark, typically Sebaldian, alluded to Benjamin's reference to the exquisite exactitude of the machining of twelve thousand metal fittings and two and a half million rivet marks in the new technology of iron construction, in Benjamin's article called "The Ring of Saturn" (2002, 885). Peter Heinegg quoted Sebald as having said, "When I began to write at forty, at first it was only to carve out some free space for myself in the everyday world" (Heinegg 2002, 126). Readers around the world, according to reviews and articles, were being teased, "taunted" in his colleague Professor Michael Robinson's word (Jaggi 2001a), and seduced into speculative and imaginative engagement with his elegant, highly aesthetic prose. Sebald's was an unusual *début* as an imaginative writer, an extraordinary sequence of production, and a revival of discussion, at the end of one millennium and the beginning of the next, about the very nature of literary fiction, that "vast net" of "possibilities" (Calvino 1992, 124).

3: Views from a "Coign of Vantage"

> It's hard on publishers . . . you have to make sure it doesn't get in the travel section.
> — Sebald in conversation with James Atlas, 1999

> Literature . . . allows us vicariously to *possess* the continuum of experience in a way we are never able to in reality.
> — David Lodge, *Consciousness and the Novel*

> Sommes-nous fatalement des esclaves de l'image? Ce n'est pas sûr, répondent les philosophes, par métier incertains, l'image est potentiellement un espace de liberté: elle anéantit la contrainte de l'objet modèle et lui substitut l'envol de la pensée, le vagabondage de l'imagination.

> [Are we fatally enslaved by the visual? That's not always so, say the philosophers, professionally uncertain — the image is potentially a site of freedom: it annihilates the constraint imposed by the object which it represents, and puts in its place the line of flight that is thought, the wandering that is imagination.]
> — Julia Kristeva, *Visions capitales*, 1998

Setting Out: *Vertigo, The Emigrants, The Rings of Saturn, Austerlitz*

IN THIS SECTION, which suggests a reading practice, I argue that Sebald's reader is positioned to be disobedient, interrogating and constructing images according to his or her own engagement with the destabilizing and disconcerting verbal text. I consider three aspects central in the production of Sebald's disobedient reader.

First, Sebald's fiction eschews narrative in the conventional sense, abandoning conventions of plot and character, and employs a curiously homodiegetic first-person narrator, my focus in stage 1. This narrator is a solitary, soliloquizing writer, not interested in engaging the reader directly in a narrative contract of the usual kind, absorbed instead in the practice of writing which memorializes his own subject, a kind of spectral annunciatory presence that engenders the texts. The Sebaldian narrator is, a little like the Lucan archangel, mediating between two worlds: the textual imaginary and the historicity of prior reality. The disobedient reader, a funambulist too, balances artfully on the verbal tension which connects

these two poles. He or she is free to locate his or her own position trans-
gressively, both inside and outside the textual economy, seeing things on
the journey in each text from her own "coign of vantage" (*Macbeth*,
1.6.9), sometimes but not always by the narrator's side.

Second, the photographs invite disobedience by withholding explanation. I argue in stage 2 that Sebald's use of photographs is primarily ludic,
calling the disobedient reader's attention to the way in which the images
open up a dialogic space between the reader and the text. The reader must
construct the photographic image, whether it appears to need construction
or not, because the text only *suggests* its imaginative or signifying potentiality by offering a context.

Third, the fictions construct place as a poetic space in which, as I argue
in stage 3, the disobedient reader becomes implicated in what Raymond
Williams called a "common culture." In each text the narrator is a restless
traveler, a kind of afflicted Beckett-character who "gets out of the house a
little more" (anonymous interjection, Davidson Symposium 2003), a
note-taking, photograph-collecting restless *Wandersmann* who seems like
a *revenant* pursuing traces of the past, constructing his own European
"songlines" (Bruce Chatwin's appropriation of Australian aboriginal
ethnography) out of the traces of literary and historical culture with which
his memory engages. The disobedient reader, prompted by the highly allusive intertextuality produced by the traveler-narrator, is pushed into travels of her own through the cultural archive.

These three elements, the narrators of the texts, the use of photographs, and the construction of place as poetic space, call the disobedient reader into existence because Sebald positions her as uncertain, in a
space (perhaps *une salle des pas perdus*) where she is left to assume collaborative authority for the textual imaginary by reading contestatively, inter-
rogatively, as a consequence of which she sets off on, and takes responsibility
for, her own *envol* and *vagabondage*. These are, after all, books *pour ceux
qui savent lire*.

Stage 1: The Traveling Narrator
and His Disobedient Companion

When will someone write from the point of view of a superior joke, that
is, as God sees things from above?
— Gustave Flaubert, *Préface à la vie d'écrivain*

We explore the world by seeing actual patterns as contingent variants
of deeper factors, and these we explore by rearranging actual patterns,
in real or imaginary experiments.
— Ernest Gellner, *Language and Silence*, 1998

Is the subject I speak of when I speak the same as the subject who speaks?

— Jacques Lacan

Je est un autre — [*I* is an other]
— Arthur Rimbaud, Letter to Paul Demeny, 15 May 1871

The Sebaldian narrator, what Sebald called that "narrator-figure" (Zeeman 1998), in each of his four writerly manifestations is a fictional screen (Guido Almansi's term) behind which the autobiographical narrator is "hidden," hidden because the narrator's life is so "insinuated" (Craven 1999) with the author's own, that only a very disobedient reader, armed with biographical details about Sebald, can be even partly certain of distinguishing between them. The text cannot disclose the spectral "dead author" (Barthes 1977), without evaporating itself. This fiction is not memoir, not autobiographical writing, not a set of essays, even though it teases the reader with suggestions of all of these discourses in the fragments of them that the narrator is "translating" into something else: "his" beautiful prose which makes a virtue of anachronism.

What Genette calls the diegetic, first-person narrator who "writes" each of Sebald's four fictional texts and whose different journeys offer the reader adventure in his oddly self-contained and ruminative company produces a disobedient reader, what Sebald termed "the reader [who] must constantly be asking, is this so?" (Zeeman 1998).

In his last interview in London (Jaggi 2001b), Sebald observed that "ever since realistic writing moved to center stage, authors are always at pains to say . . . this is not just an invented tale. . . ." This is the traditional novel's generic nature, that perpetual shift between "truth-telling" representation and the rhetorical nature of language used by an imaginative writer. In an earlier interview (Zeeman 1998) Sebald had remarked that in the nineteenth century an author would write that a manuscript had been found, that a text was "recording real life," and he added, "We still have that problem as narrators." The problem seems to be the reader's imaginative bad faith.

The narrators of these four texts engage self-reflexively in the writerly business of crafting the foregrounded prose. "The precedence of the carefully written page of prose over the plot" and "a high intensity in the prose . . . to which a good deal of attention is devoted, much like a poet" (Silverblatt 2001) is each narrator's particular focus as "writer." The reader, as an attentive companion, is made aware of the artifice being practiced, and is free to slip outside the textual economy that the narrator "creates," to interrogate it and thus to set off on her own contemplative and imaginative paths in her reading journey.

The narrators' experiences consist almost entirely of their encounters with stories, the business of language. Some are literary, some historical, some transmitted by people who speak as eyewitnesses and whose paths have intersected with that of the narrator. Some of these people are identifiably historical persons, some of them are not, and the vigilant reader has grounds to suspect fabrication even when, perhaps especially when, imaginative invention is imbricated in a pattern of historical detail. This creates an "unsettling" (Zeeman 1998) of the reader, so insistently disconcerting that the reader desires a little distance to afford her perspective, so that she might ascertain the nature of her relationship with this intense and seductive quasi-authorial narrative voice. In this desire to preserve the distance of autonomy lies her potential for disobedience.

As McCulloh observes, "to read Sebald is to make a journey," the act of traveling "physically as well as mentally through time" (6), and the reader's position as "Fahrgast" (Williams 1998, 110), as traveling companion, is one which I argue in this section is disobedient, whereby the reader, aided, abetted, encouraged (but not commanded) by Sebald's "*ceux qui savent lire*," keeps straying away from the narrator's side into side paths of her own, offering a different perspective, before returning once more to follow the *Wandersmann*-narrator's itinerary. The excitement of adventure, of traveling into the unknown and the future, has been inverted here, for the journey's forward movement, an inevitable trajectory, is disguised by the narrator's insistently reiterative sojourns, those fragments of journey into the past, into its silence and its determination of the future.

The postmodernity of these narrators consists in part in their appropriation of various fragments of the cultural archive (Derrida's term), the *bricolage* of Lévi-Strauss, but their self-reflexive reconstitution of them in a new unity, a cinematic literary montage, is particularly Sebaldian. His discourse restores the possibility of redemption, both in the elegiac sense of redeeming what might otherwise be lost, "to rescue something out of that stream of history that keeps rushing past" (Zeeman 1998), like the dissolving images Kafka saw *im Kino* as a metaphor for his own death (Sebald 2005, 165), and perhaps also, in an oblique New Testament sense of renewal or change, the affirmative making of something new (Revelation 21.5), the business of art.

The narrators' postmodernity is also reflected in what McCulloh perhaps a little broadly terms "the postmodern obsession with ambiguity in general . . . narrative uncertainty" (12), and it is this "ambiguity" and "uncertainty" that characterize the disposition of these narrators and destabilize the reader, further encouraging disobedience. In part this is connected with a deeper sense of uncertainty, the "writer"-narrator's habit of storytelling itself, reflected in Ivor Indyk's formulation that "the act of recovering the past occurs in the shadow of death," after Benjamin's "death is the sanction of everything that the storyteller can tell" (1991, 247).

There is in this a distinct echo of the spirit of Kafka's narrative art, couched in the words of Ritchie Robertson (whose work Sebald admired) in his introduction to the English translation of the equally admired Klaus Wagenbach's book on Kafka (2003) and dedicated "to the memory of W. G. Sebald": his "giving fictional form to the metaphysical uncertainty and spiritual homelessness that was considered characteristic of modern man" (viii). In Sebald's fiction, in the narrator-figure through whom the stories are told, this "modern man" is still at issue, suggesting that "postmodernity" might indeed be "late modernity," an articulation that is reflected in the Sebaldian narrators: storytelling, uncertain and homeless. Sebald's own well-documented distaste for the trappings of what he calls high capitalism in a secular late modernity connects with a nostalgia in his texts for a slower world, where nature is privileged over consumption, where the individual, his subject and his story, are valued and honored. A complex and sensitive sensibility, like Sebald's, like those of his narrators, like those of the writers and artists he admired, is exiled, so many of these spirits "uncertain" and "homeless" in a world in which the human species seems intent on destruction. They, as creative people, are impelled to make a place for themselves in their art.

The disobedient reader who resists, in that literary modality of resistance outlined by Culler, what she "ought" to be reading, in obedience to the text's apparent authority, is a literary reader, predisposed to resistance, to scrutiny, to interrogation and contestation. She is compelled to disobedience because of her engagement with narrative uncertainty and ambiguity which wind back to the matrix of the eccentric and exceedingly melancholy writerly narrator, metaphysically uncertain and spiritually homeless. She is aware of the irony of these qualities being attached to the disembodied voice of a spectral figure, an annunciating voice, but she is mindful that the narrators themselves do not share her distance from, or the view from her perspective over, the texts they "write." So much is withheld, untold by the narrators, that the reader must collaborate imaginatively and thoughtfully in the authoring of texts whose verbal "lost and found" edges (the technique referred to earlier that an artist uses, relying on the viewer's imaginative capacity to complete the missing or absent portion) consistently invite her disobedience.

In *Vertigo* four stories are told by a writer who seems afflicted with a psychic disorientation. Chapters 1 and 3 present like essays, one on Marie-Henri Beyle (whom the "writer"-narrator never names as Stendhal) and the other on Dr. K. (K. is the name Franz Kafka gives to his fictionalized self in *The Trial* and *The Castle*). These seeming essays blend the memory of the real and the imagined in a foregrounding of fiction as a kind of mental alchemy whose disorienting effect strikes the reader as seductive but also suspicious. Chapters II and IV are presented as autobiographical accounts of the writing narrator's observations and meditations as he undertakes a literary pilgrimage in the footsteps of other writers whose lives he weaves together with his more recent empirical past. *Vertigo* is a kind of *Bildungsroman/Künstlerroman* which conflates writing with madness in the figure of the writerly narrator himself, a splendid Sebaldian irony.

In *The Emigrants* four stories of others whose paths have intersected with his are told by a narrator. The authority of the framing narrative is vested in the narrator's own journey (not revealed sequentially) as a European emigrant from alpine Germany to England, first to Manchester, then to Norfolk. The others' stories end in suicide, death by abjection, bleak and possibly terminal hospitalization. Though less marginalized and despairing than those of the persons whose lives he tells, the narrator's telling is inflected nonetheless with a greyness of tone that implicates him in their stories in a way that is unspoken or withheld, untold. The narrator, brushing against loneliness and despair and with an unspecified dependence on a Foucault-inflected academic institution himself, "writes" a seemingly therapeutic text, in which, perhaps, he "can once more carry on a conversation with himself" (Kafka quoted in Wagenbach 104).

The Rings of Saturn is a solitary, poetic book whose stories are chiefly those told by the narrator, a solitary rambler. There are embedded narrators too, but this text is predominantly the writing up of "notes" made during the narrator's meditative pilgrimage across Suffolk to the extreme point of the east coast of England. Lying in Thomas Browne's hospital in Norwich, the frame narrative of the text, the narrator reflects on death and destruction, on the idea of the world as a hospital, using the extended metaphor of silk to trace a textual pilgrimage, to bind the world.

The framing story of *Austerlitz* is a set of encounters between an unnamed, French-English-German-speaking narrator who lives in the north of England but travels quite often to Europe, and a London-based architectural historian named Jacques Austerlitz. These encounters take place, firstly in French and then in English, over a period of thirty years, with a twenty-year interval in the middle. The narrator becomes the writer of this story because Jacques Austerlitz, the historian, can no longer write because he suffers from a literary paralysis, induced by despair. There are embedded narrators, nested in Austerlitz's account as reported by the narrator. The journey traced by the narrator is circular, beginning and ending in Belgium, the promise of the fulfilment of the writing task at the end signaled by the return to the railway station that figured at the beginning.

In each of these books the narrator leads the reader through landscapes and urbanscapes in England and Europe, and simultaneously through the diegetically rendered topography of the narrator's mind. McCulloh writes: "Accompanying the peripatetic narrator on his journey, the reader participates in an act of studied observation at every juncture" (6). This participation is, initially, obedient, considering some vector of remembrance or association under the narrator's guidance. The narrator's journey in each text, however, has always another strand to its itinerary, the writing journey of the text's production, the self-reflexive and metafictional dimension of the carefully attentive weaving of the prose enterprise itself, foregrounded so that the reader cannot help but consider it, and in so doing, step a little away from the thraldom of the narrator's voice and the imperative of his itinerary. This is the site of disobedience.

The narrator's focus is shown to be not authoritative, in the sense that a historical text is authoritative. His perceptions are intensely subjective because this is "his" scriptural economy. Even more disobediently, as McCulloh and Brookner among others noted, Sebald rejected "traditional narrative conventions" (19) represented by what is still called, now somewhat ironically in Sebald's view, the novel. The reader must negotiate a way into the adventurous travel that reading these texts also represents because the narrator is presenting them as real journeys, indexed in ways, topographically and historically, that are beguiling.

The *truc* of Sebald's narrator's destabilizing of the reader, and therefore his calling the disobedient reader into existence, lies primarily in his subversion of referents, of documents. Because he is not a historian and is therefore neither writing history nor claiming to do so, his exaggerated or hyperbolic use of referential material, his hyperrealism, is problematic unless we see it *as* exaggerated, rhetorically heightened, just as Sebald sees Tripp's pictures (2005). This exaggeration reinforces the reader's understanding that the legitimation or authority of institutions is artificially constructed, like the institutions themselves, an illusion of certainty and stability, possibly absurdly deficient.

McCulloh is right when he defines Sebald as "a modern pilgrim" (25), but the shrines at which his narrators seek to worship, places hallowed by time and habits of contemplation, are endangered by a secular late modernity which might consign them to desuetude and ultimately oblivion. The disobedient reader is called into existence to retrace those routes of pilgrimage herself as though by deepening the old paths to those shrines of cultural knowledge, the past, and the self-reflexive contemplation that is possibly the only way out of the harmful, potentially destructive present, some kind of salvation from our anxiety, our uncertainty and homelessness, may be possible. The reader, undergoing a kind of education at the hands of the narrator and sent off into her own self-educating pathways, is herself both preserved and revitalized, saved, but very often the effect is also one of destabilizing, of unsettling.

Although Sebald observed that "In one sense the future doesn't interest me, or that narrator-figure" (Zeeman 1998), he also talks about the past as "some kind of refuge" (Zeeman 1998), something which offers sanctuary from both the present and the future, with its ambivalent "weight" (the "dark centre . . . 1925 and 1950 in Germany") and also "liberation from present constraints" (Zeeman 1998), which for him includes the distasteful aspects of contemporary life. Without history and without community, we wander, as de Certeau observed (1986), in a solitary, purposeless way, telling increasingly meaningless, incomprehensible stories to ourselves on the road to pass the time until our inevitable and possibly absurd end. Reading Sebald is more fulfilling than that, more purposeful, and much more affirmative.

The apparent emotionlessness of the narrators, their lack of detailed engagement with anyone, including with the reader, is counterbalanced, and obliquely substituted, by the extraordinary poignancy and intensity of "their" prose. What McCulloh calls its note of reverence (20) is reflected in an elegiac, Virgilian sense of "*sunt lacrimae rerum*" (life is distress and sorrow), the narrator's refrain, met antiphonally by the reader's elicited empathetic response, "*et mentem mortalia tangunt*" (and pity for short-lived humanity; *Aeneid* 1.462). The deep resonance of this in the prose contributes to the illusion of the first-person narrator being Sebald, as though the "authentic" Sebaldian voice comes through unmediated by his fictional narrator. In Sebald, unlike Virgil, there is concomitant irony and humor, but his language, like Virgil's, hallows the poetic space it creates.

Part of the rhetorical trickery of Sebald's style, wily Odysseus, lies in his narrators presenting themselves as deeply melancholy spectres from whom the vitality of the moment has been leached. The disobedient reader, however, is aware of the comic leaven in the writing, the "irony" and "amusement" that Sebald said was vital to keep the readers engaged (Zeeman 1998), reflecting Flaubert's "superior joke" (Barthes 1977, 110), together with the affirmation of the consoling aspects of the past (including the fact that it is over, as Sebald archly observed), the beauty of the natural world and of art, mainly painting and literature, in a more explicit way than the narrator allows himself.

The grieving narrators do not bear Sebald's name, nor any name. In that condition of namelessness they remain rhetorical tropes, disembodied voices through which the texts are mediated. These voices are characterized by pity, an obliquely uttered empathy, an acute sensitivity to both the human condition and beauty's consolation. They privilege the attempt to create some reflection of that in art, their own writerly preoccupation: ". . . primarily an aesthetic sense . . . to make a decent pattern of whatever comes your way" (Zeeman 1998). What they do above all, in their nameless alterity, is foreground the reader's dialogical self, an ontological or empirical reality, and offer a consciousness whose embodiedness has been relegated to the periphery.

Because the narrator's first-person voice is a self-constructed fiction, the reader is free to play in the textual spaces he "creates," free to disobey the seeming authority of a voice writing artifice. From her own "coign of vantage" the reader's view is not the same as the narrator's. Her independence is guaranteed as long as she "questions authority," as long as she "reads vigilantly," keeps that "narrator-figure" (Zeeman 1998) under scrutiny (Jaggi 2001b). Sebald's narrators encourage readers into positions of disobedience from which they exercise constructing powers of their own, their (ultimately) uncertain subjectivity elicited so explicitly.

Apples of Disobedience

> Speaking about Bishop Berkeley . . . I remember he wrote that the taste of the apple is neither in the apple itself — the apple cannot taste itself — nor in the mouth of the eater. It requires a contact between them. The same thing happens to a book or a collection of books, to a library. For what is a book in itself? A book is a physical object in a world of physical objects. It is a set of dead symbols. And then the right reader comes along, and the words — or rather the poetry behind the words, for the words themselves are mere symbols — spring to life, and we have a resurrection of the word.
> — Jorge Luis Borges, *This Craft of Verse*

> Art consists in a process of forcing the spectator to look at the apples, not in inviting him to salivate at chewing one.
> — Guido Almansi, *The Writer as Liar*

In Sebald's texts the "right reader" (Borges 2000, 4) is the disobedient one, the one who does not "obey" the reading protocols which the narrator presents, as nonfictional ones, but who elicits the poetry behind the words of the *ficciones*. In Almansi's sense (1975, 14) the narrator's "apples" require the reader's scrutiny, her interrogatory vigilance.

The reader too well trained by institutional reading practices and convention can find herself disoriented. This writing looks like nonfiction at first, but we come to realize it can't be read as other than a fictional artifice because of the pervasive presence of a focalizing "narrator-figure" (Zeeman 1998), who keeps drawing our attention to the literariness of his language, as a poet does. This is fiction as art, that we seem to need also to look at "awry" in Frank Kermode's sense of coming at things aslant (2000), because trying to look at it directly is less productive, as many now note.

Destabilized and uncertain, the reader becomes proactive, disobedient, after Umberto Eco's notion of the "very obedient reader" in his Norton Lectures, *Six Walks in the Fictional Woods* (1995, 16). Because the text itself seems to refer its destabilized locus of authority embodied in the narrator to the reader, this is a textual authority constructed, as Roland Barthes articulated prophetically in the seventies (Barthes 1975, 4), by the reader's engagement with the text's language, a reader who is free, in Gerald Prince's formulation (McQuillan 2000, 102) to read in new ways, including perhaps free to be uncertain, to wander in "a galaxy of signifiers" (Barthes 1975, 5). The dialogue of the reader is with the text, whose language both veils and signifies two spectres: the author (already dead, theoretically speaking and in the archive of the future, represented by the text itself) and also the (now dead) narrator, that ironic reflection of the author represented by Sebald's prose.

The Sebaldian narrator who "writes" each of the four fictional texts does not play Borgesian games with a reader accustomed by convention to look at fictional apples as real, that is, apples which look real but aren't. The reader finds herself confounded by being confronted with what seem after all to be real apples: a discourse on Rembrandt's painting *The Anatomy Lesson of Dr. Nicolaas Tulp* in the Mauritshuis; the tale of the odyssey of Sir Thomas Browne's skull; a description of contemporary Terezin, the former Theresienstadt; the account of a visit to the Giardino dei Giusti in Verona; a photograph of Vladimir Nabokov standing with a butterfly net in an alpine summer. It is the (dead) author who, spectrally, through the medium of his language-constructed-and-constructing narrator, plays that game, by indicating that some of the apples are real, and some are not. That which looks real may in fact be fiction, just like the narrator-figure himself. This is a moment of Sebaldian theoretical comedy, not least because Sebald is actually writing himself into W. G. Sebald, writer, and away from Professor Max Sebald, academic.

So, what is a reader to make of all these "apples" when they are mediated by a writing narrator whose immanent presence, psychologically afflicted and writing in anachronistic prose, seems remarkably like the author and yet is not that authoritative presence, just a "figure" (Zeeman 1998)? The answer is that this is the author's game, the far wittier author, capable of irony, whom we glimpse from time to time, that "ontological flicker" (McHale), and whom we, in Wayne C. Booth's formulation of 1961 in *The Rhetoric of Fiction*, are still seeking as we read, "craftily" (Robert Scholes 2001). Sebald is subtle about his own slippery and artful dodging in one sense, and unsubtle about it in another. His narrators' habitual use of photographs in "their" texts, for instance, is the most obvious indicator of Sebald's ludic brinksmanship with the reader. These appear to serve as documenting prior reality; in fact they are coded signifiers for Sebald's metafictional practice, as I discuss in stage 2. They are also unstable: some need constructing, some do not; some appear to be unmanipulated, others clearly are. It's a game.

The reader must be agile. Sebald's use of photographs gradually becomes more audacious as he continues to position them in his texts, finally absorbing them into the narrative itself in *Austerlitz*. Their changing relationship with the verbal text becomes another dimension of the reading problematic appertaining to the "narrator-figure": what is the reader to make of this "unsettling" (Zeeman 1998) practice of the delphic narrator who writes and its destabilizing effect on the verbal text? The reader must take matters, these images of apples, into her own hands, at least from time to time, and scrutinize them for herself. Sebald's textual practice is a postmodern fusion of old and new, that effaces the old rigid conventions of fiction which have lingered on, in Sebald's view, in outmoded mimetic narrative practice and which seeks a more authentic but still literary form of engagement. We are invited not only to scrutinize the means of construction but to collaborate in it by applying our own imaginative intellects.

Our relationship with the Sebaldian narrator is always provisional: he withholds a great deal and does not address the reader directly. He is also mysteriously private, reticent about his life. He creates the text. We know him only in the language with which he shapes his text, in the pictures which are fused with it, in the fact of his deep melancholy, his sensitivity to destruction, suffering, loss and death, and some pervasive sense of care and compassion, curiously attenuated, inflected by a suggestive immanence rather than a real presence. He is everywhere and nowhere; he is the language of the text.

It matters to the reader that the narrator is a writer, for it is the only way, in the language of consciousness that speaks him (the ghost of both Wittgenstein's "*Die Sprache spricht*" and the Lucan "*logos*"), in which we can know him, in the abstracted pictures which his scrupulous use of language "paints." We scrutinize them, and in doing so, his authority. It matters that the writerly narrator is also a traveler who takes us on quite different journeys in four different texts, for we too are moving through space and time as readers, in the narrator's presence and in the text which utters him, but we are also free to take off on our own trajectories. Like the spectator in a gallery we too have traveled to stand in front of the picture. This is quite possibly what Sebald means by "authentic" writing, what Martin Buber means by encounter, that transactional dialogism of "I" and "thou."

In this self-reflexive, metafictional discourse (in Linda Hutcheon's sense of the postmodern) whose primary trope is travel, the reader is a nameless companion, Williams's "Fahrgast" (1998, 110), of the nameless narrator. This is suggestive of the dialogically imagined couplings of Dante and Virgil, Don Quixote and Sancho Panza, Diderot's Jacques and his master, Plato and Socrates, those conversational and interrogatory couplings which produce texts.

In his 1982 essay "Between History and Natural History: On the Literary History of Total Destruction" (2005, 68–101), Sebald observes that those who have survived "collective catastrophes have already experienced their death" (73). This goes some way to identifying the nature of Sebald's narrators, and melancholy in his texts as a "perimortal" condition. It also adumbrates the curious space between a vividly and actively engaged sense of life and the exiled, detached quality shared by those shadowed figures in his books.

Itineraries

Each of the four texts comprises a different journey, and a different kind of journey, but all of them journeys which travel backwards into the past as much as they trace itineraries across the earth and across the page. In *Vertigo* the narrator sets out on a writerly pilgrimage which ends infernally with a dream of fire and ice, Pepys and an apocalyptic vision, but begins with Beyle and Napoleon's transalpine expedition. *The Emigrants* is a writer's journey from central or eastern Europe into exile, with destinations various and individuals subject to further psychic displacement. In *The Rings of Saturn* the writer's journey is recollected, relived from a position of near-paralysis in a hospital bed located in the city from which the elliptical journey had begun and to which it returns, Goethe's center and bourne expressed, ironically, as Norwich. *Austerlitz* is an iterative and circular journey, spiraling and revisiting different stations in two parallel journeys which intersect at various points, voices traveling backwards into the past, the writing speaking another's aporia, the ghostly future.

In their melancholic ruminations on the past, the narrators of all four journeys are in some ways static, like the gravity of a collapsed star threatening to pull into its orbit all other travelers who risk treading too close to the event horizon of the black hole. The texts' humor and wit, though signaling that other presence in the prose, the author playing his "game of hide and seek" (videotape of Sebald interview by Maya Jaggi, London, 24 September 2001, Turner 2003), enables the disobedient reader to keep free of the narrator's gravitational pull of self, to maintain her own position, her dignity, because she travels with an awareness of the author's stylistic wit and her own ontology, her alterity. She can intersect the path of the narrators' elliptical traveling without risk to her own integrity, her autonomy, because of her disobedient reading which resists the narrator's self. In this tension the dialogism of the Sebaldian reader exists.

In the Knapsack:
The Iterative Journeys of *Austerlitz*

> . . . I always felt the piercing, inquiring gaze of the page boy who had come to demand his dues, who was waiting in the grey light of dawn on the empty field for me to accept the challenge and avert the misfortune lying ahead of him . . . that evening in the Sporkova when the eyes of the Rose Queen's page looked through me. (*Austerlitz*, 260–61)

Austerlitz is a dialogical text, which mirrors that primary dialogical transaction, reading. The "I" of Sebald's text is quite literally an "other," as Rimbaud suggests (1960, 128), an externalized constructed other able to engage with a phantom voice retained in his memory, in a sleight of hand that blends the narrator's voice with that of his friend Jacques Austerlitz so effectively that they are virtually indistinguishable. What makes them so is the narrator's text, "his" diction, "his" syntax, "his" style, "his" crafting of language.

If we consider the narrative bones of *Austerlitz*, we find this: a diegetic narrator, specifically a homodiegetic one, formerly a listener and now a "writer," reporting what he has heard and seen. The task of telling in writing another's story has been delegated to him by that individual himself, he being rendered incapable of doing so by life's cumulative wounding of his sensibility, and ultimately by his death.

Austerlitz has already been the narrator of his own life in the pretextual past, in the storytelling the narrator heard. This is represented in an episodic series of performative and temporalized utterances, carefully indexed by the narrator: "in the second half of the 1960's" (1), "in the winter of 1996" (7), repeating Austerlitz's "in the early summer of 1967" (31), "in the years that followed" (43), "at the end of 1975" (45), "scarcely a year later" (46), "in December 1996" (46), "on that December evening" (106), "the next day" (138), "three-thirty in the afternoon" (144), "Almost a quarter of a year had passed" (165), "Saturday 19 March" (166), "that evening in the late winter of 1997" (232), "in the morning" (234), "that morning in Alderney Street" (255), "in September of the same year" (354). Correlated with this rhetorical indexing of temporal certainty by the scrupulously sequencing narrator, the powerfully evocative memories and associations that Austerlitz has recounted have an air of timelessness, despite their being situated at some particular point in his life, when a schoolboy or a university student.

Austerlitz's stuttering flow (because these episodes were surely not as elegantly sequential and poetically articulated as the narrator's text explicitly makes them out to be, 14) of episodic monologic narratives delivered to the listening "writer" are unavailable, and unverifiable, translated into the embedded discourse of a text which frames them within the writing narrator's own dutiful sense of task, his obligation to his friend, the other. Hamlet's "tell my story" is an intertextual ghost here.

In his language net he captures the metaphysical phantom that is Austerlitz's consciousness, his mind, his memory, as it encounters him, his own memory, on several occasions, sometimes serendipitously, sometimes by design. Although no paragraph convention is observed by the narrator — whose nonlinear, temporally iterative narrative habit with its digressive associations and recollections contrasts with the linearity of his precisely indexed construction of the encounters and meetings he has with Austerlitz, — the reader is in no way discommoded.

This is because the itinerary of the pattern's design is woven obliquely over the top of the background warp and weft grid where the conversation takes place, which we very quickly forget as readers, in the gradual dissolution in our minds as readers of the bar of Liverpool Street station in London, when we listen to and follow the patterns of story. The narrator's discourse is indexed temporally, in his "writing," because the frame story is (albeit slenderly) mimetic. Austerlitz, or rather his consciousness, exists outside time in the narrator's memory, just as the reading (and listening) strike the reader as atemporal, occurring in the illusion of stasis that the narration, the reported speech, the station itself creates. The memory of Austerlitz and the voiced conversations, though themselves now timeless in the narrator's mind, are fixed in the text that records them, before they are brought to life again in the reader's mind.

A key moment for understanding the fictional strategies in *Austerlitz* occurs in a section about Andromeda Lodge, the house in Wales belonging to Gerald Fitzpatrick's mother Adela. The narrator recalls visits there with Austerlitz. On long summer days they played badminton in the ballroom:

> After our game we usually stayed in the ballroom for a little while, look-ing at the images cast on the wall opposite the tall, arched window by the last rays of the sun shining low through the moving branches of a hawthorn, until at last they were extinguished. There was something fleeting, evanescent about these sparse patterns appearing in constant suc-cession on the pale surface, something which never went beyond the moment of its generation, so to speak, yet here, in this intertwining of sunlight and shadow always forming and re-forming, you could see mountainous landscapes with glaciers and icefields, high plateaux, steppes, deserts, fields full of flowers, islands in the sea, coral reefs, arch-ipelagos and atolls, forests bending to the storm, quaking grass and drift-ing smoke. And once, I remember, said Austerlitz, as we gazed together at this slowly fading world, Adela leaned towards me and asked: Do you see the fronds of the palm trees, do you see the caravan coming through the dunes over there? (158–59)

Here individuals are experiencing the moment by transforming its patterns into memories and associations of their own. The passage ends with a per-sonal invitation from Adela to the narrator, here the embedded Austerlitz, to see what she sees, to claim meanings for the empirical moment in the ballroom by reference to worlds elsewhere through concatenations of associ-ation. This invitation extends to the reader, who is encouraged to go off on the same travels of association, quite different to the reader of Flaubert or Dickens.

These fictional strategies, not least because they also invoke inter-textual associations (that Proustian hawthorn or that caravan of Edward FitzGerald or the spiraling patterns in Parc Monceau in Vladimir Nabokov's memoir), encourage the production of the disobedient reader through their soliciting of an active response from the reader. The narra-tor constructs a sequenced discourse, the frame of his diegetic text in which the mimetically represented meetings between Austerlitz and the narrator occur, but this is always less compelling than the vivid images that Austerlitz's memory evokes in the narrator's retelling within that frame. The past is constructed in exquisite detail. One of the finest examples is in these sequences at Andromeda Lodge, the beauty of its setting, the night expedition to watch moths with Uncle Alphonso, and the shadow play of the setting sun with Gerald Fitzpatrick's mother.

On the walls of the ballroom in Andromeda Lodge in Wales, as shadows of the setting sun trace "through the moving branches of a hawthorn" (158), Adela summons "the camel caravan" (159) of the Arabian desert, which connects in the disobedient reader's mind with the section from *The Rings of Saturn* and the description of the Suffolk writer Edward FitzGerald's translation of *Rubaiyat of Omar Khayyam*, with its image of the morning summons likened to the flinging of a stone in a metal bowl whose ringing sets the caravan in motion across the desert sands like the constellations of stars in their stately gradual motion across the deserts of the night sky. This too connects with Gerald's subsequent career in astronomy, with the tellingly named astrophysicist Malachio in the bar in *Vertigo*, the midnight ferryman across Stygian waters; these echoes reinforce the sense of conversation that exists between Sebald's books, as well as intertextual ones.

These intricate images, summoned in the disobedient reader's mind as vividly as the "mountainous landscapes with glaciers and icefields . . . fields full of flowers . . . coral reefs . . . quaking grass and drifting smoke" (158) form an imagined topography in Austerlitz's mind, weaving associative links, but the image of the narrator's childhood memory, also in *The Rings of Saturn*, of imagining that the evening flight paths of swallows wheeling in the alpine valley that was his home are somehow binding up the world evokes the desire for reassurance and consolation, some kind of meaning, however mysterious and insubstantially shadowed, that Adela's game creates. The overwhelming sense here for the disobedient reader is the richness of the imaginative capacity of the human mind summoned by the narrator, effected by the narrator's voice.

The strategies here are complex and nested. The voice of Austerlitz represented by the narrator's exquisitely evocative prose takes the reader up the Dee Valley to Barmouth by train, on more than one occasion, for there are several visits to Andromeda Lodge, by pony trap along the road that follows the Mawddach, up the graveled drive and through the wild and exotic garden with its Moluccan cockatoos and New Zealand man ferns, into the grey stone house and into the ballroom, one late summer afternoon. In a brilliantly understated, barely existing communication caught in the metaphor of the feathery to-and-fro trajectory of the shuttlecock, with its elongated temporal metronome, between the sensitive, serious young man, now a student at Oxford, and the beautiful, slightly

mysterious, gracious widow Adela, who gave sanctuary to the lonely former schoolboy, Dafydd Elias, her son's friend, from Stower Grange, the
reader is taken out of mimetically represented place and into the imaginative trajectories suggested by Adela and traced by the shadows playing on
the wall. The disobedient reader eventually steps back from the decelera-
tion of time, having been momentarily completely absorbed into this
seductive and enthralling space in the prose, by being "vigilant," by questioning its authority.

Is this the narrator, or Austerlitz, or Adela, or is it the sinuous thread
of the prose itself weaving its spell? If it is the latter, whose language is it?
It is the "writer"-narrator's prose, in which the voice of Austerlitz, and
the embedded one of Adela, is represented in such an insinuated way that
we cannot really tell where one starts and the other stops, except with the
most careful scrutiny of the tag "he said," and even then it is almost
impossible to be certain, as it is almost impossible to be certain where
mimesis shades into diegesis, where the threshold is and where intersection lies. Careful scrutiny can reveal that, and careful scrutiny can reveal
how artfully the aesthetic richness of the prose is wrought, and how
lightly it nets us.

The Turner watercolor, *Funeral at Lausanne* (1841), which exists in
the reader's empirical reality as one of Turner's late series of Swiss and
German watercolors (1840–48), as the beauty of the Mawddach estuary
also does, offers another example of this fictional strategy (155). Austerlitz
is reported by the narrator as "rediscovering . . . this almost insubstantial
picture" and reflecting that, judging by its date, it came "from a time when
Turner could hardly travel any more and dwelt increasingly on ideas of his
own mortality" (155). Austerlitz's reference to this watercolor is prompted
by the scene at the Cutiau cemetery where the funeral procession for
Evelyn and Alphonse is heading one misty morning in autumn (154).
Austerlitz's verbal sketch of the Mawddach, the massif of Cader Idris, the
"few dark figures, the group of poplars, the flood of light over the water"
(154), is a preview of the watercolor which is reproduced by the narrator
on the page (155). The disobedient reader aligns the details of Austerlitz's
description of the Welsh scene with the reproduction of Turner's watercolor of the scene in Switzerland. They match in such a way that the connection between the scene above the Mawddach estuary (a place Turner
also painted in 1798, as Austerlitz observes) (156) and the Swiss scene is
uncanny, as it was for Austerlitz, but whether this is exactly what Austerlitz
said or compared, the reader cannot know, because the narrator has
reshaped that prior moment of telling in "his" prose and with the insertion
of the reproduction of the watercolor. The narrator then reports
Austerlitz's speculation on the provenance of Turner's "almost insubstantial picture" in which the observed, remembered and imagined (literally
imagined) are inextricably fused:

. . . perhaps for that very reason, when something like this little cortège in Lausanne emerged from his memory, he swiftly set down a few brush-strokes in an attempt to capture visions which would melt away the next moment. What particularly attracted me to Turner's watercolour, said Austerlitz, was not merely the similarity of the scene in Lausanne to the funeral at Cutiau, but the memory it prompted in me of my last walk with Gerald in the early summer of 1966, through the vineyards above Morges on the banks of Lake Geneva. (155–56)

Turner's watercolor, an image created out of observation, memory, contemplation, imagination and painterly artifice, becomes here in the narrator's reported telling a "vision which would melt away again the next moment" (155), precisely what the reader of Sebald experiences as she follows the itinerary of Austerlitz's thoughts and their associations as they are constructed by the "writer"-narrator's prose. Painted by a man who went walking all his life in beautiful places, making "notes" or "rapid watercolour sketches . . . noting down what he saw either from life or looking back at the past later" (154–55), Turner's watercolor, for the vigilant Sebaldian reader, that adventurous and disobedient reader, can never now be separated from the misty autumn morning above the Mawddach, the double burial of the two great-uncles, the miserable religious brother and the joyful naturalist-artist brother. Who can say, even with the questioning reader's eye, whether the Turner watercolor of Lausanne is more or less real than the funeral at Cutiau, now that that particular watercolor is forever fused with Sebald's literary appropriation of it, calling to mind Turner's other drawings and paintings of the Mawddach valley?

Austerlitz's imaginative, contemplative speculation about the artist's empirical reality and its informing the painting licenses the creative reader to accept this as an invitation to her own active interpretative response to this section of the text. The thread which connects Turner and Austerlitz's speculation also connects Austerlitz's two memories, the double burial at Cutiau and the intense poignancy of his last walk with his life's friend, Gerald, in the Swiss Alps before he dies prematurely in an aircraft accident, not recounted here in this section of the text (156), although the irony of flight affording Gerald escape from the damaging misery of school and his decision "to study astronomy" (157) is suggested. Death and beauty, travel, art and culture come together here in a fictional lode that makes this too a key passage in identifying Sebald's fictional strategies and the ways in which they produce the disobedient reader, her vigilance, her questioning of authority, her own imaginative and contemplative traveling into other pathways, including into Turner's watercolors.

It is his awakening sense of natural beauty that Austerlitz remembers, his staring out at the Irish Sea from his bedroom window at Andromeda Lodge, "unable to think coherently in the face of this spectacle, which was never the same twice" (134). Describing with the precision of a painter or a scientist, whose "eyes" the narrator alludes to at the beginning of the text (3), the changing scene at different intervals of the day, Austerlitz's final verbal painting in light suggests the impact of the beauty of the natural world on him:

> But on bright summer days, in particular, so evenly disposed a lustre lay over the whole of Barmouth Bay that the separate surfaces of sand and water, sea and land, earth and sky could no longer be distinguished. All forms and colours were dissolved in a pearl-grey haze; there were no contrasts, no shading any more, only flowing transitions with the light throbbing through them, a single blur from which only the most fleeting of visions emerged, and strangely — I remember this very well — it was the very evanescence of those visions that gave me, at the time, something like a sense of eternity. (135)

The role of beauty for the narrator here, in this verbal Turner watercolor, is to transport both the teller and the listener, and the "writer"-narrator and the reader, out of the mimetic representation of the bedroom on the upper floor of the grey stone house, and even more so out of the bar of Liverpool Street station, into the intense experience that the "prose of high intensity" (Sebald to Silverblatt 2001) invites, the liberation of consciousness from the everyday, the poetic effect of the prose, a version of the kind of painting in which Turner, while never losing sight of the reality he is observing, creates a poetic freedom, the kind of funambulist aesthetic that we can recognize also in Sebald.

Sebald's prose shifts between temporal planes here in a way that the reader cannot, and does not want to, hold fast to. We have forgotten, in this marvellous telling, where the narrator and Austerlitz are, for we too are standing at the bedroom window overlooking Barmouth Bay and the Irish Sea, watching the play of images on the ballroom wall at Andromeda Lodge, sitting on the side of the hill above the Mawddach estuary as ten thousand moths stream past us in a kaleidoscope whose complexity we cannot fix. We are, as the narrator was in that prior telling, transfixed as Austerlitz was empirically transfixed even earlier in his boyhood, by the power of seeing, and the power of the imagination, and by the language which acts as the vector for that experience which collapses time, making manifest the idea that human consciousness, or the mind, is not only its own place, but is constructed in and communicated by words and images.

We see this again when great-uncle Alphonso takes Austerlitz and Gerald "up the hill behind the house on a still, moonless night to spend a few hours looking into the mysterious world of moths" (127). Guided by Alphonso's knowledge, the scientific scrutiny of these "invertebrates, which are usually hidden from our sight," is invested, as is the mantra of their beautiful names ("China-Marks, Dark Porcelains and Marbled

Beauties, Scarce Silverlines or Burnished Brass, Green Foresters and Green Adelas . . ." 128) and painterly characteristics ("oblique and wavy lines, shadows, crescent markings and lighter patches, freckles, zigzag bands, fringes and veining and colors you could never have imagined, moss green shot with blue, fox brown, saffron, lime yellow, satiny white, and a metallic gleam as of powdered brass or gold" 129), with a sense of the astonishing variety and beauty of the natural world. Alphonso's lesson in seeing, for that is what it is, is imbued with a sense of the marvellous, as he tells the boys "how each of these extravagant creatures had its own character" (129). There is scientific wisdom too as Alphonso describes the body temperature of moths at "thirty-six degrees, like that of mammals" as they are coaxed back into life from their dormant state during the day. "Thirty-six degrees, according to Alphonso, has always proved the best natural level, a kind of magical threshold, and it has sometimes occurred to him, Alphonso, said Austerlitz, that all mankind's misfortunes were connected with its departure at some point in time from that norm, and with the slightly feverish, overheated condition in which we constantly found ourselves" (131). Austerlitz's memory is imbued with a magical oneiric quality as he describes it:

> On that summer night, said Austerlitz, we sat high above the estuary of the Mawwdach in our hollow in the hills until daybreak, watching the moths fly to us, perhaps some ten thousand of them by Alphonso's estimate. The trails of light which they seemed to leave behind them in all kinds of curlicues and streamers and spirals, and which Gerald in particular admired, did not really exist, explained Alphonso, but were merely phantom traces created by the sluggish reaction of the human eye, appearing to see a certain afterglow in the place from which the insect itself, shining for only a fraction of a second in the lamplight, had already gone. It was such unreal phenomena, said Alphonso, the sudden incursion of unreality into the real world, certain effects of light in the landscape spread out before us, or in the eye of a beloved person, that kindled our deepest feelings, or at least what we took for them. . . . (131–32)

Alphonso deepens the mystery:

> . . . there is really no reason to suppose that lesser beings are devoid of sentient life. We are not alone in dreaming at night for, quite apart from dogs and other domestic creatures whose emotions have been bound up with ours for many thousands of years, the smaller mammals such as mice and moles also live in a world that exists only in their minds whilst they are asleep, as we can detect from their eye movements, and who knows, said Austerlitz, perhaps moths dream as well, perhaps a lettuce in the garden dreams as it looks up at the moon by night. (133–34)

This (partly comic) metaphysical speculation is based on close scrutiny but capable of admitting the possibilities of uncertainty and doubt, imbued with imagination born of observation and the productivity of open-ended uncertainty, rather than closed down by logical rationalism or determinism of any kind. Within the terrible story of Austerlitz's life, its dislocations, its breakdowns, its anguished search for the truth of its beginnings, Sebald has captured a consciousness and a sensibility, and memorialized them through the medium of his narrator. Mind to speech to writing and the vivid magic of reading: this is no scientific formula but is rather the bedrock of Sebald's textual practice, intrinsically poetic in its fictionality. The disobedient reader elicits that poetry by disavowing its presentation as nonfiction, questioning the authority of the narrator and reading with a vigilant eye to the way language is being used in that uncertain, adventurous discourse we call fiction.

In a Small Suitcase: *The Emigrants*

During the winter of 1990/91, in the little free time I had (in other words, mostly at the so-called weekend and at night), I was working on the account of Max Ferber given above. It was an arduous task. Often I could not get on for hours or days at a time, and not infrequently I unravelled what I had done, continuously tormented by scruples that were taking tighter hold and steadily paralysing me. These scruples concerned not only the subject of my narrative, which I felt I could not do justice to, no matter what approach I tried, but also the entire questionable business of writing. I had covered hundreds of pages with my scribble, in pencil and ballpoint. By far the greater part had been crossed out, discarded, or obliterated by additions. (*The Emigrants*, 230)

Niall Lucy observes that fiction, both in essence and its form that we have called the novel, was always an essentially hybrid form, an unstable structure. Mapping the "blurring of generic boundaries" and the blurring of the "distinction between fiction and non-fiction" in American writing in the sixties and seventies (85), Lucy asserts that "the notion of literature expanded to become a kind of 'writing' in general" (1997, 85). Lucy points to the dynamic mutability of what we call the literary, which embraces the construction of prose fiction as a way of negotiating a relationship with the world in which we live, whether we feel at home in it or not.

The narrator in *The Emigrants* is not at home in the world, as the subjects of the four stories he tells are not, but the narrator finds a home for himself in the negotiation of the relationship between his implicit story of emigration, and its threat of despair, and the writing of the stories of four other emigrants in the discourse of his text. Lucy's formulation of writing adduces the author, Sebald, who translates his own carefully edited empirical reality into the fictionally constructed voice of his figure of the "writer"-narrator. This kind of writing, in which the boundary between fiction and nonfiction is elided, becomes "a way of [the narrator] negotiating a relationship with the world" (85). The narrator's presence in each story in *The Emigrants* is shaped by a sense that decenteredness, eccentricity, or marginalization, whose corollary is a despair which can over time become a mortal wound, is a fate that he has managed hitherto to avoid.

The first story in *The Emigrants* is prefaced by an epigraph: "And the last remnants memory destroys." This suggests that narrative, which draws on memory, engenders *amnesis*. This is both ironic and ambivalent. It suggests that the actual traces of the past are displaced by the construction of memory, in this case narrative, although also in a painting or a photograph. In varying ways each of the stories here is partly the narrator's story, and the reader, the disobedient reader, is always mindful of that.

The shapelessness or indeterminacy of memory has been materialized as shaped, sequenced discourse, which belongs, within the text's economy, to the constructed narrator, even though there are many embedded narratives within it, spoken by the emigrants themselves, who appear to have been given their "own voice" either as historical or fabricated individuals, for we cannot easily distinguish them. The first story begins with the homodiegetic narrator's "I": "At the end of September 1970, shortly before I took up my position in Norwich, I drove out to Hingham with Clara in search of somewhere to live" (3).

The reading problematic of Sebald's textuality begins here. Staying obediently inside the textual space of the story, the reader has no idea who the speaking voice of the narrator belongs to, except that he is a married man who has come to Norwich to take up some kind of position, coming from a mountainous region near Berne to the flat country of Norfolk, in need of rented accommodation until he and his wife are able to find a more permanent home. It is "the end of September 1970" and the village of Hingham is about "25 kilometres" from Norwich. Apart from the historical facts that Abraham Lincoln's forebears emigrated from Hingham to America in the seventeenth century, and that Hingham is a small market town rather than a village, unmentioned in the story and discoveries of associating threads that a curious reader makes on her own side-trips, it is a disorienting beginning just as it may have been for the narrator. That the house is called "Prior's Gate," a name which invokes the hospitaler monastic foundation of great cathedrals like Winchester, not Norwich, suggesting sanctuary and protection, commends ironically the narrator's choice of "temporary accommodation" at this transit stop on his journey from the alpine landscape he has come from to wherever it is that he is going. That is subverted when the reader discovers that while it may also be a protective sanctuary for the curious Elaine, it is a rather dismal, lonely place for its principal inhabitant, Dr. Henry Selwyn, who retreats even further into the sanctuary of his flint hermitage, a veritable monk.

Contextualized by the other stories of Paul Bereyter, Ambros Adelwarth, and Max Ferber, Henry Selwyn's story belongs to a metanarrative which appears to be invested less in the individual stories of emigration which have somehow intersected the narrator's own thinly and partially told story of emigration than in the marginalized and displaced lives whose psychic wounds have etiolated them, reducing them at last to the paralysis of melancholy and in several cases a final act of despair. It is the tone of the narrator's voice, the grey, melancholy tenor of his prose, which suggests that he too is vulnerable to this decenteredness that he observes in others, whose stories he has connected, threaded tenuously together for survival.

The obedient reader waits in vain for the narrator's voice to link the stories more explicitly, and to his own. We never know precisely why the narrator, whom we discover in the second story was schooled by Bereyter in Bavaria, has come to Norwich in 1970, or why, as he tells us in the last story, he moved to England in 1966 (149), leaving from Kloten airport in Zurich. We do discover in that last story, Max Ferber's, the depths of the narrator's own capacity for melancholy on the bleak Sundays he spends walking to fill the emptiness of the lonely hours experienced in his early days in Manchester. His journey of displacement into solitude connects with the four stories he tells of others, as though through his empathy he can project imaginatively into lives which have been marginalized by circumstance, which end in ways that are at least poignant if not tragic, his empathy evinced in his narration.

His writing of these lives is described by one French reviewer as a "requiem" (Spozio 2003). If this elegiac quartet, *The Emigrants*, is played in a minor key, it is the narrator himself who is responsible. There is enough silence, apparent unspokenness, in these stories, including Henry Selwyn's, for the reader to be puzzled by the narrator's position. An informed reader stepping outside the textual economy will know that Max Sebald moved to Manchester in 1966 for postgraduate study, before he was married, having finished his undergraduate degree in Switzerland. That reader will also know that by the time Sebald was appointed to a position in Norwich in 1970, he was married (not to "Clara" but to Ute), and may know that W, in the Ambros Adelwarth story, conjures the village of Wertach. This is not just coyness, or an easily exposed attempt at privacy. We are lured, as readers, by the aura of the real, but it is a deceptive glow, because it is a reflected light, as all art is.

The highly visual nature of the narrator's description of the first sight of the setting of the "large, neoclassical house" (4), with the graveyard, the Scots pines and yews, the shrubbery of hollies and Portuguese laurel, the stand of beeches, the Virginia creeper, the lime trees, elms and holm oaks, the "gentle undulations of arable land and the white mountains of cloud on the horizon" (3–5) tells us far more about the narrator than it does about Henry Selwyn, even when the narrator introduces us to him "lying in the shade cast by a lofty cedar" in a corner of the garden (5). It is not difficult to think here, in this precisely indexed landscape, of Thomas Hardy's line, "he was one who used to notice such things," in the poem in which Hardy writes his own epitaph ("Afterwards," Hardy 521), partly because the narrative began with a graveyard, partly because the narrator as a traveler is keenly observant and partly because the narrator's combination of these two things sets the tone for the book as a whole, its uttering of him, especially as most of the people whose stories he is recounting here are dead.

The free indirect discourse of Selwyn's speech is less a vivid characterization of Selwyn (5) than a testament to the narrator's powers of recall. The narrator's sense of engagement with Selwyn, as we discover in the last story and in the description of Gracie Irlam's salvific teasmaid (as Lilian Furst pointed out in her McGaw Lecture at Davidson College, 2003), is shaped by a shared experience of deep loneliness that in the narrator's case has passed, which is why perhaps the text begins in 1970 and ends in 1966, and in Henry Selwyn's story ends in his uncharacteristically violent suicide.

This grimness is alleviated by the narrator's reference to Selwyn's quirky description of himself as "an ornamental hermit" (5), although the truth is that, estranged from his wife, he lives virtually alone, purposelessly and lovelessly (unlike the narrator with his new wife) in the empty house and derelict garden with an odd, silent female servant, Elaine, whom the narrator describes as resembling the inmate of a lunatic asylum. Why she is there and whose charity enables her to be there, like the aged horses, we are never told. On Sundays she appears in a Salvation Army uniform (the kind Gracie Irlam's youthful affiliation also) — here a nice irony: saved or saving? Against the dereliction of the garden and the house the narrator sets his own domestic efforts of repainting the bathroom and the staircase to the east wing of the house where his flat is located, an oddly pointless act of domestication in a tenancy of short duration, but it serves to contrast the dereliction of Selwyn's life with the narrator's hopeful making of a home for his wife and himself.

The narrator's description of the unusual dinner to which he and "Clara" are invited when a friend of Selwyn visits is oddly restrained. His description of the flint folly in the garden, Selwyn's "hermitage" where he spends his days in clement weather (10) suggests a personal refuge, a shelter from the empty and uselessly large marital home. The terrible loneliness of the former surgeon, the Lithuanian child refugee, is the context for the narrator's depiction of him as a gentle, courteous man whose instinctual warmth and generosity have somehow been betrayed by life.

The evening scene of the dinner, its frugality of vegetables harvested from the derelict garden and served by the silent and grey-aproned Elaine, is both cinematic and oneiric, as though the vividness of the narrator's recollection has heightened the details to a kind of hyperrealism that is at once beautiful and disturbing. The description of the dark dining room with the oak table that could accommodate thirty, with the surgeon and his friend the botanist and entomologist, Edwin Elliott at either end, and the narrator and his wife on one side facing the darkened windows looking out onto the garden, with Elaine lighting the candles in the two silver candelabra and pushing a "serving trolley equipped with hot plates . . . dating from the Thirties" (13) is, like many scenes in Sebald, evocative of films in which the cinematography privileges shadow and the soundtrack silence, as in Werner Herzog's *The Enigma of Kaspar Hauser*, which the narrator alludes to later (17) and in which roles are played by the people, including the Elaine-like Kaspar, whose lives the film depicts.

The narrator slows down the pace of the prose by lingering over the detail in a way that demands the reader's scrutiny, just as the camera zooms in and pans across the ritual of the dinner table. Over these images the narrator plays the soundtrack of Dr. Selwyn's story, inserting verbal-stills of his spending the years of the First World War, after "completing his medical studies in Cambridge" (13), his climbing in the Bernese Oberland and meeting the alpine guide who becomes his great friend and with whom he shares the climbing expeditions. Naegeli's alpine disappearance, and presumed death, has caused Selwyn such grief that he falls into a profound depression, from which he seems never to have recovered.

We are prepared for the end of Selwyn's story here, in the middle of its chronic despair, by the narrator's lingering over the melancholy reminiscence of Naegeli's fate, with which the story will conclude, itself a metaphor for the "return" of the dead Selwyn in the story that the narrator, whose own former home was "near Berne," tells. We are not prepared, however, for the whimsy and the irony of the next section, in which the narrator describes seeing the film of Selwyn's and Elliott's "last visit to Crete," some ten years earlier. The shot of Selwyn, with his "knee-length shorts, his shoulder bag and butterfly net," is compared by the narrator with a photograph of Nabokov "in the mountains above Gstaad" (16) which he has "clipped from a Swiss magazine a few days before" (16), and indeed that is the photograph that the narrator has inserted into the text, recording not Henry Selwyn's story but his own, just as the view of the graveyard with its evergreen holm oak, the whitewashed wall of the tennis court, the derelict garden, and the flint-built hermitage are records not of Henry Selwyn's story but of the narrator's engagement with Henry Selwyn.

After the narrator and his wife leave the house "in May 1971" (18), Selwyn visits them "at fairly regular intervals" and one day tells the narrator the story of his family leaving their Lithuanian village to travel to America, finding themselves, by an absurd, even ridiculous mistake, in London. He also tells the narrator about the failure of his marriage to wealthy Elli, and his retreat from the world. The beautiful image of his gift of white roses twined with honeysuckle (21–22) is shockingly juxtaposed with the narrator's brief account of Selwyn's suicide, and the curious discovery in 1986, as the photograph tells us, of the body of Selwyn's great friend, the alpine guide Naegeli, who had disappeared in 1914.

It is the uncanniness of these juxtapositions, for which the narrator is responsible, and the coincidence of his being in Zurich and buying a newspaper from Lausanne, which prompts the "memory of Dr. Selwyn" to return "for the first time in a long while" (23). That "the dead are ever returning to us" (23), both Naegeli and his friend Selwyn, serves as the prelude to the other three stories in the collection in which fragments of the narrator's life are embedded.

How do we construe this story as fiction, if it is drawn from the narrator's memory and indexed so precisely by empirical sources which can be interrogated by the disobedient reader's trip to the village of Hingham in Norfolk; an archival search for Véronique Tissières's article in the Lausanne newspaper of "23. juillet 1986"; a biographical check of the details of Sebald's movements; an archival search of the academic records of the medical school at Cambridge; the scholarship lists at the Merchant Taylors' school; and the shipping records for the Port of London in the autumn of 1899?

The disobedient reader, prompted to step outside the textual boundary to watch Werner Herzog's film or source the photograph of Vladimir Nabokov hunting for butterflies in the Alps, engages with the narrator's fictionally reconstructed reality. This section of *The Emigrants*, like the others, is a constructed text in which the disobedient reader is free to play in the same space as the narrator — the subjective recollection and contemplation of the images of the past that haunt his mind, not just the historically indexed documents which are remnants of the past, but the seeming living encounter with Henry Selwyn mediated by a narrator whose sensibility and subjective consciousness and artful use of language breathe life into the "polished bones and the hob-nailed boots" which the melting of the alpine snow has revealed.

A temporalized discursive process in which the reader is disobediently aware of this language-shaping task that the narrator has set himself can be seen at the end of the last story in *The Emigrants*, Max Ferber's, where the narrator sits "in one of the plush armchairs" (234) in the dilapidated Midland Hotel, imagining that he hears the orchestra tuning up, arias from Wagner being sung in the Thirties before the war changed everything, and where he describes to himself the stage flats, a pure figment of his imagination, on which he sees the photographs of the Litzmannstadt ghetto "established in 1940" in Lodz displayed at an exhibition in Frankfurt "the year before" (235). These photographs, which turned up by chance like ghosts of the past in 1987, much like the bones of Naegeli and the narrator's memory of Henry Selwyn, occupy the mind of the narrator as he sits in the Midland Hotel after visiting Ferber in a Dickensian public hospital, meditating on the difficulty of writing his friend's life, "the entire questionable business of writing" (230).

The Emigrants concludes with the narrator disappearing into his own mythic construction of one of the photographs, which he describes as a depiction of the three classical Fates, the Erinyes or Eumenides (ambivalently both the Furies, wreakers of havoc, destruction, and horror, and the Kindly Ones, bringers of balm, consolation, and beauty), whose task in the contingent present of the narrator's mind is to decide whether Ferber will set out on his final journey now or later, and whether that death, like Selwyn's, like Bereyter's, like Ambros Adelwarth's, like the narrator's, and like the reader's, will be another instance of horror and destruction or balm and beauty. The complicit silence of the legion dead, whose souls ghost through these pages, sustains that dualist tension. The determinism of Ferber's ending is suspended just as the text's is, and it is the imaginative resurrection of the past in the narrator's telling and the iterative habit of the dead in "ever returning to us" (23), as emigrants from some unknowable other world, which confirms the imaginative possibilities of literary fiction in this text for a disobedient reader prepared to question "the business of writing" that the narrator has made his own.

At the Threshold of an Underground Station: *Vertigo*

> I could not then and cannot now recall whether I was even in the Krummenbach Chapel as a child with my grandfather, who took me with him everywhere. But there were many chapels like that of Krummenbach around W, and much of what I saw and felt in them at the time will have stayed with me — a fear of the acts of cruelty depicted there no less than the wish, in all its impossibility, that the perfect tranquillity prevailing within them might sometime be recaptured. (*Vertigo*, 179–80)

Sebald's first work of fiction, a four-part book, begins with what seems an authoritative, third-person, historical account. The reader has no idea what the context for this first section is until she begins the second, where the narrative shifts to the first person, the unnamed narrator revealing that his habitual tasks are "writing and gardening" (33). This is deliberately foxy. Where does this journey begin?

The first section prepares us, in a long prolepsis, for the revelation of the "grey *chasseur*" in the attic of Mathilde Seelos's former house in W (228), a ghost of the narrator's imagined fear in childhood. This Tyrolean *chasseur* connects Napoleon's Battle of Marengo in the first section, for which Beyle arrived too late to help defeat the Austrians. The disintegration into dust in 1987 of part of the narrator's imagined past, now more real, is the journey's closure, where the text began, with a European itinerary, writer bookended to writer.

Like Flaubert's shift in the narrative person at the beginning of *Madame Bovary*, from first to third (1961, 18), Sebald's shift here (Sections 1 and 3, and Sections 2 and 4) requires a close scrutiny of the language in order to establish bearings at the beginning of the text's journey. The reader finds herself expected to change gear without explanation, confronted by sections of text whose juxtaposition is unexpectedly disjunctive. She has to construct for herself the linking that we expect of narrative's "and then" (Forster 83), of "the backbone" of story (Forster 29), its stable narrative voice withheld. The discourse of the first section of *Vertigo* is problematic for the reader only until she construes the narrator as a writer, a writer for whom Beyle and Kafka offer a way out of the autobiographical tyranny of fact that the final section, *Il Ritorno in Patria*, represents for a narrator constructing himself as a literary writer, not least because he seems to be an academic by training — those "troublesome facts" again.

"Beyle, or Love is a Madness Most Discreet" appears, looking back from page 33 and the subsequent journey "*All'estero*," to be in some way part of the narrator's writing life. This narrator is in need of refreshment, of change, a new perspective and sense of self that travel provides. The reader does not fully realize that the journey of *Vertigo* has begun until after the first section is read. It is this first section devoted not to the unnamed writer of the "great novels" (29) but to the traveling Beyle, the Napoleonic dragoon, European diplomat and writer of fiction disguised as nonfiction, that initiates the pilgrimage which is the journey of the text.

Only the inquisitive reader can know, for the text is silent and withholds that logical connection, that Beyle is Stendhal, the writer of *Le Rouge et Le Noir* and *La Chartreuse de Parme*. The fictionalized autobiography *La Vie de Henri Brulard* (whose drawings appear in this text) and the audacious fiction of the so-called treatise on love, *De L'Amour*, are mentioned instead. These are diegetic works that play fast and loose with the boundary between fiction and nonfiction, a metafictional tactic that draws the reader's attention to the fictionality of the text. The narrator produces a quirky, offbeat portrait of a writer whose amorous exploits and four decades of self-medication to cure his chronic syphilis "undo" him, provoking the fit he suffers on the Rue Danielle-Casanova from which he dies. A writer is "undone" by imagination and death, a witty gloss echoing Flaubert's "feeling so deeply what my little Bovary was going through" (Steegmuller 203).

Stendhal's use of his experiences as a Napoleonic soldier in his fiction is the unspoken, withheld dimension of this first section engaged with Stendhal's capacity for self-deception, and his deception of the reader. This links up with the third section, "Dr. K. Takes the Waters at Riva," an oblique account, as the engaged reader knows from her own research and reading, of Kafka's flight from his fiancée, Felice Bauer, who writes imploring letters to Kafka while attempting his self-cure at Riva, falling in love with a young, Swiss, Christian woman. Like Beyle's, and Bovary's, this is the ironically ambiguous cure of the *pharmakon*, poison and drug, "curing" the malady of love with more love, like writing one's way into literary fiction out of academia or writing against one's fear of death by writing about it.

Like Kafka, the "writer"-narrator is undertaking his own "cure" by setting off, in the second section "*All'estero*," to overcome the effects of living for a quarter of a century under "grey skies" and a "difficult period" in his life (33). The narrator's serious sense of self, like Beyle's and Kafka's, is ironized in subtle and ambiguous ways that the reader has to construct, guided by the juxtaposition of afflictions, "discreet madness[es]," in Stendhal, Kafka and the narrator. In all cases the destination appears to be a therapeutic place of cure. For the narrator, this seems to be the place where he can complete the writing of his book, *pharmakon* the discreet madness of obsessive love of literature and language, a Flaubertian touch.

Only when the first-person narrator actually appears in his own voice at the beginning of the second section and sets out on his journey "*All'estero*," in Sebald's insistently untranslated way, and then returns home like Ulysses in the fourth section in Monteverdi's "*Il Ritorno in Patria*," firstly to southwest Germany and his former home in childhood, then to London where he catches the train to Norwich, does the reader (disobediently mindful in her own imagination of British postboxes marked "Home" and "Abroad," reversed in the narrator's case) see the shape of the itinerary, which is why it is so disorienting, or "vertiginous" (Brookner 2001). That the melancholy narrator did not succumb, on his way home, to the alternative of the entrance to the underworld, "Mind the Gap" (259) indeed, is a relief (a safe return, not the final journey with no return) and a joke which the reader can spool back to the gaps between fiction and nonfiction, reality and dream/memory, connecting the end of the text's journey with its beginning, in the Alps.

The text concludes with the narrator's apocalyptic, infernal dream combining a memory of the frozen wasteland of alpine scree with the Great Fire of London recounted in Samuel Pepys's eyewitness diary, a terrible and haunting metaphor for the Blitzkrieg in London and the burning cities of Germany. If this is a circle of hell that we have just passed through in the company of the narrator, like Dante with Virgil, then no wonder the reader feels destabilized, disconcerted, with no certainty of a Celestial City on the horizon.

This "discreet madness" of the narrator is always in the reader's view. The disobedient reader wants to know what the "difficult period" in the narrator's life actually was, what caused the narrator to be so disoriented in Vienna that he wandered back and forth in the quarters of the city named after the Habsburg emperors near where Freud practiced psychiatry, tracing the pattern of a smile in a trajectory whose coordinates are an amusement ride in the Prater named after a Venetian instrument of torture, "the Venediger Au," to which Casanova was exposed in the Doge's Palace dungeon, and "the great hospital precincts of the Alsergrund" (34). Foucault lurks here, especially his *Discipline and Punish*, and imperialism seems to induce a kind of madness in those who are exposed to it. The psychically afflicted wander in patterns of repetition, one of whose forms is intertextuality.

The title of the first section, drawing on Shakespeare's *Romeo and Juliet* (1.1.191), with a proleptic reference to Verona, and an invocation of the ambivalent bittersweet nature of love's obsession ("A choking gall, and a preserving sweet," 1.1.192), now seems, in retrospect, a gloss on the narrator's weaving together of love and death (those two great German Romantic themes of *eros* and *thanatos*), of madness and writing. These itineraries of association beckon the disobedient reader deeper into Eco's "woods," that other place, that one text, where the reader either "play[s] the game" of reading obediently ("as a model reader," Eco, 10) or, as Sebald's reader does, "leave[s] the wood" at any time and "think[s] of other woods, of the infinite forest of universal culture and intertextuality" (Eco, 110). Kafka's "Dr. K.," a figure constructed by the narrator blending Kafka the historical person with the fictional *persona* from his own fiction with yet another figure who writes *The Hunter Gracchus* set in Riva, is both in flight from "the terrors of love" (167) with one woman and falling in love with another, an experience he commemorates obliquely in the fiction of *The Hunter Gracchus*, the story of a corpse's endless journey in its ship of death, condemned to travel perpetually in search of a final resting place. The hunter from the forest, the hunter after love, the hunter after the text, and the hunter in pursuit of home are single strands in the narrative thread.

In the second section the narrator is in a disoriented state, like Beyle unable to distinguish at times between "the images in his head" and the reality which is before him as he travels in Europe. This dislocation or perceptual disorder can be partly attributed to what McCulloh describes as Stendhal's syndrome, "a psychosomatic illness" which causes "dizziness, confusion, and even hallucinations" (86) when the individual is exposed to an overdose of beautiful artefacts, referred to by Stendhal in his book *Naples and Florence: A Journey from Milan to Reggio* recording his journey in 1817.

Reading masterpieces may also have produced in the intertextualizing "writer"-narrator a similar tendency, accounting for the hallucinations and delusions he suffers in the next three sections. The disobedient reader constructs this as a self-reflexive irony, these patterns eliciting, as they did in Anita Brookner (2001), another version of Stendhal's syndrome. It is an outrageous boldness.

There are other reasons for disorientation, in the glimpses of the human history of cruelty and persecution and horror. The reader, ambivalently disobedient sometimes to the serious intensity, sometimes to the humor of the narrator's tone, catches sight of a distancing irony in the narrator's voice in *Vertigo*'s second section, "*All'estero*." The narrator's discreetly strange behavior is "mapped" on the grid of the city as a "precisely defined sickle-or-crescent-shaped area" (33–34), a mad flash of the emblems of Communism and Islam, elements which appear later in Verona, but suggest also the shape of a vacuous or sinister smile, echoed later at Klosterneuburg where the narrator visits Ernst Herbeck, the poet whose life has been spent confined in a mental institution. What exactly are the links between creativity, madness and persecution that are being braided together here?

Napoleonic imperialism, Milanese syphilis, Venetian torture, Viennese mental hospital and asylum, all underpinned by writerliness, prepare the reader for the strange hallucinatory section in Venice. The narrator, in his "muted condition" (34), sees visions of dead people from his own past, "Mathild Seelos" (whose last name, ironically, suggests soulless, or sea-less, in German — she was a member of a convent which damaged her, Kafka's "frozen sea within" glossing soul) and the "one-armed village clerk Fürgut" (another name worthy of Dickens, inflected with Flaubert's and Swift's and Voltaire's more savage irony — maiming is good for you, it's all for the best, suffering is the means to grace). He sees Dante, in the street named after his exiling persecutors, Gonzagagasse, and the Winter Queen, the English Elizabeth of Bohemia, on the train traveling out of Germany back to England. The sequence of literary-historical "visions" suggest that he too is "discreetly mad," in a writerly way. For the disobedient reader, these are glimpses of Sebald, her own visions of another writer.

The narrator describes the experience of these "hallucinations" as producing a feeling of "vertigo" (35). How can the reader trust this mad "writer"-narrator as a guide, particularly if she knows that in German the pun on vertigo means being conned? Is this an "antic disposition" (*Hamlet* I.5.172)? But if the narrator is untrustworthy or mad, what is the reader to make of the apocalyptic vision at the end which is also horrendously real? A more pathological reading of the narrator's condition would suggest that he is wandering in a state of dis-ease, psychic dis-ease, disoriented by oneiric states of consciousness in which his fear of the future and the rich interior life composed of scenes and memories from the past combine in a compelling vividness which seduces him into exile in his mind, in psychic retreat from the disturbing and destabilizing contingency of living in the present surrounded by what he will call in *The Rings of Saturn* "traces of destruction" (3).

This "writer"-narrator, as he reveals himself to be (33, 94, 252), is mapping a different kind of trajectory as he travels, "drawing connections between events that lay far apart but which seemed to me to be of the same order" (94). From this archive he has retrieved Stendhal, Kafka, a painting by Tiepolo seen through "a veil of ash" (51) in Würzburg, Shakespeare's Prospero in exile from Milan, Jewish children singing Christmas carols in English in the middle of Vienna, and a poet institutionalized in a mental asylum for over thirty years. That woman in a brown beret is the Winter Queen, Elizabeth, the daughter of James I for whose wedding to the man who became King of Bohemia Shakespeare wrote *The Tempest*, a play in which the coordinates of the real are displaced by those of the imagination, by dream. The woman is reading a book, *The Seas of Bohemia*, by a writer called Mila Stern whom the narrator cannot trace anywhere, neither writer nor her book. The reader, baffled by this whirling kaleidoscope of images and associations, will search in vain for the book, whose title suggests a black joke, Bohemia's frozen seas, and the author's name, connoting the Jewish "star" in German, a tragedy.

Where is the reader to go? If she follows a "mad" narrator, won't she be implicated in his pathology? This is a nice Sebaldian irony, and one with real moral bite. Is the genesis of the madness in the very act of writing? "Live like a bourgeois, and think like a demigod," Flaubert wrote (Steegmuller 197), drawing madness and writing together in his own intensively researched fiction. The narrator has traveled from England, where his "customary routine" was "writing and gardening" (33). In Vienna he has no routine, no vestige of the bourgeois. It is not entirely clear whether it is the writing that has destabilized the narrator or whether the narrator, destabilized, is driven to write, in this city of Freud and Hitler. The connection between writing and madness seems nonetheless to be a crucial underpinning of this first fiction.

In *Vertigo*'s third section, "Dr. K. takes the waters at Riva," Sebald has returned his narrator to embedded writing practice. Kafka took his doctorate in law in 1906 in Prague. In 1913 "Dr. K." traveled to Vienna, then to Riva on the shores of Lake Garda in Switzerland, to "escape from this first decision-making" between life and literature (Wagenbach 2003, 101) by putting a distance between himself and his fiancée, Felice Bauer. There Kafka met a young Christian woman, Gerti Wasner, and he alluded to this as one of two instances in his life (the other not with Felice either) as the "sweetness in a relationship with a woman one loves" (Wagenbach quoting one of Kafka's letters to Max Brod, 101), experienced at a time when he was "altogether confused and sick in every possible way" (101). Love is a discreet madness indeed, as it is for Beyle. The "small indirect memorial" he creates to this love which had to be kept silent, as he promised Gerti, was the setting of *The Hunter Gracchus* in Riva, "Gracchus" being one of the code words for Kafka himself, as "in Czech *kavka* means 'jackdaw,' which in Italian is 'gracchio'" (101).

The reader is able to associate Kafka's fictionalizing of himself with Stendhal's and with Sebald's. "Schwindel" is a codedness. It is tempting to consider that the German pronunciation of "K" is "ka," the Egyptian hieroglyph for soul or psyche, that part which lives on after death, surely not overlooked by the death-haunted Sebald who points to the Egyptian cultural predilection for death (1999a, 136) and another writer whose story of the hunter, Gracchus, takes as its central image the ceaseless journeying of a corpse who can find no resting place, the "fate of being unable to depart this life" (167).

The image of Kafka apparently taken in Vienna at the Praterstern is falsified to misrepresent Kafka with his companions "flying" like a company of unusual angels above "the spires of the Votivkirche" (144). The reader cannot see these spires in the photograph, but if sufficiently disobedient, thoughtful and imaginative, might pick up this thread of Christian devotion ("Votivkirche") from the narrator as a hint of the affair of the heart with "the [Christian] girl from Genoa," the "mermaid" (160), that awaits him while he is taking the saving cure at the sanatorium in Riva, another site of splendid ambiguity, and another conversational link with *The Rings of Saturn*, in which the narrator waits for his wife, "Clara" here too as in *The Emigrants*, to collect him at a pub called "The Mermaid," that Shakespearean place name, at the end of his pilgrimage.

Dr. K.'s vision in Verona of one of the Scrovegni Chapel angels of death and mourning, one of whom has already appeared in the previous section of the text in Salvatore's narrative in the piazza (134), is revealed to be the coarsely worked figurehead from a ship "such as hang from the ceilings of sailors' taverns" (146) — another Sebaldian irony reflecting on the withdrawal of the imagined and its revelation as a tawdry reality, the obverse of the writer's capacity to inflect the banal with a sense of awe, to infuse the familiar with a sense of the uncanny, to cause "Schwindel. Gefühle," the feeling of vertigo, to expose, like Romeo's discovery of the difference between Rosaline and Juliet, the difference between lust and love. It is a complex joke, not least because it exposes the gap of irony between the real and the imagined — tantalizing for the disobedient reader who might well think of Kit Marlowe's death in a tavern brawl.

Dr. K.'s dinner companion at the sanatorium, General von Koch, shoots himself "both in the heart and in the head" (162), achieving a reconciliation between the real and the imagined, of which neither Kafka nor Stendhal was capable, Stendhal's novel (unidentified by the narrator), *Le Rouge et Le Noir*, open on his lap. Koch seems to have reached that point of "understanding" that connected Napoleon's failed battle plan at Waterloo, the deaths of "50,000 soldiers and horses" (157), with the demonstration of his own ability to "influence the course of events by a turn of the helm, by will-power alone" (157). He kills himself in a chair in a Swiss sanatorium, reading a fictional account of one of the world's great battles which changed the course of history. This produces a very disobedient reader, one who slips out of this text and into history (just as General von Koch does) even though he is, possibly, not a historical person in the first place. This is a profoundly skeptical reader less vulnerable to madness than General von Koch, whose destruction of both heart and head effected a horribly permanent cure.

Life is also transmuted into art in the "three whole years" that it takes the barque containing the corpse of Gracchus to appear at Riva, announced in fairytale mode by a speaking "pigeon the size of a cockerel" (164), the actual interval of time it takes Kafka to write the story after leaving Riva and Gerti (Wagenbach 101). Love and death are interwoven here in a compressed complexity which leaves the reader's head spinning, not least because it is fiction which seems to have killed the General and love which produces death in *The Hunter Gracchus*: more Sebaldian irony.

"Dr. K. Takes the Waters at Riva" is the sidetrip made by the Deputy Secretary of the Prague Workers' Insurance Company on a journey to Vienna to attend a "congress on rescue services and hygiene" (141), an oblique and ambiguous reference to the "cleansing" of Europe. Dr. K.'s own unwellness, that prophetic quality in his writing that causes the ship of death to arrive at the sanatorium bearing a corpse for whom no salvation, no redemption, is possible, suggests "Our sickness" (167) cannot be cured, as Swift, Voltaire, and Flaubert all knew. Love, it seems, is not enough.

The final section of *Vertigo* positions the speaking voice of the narrator within his own past. Walking through the valley, he arrives in November at the village where he was born, the metafictional W, and books into the Engelwirt Inn, its name an ironic reference to all the preceding angels in the text. "Forever bent over his papers," the narrator concludes that "solitary commercial travellers" would assume that his "was a different a more dubious profession" (252), a nested metafictionality in the authorial irony about "the questionable business of writing" (Sebald 1997, 230), reflecting the dizzying confusion of the title's pun and the ambiguity of "I resolved to leave, particularly as my writing had reached the point at which I either had to continue for ever or break off" (252–53).

The narrator's journey back to London "in the Hook of Holland express" (253) brings on another destabilizing episode triggered by the fact of traveling through "the German countryside," the narrator reflecting that what he saw suggested "mankind had already made way for another species" (254). The mantra in his mind of "south-west Germany," which is the sound made by the train's wheels on the railway track, reinforces maniacally both where he is and where he has come from, where he was born. Madness threatens: "something like an eclipse of my mental faculties was about to occur" (254).

On arrival in London the narrator visits the National Gallery to look at Pisanello's painting of St George killing the dragon. The ironic depiction of St George wearing an antic straw hat with a large feather, "such inappropriate and positively extravagant headgear" (258) given the seriousness of his undertaking is a kind of madness, but Pisanello's or the spectator's? The vision of shipwrecked Prospero selling chrysanthemums at the entrance to the underworld perhaps on this enchanted island — "a scent which might stir the imaginings of an oarsman far out to sea" (258) — and the glimpse of a yellow brimstone (underworld) butterfly "flitting about from one purple flower to the other" (not so much a Nabokov intertextual moment as a suggestion of the dead children of Terezin whose book of poems and drawings is called *I never saw another butterfly* . . . De Silva 1996, xiv) shadows the liminality of life and beauty with horror and fear and oblivion. These are madnesses which might well be real, which exceed imagining or dream.

The 1913 (Kafka's visit to Riva) India-paper edition of Pepys's diary, fragile butterfly pages, sets off the narrator's dream (261) as he travels home on the train, suspended in a dreaming, fearful vision of Dante's hell. This too is a real dream, as the disobedient reader knows all too well from her slipping out of this wood into another — that of history.

That Undiscovered Country from Whose Bourne No Traveler Returns: *The Rings of Saturn*

> Apollo had burnt all of his own manuscripts in the fireplace. At times, when he did so, a weightless flake of soot ash like a scrap of black silk would drift through the room, borne up on the air, before sinking to the floor somewhere or dissolving into the dark. (*The Rings of Saturn*, 108)

There is a little of Hamlet, the brooding scholar, in the traveling narrator of *The Rings of Saturn*, not least because his serial soliloquies focus on "the paralysing horror that had come over me at various times when confronted with the traces of destruction" (3). For the narrator in this text, death is, as it was for Hamlet and for Sir Thomas Browne, a preoccupying subject.

The opening of *The Rings of Saturn* is an ironic reflection of Browne's bleak but comic saw from *Religio Medici*, that "the World . . . [is] not an Inn, but an Hospital; and a place not to live, but to dye in" (1947, 83). This is a hidden German pun in the English version, for the word *Wirtshaus*, inn, means literally host's house or hospital. A hospital, originally an inn for pilgrims (from the Latin *hospes*, guest) and run by religious communities, draws together, in Browne's title (1642) "the scruples/ superstition/ piety/ reverence" (William Smith 629), the many facets of the Latin *religio*, of "a medical man," *medici*. These etymological associations are set spooling in the disobedient reader's mind by the pilgrim-"writer"-narrator of this poetic work of fiction, as long as she is reading slowly.

The actual journey that the invalid pilgrim had taken in the late summer of 1992 is taken again "in my thoughts" while he is lying paralysed, a year later, in a hospital bed in Norwich, in Thomas Browne's hospital. Further on the narrator writes: "Now that I begin to assemble my notes, more than a year after my discharge from hospital . . ." (5). It takes the reader a little time to follow, to see that this is an iterative journey, a meditative pilgrimage, that ancient pattern of prayerful meditation that pilgrims walked through Western Europe in a symbolic journey which represented the pilgrimage to Jerusalem, representing in turn the pilgrimage to the City of God. This meditative iterative traveling, a journey of spiritual healing, by the narrator in *The Rings of Saturn* is what produces his text.

For the narrator, in this outer ring of frame narrative, the Suffolk walk has provided freedom from care, "an unaccustomed sense of freedom" (3), but ironically and not without amusement for a disobedient reader, what has healed his "spirit" (3) has afflicted his body, confining him a year later to his hospital room in Norwich. This dualism is suggested by Browne's specter which haunts these pages, the physician who wrote on metaphysical matters. That brooding scholar, the narrator, has lost two of his academic colleagues, both literary scholars who have died in the interval between his own hospitalization and his turning to his notes. The disobedient reader, drawing a little away from the narrator's voice, can't help but see these connections in the textual fabric.

The two unexpected and premature deaths sharpen into grief the more indeterminate sense of melancholy articulated at the outset of the textual journey. For the narrator-writer to turn to Sir Thomas Browne for healing, aka literary guidance, is not surprising. Healing appears to lie in the therapy of writing prose, prose which reflects the physician's digressive, contemplative Cartesian wrestling, against all the physical evidence of doubt, including material corruption, with his assertion of Christian belief in the afterlife of the soul, in prose held up after more than three centuries as a paradigm of style. The physician's ironic dilemma is that he cannot, ultimately, save the body. Dakyns and Parkinson are dead. The hope of the soul's salvation, its continuing existence, is the preoccupation of Browne's writing, which shapes the narrator's tribute to his dead colleagues.

The narrator has used, in his chapter summaries, the convention of historical and philosophical writing that Browne employed, key terms advertising the content of each section to the reader, but not without inculcating in the disobedient reader's mind that all the material evidence in the world, including Sebald's scientific, historical and aesthetic trinity, can neither confirm nor deny the existence of the soul, the possibility of its transmigration to another place. These chapter summaries are therefore only seeming bearings for the reader, created by the narrator as the stages of his subjective journey, destination undisclosed.

The chapter summaries suggest that this is a collection of essays, a suggestion apparently confirmed by the book's two epigraphs. The Conrad epigraph in untranslated French refers to pilgrimage. (In the English translation, the German subtitle, "An English pilgrimage," was omitted, as was the third epigraph in English, "Good and evil we know in the field of this world grow up together almost inseparably," from Milton's *Paradise Lost*, McCulloh 67). The disobedient reader must translate for herself the excerpt from the letter that Conrad wrote to his aunt, Marguerite Poradowska, in March 1890:

> Above all one must forgive those unhappy souls who chose to make their pilgrimage on foot, who hug the shore and look on, without understanding, at the horror of the struggle, the joy of conquest, and the profound despair of the conquered. [My translation]

What is the reader to make of this, once she has translated it? It sounds a clarion call to adventure, to a sailor's life full of risk-taking engagement as opposed to that of those timorous souls who take no risks and who never understand what it is to feel the extremities of the human. Was this Parkinson and Dakyns in *The Rings of Saturn*? Surely not, given their fates and sensibilities. It also contains, however, a self-reflexive irony here, for it is perhaps this academic narrator, the scholar, who "hugs the shore."

The narrator's book, the book of a scholar, is also the work of a pilgrim who travels on foot. His journey with its "stations" (86) of meditation is built on the same platform as that of a traveler avid for the "nexus" of knowledge of self and other (Blanton 2002, 3), but the reader is made uncertain about the decentered authority of the narrative as it pivots on the subjective axis of an afflicted narrator who is an ambiguous, and possibly ambivalent, scholar. Because contextualizing details about the narrator are sublimated in the narrative, the reader is made to feel more uncertain about the identity and the reliability of her companion-cicerone. If the narrator as traveler is avid for the "nexus" of Buberian encounter, then it is a strangely, even uncannily, detached nexus.

The book's second epigraph quotes from an entry in the *Brockhaus Encyclopedia* about the rings of Saturn. The entry describing the Roche limit alludes to the gravity (possibly an implied pun) of a planet maintaining fragments of destruction in its own orbit, a metafictionality that also keeps Dakyns and Parkinson, their literary passions and personal qualities, in the writer's field. This suggests that Sebald, rather than the scholarly narrator, who is too melancholy, is playing a game with his reader, with these digressive essays or meditations written by a Coleridgean or Wordsworthian walker with a Romantic sensibility. (The author revealed, foxily, in an interview that he wrote this book to make enough money to cover the costs of his "rambling tour," an intertextual slyness, a reference to the authors of *The Lyrical Ballads*, who had initiated that particular game plan over two hundred years earlier.)

The "writer"-narrator's walk to the coast of the ancient kingdom of East Anglia, settled by the Angles of Jutland and Denmark and the Saxons of Germany whose Rhine empties itself into the North Sea on the opposite shore, will enable him to meditate on the absurd horrors of the Second World War. The image of both the imminence of further destruction kept at bay and the preservation of traces of previous destruction that is the dualism of the Roche effect, the gravitational explanation of how the rings of Saturn are formed, is one of an arrested state of ruin, and one which it is tempting to suppose produces both a metaphorical power and a metafictional effect here, especially as the narrator's reference to Saturn, that paradoxically dark planet, the Dog Star (3) which governs him and his "black dog" (Storr 5), comes so soon afterwards.

For the disobedient reader, the planet Saturn, whose dark influence instils melancholy and is connected with the "scythe" of death (79), is an image of the essential mood of this text, the elegiac contemplation of various kinds of death and destruction manifest in the fragments of the past that the narrator's subject draws into the orbit of his consciousness in his therapeutic transit through the landscape of Suffolk, and the iterative ones undertaken in his hospital bed and in the writing of "his" text.

The narrator's actual journey begins in summer, setting out from Norwich, and ends with the rites of exequy that Thomas Browne alludes to in *Pseudodoxia Epidemica*, although the narrator says he can no longer find the passage (296). This is an explicitly Borgesian invitation to the reader to authenticate the narrator's authority. Connecting the silken thread of his metaphor, the narrator reminds the reader that Browne's father was a silk merchant, thus sustaining the ubiquitous metaphor of silk used in the way that Sebald admired in Dickens's use of fog in *Bleak House* (Silverblatt 2001). The "only true book" (Sebald 1998a, 286) is the silk weavers' book of patterns, the key to creating beauty, with artifice and industry, from nature. This is the narrator's self-appointed task, and part of Sebald's perception of the essential connectedness of things, as McCulloh argues, a nagging sense of an elusive master pattern, if only we could get high enough up for an overview from a "coign of vantage."

His first meditation takes place in Browne's hospital that is the end of one journey and the beginning of the next. For the vigilant, questioning reader, this is the matrix of Sebald's text. Because the narrator never tells the reader what the actual cause of his own paralysis is and because he likens himself to Kafka's Gregor Samsa from *Metamorphosis*, the reader feels understandably uneasy. This is a pilgrim who may have been transformed by the experiences he is now recounting.

The narrator, researching, has discovered that Browne had journeyed to Holland to pursue his medical studies. The narrator takes the reader there, to the Waaggebouw in Amsterdam on the morning of the public dissection of the corpse of Adriaan Adriaanszoon, alias Aris Kindt, a scene memorialized in Rembrandt's painting, *The Anatomy Lesson*, which fixes forever the image of a victim whose corpse is harrowed in Michel Foucault's formulation after society's own institutionally sanctioned sickness (*Discipline and Punish*, 1979). That the narrator names the body, and his alias, suggests he wants to tell a story which is far greater reaching than the aggrandizement of scientific progress and increase in knowledge that the painting records. The disobedient reader must connect the "lost and found" edges of the two stories, the occasion of the painting and Browne's being in Holland, and can only do so by undertaking more research of her own, contemplating and imagining in her own empirical reality.

The "writer"-narrator's careful contrast of the conjecture he makes (which the disobedient reader preserves her skepticism about), that Browne was present that morning, the scientific progress that the commissioning of the painting celebrates, with his reading of the painting, Rembrandt's subversive compassion and moral critique of his patrons, is a telling example of the kind of layering of the three strands that Sebald is in the habit of bringing together: the historical, the scientific, and the aesthetic, the original paratextual formula in his poem *After Nature*. The narrator wants the reader to see what he believes Rembrandt saw, really saw, that morning in the Waaggebouw.

Where does this position the reader, when she has been placed in front of the painting in the Mauritshuis, a house built from the wealth acquired from colonial exploitation in the sugar industry? Why is she in the Waaggebouw with Dr. Nicolaas Tulp, the President of the College of Surgeons and possibly with Dr. Thomas Browne, a writer inclined to poetic uncertainty and Descartes, that amateur surgeon, in January 1632? Why is she too, in a cinematic jumpcut, at Rembrandt van Rijn's easel as he deliberately transposes the tendons on the anatomized hand and forearm, making those of the right appear on the left? Is it a joke, that the right hand should know what the left hand was doing? Was Rembrandt mocking the surgeons' anatomical knowledge in the context of moral blindness? Should the disobedient reader remember that Rembrandt painted the Jews "van Rijn," from the Rhine, and reflect that Aris Kindt, the alias of Adriaan Adriaanszoon, is a Jewish name? Is the historical context of the persecution of Jewry in Holland in the sixteenth and seventeenth centuries at issue? Is the Cartesian gaze of reason the one that overlooks the individual story, what lies behind the merely material corpse here? The life that has been extinguished, "discipline[d] and punish[ed]" (Foucault)?

The reader is in all these positions at once, asking vigilant questions about the authority of the narrator whose scholarly conjecture these questions pivot on. She is in a position to interrogate the authority of the writing: no historical evidence here suggests that Browne was there that

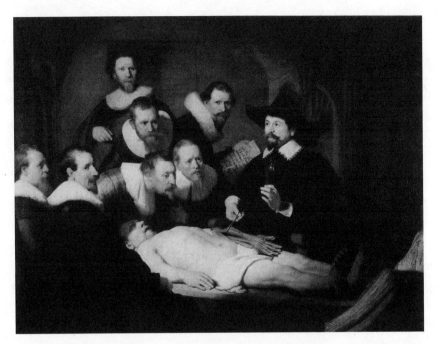

morning. On the other hand, the narrator's account of the painting is compelling: Rembrandt has exposed the Pharisaical self-righteousness of the College of Surgeons in the dehumanizing abjection of the petty thief's corpse.

The narrator seizes this opportunity to reflect on the "verisimilitude . . . more apparent than real" (16) of Rembrandt, suggesting that like Flaubert, as he has already reminded us, a grain of reality in the fictional hem is enough to suggest the stupidity of the masses (8). Are we beguiled as readers here, like the College of Surgeons? How can we tell? This is a link to the end of the narrator's book and the reference to *Pseudodoxia Epidemica* (The Spread of False Doctrine) but also to *Musaeum Clausum or Bibliotheca Abscondita* (271), this last a Borgesian phantasmagoria, "a catalogue of remarkable books . . . listing pictures, antiquities, and sundry singular items . . . more likely products of his imagination, the inventory of a treasure house which existed purely in his head" (271). In this inter-woven space of the real and the imagined, the researched and recalled, scholarly conjecture and documented historicity, the disobedient reader is set free to play.

Is the narrator, too, interested in leaps of historical conjecture, that imaginative, fictionalizing impulse, wedded here fantastically to Browne's reference to the mysterious piece of purple silk in Patroclus's urn? Is it actually there in Browne? Why mention Browne's capacity for doubt, his peregrinations before and, disconcertingly and ironically, after death? These are areas of quicksand on the narrator's path which the wary reader needs to sidestep, despite the narrator's hypnotically steady, grave voice.

Another invitation to disobedience is extended by the narrator's conversation with William Hazel, the gardener at Somerleyton, the context in which the narrator listens to and represents the history lesson he is given with a statistical scrupulousness that suggests eyewitness authority and retentive reading:

> In the course of one thousand and nine days, the eighth airfleet alone used a billion gallons of fuel, dropped seven hundred and thirty-two thousand tons of bombs, and lost almost nine thousand aircraft and fifty thousand men. Every evening I watched the bomber squadrons heading out over Somerleyton, and night after night, before I went to sleep, I pictured in my mind's eye the German cities going up in flames, the firestorms setting the heavens alight, and the survivors rooting about in the ruins. (38)

Can the reader trust the gardener as a historian, trust the accuracy and reliability of his meticulously exact figures? Were these Hazel's exact words or has the narrator, assembling his "notes," polished his prose with a little scholarly historical research of his own? The disobedient reader can corroborate the figures with her own research. What she cannot corroborate so easily is William Hazel. What does it mean that an English gardener can quote with such precision these quantitative indices? Standing there with the narrator and the patriotic Hazel in the garden at Somerleyton is a slightly unsettling experience. What makes it so is the narrator's telling, with space for the reader's construction. A questioning reader might consider the following: the furnishing of historical detail by Hazel rides on a cushion of air, Hazel's imagined images of the consequences, themselves resting on the documentary photographs suggested by Hazel's description, because that is what he actually saw.

The "German cities going up in flames" — first picture; "the firestorms setting the heavens alight" — second picture; "the survivors rooting about in the ruins" — third picture. What does it mean if the eyewitness is more an eyewitness to his memories of what happened, images gleaned from seeing pictures in the newspapers or the newsreels at the cinema?

What matters here to the vigilant reader is that the narrator who, the gardener has realized, is from Germany (31), is absorbing without comment the gardener's remark that "sixty-seven" airfields were established in East Anglia by 1940. Recognizing the narrator's origin, Hazel has embarked on what can only be described as a shameless orgy of victory talk, "la joie de vaincre" as opposed to the "le profond désespoir [d'un] vaincu" (Conrad epigraph to *The Rings of Saturn*). It is the prose, the narrator's reconstruction of the voice of Hazel, which tells us how the narrator feels, if we are reading vigilantly, and in this moment, surrounded and diminished by the great height of the beautiful trees of Somerleyton's park, this litany of destruction, and the additional horrid little story Hazel tells, appears like metonymy, speaking the terrible burning deaths of tens of thousands, making what was real seem like an impossible nightmare, one which heightens the dreadful reality.

Before the narrator leaves Lowestoft, in a remark that begins curiously with the word "once" (44), suggesting a previous visit, an iterative pilgrimage, he observes a hearse "right by Lowestoft Central Station" (44), a conjunction of two quite different journeys, the wryness a glimpse of the author. The more earnest narrator, projecting imaginatively into the unseen, fashions a neat little image of the decorous corpse, a study of stillness with "the tips of his toes pointing up" (44). Disconcerted by this, the obedient reader is solemn and disquieted; the disobedient reader is inclined to smile, however inappropriately, at the absurdity of the narrator's image. Apart from the contrast this anecdote affords, fruitfully for the intelligent reader, with Lowestoft's having "reawoken to life" that morning, the reader is now uncertain whether or not the hearse had been there in a previous visit or was seen by the narrator that very morning as he was leaving the ironically named Albion Hotel. Memory itself is uncertain.

Walking further with the narrator the reader encounters a field of swine, with a metonymic view of Covehithe Church in the distance, and resting, watches the narrator pat one of the swine which, he observes, "sighed like one enduring endless suffering" (66). This invokes, for the disobedient reader, Coleridge's account of the Ancient Mariner's redemption through his ability to "bless . . . unaware" the beauty of God's creatures the water-snakes, unlike the captive swine, "happy living things" (198). In the narrator's construction of this moment, his pity for the abjection of the swine and the disappearance of the "boat . . . barque" (66) give way to his retelling of the parable of the Gadarene swine in Mark's Gospel.

The narrator meditates on the meaning of the marginalized story, decoding it in two ways but contextualizing it by referring to his sitting "overlooking the German Ocean," a question of perspective (and the former name of this stretch of water), although McCulloh, possibly a disobedient reader himself, researched an interesting historical explanation about German royalty holidaying at Felixstowe (76–77). The first reading is ironic, that "Our Lord committed a serious error of judgment" in healing the Gadarene swine, because, by nature condemned to self-destruction for being afflicted with violent and "unclean spirits," they did not merit redemption or healing; secondly, that the evangelist had made up the parable to "explain the supposed uncleanliness of swine," to justify their being "inferior and thus deserving of annihilation" (67). This is a sharply defined *locus* of Sebald's provocative ambiguity and dualism.

It is not difficult for the disobedient reader to make associations here as she continues the journey, in the company of a German narrator steeped in English literature, along the precarious edge, a coded liminality, of the Covehithe cliffs overlooking the "German ocean," reflecting on the narrator's first reading of the parable as a bleak vision of mankind's capacity for self-destruction and God's error in sending Christ to save us. The narrator's silence prompts the reader's disobedient contemplative arrest of the narrative, the narrator stopping to observe the sand martins. These recall a childhood memory when he "had watched from the valley as swallows circled in the last light," imagining that "the world was held together by the courses they flew through the air" (67). This image, the world bound by the trajectories of birds ribboning across the late afternoon sky, summons a disappeared innocence and a sense of security quickly displaced by the reader seeing, under the narrator's direction, the menace of the sand martins eroding like "bullets" the safety of the cliff top, connecting their depredations with the "empty space," level in a menacing way with the eye of the narrator standing on "perforated ground" (68).

The reader is made here to feel uncertain, unsafe. This metaphoric intensity suggests another kind of sniping, ironic in this context, directed at the coast where the Allied Bombers took off. The narrator calms himself by recalling a childhood dare, staring first at the zenith and then at the horizon, the extreme points of perceivable distance. Who will lend the disobedient reader this momentary, steadying sense of perspective, these bearings from which she might take her position safely? This is profoundly unsettling.

Ten years before this pilgrimage, the narrator had visited Admiral Sutton's Ditchingham Park, and he uses an embedded story about the love between Charlotte Ives/Lady Sutton and the writer/diplomat Chateaubriand as the context for his second visit, for writing about the sickening of the trees infected with Dutch elm disease in Norfolk, and the arrival of the extraordinary phenomenon of the "hurricane" of the "autumn of 1987" (265). The disobedient reader has to connect for herself the links between the narrative threads to make the pattern of destruction complete. The narrator's description of the effects of the hurricane on the susceptible trees reads like a report of warfare and an account of the fallen: "over fourteen million mature hard-leaf trees fell victim to it" (265).

The prose rhythms of the description of the approaching storm suggest the arrival of an unstoppable force, an invincible enemy whose presence is truly terrifying. This is death's dominion. The narrator creates both a half-dreaming sleepiness and a menacing tension in the pace of events by slowing his prose: "I woke at about three in the morning, less as a result of the thunderous roar than because of the curious warmth and the increasing air pressure in my bedroom" (265–66). It is as though this barometric explanation can account for not just the conditions under which natural destruction took place, but the narrator's foolish hope that it can account also for destruction itself, the decimation of living things. The narrator does not voice what the disobedient reader must construct for herself: the postapocalyptic vision in which, in a Baudelairean *correspondance*, "there was now not a living sound" (268), the unearthly silence which marks the end.

The exquisitely rendered detail of the scene is like a painting: "entire tracts of woodland were pressed down flat as if they had been cornfields," and a scientific explanation, the root systems preserving the trees so that they "toppled only gradually," "forced down so slowly" (266) that their crowns were preserved, adds depth. The anthropomorphized "ancient trees on either side of the path . . . lying on the ground as if in a swoon" (267) and the sun rising over the horizon onto this scene of arboreal carnage and postapocalyptic silence suggest the destruction of time itself.

The reader's disobedience here is like that of a spectator of a painting, recomposing in her own mind the image before her. The description of the destruction of these trees, weakened by invasive disease and subject to the unpredictable forces of nature, is so powerful in its effect on the reader that she becomes disquietingly aware of the immensity of loss, of destruction, of death, of her own implicated vulnerability, and the poetic intensity of the metaphor here.

Like the narrator who stood within the mythologized sanctuary of the Lebanese cedar in Admiral Sutton's Ditchingham Park ten years before the great storm, the disobedient reader cannot help but feel the destruction of an illusion of security, the authorized sanctuary of hallowed ground, in this actual destruction of the trees of Norfolk. It is profoundly disquieting. The disobedient reader cannot, perhaps should not, trust authority, or the illusion of sanctuary.

* * *

Displacing his authorial self, the voice we would have heard if he had been writing as Bruce Chatwin, Jan Morris, Virginia Woolf, Thomas Browne or Michel de Montaigne in their essays or their travel writing, Sebald has fictionalized his diegetic discourse so that it is mediated by a narrator who is aware of his own practice as a writer. It is this self-conscious writer, this constructed "I," which we construe as generating the texts we read, not a stable authorial figure. In mannered, hypotactic syntax as distanced from contemporary writing as it is from speech, the narrator's elegant ruminative discourse privileges the memorializing acts of his own imaginative contemplation. The reader, his companion, operating both inside and outside that language economy, is positioned to be disobedient by the foregrounded literary language that the narrator employs and from which the reader sets off on her own.

These self-consciously literary texts of Sebald do not play, in their narrator's complex, highly allusive way which segues from one episode of thought in the narrator's mind to another as memory does, to a marketplace readership at the beginning of the twenty-first century. They do not seek to engage a reader as narratee in a conventional narrative contract (see Genette, Prince, Chambers). These are diegetic fictions, producing a disobedient reader who questions the authority of a destabilizing, withholding narrator because his prose requires a vigilant literary reader.

This kind of postmodernity calls into question the nature of narrative when it relies, as Sebald's does, on subjective sequences of coincidence and association arranged into itineraries by a traveling "writer"-narrator rather than a unified drama enacted on a single stage. This is no textual space in which the reader can obey the reading protocols, for in Sebald these are ambiguous, the reader consistently destabilized. The language of the "writer"-narrator's text is always transporting the reader to other places and other times.

This writing practice is made to seem a displacement activity for the despair that seems to threaten to overwhelm the narrator, and his grey voice mediates everything we read. This section argued that this static, unchanging voice has the same tenor in every text, despite the differences between them and the different kinds of journeys they represent. What licenses the reader to be disobedient, to step outside the melancholy textual spaces which the narrator is constructing, is the corollary of irony and amusement, represented by the playful literariness of the texts themselves, which the narrator himself cannot express. This disobedience manifests as the reader's construction of the text, her own collaborative engagement, her *envol* and *vagabondage*.

Sebald makes it possible for the disobedient reader to glimpse the fleeting presence of the author, a flash of wit or humor which ironizes the narrator's Benjaminian melancholy and his preoccupation with the obsessive task of transforming the flickering film of his mind into the language of the page, in words and images.

It is largely these photographic images which reflect much of that irony which distances the reader from the narrator, distinguishing the author from the narrator. The playfulness, the uncertain status of the photographs in the texts, chosen and inserted by the narrator within the textual economy and therefore fictionalized in their contextual emplacement by a metafictionally aware narrator in a constructed text, will be the next focus in this study.

There are also from time to time slips, as it were, in the grey silken filter over the narrator's focalizing lens through which we see the text, by which we also see the narrator reflected, and occasionally a saccadic flash of lightness alleviates the burdensome nature of the ur-earnest narrator's voice and his beautiful but elegiac prose. In these more generous textual spaces the disobedient reader is authorized to construct her decentered response.

In Barthes's sense this is not only the death of the author and the birth of the reader (Barthes 1977) — (and Sebald's spectral narrator as the author's ghost is a witty irony) — but it is the birth of a particular kind of reader, a disobedient reader free to be uncertain about the text and the text's authority, free to construct a textual reading that is liberated from the tyranny of a totalitarian and centered authority.

Stage 2: Traveling with a Cheap Camera — Imagine That!

... if there is a narrative form intrinsic to still photography, it will search for what happened, as memories or reflections do. Memory itself is not made up of flashbacks, each one forever moving inexorably forward. Memory is a field where different times coexist. The field is continuous in terms of the subjectivity which creates and extends it, but temporarily it is discontinuous.
— John Berger and Jean Mohr, *Another Way of Telling*

I always have one of those small cheap cameras in my pocket.
— Sebald to Joe Cuomo, New York 2001

In this section I will argue that Sebald's fictional enterprise is marked by a duplicitous relationship with the reader, presenting as nonfiction what is constructed and mediated by a fictionally constructed diegetic first-person narrator, also the "writer" of the texts. This fictional practice inaugurates a disobedient reader, a reader who is free to be uncertain, free to resist the authority of the text and free to construct for herself a textual imaginary afforded by richly layered discursive language employed in a poetically ambiguous, playfully postmodern, self-referential way.

I argue that the fictional narrator whose discursiveness remembers aspects of the cultural archive of Western Europe is also constructed as a collector and manipulator of images. This writerly narrator deploys those images in a way that reinforces the concealment of the author's presence in constructing, sequencing, and illustrating "his" texts, and ambiguously in a dualist fashion utters the silent presence of the author in the ironic, subversive, and often humorous sense of play that some of the images can give rise to. I am arguing therefore that Sebald's peculiar use of black-and-white photographic images, whether actual photographs or photographs of paintings, drawings or objects, in his fiction is part of the ironic foregrounding and self-reflexive constructedness of his fictional texts. If the narrators with their richly imagined associations, memories, and cultural knowledge invite and encourage disobedient wanderings from their readers, the photographs insist on them. They actually compel the reader to construct for herself, in an intriguing way. Only when the disobedient reader joins the Sebaldian narrator is a collaborative freedom of play possible.

Although the photographs appear at first to document and illustrate the texts in a conventional fashion, they do so in an artful and playful manner, subverting the reader's habitual expectations of their relationship with the texts as passively illustrative or documentary. They are made to appear to document the texts' "authenticity," inserted by the narrator for his own illustrative or documentary purposes, but I argue that in fact they make manifest the fictional game that the author, as distinct from the narrator, is playing with the reader. As a consequence, the reader's disobedience is invited in the construction of many of the images, although cleverly not all, as discursive elements in these fusion texts.

Sebald's wit subverts the privileging of the image over the word in contemporary culture, positioning the reader to construct the sometimes enigmatic images in ways which reveal that the verbal text amplifies the discursiveness of the images. In Sebald's texts, images are appropriated by and contextualized within the fictional economy of his discourse. They are no longer merely individual images, but inserted, sequenced, and expanded discursively by the text in which they are embedded. In one sense Sebald's fiction employs an idiosyncratic, ludic version of the sequential and temporalized technique of film: a series of still images run through a projector at twenty-four frames per second. Sebald's images are frozen instantiations of single frames that have been fragmented from their sequences, and his verbal text restores sequence to them, not of the impossible original kind now forever lost, but of another archival kind, using the memory and the language of consciousness of the "writer"-narrator.

Wittgenstein argued in his revised or second theory of language that language is a set of tools able to be deployed in different contexts and according to different sets of rules in different language games (Gellner 154–55). Sebald employs photographs in the language game of his fiction as constructed figures rather than merely as documentary evidence of a prior reality that has in any case been withdrawn by the passage of time and the subject's eye (potentially many subjects and mostly unknowable) which first looked through the camera's viewfinder. The images, as discursive tools or as the instantiations of memory which Sebald or the "writer"-narrator position them to be, are inflected by the fictional context in which they are deployed. By employing photographs in this way, Sebald has foregrounded the constructivist elements of his own writing practice, as he weaves the associations in the narrator's self-consciously contemplative, imaginative use of language between the images and makes, in a sleight of hand, "connections" between the text and the images which appear then to offer a system of meaning to the reader, although it is, like story in the more conventional sense of the novel, withheld or unavailable, offered only in episodic fragments.

In addition, I argue that Sebald deliberately teases the reader by subverting the conventional use of photographs as documentary records of the past, offering them instead as discourse, that is, as a fusion text available for analysis and construction. While they seem to offer tangible memories of the past, these memories are lost or unavailable, displaced by the images themselves and subject to manipulation. Moreover, the scrupulously indexed descriptions of the narrator's perceptions of the natural world and other observations and recollections, the far more textured and much more vividly realized images in the texts' prose, mock by contrast the imaginative poverty of the images he employs, thus privileging the affective power of the written word over that of the image, which, alone and without context, is delphic or shallow.

Finally, I also argue that in each successive prose text, Sebald's use of images changes slightly in ways that reflect his increasingly sophisticated use of this device and reinforce the metaphysical suggestiveness of his fiction. It is more than a representation of reality: the reader who is actively encouraged to be disobedient looks beyond the exquisitely drawn surface of the text as it is presented by the narrator in his meticulous prose, the discursive hyperreality of his exquisite descriptions, to peer beyond it in a contestatory, interrogatory way that signals the reader's disobedience as a contemplative and imaginative collaborator in the construction of the textual imaginary.

A Helpful Little Device

I've always liked image-text relationships. In the '70s there were very interesting things written about photography by Susan Sontag, Roland Barthes, John Berger. I felt a direct rapport with things said in these essays. . . . The writer's curse is that he doesn't work with tangible matter of any kind, and this is a little device that helps.

— Sebald in a telephone conversation
with Kenneth Baker, October 2001

Roland Barthes in *Camera Lucida* draws a distinction in the "affect" of photographs on the viewer, between what he calls *studium* and *punctum* (1990, 26). The first, *studium*, is what draws the viewer's interest: the landscape, the scene, the "kind of general enthusiastic commitment" that enables the viewer to participate culturally in what the photograph offers by way of figures, faces, gestures, settings, actions (26). This characterizes the relationship between the viewer and the photograph in a very general sense — it's what the reader (the obedient reader) sees as the page is turned and the photograph appears, seducing the gaze away from the work of constructing the verbal text. It is "this kind of human interest" (26) which characterizes the seduction of our gaze.

The second, *punctum*, is according to Barthes the element in the photograph that "will break (or punctuate) the *studium*" (26). Barthes explains it further: "This time it is not I who seek it out (as I invest the field of the *studium* with my sovereign consciousness), it is this element which rises from the scene, shoots out of it like an arrow, and pierces me" (26). This "wound," as Barthes calls it, is what Sebald's narrator, as the constructed viewer, selector and inserter of the images, has already "experienced" in some way, as his insertion of these images into the texts suggests. This is the defining point from which the relationship between the images and the verbal text begins, within the economy of the text constructed by the first-person narrator. The verbal text which frames the images or better the images which frame the verbal text (for it is always the prose which has priority in Sebald) then creates the context in which the reader (the disobedient reader) is implicated in the *punctum* of the photograph, not just the obedient observer of the *studium* but the "accident" of the photograph which can prick or bruise, whose image carries the power of poignancy out into the reader's empirical otherness (27).

Sebald creates the sense of coincidence that the images in the texts manifest through his constructed narrator, their sitedness within "his" written text. The immediacy of the narrator's empirical sense that we see reflected in the text, his "sovereign consciousness" (26), invests the photographs with a more immediate sense of *punctum* by virtue of their being redeemed or resurrected from the oblivion of the past, of forgetting, and their annunciative presence in the text as invested with a meaning that often appears to need further constructing by a reader. What they annunciate is the presence both of the narrator and of the author, the strange dualism of the constructed voicing of the text (the narrator) and that which that voicing represents but which is always withheld (the author). This lends the texts much of their sense of the uncanny.

The disobedient reader might well be aware that in this Sebald is subverting Barthes's assertion that "every photograph is contingent, and outside of meaning" (34), whereas the obedient reader looks only at the *studium* and sees what Barthes calls the *noeme*, that is, the "reference" of photography (76–77). In Sebald, contingency is reconstructed and embodied in the narrator's memory shaped by the text. Consequently the photographs, contextualized within a constructed text, are implicated in the signifying practice of that text, even though that too in Sebald is made problematic because there is nothing outside the narrator's elegizing consciousness within the textual economy.

For Barthes, photography is essentially melancholic, and for Sebald too, because it represents the real, or reality, in a past state (82). Because it is both past and real, Barthes said that photography "raises metaphysical questions" (85). In Sebald's fiction the "metonymic power of expansion of *punctum*" (45) captures that metaphysical resonance and invests it in the disobedient reader's capacity to contest and interrogate the relationships between image and text, and between reader and fused text, image and prose. In Sebald that can also become a ludic relationship because of the witty way he destabilizes the photograph as referent, appropriating it aesthetically and investing it with a sense of aura by virtue of its positioning in the prose text.

For Sontag, photographs are many things, but primarily evidential (1979, 5). She describes them as the most "innocent" of mimetic techniques (6), "memorializing" (8). More pertinently for Sebald, she describes them as "appropriating place," enabling insecure people to "take possession of space" (9), "soothing" and assuaging "general feelings of disorientation" (9) that the experience of travel in particular gives rise to, a quality that characterizes the Sebaldian narrator. If, as Sontag claims, photographs also "actively promote nostalgia" (15), then in Sebald this nostalgia is cauterized by the manipulative way they are used to elicit a response that cannot be nostalgic because the narrator steps between the viewer and the photograph. "All photographs testify to time's relentless melt" (15) as Sontag asserts, but Sebald's narrator's use of photographs engages the disobedient reader in a contingent act of construction that is more ambiguous, engaged in the salvation or redemption of at least these fragments, these temporal ruins. The photographs are lifted out of their role as referents and redeployed in the eternally contingent moment of construction that engages the disobedient reader, who ignores mere *studium*, accepts perhaps that *punctum* is either unavailable or a fiction, and constructs the text for herself by interrogatory and contestatory means: why this photograph in this position in the text? The cultural memories in these texts are only ours, as readers, by association, thanks to the texts themselves. They may also be memories that lure us to further research of our own, disobediently transgressing the borders of the texts and pursuing threads of association after our own fashion.

In a more specifically cultural way Sontag excepts the unspeakable photographs of the death camps and related atrocities (which affected her so profoundly and so permanently when she saw them at age twelve in a bookshop in Santa Monica), when she says that photographs do not keep their emotional charge. Sebald uses only three such photographs. Two are in *The Rings of Saturn*, the first a double-page photograph showing strange rows of mounds under the trees, like a burial ground in which all the bodies are coffinless (60–61), and the second a line of hanging bodies (97). In *Vertigo* there is a small photograph of an oddly smiling gypsy woman in front of whom the barbed wire is only just visible (184).

"Time," Sontag adds, "eventually positions most photographs, even the most amateurish, at the level of art" (21), which is where Sebald's intratextual photographs are positioned. Even the one of Sebald standing underneath the Lebanese cedar at Ditchingham Hall (*The Rings of Saturn* 263), redolent with the Biblical suggestion (Ezekiel 31:1–18) of the mythical properties of that particular world-history tree (*Vertigo* 69) offering sanctuary from evil to those who shelter beneath it, is in the process in the text, let alone after Sebald's premature death, of being both ironized and aestheticized, the "I" of the narrator twinned with the young man who had by the time of writing already vanished from Admiral Sutton's eighteenth-century park.

Sontag's notion that "Through photographs, the world becomes a series of unrelated, freestanding particles; and history, past and present, a set of anecdotes and *faits divers*" (1979, 23) catches with uncanny exactness the form of Sebald's texts in which the disobedient reader, like the constructing narrator, is free to construct the associations and relationships that weave the threads into the textual fabric. Sontag observes that this "is a view of the world which denies interconnectedness, continuity, but confers on each moment the character of a mystery" (23). It is part of Sebald's aesthetic enterprise to make connections, to construct a kind of continuity, but to continue to allow "each moment" (23) its mysterious character. This is the balancing act of his aesthetic practice.

Sontag also describes photographs as essentially "surreal" (51), the surrealism lying "at the heart of the photographic enterprise: in the very creation of a duplicate world, of a reality in the second degree" (52). This too catches at Sebald's use of the narrator figure, that authorial double, which creates such an odd dualist sense, in the photographs as well, of presence and absence. "What renders a photograph surreal is its irrefutable pathos as a message from time past" (54): this is, one suspects for Sebald as well, that strange annunciatory quality, the rupture of the membrane of contingent certainty, a spectral messenger which seems to fulfil the prophecies of the past simply by speaking to us in the present about the mystery of our own future and our uncertain present. The elegiac note so often struck in *The Emigrants,* for instance, draws on the dialogism set up between the narrator's perspective of the lives of the four emigrants and his own whereby his preoccupation with their marginalization and despair emphasizes both his empathy and his own escape from the possibility of the same fate. By transforming their lives into text the "writer"-narrator has memorialized them in his art and constructed himself as the agent of their temporal redemption or salvation.

For Sontag, photographs "trade simultaneously on the prestige of art and the magic of the real" (1979, 69), the kind of fusion that also describes Sebald's aesthetic practice. The photographs' dualism is echoed in the dualism of the verbal text, combining the "prestige of art" that the "writer"-narrator has self-consciously in his sights, to which end he crafts his highly wrought prose and the "magic of the real" that is sustained by Sebald in the funambulism of his narrator figure, art and reality held in a kind of tensile balance. Whatever the original intention of these photographs that Sebald gives his narrator to employ in his texts, their appropriation and assumption into a work of fiction has made them new, also a kind of redemption — an aesthetic one.

If Benjamin collected quotations, as Sontag quotes Hannah Arendt as saying, like "netted pearls and corals" (75), then Sebald collected photographs in a similar way, in the hypotactic-paratactic net of his prose syntax. Sontag writes of Benjamin: "In a world that is well on its way to becoming one vast quarry, the collector becomes someone engaged in a pious work of salvage. The course of modern history having already sapped the traditions and shattered the living wholes in which precious objects once found their place, the collector may in good conscience go about excavating the choicer, more emblematic fragments" (76). This is very close to the Sebaldian textual exercise, not least because it is inflected with some suggestion of Sontag's sense of the loss of the past. "Like the collector," Sontag goes on, "the photographer is animated by a passion that . . . is linked to a sense of the past. But while traditional arts of historical consciousness attempt to put the past in order . . . the central from the marginal . . . the photographer's approach — like that of the collector — is unsystematic, indeed anti-systematic" (77). Sebald, who voiced a preference for the "unsystematic" or even "anti-systematic" (see stage three), demonstrates in his prose fiction, with the use of photographs and what appears to be, in the narrator's consciousness, the segues of memory and thought, an ordering that is contained within the orbital path of the journeys that the "writer"-narrator makes in each of the texts.

Sontag may be right when she says of the twentieth century that "the new age of unbelief strengthened the allegiance to images" (153), but in Sebald these very images are themselves destabilized, rendered uncertain or unreliable. This is an intrinsic part of the gamesmanship (in Eco's sense of the game of reading) of his fiction. The reader, unable to be obedient because of this rather marvellously destabilizing uncertainty, can only look to the text, and the text's dialogical relation with the images, and construct for herself a dialogical relationship with the text's audacious fusion of word and image. In Sebald the image too is shown to be very possibly an illusion, or at least a playful instantiation of the unseen author's constructing practice.

A Viewfinder

In a culture which prioritizes the visual in a competing discourse of signification, we are becoming more skilled at reading images. As a form of documentation the photograph can bring the past into the present in a disconcerting and often deeply affecting way. The spectator's relationship with the photographic image can be a curiously intense one, largely because of the realism, even hyperrealism, of its instantiation of a moment in time that is lost to time's attrition and yet which seems, in a disconcerting sense in the affected spectator's present, to have been resurrected. This can be both unsettling and mysteriously affecting.

For Peter Conrad, "Photography is a quest for those 'objective correlatives' that T. S. Eliot thought Hamlet was ineffectually seeking: an attempt to locate aspects of reality that turn, when the photographer looks at them, into symbols. It creates what Baudelaire called '*correspondances*': how else can we feel that we belong in the world?" (2003, 20). In Sebald's texts these "*correspondances*" or "objective correlatives" are made disjunctive because the photographs have an uncertain or labile relationship with the narrator as the authoring presence in the text as far as the reader is concerned. To some extent the sense of displacement and curious distance in the texts is created by this disjunctive effect. What might have been markers or bearings turn out to be stations, places of arrest where the text stops and the reader contemplates the stasis of the image.

In the first of Sebald's prose texts, *Vertigo*, the disobedient reader is on her own with captionless images, constructing them as they occur so that the text becomes the caption for the images. There develops a growing sense of their unreliability or at least their capacity to utter what the verbal text does not. By the time of the last prose work, *Austerlitz*, the photographs have become an embedded and self-reflexive fictional technique: the narrator has been given a collection of photographs by Austerlitz, "all that remains" of his life. Nonetheless, this does not in itself account for the fact that some of the photographs seem to have a more direct relationship with the mediating narrator than with the narrative subject of the text, Jacques Austerlitz. Several of them are doctored, suggesting that their manipulation, by the narrator perhaps, is itself a voicing of a presence in the text that destabilizes the reader with its uncertain status — author, or narrator, the intention or effect unclear.

In *The Emigrants*, as Jonathan Long discusses at length (2003), the form seems to resemble a photograph album, the photographs memorializing what the text constructs as the associations between the photographs. Closer scrutiny suggests, however, that here too some of Sebald's images are working on an ironic level. *The Rings of Saturn*, also, offers the reader images that enhance the poetic and meditative qualities of the lyrical verbal text, but Sebald invests many of them with a haunting quality that expands the elegiac tone of the text in unusual ways.

Sebald's idiosyncratic use of photographs becomes part of the reading problematic or "reception dilemma" (Hoesterey's term) presented by his work. How do we read these photographs as imbricated in the text, given that they are too quixotic to be merely illustrative, often just too grainy or deliberately poorly exposed to be documentary? What exactly is their relationship, as images, with the verbal text? Sebald's own admission that his reading of Berger, Barthes, and Sontag in the seventies was of particular interest to him suggests a deliberate experiment with textual discourse.

Like the fictionally constructed narrator, who is and is not Max Sebald and/or W. G. Sebald, the photographs are "but also are not" documents relating to a prior reality. What they once were, these orphaned fragments of someone else's memory of the past, has been replaced by what they now mean within the textual economy of Sebald's prose practice. The question is: whose prior reality do these photographs actually utter and in what sequential context do they take on their acquired meanings, their inaugural one being no longer available?

While we as readers accept that a writer makes use of prior experience, knowledge, and research in the writing of prose fiction, fusing these heterogeneous elements into his artefact, we are not used to seeing, as a contingent visual experience rather than an imagined one, the collected and recollected fragments of prior reality upon which a writer draws, that is, as photographs. This foregrounded appropriation of images is a postmodern *truc* that emphasizes the *bricolage-collage-montage* fusion of the creative process. Agile and witty, this is in large measure the source of Sebald's curious affirmation of the human. Juxtaposed with the often profound moral seriousness of Sebald's writing enterprise but also his capacity for a Menippean sense of carnival in the gamesmanship of fiction itself (Bakhtin 1981, 106–11) and those saccadic flashes of wit and humor which alleviate his narrator's melancholy, this dimension of his textuality seems to partake of the same broad range of response, that Terentian humanism again.

Black-and-white photographs exhibiting curios and mementos like train tickets or pizzeria bills, newspaper clippings and autographs, recording scenery and persons, make visible what Peter Conrad calls "the refraction of reality" and "a startled, mystified deracination" (2003, 24). The ways in which images are used in Sebald's four books are as much part of the process of fiction, defamiliarizing and refracting reality to represent it as something uncanny or strange, as Sebald's use of a constructed narrator is, in re-presenting fragments or instantiations of his own consciousness as vivid and strange. Proust interleaves his diegesis with mimesis, so that his narrator is present in an ambiguous way; Sebald dispenses with that dualism by absorbing mimesis entirely into the diegetic narrator's consciousness, including the photographs.

Because we are never quite certain about just whose prior experience of reality is being documented, the photographs themselves are an invitation to disobedience. There is no narrative contract between the photographs and the reader as narratee because they are so "other"; they resist being appropriated and they resist "translation" except by being embedded in the narrator's verbal text.

But not all readers have understood this. Critics and reviewers have commented on the "odd," "cryptic," "nervous," "delphic" or "mysterious" photographs, "murkily reproduced" (Kunkel 2002; Strawson 2001; Di Piero 2000; Iyer 2000; Brookner 1999) with more than one reviewer saying they document uncertainty (Eder 2000; Lewis 2001). To read them as markers, or as signposts that give bearings in the textual landscape, is a false mapping. Their witness is to the fictional process itself — subversively self-reflexive, they are of no avail to an obedient reader who seeks to take direction from what appear to be reading protocols. They are the very site of ambiguity, of duplicity.

When the Australian writer Philip Gwynne referred to Peter Robb's listing of W. G. Sebald's *The Rings of Saturn* as a work of nonfiction and its sending him "off to the library to look up all the things" mentioned in the book (*The Age* 7 August 2004), he revealed that he had in part been duped by the game Sebald is always playing with the reader. Sebald's narrator's historically corroborated facts about Thomas Browne, the last Dowager Empress of China, Joseph Conrad, Roger Casement, or the rise of the silk industry in Europe in *The Rings of Saturn* are, as Gwynne suggests, excellent, even tantalizing, spurs to our readerly and contemporary thirst for knowledge, our research into the cultural archive of the remembered past resurrected in Sebald's text. This is part of the considerable pleasure and great richness of reading Sebald's highly allusive, intertextual prose. But not to recognize that this knowledge is embedded in an aesthetic construction, in fictional prose practice, of consciousness and self-consciousness as discursive practices, is not to read the whole text.

One wants to ask, what might obedient readers like Philip Gwynne or Peter Robb (author of *Midnight in Sicily* and *M*), for whom Sebald's texts are "non-fiction," make of the first photograph in *The Rings of Saturn*, for instance? It seems at the very least unnecessary to provide a photograph of the sky seen through a window over which some form of black netting has been stretched, the kind of thing that an editor might scrap. The disobedient reader, however, jumping from one text into another in the conversation between all of Sebald's prose fiction, will recall that a similar, but larger grid, was drawn over the face of Beyle's "Angela Pietragrua" (Sebald 1999b, 12), whose angelic stoniness as the mistress of "his fellow-soldier Louis Joinville" (13), makes her both unavailable and all the more desirable. But what meanings attach to the clearly amateurishly inked grid over the drawing of Angela?

Similarly, what are we to make of the photograph of sky? Who took it from that strange angle? Whose point of view, whose focalizing perspective,

*Copyright © 1998 W. G. Sebald, reprinted with permission
of the Wylie Agency, Inc.*

is foregrounded here if not the artful invalid himself, the Sebaldian narrator? What is the Sebaldian narrator actually documenting? His own precarious and absurd position? Is he also documenting himself documenting his absurd position? Is this a moment when we glimpse the author's wry smile at the intensity of the narrator's self-preoccupation and his search for understanding? Is this a coded joke for the necessarily subjective view of man's relationship with the cosmos, contextualized by Sir Thomas Browne's hospital as "the world" in which we, as invalids, are destined to die, yearning all the while for what may (or may not) lie "beyond"?

The ruminating writerly narrator seems exposed here by a latent humor that subverts the seriousness of his melancholy contemplation, partly through the odd use of the photograph. The absurdity lies in the reader's imagining the paralysed narrator somehow managing to photograph (hence the odd angle) his own view of the sky through the hospital window in Norwich which nets the image of the clouds passing, that vaporous mist that figures so often in Sebald, as a temporal instantiation which yields only mystery, that which obscures our vision, and our understanding. It is, at the very least, a focalizing joke about focalization, a far more mysterious and uncanny photograph than an obedient reader might perhaps construe.

Traveling Toward the Image

On several occasions Sebald referred to the fact that the photographs, some taken by him and some collected by him in secondhand shops as curios, functioned as constructivist elements in his writing: ". . . in prose fiction: you have to elaborate. You have one image, and you have to make something of it — half a page, or three quarters, or one and a half — and it only works through linguistic or imaginative elaboration" (Cuomo, 2001). It is not unreasonable then to argue that Sebald's fusion texts are a form of prose fiction which leaves the constructivist elements in, using the Beaubourg architectural principle of exposing all the utilities that make the building work on the outside, featuring them as foregrounded aesthetic elements (all those red, blue, and yellow pipes for instance) in the façade of the building. In Sebald's texts the photographs function both as decorative elements which seduce the reader's gaze from the harder work of constructing the verbal text and as the constructivist elements, the stations on the (writerly and readerly) journey as it were, out of which the textual discourse, and the final object of the text itself, is made.

Sebald himself commented upon that "building" process: "what the image always does is arrest the text. The narrative moves in time and slides toward its own ending. The visual arts have the capacity to lift you out of time" (Cuomo 2001). Sebald's images arrest time, and it is time, its ineluctable passage or what Susan Sontag called "time's relentless melt" (1979, 15), that is, twinned with death and memory (a constant preoccupation in all his texts) which also makes Proust's novel and Nabokov's memoir such spectral intertextual presences in Sebald's prose fiction.

By employing this quality of the visual, temporal arrest, Sebald pushes the fictional envelope out into a new dispensation. This is prefigured in Walter Benjamin's discomfort with the constraints of mimesis and historicism, in Benjamin's desire for the transformation and translation of the coordinates of the subject's engagement with alterity: memory of the past, a sense of the present, and confidence to imagine the future in some other form. Sebald's expanded notion of a fictional text embraces the technology of the image in a postmodern and ironic sense as well as a form which catches something of man's innate desire to arrest time, to prevent the future, to live more intensely in the contingent moment, to console himself with the past, at least the "beatific moments" in it (Silverblatt 2001). This too shapes the melancholy of Sebald's writing.

The reader's uncertainty in this textual economy is, in Sebald's terms, a more authentic reading experience, precisely because the narrator, and for that matter the author, is profoundly aware of the provisional nature of construction and this wager against time's "relentless melt." The constructed artifice is consoling but consoling because it is constructed, more resistant to temporal attrition or entropy. It is a *bricolage*, a *collage* and a *montage*, because this is what memory and recollection do, what consciousness does, as in the Cartesian notion of thought, concepts or ideas, or memories for that matter, as images, strung along a thread of association that the thinker makes between images. It is not difficult to see this too as the Sebaldian narrator-writer's *modus operandi* in all four texts. The images are not so much determining as the technical stations on the journey toward the text's consummation. If they are epiphanies, or annunciations, they resist meaning in the usual sense, offering the disobedient reader a transit pass across the border between the real and the imagined.

Julia Kristeva caught some of this in her text in the Louvre exhibition catalogue, *Visions Capitales*. She suggests that rather than being "slaves of the image," the viewers see that "the image is potentially a space of freedom" because it has effaced, once and for all, whatever has been depicted in it, substituting for that prior materiality the trajectory of thought and the errancy of the imagination that it both utters and inspires. This is what happens in reading Sebald. Sebald's narrator, and Sebald's disobedient reader, play in the textual space that Sebald constructs in language and images, engaging collaboratively in the freedom of contemplative and imaginative responses.

The photographs, with their mysterious provenance, also serve as a means of resisting autofiction, the confessional writing that Sebald says he does not want to write: "I would find it hard to write anything confessional. I prefer to look at the trajectories of other lives that cross one's own trajectory — do it by proxy rather than expose oneself in public" (To James Atlas 1999).

The photographs as proxy leave only spectral traces of the author and his temporal act of textual production. The author as specter might haunt the reader in the text (and it is not difficult to see a Sebaldian witticism at Barthes's expense here, in the "death of the author"), but the constructed metaphysical object that is the text (Borges's dead object that is waiting for the reader to animate it, in *This Craft of Verse*) is the constructed space in which the author hides and the reader plays. It is a vertiginous set of dualities.

Because the photographs are black and white, or finely graded greys, they echo the predominant leitmotif or metaphor in all Sebald's texts: the word "grey," the mist which clouds our vision, the grey patches of amnesia, the death-in-life or life-in-death monochrome, the strange interstitial grey silk scrim that separates the living and the dead. They speak presence and absence at the same time. The sand in the desert photograph is not medium grey; the canopy of the tree is not grey inflected with lighter shades of grey. These photographs are themselves not truly representational, not truly mimetic. Simulacra, they are images which require our imagination to convert them into greens and ochres. This is precisely what we do when we read the inked symbols of words, converting their conceptual symbolism by mysterious contemplative and imaginative acts into our own images. The image, in Flusser's estimate, "produces magical — not historical — relationships between elements of the image and the reader" (60). This sounds like reading Sebald.

Vertigo: Everything out of Focus?

This is the first fiction in which Sebald employs photographic images. His use of them is less consistent than in subsequent books. Here he is experimenting with the various ways in which they might work in the verbal text and engage, puzzle, or destabilize the reader. In *Vertigo*, sixty-eight photographs appear, none with captions. An obedient reader might expect to pick up signals from the generic conventions of the prose. Photographs in sections II and IV might serve as illustrations for the travels of the "writer"-narrator, while those in sections I and III might be read as evidence supplied by the narrator in documentary support for the historical essays he is writing about Beyle (Stendhal) and Kafka. But this is Sebald, and the reading experience of *Vertigo* is much less straightforward — and far more fascinating. From the obedient reader's point of view these photographs are unstable. To suggest how a disobedient reader might make her way through the photographs without succumbing to vertigo, I will focus on the ways in which the photographs resist the generic conventions of the prose into which they are inserted, soliciting the reader's interrogating scrutiny.

The book opens with the photograph of a painting. Beneath the image comes *Vertigo*'s first sentence: "In mid-May of the year 1800 Napoleon and a force of 36,000 men crossed the Great St Bernard pass, an undertaking that had been regarded until that time as next to impossible" (3). In the informed reader's mind the most famous painting of the transalpine crossing is that of Napoleon in full uniform on a rearing horse in which Jacques-Louis David has captured a sense of the historical grandeur of this "next to impossible" undertaking. David's painting was a glorifying falsification of the reality — a dusty and travel-weary Napoleon crossed the Alps on a mule. In the unreferenced painting of *Vertigo*, men and horses are dwarfed by majestic alpine scenery. The tricornes of Napoleon's troops seem miniature absurdities in a landscape which pits men against Nature. In the small and grainy photograph, grandeur belongs to the mountains, not the men, so that the image belies the admiring prose.

The narrator layers complexity of his own in the painting: he names one of the miniature figures as Marie-Henri Beyle, the seventeen-year-old who will translate these experiences as the writer Stendhal into those of his fictional character in *La Chartreuse de Parme*. The anonymity of the historical event is reduced to the particularity of the micro-narrative of one ambitious Swiss boy who will, through the lens of fiction, give these historical events an affective and ongoing influence, as we will observe in section III of *Vertigo*. One of those tiny figures in the painting (apart from Napoleon himself) will assume an identity, much as Robert Lowell suggests that the business of art, given that "we are poor passing facts," is imagination, to "give each figure in the photograph his living name" (from "Epilogue" 1978, 127).

On *Vertigo*'s second page come two more images, photographs of sketches. Between the top sketch of a boy cocking his snook and the lower sketch of a dashing youth in his cravat with a valorous ink-blot come the words "childhood and adolescence." They are part of the sentence framing the two images and yet seem to serve an entirely separate function, as if constituting a descriptive caption. The lower photograph contributes its own words to the image of the dashing youth. Sebald does not tell us that both images come from Stendhal's fictionalized autobiography, *La Vie de Henri Brulard*.

On page 14 there is a strip photograph of a different kind, its playfulness impossible to ignore. What is a reader to make of this pattern of repetition, the photograph of a medical drawing showing the interior of a man's mouth replicated three times? The erotic suggestions in the text have been subverted by this ironic comedy of a different anatomical view. The narcissistic repetition is rhetorical, suggesting a chronic condition and anxiety. The text amplifies the diagnosis of ulceration by adding "inflammations" (14) to the monochrome image, framing it by suggesting that these are symptoms relating to a "venereal infection" (12) contracted by Beyle from his "apprenticeship" in Milan's brothels (11–12). Puns, visual and verbal, hover around the real consequences of youthful fancies.

Less comically but still ironically, this is a retrospective prognosis, the beginning of the end of Beyle's journey, and proleptically the narrator's textual one. Forty years of self-medicating practice with "quicksilver and iodide of potassium" (12) will bring on the fatal fit that Beyle suffers on a Paris street, the great writer "undone" by both the disease and the cure, life/love and death. This is, for the disobedient reader, an intricate joke juxtaposing comedy and tragedy, amusement and distress: love, madness, writing. The image sends the disobedient reader down associating pathways mapping the text, keeping her from surrendering to the threat of vertigo.

In the vertical strip photograph on page 18, a cropped detail from another unreferenced painting, formatted on the margin of the page (Sebald often uses page space playfully), we see the spectral figure of a distant "mean" monument which, according to the text, memorializes the dead in the Battle of Marengo (18). A single military figure, foregrounded, is slightly absurd, its bold arm raised, its independent flair recalling the pair of mischievous self-portraits (4). According to the adjacent text this might be either the battlefield of Marengo with the spectral memorial column, or the "turbulence of the Battle of Marengo" itself (18). This is a disturbing temporal superposition. The monument could not have been erected during the Battle itself. This contains the suggestion of Sebald's "writer"-narrator, like Stendhal but not when he was Beyle, reconstructing the past in temporal layers, a palimpsest of memory. Here in the narrator's ironic and manipulated construction of a moment of epiphany in the *tranche* of the painting, the figure of Beyle, who will translate himself into Stendhal, "in the autumn . . . he resolved to become the greatest writer of all time" (18), has become the agent of his own salvation, escaping Waterloo to write "the great novels between 1829 and 1842" (29), different kinds of memorials entirely.

In these first pages the photographs have begun to produce a kind of parallel text, its meanings more confusing than elucidating to the reader. The photographs are not passively responsive to the generic conventions of the historical essay, as section I of *Vertigo* might seem to be, by being merely evidential or illustrative. The reader is being provoked, teased, a different kind of engagement. The problems for the reader include the resistance of the photographs to "what they are supposed to be saying" (Culler 2000, 290). Cropped, repeated, reproduced indistinctly, they resist being read purely as illustrative or evidential. They offer the reader an additional interpretive site, and doing so, complicate the reader's engagement with the verbal dimension of this fusion text. The reader is not able to read this first section of *Vertigo* as a historical essay. For precisely the same reasons the photographs in Section III pose similar problems. Mystification rather than clarification prevails.

In Sections II and IV, what seem to be autobiographical travel essays, the photographs also pose problems. In "*All'estero*" the narrator has traveled

along the Danube by train with Ernst Herbeck to Altenberg. They climb "a shady path to Burg Greifenstein," a "medieval fortress" which the narrator tells us played "a significant part" in his own imagination, and continues to do so "in that of the people of Greifenstein" (40–41). The photograph inserted here seems to be of a building which could pass as "a medieval fortress," but on closer scrutiny reveals itself to be a kind of fanciful pot for containing cacti which grow out of its central courtyard like unclimbable versions of Jack's beanstalks. This may be imaginative, but here it is also crazy, a distortion of reality. The disobedient reader might construe that the narrator's companion, Herbeck, has had a disorienting (or creative) effect on him. Why is this photograph here? We never find out, because the current of the prose moves backwards to a memory of the narrator's in which he "visited the castle in the late 1960s, and from the terrace of the restaurant had looked down across the gleaming river and the waterlands . . ." (41).

The next photograph is not of the view that the narrator and Herbeck see "on that bright October day" (41), but of one that the narrator's memory summons up from "the late 1960s" (41), "on which the shadows of the evening were falling," or perhaps one that Herbeck, who "At times . . . was very far away" (41), may have seen on another occasion entirely. Is this perhaps a view that existed only in the childhood imagination of the narrator, one which the actual glimpse of the river in the "late 1960s" (41) displaced? Where do these photographs come from and what are they actually documenting? The disobedient reader might construe that what is documented here is not the recent past of this trip, but a more remote past. The problem is a confusion about the priority of empirical experiences, memories, and images. What comes first, and in what sequence?

Copyright © 1999 W. G. Sebald, reprinted with permission of the Wylie Agency, Inc.

The photographs increase the complexity and confusion, like a temporal disordering of a film sequence.

The autographed and dated note that Ernst Herbeck has written in the narrator's notebook, just as the text translates it from the German, appears to be an authenticating document, but by now the reader is suspicious. The disobedient reader may note, without knowing why, that Herbeck rests "his left hand on the open page" to write, which summons the "decapitated" photograph (39), tantalizingly withholding identity. In it the man's left hand is held at an angle that recalls the plaster cast in the photograph of (is it?) Méthilde's left hand. What is the withheld significance of this detail? Why has the text, through this repetition, emphasized it? What private memory has the narrator shrouded here? Too much is unexplained, turned to enigmatic metaphor, resisting the generic conventions of the autobiographical travel essay.

Is this actually a picture of Herbeck, the poet institutionalized for thirty-four years until his discharge into a home, whose demeanor suggests to the narrator that he has "travelled with a circus for many years" (49)? We can't tell whether the suit is "glencheck" and there doesn't seem to be a "hiking badge on the lapel" (39). Herbeck's carrying his hat reminds the narrator of his grandfather's habit. The disobedient reader, recalling that Sebald's beloved grandfather's photograph stood on the author's desk (Turner, Davidson College, 2003) suspects that memory is odd and deceptive. Has Herbeck recalled, momentarily, the narrator's grandfather so that the narrator has represented that trick of memory rather than the person? The reader is confused then about what the photograph represents: Herbeck, the narrator's grandfather, the memory that the one evoked of the other, the writer's own hand as a genetic evocation of the absent one? In fact, it seems to be a photograph of Robert Walser, like the one used on the cover of the American edition of his stories. A Sebaldian tribute.

This confusion stretches backwards into the text, potentially disconcerting for a reader who generally travels forwards. Stendhal's memory of his imaginary beloved was displaced by the artifice of the plaster cast, so that the simulacrum (the cast) represented a simulacrum (the imagined love). Whose hand was cast? Was it merely that the crooked little finger recalled Méthilde to mind, even though Méthilde was not really Beyle's beloved? The photograph of the cast (an invocation of Jean Baudrillard's simulacrum) becomes a fantastic object of Beyle's devotion (like Romeo's for Rosaline, or Félicité's for the stuffed parrot in *Un Coeur Simple*). What is the connection here? "The left hand" on the open page alerts the disobedient reader.

Is this, like Barthes's withholding of the last image of his mother in the winter garden in *Camera Lucida*, too powerful a memory of personal grief that love inspires to be exposed to the reader? Is the narrative screen in danger of slipping here to reveal the author? So much for the conventions of an autobiographical travel essay. By cropping the photograph, the narrator has created his own simulacrum which displaces actual memory, a photograph rendered mysterious, foregrounding the left hand, the half-hidden hat carried in the right. This is no document.

Sleight of hand is used again in the photograph of the author's German passport reissued in Milan on 4 August 1987 (114). It is not difficult to see that this is a photograph of a more youthful Sebald, partly obscured by the vertical black line, the signature cryptic but identifiable as "W.S. . . ." What is the reader to make of this? Is this an absurdly obvious indication that the author's identity has been canceled, but suggesting also that the author's identity can only ever be partly hidden? The identity of this individual is subject to institutional determination, constructed as "freedom to come and go" (115), to appear and disappear, to cross borders. Is this important? Does this include the borders between the external world of reality and the rich interior space of one's conscious self, one's imagination? Could this little narrative and its passport photograph be a metonymy for Sebald's fictional "game of hide and seek" with the reader (videotape of Jaggi interviewing Sebald, 24 September 2001, London, Turner, Davidson College, 2003)?

In Venice, where the narrator has traveled to after leaving Vienna (as the bafflingly empty page of the travel diary shows on page 60 of the richly imagined written text), several mysterious and uncanny things occur. The first is that there is not a single photograph of this most photogenic place. It evaporates into the virtual reality of the words of the text. There is a cryptic note underneath October 31, the date of Hallowe'en or the night before All Souls (the Christian holy day for the commemoration of the dead). This reinforces the spectral quality of the city. The note, "Riva degli Schiavoni," the most recognisable part of Venice, painted twice by Canaletto and several times by Turner, suggests an assignation, with the mysterious "M," the code name of Caravaggio. This is a puzzle that dissolves when Malachio appears, the conversation in "the bar on the Riva" which the narrator has with "a Venetian by the name of Malachio, who had studied astrophysics at Cambridge" (60), leading to a midnight ferry ride past the Venetian crematorium. Here the travel diary, like the "cancelled" passport, is an empty document, a prompt to memory, a license to travel, and a duplicitous lure.

In Verona, the city of Romeo and Juliet, the narrator spends "the hours of the early afternoon" (69) lying on a stone bench in the Giardino dei Giusti. A photograph of the ticket which permits and regulates entry appears. Why is the reader shown this souvenir? Is this to document the narrator's visit to the garden? Why is it deemed necessary for inclusion here? It records a number ("No. 52314," 69), denoting the "very long-standing habit" of admitting people, including the narrator, to the garden. These include, the disobedient reader knows, the English essayists Coryat,

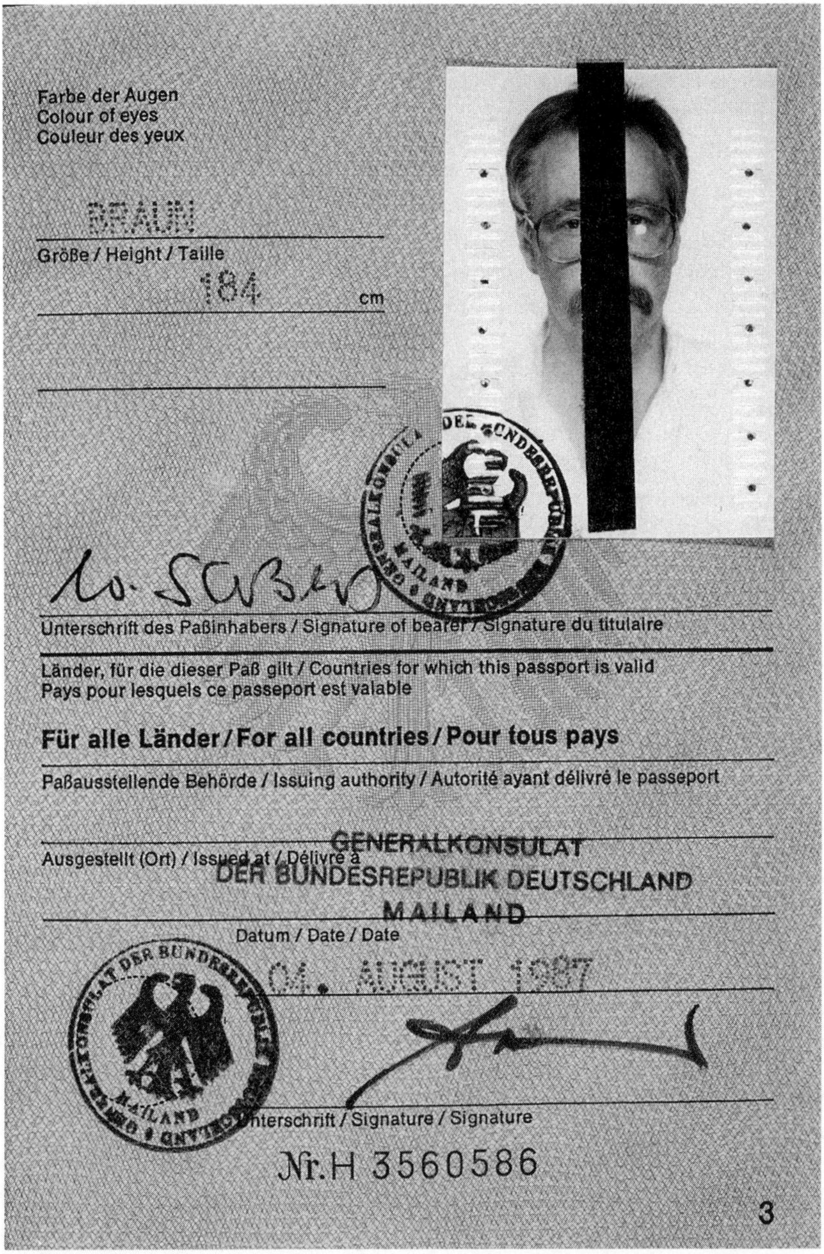
Farbe der Augen
Colour of eyes
Couleur des yeux

BRAUN

Größe / Height / Taille

184 cm

Unterschrift des Paßinhabers / Signature of bearer / Signature du titulaire

Länder, für die dieser Paß gilt / Countries for which this passport is valid
Pays pour lesquels ce passeport est valable

Für alle Länder / For all countries / Pour tous pays

Paßausstellende Behörde / Issuing authority / Autorité ayant délivré le passeport

GENERALKONSULAT
DER BUNDESREPUBLIK DEUTSCHLAND
MAILAND

Ausgestellt (Ort) / Issued at / Délivré à

Datum / Date / Date

04. AUGUST 1987

Unterschrift / Signature / Signature

Nr. H 3560586

3

Evelyn, Addison, the German poet and traveler, Goethe, and even more suggestively perhaps, Stendhal (Masson 1961). The photograph of this numbered ticket is a fleeting Sebaldian witticism perhaps, but it is edged with a sinister echo. The narrator's blissful experience in the paradise-garden is only for the elect, those who have a ticket. The well-being and refreshment that the narrator enjoys, in a reverie on his stone bench, painted in his lyrical description of "a pair of white Turkish doves soaring again and again into the sky above the treetops with only a few brisk wing-beats, remaining at those blue heights for a small eternity, and then, drop-ping with a barely audible gurgling call, gliding down on the air in sweeping arcs around the lovely cypresses, some of which had been grow-ing there for as long as two hundred years" (69–70) is available only by ticketed admission, many having gone before. The reader's problem here is one of tone: predominantly dark or light? Are both suggested here? Is this wholly a place of refreshment, light, and peace?

The next photograph adds a further layer of irony and ambiguity to the one of the ticket by representing the enclosed garden as a garden of the dead, the entry ticket admitting the narrator to his serene stone bench, like those before him, now dead. What is the reader to make too of the darker suggestion of twentieth-century *Ordnung*, dehumanizing human beings, tattooing on their wrists a "biglietto di ingresso" to hell-purgatory-paradise, entry provided by self-appointed gatekeepers of the most terrible and appalling kind? This is no mere autobiographical travel essay, no mere snap.

Sebald keeps a fine balance here. Any more explicit and his words would be so heavily freighted with meaning that his imaginative text would founder, washing up against the rocks of referentiality. It is because his oblique suggestiveness relies on the reader's capacity to view the text as "*scriptible*" (Barthes), and collaboratively authoritative, that the imagina-tive aura of the text is strong enough to maintain its tensile relationship with the referents which have engendered it, including this sharply shad-owed photograph (70). Panoramic and taken from a point of vantage, nothing in the verbal text suggests that the narrator took the photograph. It is perhaps an old postcard, another document retrieved from the archive, but this time one, in the narrator's view, attesting to the timelessness or stasis of this place.

The photograph suggests a funerary monumentalism with what look like headstones erected on the wall, their pattern recalling analeptically Grillparzer's description of the pattern of the roofline of the Doge's Palace, "the lead-plated crocodile" (60) in this second section of *Vertigo*. It is per-haps also a prison, an ambiguous site like the Doge's Palace. To the dis-obedient reader this reading of the photograph suggests the narrator's capacity to move imaginatively beyond the contingent moment, being "abroad." The strangely elongated, pyramidal pediments on the gateposts suggest some exotic temple with Egyptian mortuary overtones, which we see again in the photograph of the second owner's pyramid bookplate in a book once inscribed as a gift to Kafka at the end of this section (136), and these are surely cemetery cypresses pointing everlastingly skywards. What kind of garden is this? The access points through the iron gates are both exclusive and imprisoning. The fountain on the left, in which the narrator performs his ablutions, is set into the wall like a stoop of holy water. This is a place where the coordinates of time and space don't work in quite the same way as they do when the narrator moves across the Ponte Nuovo and down the Via Nizza and the Via Stelle to the Piazza Bra. The "keeper of the gate" in her "gloomy cabin" (71), to whom the narrator waves in vain for human connection, is fixed forever, waiting in some indiscernible future on the threshold between the city of Verona and the paradise-garden of lost time. Like the caretaker of the Jewish cemetery in the East End of London who will disappear, in *Austerlitz*, back into the hallowed and anonymous timelessness behind the wall next to the grey-toned world of asphodel that is Jacques Austerlitz's flat, she too is suggestive of a Grimm *Märchen*, a fairytale that codes fear of disaster and anxiety about death.

This interlude in the Giardino is created as an interstitial, timeless moment embedded in the narrative, not some anecdote for an autobiographical travel essay. An imagined immanence is resurrected in the contingent moment, mediated by memory and reinforced, in Sebald's wry and ironic way, with a photograph that attests not to what the narrator has merely described but to an apprehension of some mysterious conjunction of associations. This photograph's relationship with the verbal text is what gives it depth of perspective, something that its two-dimensional illusion of perspective can only simulate. Without the verbal text this postcard too, like the *biglietto d'ingresso*, is only another empty document. The network of Sebald's poetics, that construction of the means by which the ephemeral present is netted for future remembrance, is a melancholy musealizing of fragments but also a hopeful archive that we as readers of the archive might invest with connectedness, that is, with the significance that will, in turn, ensure their preservation, and our ability, by remembering the past, to shape a better future.

The final image in *Vertigo*, in Section IV, is another tripled image. What the reader can see in the pattern of St George "forever driving a spear through the throat of the griffin-like winged creature lying at his feet" (242) is *mythos* transformed into historical portent by remembrance. This is the image painted at the end of "the high cemetery wall" (242), seen here from an upward angle, the schoolboy's perspective on his way past "the teacher's house and the curate's house" (242), on his way home from writing out the catalogue of disasters at school. The figure has been removed from its context, and on the page of the text it exists in a space of its own, the iterative struggle against the forces of darkness. This is not simply to describe one of the wall murals in the narrator's childhood home village. This is the never-ending battle to destroy evil, constructed by the narrator's repetition of the photograph. The "smell of burnt horn . . . from the smithy" (242–43) juxtaposed with this image in the reader's mind recreates the vivid lingering memory that connects the narrator's childhood with the evil that has befallen human lives in history, a litany of disastrous struggle and hope, a never-ending battle of serial victories. Like the other photographs in *Vertigo*, complete meaning is unavailable; this one too is open to the reader's scrutiny, contemplation and imagination.

The Emigrants: Like the Room in this Photograph

It is tempting to construct the photographs in *The Emigrants*, as Jonathan Long does (2003), as four album-texts adjunct to the narrator's telling of the stories of four emigrants. These photographs are not documents representing the lives of these four individuals but rather they focus the reader's attention on the narrator's engagement with the subjects of "his" stories. *The Emigrants* is a set of four stories associated with one another through the narrator's obliquely suggested and largely withheld story. In the seventy-six photographs reproduced in this text, this principle applies throughout.

The first photograph in *The Emigrants* is of a graveyard, the generous canopy of a large tree sheltering old gravestones. This is not a cheerful beginning. It might for some disobedient, adventurous readers summon Wordsworth's *Ode: Intimations of Immortality* (1802–4, 1807), as do one or two other photographs of trees in Sebald:

> But there's a tree, of many, one,
> A single field which I have look'd upon,
> Both of them speak of something that is gone:

Underneath it the text runs, "At the end of September 1970, shortly before I took up my position in Norwich, I drove out to Hingham with Clara in search of somewhere to live" (3). This is a disconcertingly black joke, if the reader applies the convention of reading the juxtaposed text as the caption to the image in an album. Later the reader will see that this image echoes the photograph of a painting by Courbet, "The Oak of Vercingetorix" (180), the only photograph with a caption in Sebald's texts. This is the image that the narrator tells us the painter Ferber is using as a model for one of his own paintings, so that this first photograph will become, subsequently, a hint of the last story, its wounded artist robbed of continuity with his own past, and the narrator's task now clarified as that of messenger: to memorialize the lives of people who are not able to tell their own stories.

Copyright © 1996 W. G. Sebald, reprinted with permission of the
Wylie Agency, Inc.

At the beginning of *The Emigrants*, it seems that this scene is what the narrator and his wife first see as they arrive at Hingham. Given the retrospective nature of the prose, though, it may also be that this is their most lasting image, a memory of the evergreen holm oak in the graveyard of the church at Hingham sheltering the final position of unrecounted lives and feeding off them is a metonymic image of the vanished lives memorialized in this book, and the final destination of those yet to join them.

The apparently documentary effect of this photograph suggests a very different kind of "emigration," particularly in hindsight when the reader is faced with two suicides, two slow deaths in a mental institution, the death of the painter's mother in a ghetto, and the serious illness of the painter hospitalized with pulmonary disease in a former Victorian workhouse. "Emigration" in this sense seems far more permanent, a journey from which no one returns, the one which inflects the etiolated lives described in *The Emigrants* by a narrator whose spectral presence is implicated in the lives of those whose stories he recounts. This first photograph is slightly shocking, the final destination of the emigrants, this final image seen by the survivor.

The photographs of the "whitewashed brick wall" of the tennis court and of the "kitchen garden . . . that's on its last legs after years of neglect" (7) are what the narrator sees at "Prior's Gate." These are metaphorical emphases for the neglected husband of the wealthy Swiss Elli (21). The narrator sees a net stretched across a lawn tennis court, still in readiness for a game, and the unkempt kitchen garden from which, nonetheless, the ingredients for an occasional dinner will be drawn, small vestiges of hope and all the more poignant for that. This will be echoed in the narrator's observation of Dr. Selwyn's caring for the three doomed horses, his sheltering of Elaine with the "whinnying" laugh (10), who cares in turn for her dolls, his welcoming of the new tenants, and his friendship with Edwin Elliott. Where there's life, it seems there is (a little) hope also.

The narrator's photograph of the flint hermitage shows an eccentric garden folly like a toy castle (11), recalling with irony "an Englishman's home is his castle" — "Dr. Selwyn was scarcely ever in the house. He lived in his hermitage" (11), an *ersatz* Englishman in an *ersatz* castle, an *ersatz* home. Its crenellated battlements and arrow slits make it look even more like a dark medieval keep, in stark contrast to what appeals to the narrator about his flat, "the view from the high windows across the garden, the park, and the massed cloud in the sky" (8). Selwyn, the former alpine climber, is both hermit in retreat and prisoner in some terrible siege, his view an inward-looking one, forever keeping his distance (he is never "Henry," like "Edwin," only "Dr. Selwyn"). These are all empty photographs, voicing the narrator's awareness of the terrible marginalization of Selwyn's life, its reduction and despair, his presence the absence the narrator has observed and recorded in these photographs.

The narrator's presence is always obliquely suggested, as the eye behind the viewfinder, or the pair of hands with scissors. The photograph of Vladimir Nabokov that he "had clipped from a Swiss magazine a few days before" (16) in order to suggest the sight of "Dr. Selwyn in knee-length shorts, with a shoulder bag and a butterfly net" (15) in the shots of the trip to Crete made ten years earlier by Selwyn and Edwin Elliott is a curious one. What is the reader to make of this? The narrator had no access to the projected images recording the trip to Crete. It's a poor substitute: Nabokov's photograph contains no shoulder bag and who knows what Selwyn, if he exists at all, actually looks like. The disobedient reader is aware that it's not Selwyn's unavailable photograph that is at issue here but the narrator's observation of similarities between Selwyn and Nabokov, curiously attenuated and perhaps only in their status as emigrants, like the narrator. There is also the alpine link, through Selwyn's friend the alpine guide Naegeli and the narrator having come from near the Bernese Oberland. These coincidences seem odd until the reader reflects that Nabokov died in 1977, and that the energy, vitality, and light recorded in the picture, together with the overexposed butterfly net which catches ephemeral beauty, like Sebald's hypotactic and paratactic networked prose, is also what he saw in the pictures of Selwyn and Elliott in Crete ten years earlier. The swift passage of time, the process of entropy, and the inevitable approach of death, that first picture, is what the disobedient reader "sees" in the narrator's clipped photograph. "And so they are ever returning to us, the dead" (23) is, as the first photograph also suggests, the strange enigma of death and resurrection in the memory.

The epigraph to the first volume of Brian Boyd's biography of Nabokov, *Vladimir Nabokov: The American Years*, is from an interview:

Interviewer: What surprises you in life?

Nabokov: . . . the marvel of consciousness — that sudden window swinging open on a sunlit landscape amidst the night of non-being. (11)

The photograph of Nabokov in this first section of *The Emigrants*, like the conversations between the narrator and Henry Selwyn, voices this "marvel of consciousness," in a sunlit landscape, the butterfly net white to the point of incandescence, as though the netting of the shimmering moments of lived experience is, like the photographs in the Sebaldian text, precisely what had been so terribly missing for the man lying under the protective shade of that holy tree, the cedar, in the garden at Prior's Gate in "Hingham." This is the narrator's perception, the narrator's story.

Sebald's use of photographs in *The Emigrants* is a metonymic use of this Nabokovian observation. These "sudden windows" onto moments now gone forever speak loss and transience and ephemerality (like butter-flies), turning Selwyn's empty life into a living death and Nabokov's (his father the victim of a political assassination in Russia, his homosexual brother dying in a Nazi concentration camp) into brilliant revenge for these madnesses. Nabokov said his "highest enjoyment of timelessness"

Copyright © 1996 W. G. Sebald, reprinted with permission of the Wylie Agency, Inc.

came when he pursued butterflies: "I experience a momentary vacuum into which rushes all that I love" (*Speak, Memory* 109–10). This correspondence, not least because Nabokov refers to folding his sense of time, his "magic carpet," in such a way as "to superimpose one part of the pattern upon another," produces "a sense of oneness with sun and stone"

(110). The narrator, given the choice, has opted for Nabokov's path in the sunlit Alps, netting timeless moments of beauty and love, and has rejected the terrible darkness and retreat into lonely interiority that culminates in Selwyn's shocking suicide.

The second story also begins with an image, this time an eye-level photograph of the left rail of a railway track which curves away into the distance beyond the horizon of the photograph. The first sentence of the story tells why: "In January 1984, the news reached me from S that on the evening of the 30th of December, a week after his seventy-fourth birthday, Paul Bereyter, who had been my teacher at primary school, had put an end to his life" (27). Disconcertingly, the viewer's eye is taken to the immediate foreground of the image, as though one were lying on the track, and then the viewer's eye follows the track, its relentless, inexorable movement out beyond the image, over the stones and past the wooded hill on one side and the wild grasses on the other, the world left behind. The narrator has placed his camera's lens on the track to record — could it ever record? — the final perspective, the last view of a man who lies down in front of a train to die.

What strikes the reader, the viewer, is that the narrator wishes to feel and wishes the reader to feel the intimate intent of this action. We cannot hear the gradually increasing hum of the approaching train, nor can we know for certain, unless we are told, that the train will come from ahead

Copyright © 1996 W. G. Sebald, reprinted with permission of the Wylie Agency, Inc.

or behind. We can glimpse only the slightest inkling of what madness or courage or fear or despair it might take to face its terrible approach, to feel the pressure of intention that holds one fast to the ground in the imminence of certain death. What sort of person might travel to S, "where the railway track curves out of a willow copse into the open fields" (27), in order to project imaginatively into Bereyter's terrible decision? This person is the narrator.

Bereyter's obituary, he tells us, makes "no mention of the fact that Paul Bereyter had died of his own free will, or through a self-destructive compulsion" (27), but more problematic is the additional comment "almost by way of an aside" (27), "that during the Third Reich Paul Bereyter had been prevented from practicing his chosen profession" (27). This nags at the narrator, who goes back to S "to get beyond [his] own very fond memories of him" to discover the story "he did not know" (28). He discovers that in Bereyter's retirement, in spite of his excellent reputation as an imaginative and dedicated teacher, he has come to be regarded as "eccentric," and someone who, always called "Paul," was somehow destined to meet the end that he did. The narrator-writer "pictured him," "stretched out on the track," having "taken off his spectacles and put them on the ballast stones by his side," everything "a blur before his short-sighted eyes" (29). Wary of "wrongful trespass" or presumptuous intrusion into Bereyter's life and death, the narrator moves into an account of his own knowledge of the man, from the outside rather than the inside, what he was trying to find in that first horrifying photograph, the sequences of deep psychological trauma.

The rest of the photographs are "external," as it were. The map of the schoolroom, possibly the narrator's (33); the casual school photograph of primary-age children (one of whom may or may not be the narrator), "taken out of the school building whenever the opportunity arose" (38) on, perhaps, one of the outings on a "particularly fine day" (39) for an "object lesson," happy and carefree (40). Further on in the story, Lucy Landau, "who had arranged for Paul to be buried in the churchyard" (42) at S, is visited by the narrator who discovers that she had been reading "Nabokov's autobiography on a park bench" (43) when she first met Bereyter in the summer of 1971, "far too late" (43), an ironic reference to the unnamed *Speak, Memory*, whose author we know from the previous story is one of the narrator's interests. She has in her possession photograph albums which "contained photographs documenting . . . almost the whole of Paul Bereyter's life, with notes penned in his own hand" (45). We see eight of these, selected by the narrator.

This is a playful teasing of the reader's expectation that the sequencing of the photographs in the text will follow a chronological order; in fact, the narrator's use of the first photograph begins at the end, which is to say that the narrative beginning is at an ending. As the reader reconsiders the alpine photographs of that happy summer which augured "the wonderful future" (48) with Helen Hollaender, Helen's intense gaze elsewhere in the larger photograph becomes suddenly freighted with uncanny meaning as though her dark Jewish features and the delicate summer dress make her seem suddenly like some exotic butterfly seen against the looming alpine peak, suggesting the doom of an inexorable fate. This is the narrator's construction of Paul's line to death. The diminished strip photographs are like the individual frames of a movie with jumpcuts, truncated, incomplete, the unfulfilled promise of a journey of companionable happiness. The railway line image at the beginning of the story is suddenly vivid in the reader's mind. The photograph which shows Paul as a house tutor to a family in Besançon is significant for the physical manifestation of his plunging "from happiness to misfortune," "so terribly thin that he seems almost to have reached a physical vanishing point" (49). This is the perspective of that first photograph; it utters the narrator's story about desire — for love, for death, for remembering, and for forgetting.

The images in the other two stories in *The Emigrants*, "Ambros Adelwarth" and "Max Ferber," catch at this marginality. The images rupture the verbal narrative with their annunciations of a prior and permanently withdrawn historical reality, foregrounding the constructedness of the verbal text crafted by a narrator whose own identity is withheld, partial, incomplete, and who does not "speak" in his own voice in the way that Nabokov does in *Speak, Memory*, for instance. The "temporal arrest" of the images, like the sudden instantiations triggered by memory or like the atemporal moments in which one reads or views a painting, are constructed simply by the narrator's selection and insertion of them into his text, the "writing . . . [of] which, as always, was going laboriously" (225).

The images require construction because it is the words, not the images, which are the primary aesthetic consideration in Sebald's texts. Any suggestion that the image-text relationship is the central feature of Sebald's aesthetic, as Long suggests, is to deprivilege the verbal text, the writing itself. The densely written prose text is far richer than any single photograph could ever be.

The narrator is no historian but rather an empathetic and compassionate bystander, someone whose own life trajectory has been intersected by those whose lives he sketches here, not from an external position of authority but as a person whose own humanity is implicated in the stories he presents in his own "laboriously" executed "writing," the discourse which constructs him as much as it constructs Selwyn, Bereyter, Adelwarth, and Ferber. In the writing of the stories of these others, he is also writing himself, in the sense that the narrator (and the author) *is* the style (Eco, 15). In "Ambros Adelwarth" the narrator is the great-nephew, the recipient of the small diary of 1913, handed to him, like the photographs, on a visit to the United States.

This section does not begin with a photograph. The space seems particularly blank in light of the earlier sections and the first sentence here: "I have barely any recollection of my own of Great-Uncle Adelwarth" (67). This blankness is a gloss on the images at the beginning of the first two sections, "Dr. Henry Selwyn" and "Paul Bereyter." It suggests, perhaps mischievously, that the images represent "authentic" recollections, memories. Certainly a great many of the photographs in this section are of places, postcards that travelers might have bought. There is one, however, in this section of particular interest here, on page 89.

Taken on "the edge of the darkness" (88), the narrator's text tells us it is of him, taken by Uncle Kasimir (89). Firstly, for the disobedient reader alert to ambiguity, the phrase "the edge of darkness" is rich with poetic reverberation. In Uncle Kasimir's sentence, recorded by the narrator's memory, it is a reference to the Atlantic Ocean (86), the spit of land running out from Barnegat Bay and Pelican Island (87) and the coastline of New Jersey. This is the place where he "often" comes: "it makes me feel that I am a long way away, though I never quite know from where" (89). This sense of nowhere is caught in the featureless photograph, taken at "the edge of the darkness" at the end of the afternoon just before nightfall, which could be on any shore at the edge of any ocean. This indeterminacy is reinforced by the narrator — it is he, much more youthful, darker of hair, than the ageing portrait of the author on the back cover — being barely discernible in the fading light. What does the reader make of this, except that this is a story in which the narrator is pursuing part of his own family's vanishing past, not just Adelwarth but Kasimir, his uncle's gold pocket watch arriving, "two years later" (89) with the photograph taken "at the edge of the darkness" (88), the narrator surviving again? It is a strangely intimate moment.

The final image in the text, in the "Max Ferber" section of *The Emigrants*, is actually withheld but described in detail, an ekphrasis: the three young Jewish women behind the loom in the Litzmannstadt ghetto morphed by the narrator into the fates, "Nona, Decuma, and Morta" with their "spindle, scissors and thread" (237). The person they are staring at is the narrator as viewer of the photograph, then by association the reader. The uncanniness derives from the narrator's sense of his own destiny, the length of his own life reflected back at him by the eyes of three dead Jewish women in a photograph pinned up on a stage flat "which did not exist" (235). It is the narrator's memory of seeing this photograph in a Frankfurt exhibition the year before, as he "sits in the Midland's turret room above the abyss on the fifth floor" (235), which causes the photograph itself to disappear, much as photographs and verbal images do in the reader's memory after she has moved on in the text, only the lingering sense of our own implication in these stories remaining.

The Rings of Saturn: No Clear Picture

In this book the narrator has transposed the images in his head, via the medium of the photographs, onto the page, precisely what he has done in the verbal text. These seventy photographs are offered for interpretation even more audaciously than the ones in *The Emigrants*.

The first photograph here, with its apparently documentary confirmation of the verbal description of the view from the hospital window, strikes the disobedient reader as slightly absurd. By the time the reader sees it on the second page, she has already determined that the curiously valetudinarian and unknown narrator is having some difficulty locating a fixed point of reference in the present, whether that present was in the past now being recalled, or in the narrative present tense of the writing itself.

As well as this temporal disorientation, the spatial collapse in the narrator's memory of the "Suffolk expanses" to "a single, blind, insensate spot" (4) segues into a view of the world as "the colourless patch of sky framed in the window" (4) — the view from a hospital bed. With the use of this image, the narrator positions the reader where he was a year after he embarked on his journey "to walk the county of Suffolk" (3), looking at the same view from the same angle. The perspectives of narrator and reader are brought into alignment but in a curiously playful way in which Sebald foregrounds, ironically with the slightly absurd image, the very fact that he is doing so.

We can view the photograph referentially, as the mimetic counterpart of what the verbal text tells us we see: a rectangle of sky seen through a window "draped with black netting" (4). The framed image of the cosmos seen through a net or, reversing the perspective, the ephemeral patient netted by some cosmic hunter suggests more interesting possibilities in the light of the verbal text. The narrator is imprisoned on the eighth floor, but he may as well be on any other as far as this view is concerned. He is immobile (although we are never told why) and likens himself to Kafka's Gregor Samsa, his body transformed into some foreign and disgusting state. This is possibly why he wonders what is real from his perspective of imprisonment in Browne's "Hospitalle."

> Several times during the day I felt a desire to assure myself of a reality I feared had vanished forever by looking out of that hospital window, which, for some strange reason, was draped. . . . (4)

Sebald sets this scene at dusk, and in this uncertain time of neither day nor night, he moves his first-person diegetic narrator with great difficulty out of bed, suffering a state of "almost total immobility" so that he can stand "In the tortured position of a creature that has raised itself erect for the first time" in order to peer out of the window. It is a faintly comic image at which the disobedient reader might feel tempted to laugh, even though the earnest and self-preoccupied tone of the narrator invites a different obedience.

Here right at the beginning of *The Rings of Saturn* the reader is free to be disobedient. With no really stable ground in the text, she must negotiate her own way through the mental landscape of someone else's subjectivity without the comforting veil of a constructed illusion. All she can do is pay closer heed than usual to the constructedness of the text in order to frame the images with context, seeing the netting of these other moments of consciousness as some kind of memorializing activity to which she is privy and in which the discourse itself makes her believe, as the considered observations of another subject. It may well be that Sebald's artfulness contrives in this way to restore the unusual power of language and of imagination in a culture dominated by the visual and the material. However contingent, the photograph is always an intrusion here and demands our attention to its intrusiveness. It demands to be read, to be constructed, especially in its being contextualized by its position in a constructed literary fiction. That it resists being read immediately as a two-dimensional representation or offers several readings makes it part of the reading problematic of the verbal text.

Like that grain of sand in Emma Bovary's skirt (8), which the narrator recalls his deceased colleague Janine Dakyns discussing as an instance of Flaubert's "fear of the false" (7), a metaphor for his belief in the spread of stupidity against which his scrupulous writing practice was the antidote, the photograph transgresses what we expect of a fictional construct, insinuating its reality, and possibly its invitation to stupidity, into an imagined or reimagined space that is being constructed by someone's "scrupulous writing practice" — the narrator's, and therefore the author's too. As we accompany the narrator on his journey into the mental landscape of his own remembered consciousness, an informed reader might recognize that the photograph has been discursively constructed by the narrator, the author's other, before being inserted into the text. It is no mere index of reality, no icon of anything firmer than a state of mind, and no symbol of an easily read kind. The photographic images in *The Rings of Saturn* are other, uncanny, open, associative, discontinuous, as is a great deal of the prose, even though it presents, at first glance, innocuously enough.

The next image is more directly unsettling. A skull is propped on top of three books, at least two of them copies of Browne's *Religio Medici*, the third teasingly unreadable. The immediate suggestion is that Browne (if this is indeed his skull) is very dead indeed but that the books he wrote, should we open and read them to make them live, as Borges suggests (2000), continue to keep his voice and mind alive, far more interesting "relics" that speak his presence in the world, much more than the empty smiling skull which produced them. The ghost of Hamlet's graveyard meditation is here. The disobedient reader may even call to mind, networking the crosslinking of Sebald's archival redemption of the literary

archive, Proust's symbol of resurrection. This is the image of Bergotte's "books arranged by threes in lighted windows keeping watch all through the dark night like angels with outspread wings over him who is no more" (my translation — *A la recherche du temps perdu*, Vol. III, 188), the writer's own desire to create beauty likened to the pursuit of a yellow butterfly that is "this little patch of yellow wall" in the *View of Delft*. This induces dizziness in Bergotte as he gazes at Vermeer's "exquisite texture," reproaching himself for failing to have "made my prose precious in itself" (my translation; 187), and then dying, as Proust was to do within days of his last outing, as recounted by his housekeeper Celeste Albaret, to see the Vermeer for the final time.

The narrator has, with the help of his language-sensitive colleague Dakyns, before her untimely death, undertaken some quixotic research in response to his discovery that the 1911 India-paper edition of the *Encyclopedia Britannica* (the last English edition) claimed that Sir Thomas "Browne's skull was kept in the museum of the Norfolk and Norwich Hospital" (9). Just why the narrator should be pursuing this research seems to have some relationship with his stay at the hospital where Browne's skull was purported to be, but this is never made clear. The "subsequent odyssey" of Browne's skull is itself, unlike the narrator's economically articulated grief at the unexpected deaths of his two colleagues, a matter of great ironic amusement. "Gnawed out of [his] grave" in a "tragical abomination" (11), Browne's skull was exhumed in 1840 from the church of St Peter Mancroft in central Norwich, passing to a "Dr. Lubbock" (10), a playful Sebaldian allusion to the Norfolk family from whom Percy Lubbock, author of *The Craft of Fiction*, was descended, who "left the relics in his will to the hospital museum" (10). The juxtaposition of Browne's own words, "who is to know the fate of his bones, or how often he is to be buried" and the facts of his birth with the material relic (body) and the books (mind) with a photograph that does not, cannot contain Browne's skull is an elaborate joke, tenor *noir*.

This brief scholarly research of the narrator, determining that Browne's skull is indeed in the coffin in the chancel of St Peter Mancroft, is a playfully updated summary pastiche of *Urne Burialle*, "part-archaeological, part-metaphysical" treatise (11). The "odyssey" of Browne's skull is a pastiche of Sebald's memorializing text, itself an odyssey of subjective mind and memory. These meditations, cultural, literary, archaeological, and metaphysical, of which *The Rings of Saturn* are comprised reflect, as the "Contents" pages suggest, Browne's own literary enterprise. In the discourse of destruction and preservation governed by an aleatory principle as much as by human determination, these particle fragments (a skull preserved from a life finished, a literary text preserved from a subjective consciousness disappeared) are suspended in the textual orbit that is *The Rings of Saturn* as fragments which cannot be restored but whose further destruction is prevented within this preserving textual economy. The subjective consciousness of the narrator, embodied in the language construct that is the text's discourse, becomes, as we read it, the relic of an absent materiality but also endures as a metaphysical presence.

The photograph on page 11 is a metafictional matrix for the disobedient reader's response. It evokes the need for a reader to bring life to the texts in which the voice of the living author has been "buried," and in which he continues to "live."

The passage from Browne and Norwich to Rembrandt and Amsterdam is effected by the narrator's discovery that Browne was in Holland when the public dissection of the corpse recorded in Rembrandt's painting, *The Anatomy Lesson*, took place at the Waaggebouw. Sebald's double-page photographic reproduction of the painting in black and white is arresting, literally, as the reader is invited to stop reading and scrutinize the image. We are prepared for this by the narrator's contextualizing of the painting not as a masterpiece which we might recognize and pass on from, but as something that continues the silk thread of association the discourse is winding from the narrator's hospitalization to Browne to Rembrandt invoking the mind-body question — the relationship between material entropy and the metaphysical nature of mind or consciousness. The narrator constructs an antithesis between the self-aggrandizing nature of the picture's commissioning by the Guild of Surgeons (and the advance of scientific knowledge) and the Foucault-inflected barbarism of "harrowing the flesh of the delinquent even beyond death" (12).

In effect, the narrator's analysis of the painting subverts its self-importance by suggesting that the anatomical error (the tendons belonging to the right hand transposed onto the dissected left hand) reveals the artist's compassion for Adriaan Adriaanszoon, a petty thief who has become "a spectacle, presented for a paying public drawn from the upper classes" (12). The strong sense of natural and social justice here critiquing social institutions in the "history of subjection" (13) is sufficiently powerful to affect the viewer's sight of the painting when the page is turned, so that the narrator's analysis of the painting in the Mauritshuis preempts the reader's response in one sense and yet licenses the reader's contemplation of the "verisimilitude" of the painting as being "more apparent than real" (16), another self-reflexive observation perhaps about the artist's (and writer's) shaping of the real to suit his aesthetic purpose.

This is a critical moment in the first section of *The Rings of Saturn*. Sebald is providing the reader with the dualist key to his own writing. "On closer examination," Sebald's apparently real textual fragment, Rembrandt's painting and his own text with its cargo of documentary reportage drawn from the scholarly world of civilization, arts, and letters, is "more apparent than real" (16), mediated by a narrative figure who is a constructed "I" just as the inserted images are brought to bear by that enigmatic literary *persona*. By attending closely to the painting the reader can see what the narrator has taught him to see: the absurd comedy of the pretensions of Dr. Tulp's hat; the ironic contrast between the rich but frail and temporary finery of the surgeons which distinguish them (but for how long?) from the naked and eternal mortality of the not-yet decomposing corpse before them; the deliberate anatomical error in the composition and the inaccurate sequence of dissection; the rationalist reductivism of the world to material terms and the invocation of Descartes ("also, so it is said, present that January morning," 13) as a kind of nemesis: the spirit of "Cartesian rigidity" (17). By attending closely to the writing the actively engaged reader can "hear" what the narrator says: in that revisiting we make to the Waaggebouw of January 1632, via the Mauritshuis (built out of the proceeds of colonial exploitation in South America) and the Sebaldian text, we see and hear the continuing and appalling story of man's inhumanity to man, however it is dressed or presented, however it is rationalized or palliated. If Sebald's narrator suffers from "the paralysing horror" induced by his confrontation with the "traces of destruction" (3) everywhere around him, then in the midst of our bemused and amused confrontation with his hypersensitive eccentricity, we as readers are engaged by something more substantial than Wittgensteinian language games, which includes his use of photographic images in presenting as real that which is only apparent. That is the ludic nature of fiction, after all. Sebald's language games are ironic and often wryly amusing but he is nonetheless playing them for real.

The "white mist that rises from within a body opened presently after death," which Browne asserted "during our lifetime . . . clouds our brain when asleep and dreaming" (17), becomes the vaporous substance seen through the hospital window, the "great fog that shrouded large parts of England and Holland on 27th November 1674" (17), the mist in Venice in *Vertigo*. Mist, like greyness, is a principal leitmotif in Sebald, as something that obscures our vision and our understanding, just as the sight through the hospital window of the sky is echoed here as a description of the sensation that the anaesthetized narrator has been floating amidst "billowing masses" of "mountainous clouds" and gazing out "at the indigo vastness and down into the depths . . . a black and impenetrable maze," and then "in the firmament above" at the "stars, tiny pinpoints of gold speckling the barren wastes" (17), free of pain.

The great richness of reading Sebald's lapidary prose includes observing these segues within sections of this text as well as across them. In the fifth section of *The Rings* the narrator falls asleep in front of a television documentary about Roger Casement, executed for treason in London in 1916. If we list the images, we see: a frontal headshot of Casement in adult life, one side too shadowed, one side overexposed, the whole effect rather grainy and indistinct, perhaps an image from the film taken "from rare archive footage" (103). The narrator's falling asleep, his "waking consciousness ebb[ing] away" (103), is reflected mimetically in the photograph's blurring. The connection in the verbal text is from Casement to Joseph Conrad, because the narrator recalls hearing, before falling asleep, that Conrad (a writer who wanted to make men "see") and Casement met in the Belgian Congo, where "Conrad considered Casement the only man of integrity among the Europeans whom he had encountered there" (104).

The narrator reveals that he has "since tried to reconstruct from the sources, as far as I have been able, the story I slept through that night in Southwold" (104). The following images reflect that research: a painting recording the eruption of Mount Pelée on St Pierre in the West Indies (110), not long after Conrad had visited in 1876; a "photograph" (which actually looks more like a damaged painting) of a ceremony in 1898 in which Franz Kafka's uncle Joseph Loewy was awarded "the Gold Medal of the Ordre du Lion Royal by King Leopold" to mark the completion of the Congo railway (122); a rather surreal pencil rendering of the "Lion Monument and the so-called historical memorial site of the Battle of Waterloo" (123); a highly stylized cartoon scene from the Battle of Waterloo which echoes the verbal text's description: "the fighting will have surged to and fro in waves for a long time" (125) and "No clear picture emerged" (126); a photograph of Casement (we can recognize him thanks to the first one in this section) followed by a policeman (130); two pages of a diary showing the dates 29 March 29 to 1 April 1903 covered with manuscript notes (132–33); Roger Casement's signature dated 14 April 1916 (134).

The effect of the images in this section is to harness the "magic of the real" (Sontag 1979, 69), the paintings documenting events as much as the photographs of a man's handwriting — his authentic trace, to the service of art in exposing, as Conrad did, the complicity and duplicity of those in power. Sebald's narrator's precise indexing of dates and places may be historically sound, but it is the affective power of the prose's decorously restrained irony and the pompous absurdity of the Belgian *imperium* in the images, together with the dignity and humanity of Casement in the photographs of the man and his manuscripts that make the appalling immorality of power so clear and the nobility and integrity of the socially marginalized so vulnerable.

In the final section of *The Rings* Sebald's narrator draws a comparison between the "weavers" of silk and "scholars and writers," all condemned both to a predisposition to melancholy "and all the evils associated with it" (283), and to the eyestrain which comes from keeping "their eye on the complex patterns they created" (283). The creation of beauty and color, the complex patterns of association as the threads are woven into fabric, is the leitmotif for Sebald's own writing, the image of the man bent over the "instrument[s] of torture" on page 282 a self-reflexive ironical observation of the writer at his desk.

Austerlitz: Study the Black-and-White Photographs

> . . . each time the narrator stops "representing" and reports details which he knows perfectly well but which are unknown to the reader, there occurs, by signifying failure, a sign of reading, for there would be no sense in the narrator giving himself a piece of information.
> — Roland Barthes, *Image–Music–Text*

In Sebald's last work, *Austerlitz*, there are eighty-seven images, of which six are double-paged. Often the photographs are separated by many pages of uninterrupted prose, and then clustered in a tighter constellation than in the other texts. In this fiction, unlike the earlier work, the presence of photographs is explained by narrative circumstances. According to the narrator the photographs were selected from the "many hundreds of pictures, most of them unsorted, that he [Austerlitz] entrusted to me" (7). Understandably, then, the photographs never show Austerlitz synchronously with the narrator. We see a knapsack, and we see what Austerlitz has seen, but we do not see him as we saw the youthful Bereyter or the soldier Bereyter or the postcombat Bereyter. Just as we saw the older Bereyter only through the literalism and the metaphor of the railway track, so we see Austerlitz only through the traces which speak his presence.

The selection of photographs is part of the narrator's self-assumed moral burden, to tell Austerlitz's story faithfully, to preserve his memory, and his memories, in a material object. Ironically, this is of course not true. Jacques Austerlitz is a phantom; Susie Bechhofer is one of the "two or three" real persons behind Austerlitz (Jaggi 2001a), whose life Sebald heard described on the radio when he was in a shop. The text is a work of fiction which looks "awry" (Kermode 2000) at what cannot, like the Medusa, be looked at directly. Sebald himself voiced this as a kind of moral decorum by saying that the story of the horror and trauma of human lives which endured and suffered in the twentieth-century could not be told except obliquely, indirectly (Jaggi 2001a). Photographs invite direct viewing; Sebald manipulates this quality by making their status uncertain, and by investing some mysterious or enigmatic quality in them which makes them appear less stable, subverting their status as documents even though they appear to be used as evidence of the life of Jacques Austerlitz. The living presence they utter is of course the narrator's.

The way the photographs are inserted into the texts reinforces their episodic quality, which parallels the longer but equally episodic reporting of the encounters between the narrator and Austerlitz. In *Austerlitz* it is the photographs that seem to order or demarcate it in some way, more than the three asterisks, by arresting it at moments for the reader's contemplative scrutiny. The photographs, in their sheer volume of "hundreds," seem to have contributed to their owner's "paralysis," preventing him from writing the narrative which he can only tell in conversation. If these photographs are, in Barthes's organic sense, narrative seeds rather than mere traces, "*memento mori*" in Sontag's elegiac historicist formulation (1979, 15), then it might be possible to argue that Sebald's narratives reconfigure the past so that it is intincted not only by the melancholy note of elegy or even despair that reviewers have identified again and again but by some sense of the rich possibility of renewal, what Gilles Deleuze in *Essays Critical and Clinical* identifies as the creative impulse.

As we try to read the resolutely silent photographs in isolation, we are partially trapped in a labyrinth of mystery that Sebald has constructed. We can never enter into the experience that the photographs represent, nor share the impulse of the recorder. For that matter we are outside the experience of the one who has selected and inserted the photographs into a verbal text which reconstructs someone else's story. We are momentarily imprisoned, in each encounter with an image, because the photographs reflect our otherness as readers in a darkly unrevealing way, as the verbal text does not to the same degree. Much like the dark mirrors which

Austerlitz photographs in the *salle des pas perdus* at the Antwerp Centraal Station, the pictures cannot reflect us in their infinite regression, and we, perhaps like the mysterious narrator of *Austerlitz*, lose ourselves in the dark collapsed star of someone else's irretrievable past.

Like a mirror, the photographs are seductive; they draw the reader's eye. If they are absent, they imply a narrative of desire. As readers, we come to hunger after the deferred image, however absorbing or attractive the verbal text. As we read, we are also aware of this invitation to disobedience, this distraction from the business of decoding the verbal text, seduced by what seems to be the less onerous task of reading the images. The narrator's task is to create the links or associative threads which sequence and order, and thereby give meaning to, these remnants of Austerlitz's life. He is helped to do so by his "notes" (10) which record the encounters he has had in nearly three decades with the architectural historian, and the seemingly *verbatim* recording of Austerlitz's autonarrative soliloquizing.

As a reader who has taken on the task of literary criticism, I too must select from the photographs and write my own encounters with Austerlitz. Boldly, and with a heavy sense of loss incurred by the need to exclude so much, I will limit my discussion to the six moments when Sebald uses an image across two pages of text, banishing the written word temporarily altogether, because this practice calls particular attention to the image. The first time shows an engraving of a scene taken from a Biblical illustration of the people of Israel crossing the wilderness, camped in the desert of Sinai, in Austerlitz's Welsh children's Bible (78–79) given to him by "Miss Parry" (76). Austerlitz identifies with the people in this image, the Jewry from which he was descended, by finding in the depiction of the Sinai desert a replicated image of the treeless part of Snowdonia at Bala where he grew up after adoption by the Calvinist preacher and his wife. The "uncannily familiar" landscape in the engraving, "the children of Israel's camp in the wilderness" (80), offered more sense of home to Austerlitz than the increasing strangeness of his life at Bala. By prioritizing the image here the narrator is signaling a decisive moment in Austerlitz's story, a moment of recognition caused by the curious coincidence of the contours of a landscape reduced by a black-and-white, or grey, etching to a spectral form which obliterates the difference between the topography of North Wales and the lake at Bala and the Sinai desert. Well before he was made aware of the truth of his background in the final year of his schooling, this image in the Bible spoke truthfully to Austerlitz, or Dafydd Elias as he was, in a mysterious way about his birth and his flight into exile that the narrator signals rhetorically in his own text. The Biblical text in Welsh, which the narrator quotes Austerlitz quoting here — "*yn yr hesg ar fin yr afon*" — alienates the reader, who may well know the story, as the image does not, looking indeed very much like the mountains of Snowdonia near Bala, for after all it is a Welsh

children's Bible, as much as the Sinai desert, therefore a far less astonishing suggestion than the Hebrew text containing the story of Moses being appropriated by its startlingly foreign translation into the marginal, very alien language of Welsh. Coincidence and startling juxtaposition, like the double-page photographs, are designed to keep the reader agilely disobedient, tracking the associations and layering that are woven into the text. For Dafydd Elias/Jacques Austerlitz the Welsh appropriation of the Biblical scene speaks weirdly in both oracular and historical fashion the story of his own flight into the wilderness, out of European culture which is his home into the barren wilderness, the strange otherness and exile, of the Calvinist household in Bala. The image here speaks powerfully but only if the reader voices it with disobedient trajectories of thought and imagination, using the language context in which it is embedded.

The second full-page "reading arrest," or annunciative rupture, is of a group of people in formal dress (120–21). Careful scrutiny reveals that the face on the male figure in the left of the photograph has been removed and replaced. The hairlines are different: a penumbra of blonde or white curls appears above the face of a man with short dark hair. Whose is this face, which appears as some silent tribute, perhaps, like those to Wittgenstein and Tripp — whose photographs appear in *Austerlitz* (3). The figure has a grey parrot on his shoulder, a bird that calls language to mind, whether it is an African parrot (known to possess a vocabulary of nine hundred words and the ability to form sentences) or not, as the text some pages earlier suggests (117), and a bird which evokes the metaphor of imitation, perhaps an acknowledgement of the debt Sebald owes to a writer, or a sly criticism of someone who "parrots" the words of others? Within the photograph the expressions on the faces of the other figures register bewilderment, dismay, suspicion, wariness, criticism, most of it directed toward the dashing and cavalier figure with the parrot on his shoulder. Is this Jacquot, the parrot retrieved from his sarcophagus by Gerald, having lived for sixty years in his Welsh exile from his native Africa, his plumage "ash-grey" and "a pale face that you might have thought was marked by deep grief" (118)? It is a private joke, a witty invitation to seek the identity of the figure, surrounded as he is by *bürgerlich* dismay. It is tempting to suggest it is Thomas Bernhard. It is a subversive and wry self-reflexive comment on the business of, perhaps the obsession with, language caught with swift irony by a manipulated photographic image. It is also a metaphor for the exiled European child also living, at least at this stage, as an unwitting exile in Wales, greyness being, as ever in Sebald's fiction, the stealthy ubiquitous metaphor for haunting grief and life-leaching despair.

This image is juxtaposed with the narrator's reporting of Austerlitz's account of life at Andromeda Lodge ("a kind of natural-history museum" 119)

near the Welsh coast at Barmouth, the curious home of his schoolfriend and fellow isolate Gerald Fitzpatrick, his eccentric relatives and his very beautiful mother Adela. The wild garden planted with exotics and the colony of white cockatoos, the descendants of the pairs brought decades earlier from "the Moluccas" (115), might or might not be the background of the double-page photograph. The immediate verbal context is the schismatic contrast between the two strands of adherence in the family: between Catholic faith ("the traditional Papist creed regarded in Wales as the worst of all perversions" 119), and natural science, as practiced by earlier Fitzpatricks, friends of their frequent visitor Charles Darwin, who had lived in the nearby village of Dolgellau "working on his study of the Descent of Man" (119). The "crazier" (119) members of the Fitzpatrick family belong to "the Catholic line" (119), and by the time the reader turns the page to the photograph, the task of construction becomes more complex. The "case of Uncle Evelyn" (122), whose younger self, the obedient reader might assume, appears in the photograph, refers to a deeply eccentric man who donates to the Mission to the Congo. Just who the individual in the photograph is is a question that the image begs, and which individuals are supposed to represent whom, the naturalists or the Papists? The picture, of course, does not tell.

The third image (150–51) is a close-up of billiard balls looking like a photograph of astral bodies. The preceding pages prepare us for this dualist reading. Iver Grove, the dilapidated eighteenth-century house in Oxfordshire ("built around 1780," 148) containing both a billiard room and an observatory, associates the stasis of the unused billiard table (since the death of the original owner and builder of the house in 1813) with the apparently eternal orbit of those astral bodies, one black and one white, therefore whimsically privileging the joke that these are billiard balls made to seem like a moon and a planet, or bodies representing, inversely, night and day. In fact the games that Ashman's ancestor used to play against himself "in this retreat" (149) all night long until dawn suggest a kind of hypnotic reversal of night and day, an insomniac's wakefulness born of a passion for selenography and hours spent in a "bunker" to which no light of day could ever penetrate: "It was as if time . . . had stood still here" (152). This is a kind of living death, reflected in the dilapidation of the great house and its desuetude. The disobedient reader extrapolates the solitude and obsessiveness of the Ashman ancestor, with his selenography and his eccentricity, finding a shadow of Austerlitz and the narrator in Austerlitz's account of this serendipitous encounter and its hold in his memory as a supraterrestrial, temporal and spatial void: ". . . it all arouses in me a sense of disjunction, of having no ground beneath my feet" (154–55).

More than a hundred pages separate this from the next double-page image, but this instance also varies the pattern. A kind of stuttering effect is created by the narrator employing firstly a near-double-page use of three images of doors and windows in dilapidated buildings in, the reader presumes, Terezin, the first two on the left separated by two lines of text: "obstructing access to a darkness never yet penetrated, in which I thought, said" (268). This has the effect of rhetorical emphasis, highlighting a fragment of the prose text which takes on the resonance of poetry, its fragmentedness, its rupture, its stuttering even, echoing those very qualities in the images themselves, whose repetition and hermetic obscurity, together with the dualism of access and egress denied, of imprisonment and permanent closure, savagely mock the architectural function of windows and doors in this terrible context of the gross deceit of the model camp for Jewry.

The bizarre details of the enigmatic numerical sequencing of the garbage collection bins, the strange apertures on either side of the temple-like entrance, and the effect of the grave vault in front of the door and window in the third, more open than either of them, are followed by the double page but single images of two interior photographs framed by the terrible blankness of the page's vertical margins, as though the sequencing of the pages has led the reader into the terrible darkness only to find, in an ironic representation of infinite regression, a nesting of doorways, the internal one set into a brick wall in a geometric pattern offset by the mocking brick arch, suggesting what? An oven vault? The arch in Raphael's *The School of Athens* foreshortened by closure, with no perspective afforded by a celestial view? The tantalizing effect of light radiating obliquely through the broken panels in the door? And then an even more appalling door kept closed with five horizontal bolts which look like nails, surely not the five wounds of Christ, and the small square panel revealing, is it, a glimpse of the sky, the cosmos? The next word which speaks after the silence created by these images, when the page is turned, is "Austerlitz" (272). The name has escaped, has survived.

Before the reader comes to these images, Austerlitz's description of Terezin, having reverted to "an ordinary town again" (266), is characterized by the appearance and sudden disappearance of a "bent" human figure. The "straight deserted streets" of Terezin that we see in photographs seem to parody Atget's views of Paris with a hyperreal absence. The appearance of a "mentally disturbed man" speaking in a kind of "broken German," the "strictly geometric grid" which is "extraordinarily oppressive," and the adjectives, which tumble one after the other: "forbidding," "silent," "blank" (266–67) are unnerving, even sinister. The reader is prepared for a place of absent presence, and the four pages of consecutive images represent a kind of cadenza in the text, a series of appalling chords, which mark the ambivalence of a fate avoided and the guilt of the survivor. The selecting and setting decisions of the narrator, that silent shaping presence, are uttered by the photographs themselves. The reader might recall Wittgenstein's "*Wovon man nicht sprechen kann, darüber muss man*

schweigen" (*Tractatus Logico-Philosophicus*) here, "What cannot be spoken
of must remain unuttered." *Unerzählt* (Unrecounted), indeed, except
that, as in the text of that name, the meticulous drawings of Tripp and the
delphic haiku-like poems of Sebald prompt the reader's response.

After these four pages, the text moves forward to an eerie image of
whitewash peeling and spiders spinning, scuttling, and hanging, a kind of

living *stasis* of dissolution and decay, made menacing by the use of the adverb "expectantly" in "hanging expectantly in their webs" (272). This gives way to a seamless linking with a recalled dream "on the verge of waking from sleep," when Austerlitz, "in a half-conscious state," "tried to hold fast to [his] powdery-grey dream image, which sometimes quivered in a slight breath of air, and to discover what it concealed, but [which] only dissolved all the more and was overlaid by the memory, surfacing in my mind at the same time, of the shining glass in the display windows of the ANTIKOS BAZAAR . . ." (272–73). Like Nabokov's memory of the little girl in the Parc Monceau which dissolves into the spiraling patterns in a glass marble, the looping spiral of the fence, and the shadows of the twirling movements of her hoop, this passage in Sebald dissolves into an ashen insubstantiality with vitreous barriers between the voice of Austerlitz and the absurd fragments of the past in the "four still lives obviously composed entirely at random" (274) in the windows of the emporium which he, Benjaminian *flâneur*, interrogates for meaning: "What was the meaning . . .?"; "what secret . . .?"; "what might be the significance . . .?" The only reply to these vain questions is his "own faint shadow image barely perceptible" among the surviving material relics of human lives now lost (275–77).

For the disobedient reader this barely perceptible shadow is echoed here both in the spectral presence of the narrator, shaping and crafting the textualization of what appears to be Austerlitz's voice telling his own story, "visible" as it were only in reflection, and the further shadowy reflection of Sebald, whose German story is told obliquely in his crafting of verbal images, his highly visual prose style, and his deployment of photographic images. The spiders' webs, layering grey upon grey in the interior of the barracks in Terezin, become also the intricately woven prose with its threading associations winding in and out of dream and memory, recollection and observation and empirical experience, a palpably imagined interior life and the dreamlike surreal and hyperreal quality of the uncanny external world. At moments like these in Sebald the spirit of Kafka is a brooding presence. These photographs are put into the service of that Kafkan imagination which sees the *quidditas* of the world as pathologically and sinisterly other.

The plan of Theresienstadt, although it is not clearly that, is spread across two pages after Austerlitz has described the winter he spent as a mental patient admitted to the hospital of St Clements adjacent to a cemetery, in London, after collapsing in Alderney Street in the final of a series of increasingly debilitating anxiety attacks. During the period of rehabilitation, when he worked as an assistant gardener at Romford, Austerlitz has begun to study a "tome" by H. G. Adler, on the "setting up, development and internal organization of the Theresienstadt ghetto" (327) published in Germany in 1955, in which the reader presumes the plan on the following pages appears. The image resembles the floorplan of the seventeenth-century fortifications at Saarlouis Vauban that the reader has seen earlier (18), a dodecagonal fortress. Michel Foucault, as author of *Discipline and Punish*, is the reference that the actively engaged and thoughtful reader senses here, in the segue from the madhouse to the fortification to the prison, all of which culminate in the layered, institutionalized horror of Theresienstadt and more ghastly others.

Closer scrutiny of the plan shows an extraordinary degree of order, including the numbering of different sections, and the labeling in German in which the Anglophone reader can make out words like Prague and Elbe and Nord as geographical indices, German words like "Krematorium," with its terrible clarity, and "Bezirk," meaning precinct or region, which carries a very different homophonic association, contextualized by Austerlitz's madness, the madness of the "Ordnung," and the deep absurdity of a fortress turned into a prison with all the ironic inversion of keeping out and keeping in. The narrator includes this image marked on the left by a stain, an indelible stain, and the barcode in the top right segment of the image is an instance of postmodern ironic hyperbole. This is a Ruskinian symbolic grotesque, a page in a book or a document barcoded for the purposes of some systematization of human misery, some cultural-historical flowering of institutionalized deceit, a fiction masquerading as the truth, concealing unutterable horror. In the heart of this slightly absurd and not so distinctive detail lies buried, somewhere, Hannah Arendt's banality of evil and its palliation in the whited sepulchre of bureaucracy and system.

For the disobedient reader of this image Austerlitz's revelation that his "poor German" had to contend with the absurdly compounded words which elevated the "pseudo-technical jargon governing everything in Theresienstadt" (330) into meaningful language, a task Austerlitz compares to "deciphering" Babylonian cuneiform or Egyptian hieroglyphic texts, is eased into the absurdity of trying to comprehend how "sixty thousand people" could be "crammed together in an area little more than a square kilometre in size" (331). That "extra-territorial place" (331), Theresienstadt, is linguistically an absurdly coded enigma, a city beyond time and place and language. An obedient reading construes the narrator's surprise at Austerlitz's competent German as he describes his battle with Adler's dense text, revealing that the narrator is a native German speaker. The disobedient reading constructs Austerlitz's bafflement at the "pseudo-technical jargon" (330) as a distancing effect, a German speaker who is defeated by the contortions his native tongue has been forced into by Herr Adler's account of the "crazed administrative zeal" (337) of the "masters of the ghetto" (336), as though language becomes a mocking parody of itself in its attempt to name the horror of Theresienstadt. The disobedient reading here confronts the unspeakable reality as a hyperreal fantasy, a terrible intersectedness where the deep skepticism of clear-sighted disobedience has some hope of distinguishing between fiction and nonfiction, fantasy, and truth.

The penultimate double-page image is curiously pixellated so that the left side is an unreadable distortion of what may or may not be a third human profile adjacent to the other two, which have not been manipulated to nearly the same extent (346–47). The manipulation of the image is unusual in that only part of it is seen in this extreme, unrecognisable digital close-up while the rest of the image can be read as two human males whose heads are seen in profile. The enigma is the identity of the third person, obliterated by too close a scrutiny. Preceding this image, the text dwells, in Austerlitz's voice, on a propaganda film that was made of Theresienstadt by the Reich in 1944, called "*Der Führer schenkt den Juden eine Stadt*" — "*The Führer presents the Jews with a city*" [my translation] (345), a film which Austerlitz discovers exists only in an unsorted series of fragments, much like his own photograph collection. This image seems to be a still from this film, a fragment of a fragment, and a distorted one at that. As Austerlitz describes the damaged film, on the following page, the reader has already absorbed the partial image, an irretrievably damaged fragment in which some individual has been dissolved.

This relic of a film catches, ironically, the damage, the destruction, the dissolution of lives that "the masters of the ghetto" (336) effected in Theresienstadt and that the film concealed with its confection of lies. The film, a document of propaganda and a witness to the extent of the deceit and the evil perpetrated by the Reich, has become, thanks to the attrition of time and its archiving as history, an authentic material fragment of the past in the 14-minute cassette stored in Berlin in the Federal Archives, ironically procured for Austerlitz by the Imperial War Museum in England, an actual document, in its foreshortened, irretrievably damaged, fragmented state, of the truth of Theresienstadt. It is a supremely ironic moment in the disobedient reading of this image.

The final double-page image is full of silence. It shows a room stacked high with shelving in which folders or dossiers are filed, and offers empty tables and chairs at which one might sit to read, an open doorway for easy entrance and exit. Just before this final "diptych," Austerlitz has been reading Balzac in French for the first time in the Bibliothèque Nationale, a break from researching in Paris for clues about his father's disappearance during the war "more than fifty years ago" (393), last sighted at a railway station, metonymically the Gare d'Austerlitz. Quoting by memory from the story (identified in Sebald's usual tantalizing invitation to further independent research only as the story of Colonel Chabert, "risen from the dead" (394) after being struck on the head in the Napoleonic battle of Eylau and returning "Years later" (394) to claim, like Odysseus, his estates, his wife, and his name) to the narrator, Austerlitz's untranslated French describes the horror of Chabert's possibly imagined experience, possibly real memory of hearing the dead groaning and sighing around him. Austerlitz dwells on this passage in his conversation with the narrator, confessing that he had always suspected that "the border between life and death is less impermeable than we commonly think" (395). For the disobedient reader, geared to the metaphoric power of fictional discourse, this speaks also of the narrator's literary resurrection of Austerlitz's presence in the text, and of the author's hauntedness.

Austerlitz describes the extraordinary coincidence of opening the pages of an American architectural journal and discovering the photograph (which appears on the following pages, 396–97) of the Records Room at Terezin, his "true place of work" (395). This place, where the "files on the prisoners" (395) were kept, suddenly becomes as we turn the page, a mausoleum of textualized lives, a historical archive to the Bibliothèque Nationale's repository of fiction where Austerlitz has been searching fruitlessly for traces of his father's fate. On the wall the clock in the photograph, a virtual clock recording a time long past in more than one sense, records the exact time that Austerlitz sees the photograph in Paris. The coincidence, another Sebaldian characteristic, speaks not only to Austerlitz, for whom it is an index of being in the wrong place. It invests the photograph with Furst's sense of Sebald's "disconcerting contingency," and destabilizes the photograph's temporal arrest by converting, for Austerlitz, what Walter Benjamin called *Erfarhrung* (language/duration/interpretation and association) into *Erlebnis* (photograph/trauma/instantaneous) (Scott 1999, 283). For the disobedient reader, who reads Austerlitz's conversation and the coincidence of the clock's time as evidence of the narrator's constructing presence in the text, the open door signals, ironically, after all the closed doors and impenetrable spaces we saw earlier at Terezin in other photographs, that the neat ordering of the documented lives, all that is left of the human, in this sterile bureaucratic space which is both museal and mausoleal, is as inaccessible, as impenetrable, and as mysterious as the undocumented life of the father that Austerlitz has been seeking. The narrator's (and Sebald's) savage indictment of the new Bibliothèque in the rue de Richelieu (another doubly witty ironical coincidence, like the rue Danielle-Casanova in *Vertigo* if we translate the French into English) on the following page ("its near-ludicrous internal regulation seeks to exclude the reader as a potential enemy," 398) suggests that reading, absurdly obstructed in the great French library, is "the living connection to the past" (398) and the enacting of remembrance, as memory is the key to the activity of writing: "Without memories there wouldn't be any writing" (Jaggi 2001b). Reading and writing are the bedrock of civilization and our common culture, in Raymond Williams's and Ernest Gellner's senses of the term, or even our being many in one body. For most of us, Nicola King observes, visual memory and imagining memory can only be represented in language (25–26). No matter how seductive these photographic images might be, the images require captions, even of the text-length kind, if we are, as Robert Lowell suggested in "Epilogue," not only "to give each figure in the photograph his living name" but to "*caress the light* . . . say what happened" (1978).

Stage 3: Spatial Trajectories — Catching Trains of Thought to Textual Spaces

> In modern Athens, the vehicles of mass transportation are called *metaphorai*. To go to work or come home, one takes "a metaphor" — a bus or a train. Stories could also take this noble name: every day they traverse and organise places; they select and link them together; they make sentences and itineraries out of them. They are spatial trajectories.
> — Michel De Certeau, *The Practice of Everyday Life*

> But travel does not merely broaden the mind. It makes the mind.
> — Bruce Chatwin, *Anatomy of Restlessness*

> Places seem to me to have some kind of memory.
> — Sebald to Jaggi, *The Guardian*, 22 September 2001

Sebald's prose is a form of fiction which, appropriating more explicitly than usual the protocols of nonfictional writing, elicits through its own subversive practice a disobedient reader. This is a reader who is skeptical about the text, engaged with it in an interrogatory, contestatory way as a collaborative author of the textual imaginary rather than the obedient or passive recipient of its authority, a reader encouraged to step backwards and forwards across the effaced or elided textual boundary from the text to her own domain.

In this final part I argue that the representation of place in Sebald's writing, in which the narrator's subject remembers, contemplates and imagines, becomes a textual space created by "his" prose. In this space the reader, destabilized by her awareness of slippage, the segue between represented place and poetic space, and by the traveling displacement of the journeys in space and time that the narrator and she are engaged in, becomes disobedient in her desire to take her own bearings, extratextually and intratextually, stepping away from the narrator's side for her own imaginative and contemplative purposes.

Because the writerly narrator is a traveler, each text presents a series of places which appear and then disappear from view, recalled intensely for a short time before dissolving into indeterminacy again. This process is memory's recollection. Tindall quotes Nabokov saying in a late-life interview, "My Russia is very small. A road here, a few trees there, a sky" (1991, 199). Remembered place is imagined in this intensity of selected detail in

Sebald too. As they come into narrative view, in Sebald's narrator's fictional, "self-appointed" task of telling, places are imbued with a mythic quality by the narrator's subject, his mind, memory, and imagination. The narratives embedded in places recollected by the narrator translate those places into poetic space, that site of dialogical engagement with the reader.

The narrator's adventures are always retrospective, so that place is temporalized in "his" text. Like Barthes's Greeks and Benjamin's Angel of History, he faces the future by turning his back on it, gazing at the increasingly long perspectives of the past which recede before him, as though he were sitting in a railway carriage with his back to an unrelenting engine. He makes thereby the future unpresentable, something Lyotard observed as marking the difference between modernity and postmodernity, which Peter Conrad's sense of the contemporary *Zeitgeist* construes as our obsession with the past. If Conrad's estimate that, "Despite its anticipation of the future, ours has been a retrospective century, telling all the past's stories over again" is even partly right (Conrad 1999, 711), the twentieth century's preoccupation with the past and with the aesthetic appropriation of remembered fragments of it is voiced in Sebald's traveling writerly narrator's discourse which temporalizes place.

Because he "constructs poetry out of the remnants found in ruins," Conrad's formulation of twentieth-century literary practice (1999, 716), in the places where memory's fragments are haunting presences, the adventure of Sebald's retrospective digressiveness explores the potentiality of fiction that Calvino outlined in his unfinished and unpresented Norton lectures: "a multiplying of time, a perpetual evasion or flight . . . From death" (Calvino 1992, 46). Poetic space offers "perpetual evasion" (46) in an antithesis to the implication in place of the subject's inevitable absence, his death, at the end of a pilgrimage-journey during which he sees, always, his own psychic reflection, that consoling confirmation of his own presence but also the imminence of its antithesis, his absence. This is the point where all Sebald's fictions conclude, with images of destruction that denote the end which, in Calvino's words, "flattens and empties out" the "dispersed" terrestrial globe (67). Sebald's narrator composes his texts on the very sites of the ruined past. This is the primary irony of his textual enterprise.

In his introduction to *Place and Experience* (1999), Jeff Malpas discusses the idea that "human identity is somehow tied to location . . . an idea that has both a long ancestry over the centuries and a wide currency across cultures" (2). The central thesis of his argument about the idea of place is that "there is no possibility of understanding human experience — especially human thought and experience — other than through an understanding of place and locality" (15). Malpas defines place as "that within and with respect to which subjectivity is itself established — place is not founded *on* subjectivity, but is rather that *on which* subjectivity is founded"

(35). In a subsequent chapter he observes that "The idea of subjective space is tied to the idea of an experiencing creature around which such a space is organised" (72). This part argues that Sebald's disconcerting construction of place, "on which [the narrator's] subjectivity is founded," calls the disobedient reader into existence. It is the disobedient reader who makes the connection between the self-aware subject (that writerly narrator), his representation of place, and the "translation" of that generative conjunction into poetic space, the site of her engagement with the text.

In Sebald the narrator is a traveler because he is never "at home" in the places represented. Places come into focus briefly, are displaced and vanish as the traveler moves on. This is disorienting for the reader. If the idea of space is that which is tied "to an experiencing creature" (Malpas 1999, 72), then the conjunction of the subject of the text-producing narrator and reader in that space, discursively organized around them, is one of the ways in which Sebald's fiction produces a disobedient reader who arrests the displacement of travel with her own contemplation and imagination. She must assert herself as "an experiencing creature" in the poetic space. This is her resistance, her disobedience in defiance of her own displacement, her own death.

That reader, confronted again and again with the narrator's stories and images of entropy, loss, and death, desires, at least in part, escape from this traveler's ruminative melancholy, like Jacques's, as Calvino observed, in *As You Like It* (4.1.15–18), "inextricably intermingled" with "humor" (1992, 19): "the sundry contemplation of my travels, which, by often rumination, wraps me in a most humorous sadness" (19–20). The disobedient reader on occasion turns the seriousness of the narrator's text into play, the Menippean carnivalesque (Bakhtin 1986, 106–11). The freedom to enact this transformation is particularly important in fictions where the pull toward melancholy is so strong.

Melancholy is inextricable from transience in Sebald's fiction, and place is the *locus* of that transience. Place gives shape to memories of the past, those ghostly traces which "haunt" the present. These ideas are not new, of course, and Philip Sheldrake seems deliberately to recall T. S. Eliot's famous metaphors when he writes in *Spaces for the Sacred* (2001) that "the present intellectual experience of place has been characterized as a movement through a wasteland among the ruins of former theories of meaning" (2). Sheldrake calls on de Certeau's suggestion in *The Mystic Fable* that "we are on a kind of perpetual pilgrimage that somehow parallels the mystical tradition. We experience dissatisfaction with final definitions or completed places and are driven ever onwards in a movement of perpetual departure" (3). The reference here evokes Bruce Chatwin, whose writing about our essential restlessness was so valued by Sebald. This characterizes the Sebaldian narrator's restlessness, in the grey and grief-stricken English pilgrimage of *The Rings of Saturn*, in Jacques Austerlitz's uncompleted journey in *Austerlitz*, in the arrested lives of the victims of despair in *The Emigrants*, and in the psychic disorientation of *Vertigo* that closes on the narrator's vision of the nightmare of history. Place in Sebald is a series of stations, each a transit stop in this kind of pilgrimage of the mind and never really a destination. Destination in Sebald is either home (always unavailable in his discourse of unbelonging except in the psychic activity of the mind or self) or death, the ultimate extratextual transgression.

For the Sebaldian narrator, however, the world is a topology inscribed with myth or story, even if these are available only as the fragments of an Eliotian modernity, "these fragments I have shored against my ruin" (*The Waste Land*), the partial traces of which memory resurrects. The connection of these fragments and episodes is the narrator's writerly task and he connects them by linking places together with the threading paths of his itineraries. The threads he uses, the associating, connecting threads, work like the linen threads in a restored canvas or a net to catch these fleeting, transient thoughts and images that are constituent elements of the narrator's mind, giving them a more permanent form in the places of his texts, ordering and sequencing their patterns, and making them into something new for the dynamically engaged disobedient reader whose collaborative authority and own agility enable her too to take up a position in the textual space.

He or she may even be lured into traveling him or herself. After all, Sebald's books have more than once found their way into the "travel" section of bookshops — and not surprisingly. As his narrators travel in Continental Europe or England or, in one instance, to America, in and out of cities, through churches and galleries, hotels and railway stations, they seem to index places so precisely that the appellation "travel writing" has even been applied by a travel writer with philosophical inclinations (De Botton 1999). Places described in the books are "real" in the sense that they have a historical presence in the world outside the texts in which they appear, much as Jane Austen's Lyme Regis or Flaubert's Rouen do. Of course, Jane Austen's Dorset and Flaubert's Normandy are peopled by individuals who are phantasms constructed by the writer's imagination, whereas Sebald's narrators stand in for a man who himself visited Venice before his narrator described the Santa Lucia railway station, and who became friends with the poet Michael Hamburger before he wrote his house into *The Rings of Saturn*. The disobedient reader might well plan her own itinerary, book a plane ticket, and set off on travels to Sebaldian sites — but she is likely to find this kind of extratextual disobedience disappointing. Not all disobedience is equally productive.

She is likely to discover that Sebald's accounts of places are far less scrupulously indexed than they seem, compared with, say, Döblin's Berlin or Joyce's Dublin or Zola's Paris. The places constructed in the texts are fragments of places. As Gillian Tindall points out, Proust's construction of the house at Combray is partial because only the staircase and the narrator's bedroom, the lamp, and the gate with the latch are retained in the memory (Tindall 1991, 222). No other image is possible or, within the text, necessary. Sebald's marvellously evocative economy of description works in the same way. This part argues that this precise indexing of place is actually a form of hyperrealist representation, employing a few selected but very sharply evocative details, as is memory's practice, creating a textual space in which different subjects, the author's, the constructed narrator's, and the reader's, are given temporary, and temporal, definition within the discourse of textual space framed by the represented places the narrator "creates." Place in Sebald affords textual space, not because it provides a context for action or events as in the traditional mimetic novel, but because it affords a temporary and temporalized *locus* for the spectral subject of the writerly narrator. In an episodic way that reflects the fragments of remembered narrative which comprise Sebald's associative texts, these places are temporarily occupied as discursive spaces before the narrator moves on, in much the same way that the momentary rupture of the photographs is also transient, those frozen instantiations of the recollected past which surface in the inky darkness of the text in their spectral grey tonality.

Sebald's construction of place presents as nonfiction in a hyperrealist fashion, not as the informative depiction of locations that one might find in orthodox historiography, but more like a painter's hyperreal representations, such as those of his great friend Jan Peter Tripp as reproduced in *Logis in einem Landhaus* and *Unerzählt*, which prompt imaginative and contemplative responses, or the oblique suggestiveness of shapes emerging from the indeterminate suggestiveness of a Turner watercolor, or a blurred photograph whose abstraction engenders fancy. This teases, slyly, the reader's instinctive desire for certainty by heightening the clarity of a few selected details and using very sharp tonal distinctions, employing what looks like at the least a mimetic rhetoric and at the most a documentary one, but deploying it in an ironized way. Gradually destabilizing the reader's confidence in either the documented reality or the meticulous realism he seems to employ by means of the curious narrator's mediating consciousness, by his quirky, unstable use of photographs suggesting flashes of possibly distorted memories, and by the heightened use of detail generated by a contemplative remembering subject who is also a writer, Sebald shapes his aesthetic practice with a sly, ludic, self-reflexive irony. This manifests in a number of ways, not least in his construction or representation of place, and can be seen to subvert the embedded prose directions to the reader, the reading protocols, in the readerly journey by exposing what appears to be nonfictional, such as historical observations, representations of travel, or personal memoir, presented by an unmediated authorial presence, as in actuality the discursive product of the constructed narrator's consciousness or subject. Mimesis is also subverted because these seem so real as to be documentary, hyperreal, but in fact they are the ways things might appear in dreams or the memory. Moreover sometimes that hyperreal sharpness of, say, Tripp, can be glimpsed dissolving into oneiric suggestiveness, the liminal site between consciousness and dream and memory. This produces a vigilant disobedient reader who endeavors to take her own bearings.

Located in the different stations of the itinerary in each text, an external, topographically indexed journey which is presented as taking place in actual and durational time ("three months later," "the next day," "in the late sixties," "in 1996," and so on) in "Verona," "a village outside Norwich," "7, Place des Vosges," "the Flamingo Hotel," "W" and so on, the topological construction of a parallel and simultaneous journey traced by the voice of memory, both cultural and personal, creates textual spaces, adding temporal layering which gives depth of perspective to the construction of place in the language of the text. Thus Liverpool Street station is not only the point of departure for trains traveling from London to Norwich and elsewhere but is also an entrance to the underworld (*Austerlitz* 180). The aeroplane's dark entrance into which Aunt Fini disappears at Riem airport outside Munich on her way to New York after what eventually proves to be her last visit to Germany is constructed as the entrance to a place of oblivion and permanent disappearance (*The Emigrants* 69). In The Hague a man with a dark beard brushes past the narrator and disappears through a doorway into which the narrator stares "for an unforgettable moment that seemed to exist outside time" (*The Rings of Saturn* 81). The threshold of an unnamed underground station in London is "the station where . . . no one ever embarked or alighted," where the platform is always deserted and where a disembodied voice says "Mind the gap" (Sebald 1999a, 259). Sebald is fond of these cinematic dissolves in prose, from the world of empirical and material reality into what the subject perceives as the mystery of spacelessness and timelessness. Even the most carefully indexed descriptions of place, therefore, become subject to this potential dissolution, both in the processes of temporal attrition or decay, in transformation or disappearance over time, and in the destruction that threatens at the edge of the material, subject to ruin, decay, disappearance, raising the Cartesian question about the mind-body split and positing a resolutely metaphysical one.

Liverpool Street station is also, historically, a structure built in the nineteenth century over the medieval priory which founded the Hospital of St Mary of Bethlehem, the site of the social wound of the appalling Bedlam, inscribing charity initially and declining into institutionalized persecution, near the London bleachfields. This is the place where a small fictional boy (now also commemorated in the glass suitcase monument at the station in London) saved from persecution in Europe by his lively vivacious mother's putting his name on a *Kindertransport* list is met by a life-denying, childless Calvinist couple from Wales, a Methodist minister and his "wan wife" (194), a "timid Englishwoman" (61), whose charitable act also appropriates Austerlitz as a simulacrum (hence his renaming) to fill the child-absence in their own lives. Both will decline into death and madness in an ironic reinforcement of the dominant emotional paradigm of grief and loneliness.

Like a film in which human actors and animated characters appear together, this kind of fiction blends history and what Sebald called "metaphysics" (Hoare 2002) with imagined, technically constructed simulacra. The sense of place with which Liverpool Street station is imbued here is slightly sinister, as though the centuries of misery and suffering of the persecuted inmates of Bedlam and their modern displaced successor-victims of another kind of persecution have somehow soaked into the site, both hallowing it with their presence and haunting it with their history. Austerlitz's memory is eventually triggered by the exposure of the disused Ladies' Waiting Room during the renovation of the station, so that he can "see" in his memory the small boy with the green rucksack and the dour middle-aged couple from Wales who speak to him in a language which he cannot understand, as though in late adult life he is standing outside or above a scene from his own childhood. Sebald ironizes the communicative limits of language to render experience in this interstitial space. The recovery of the past through memory is a series of snapshots, an incomplete set of discrete instantiations which, thanks to the attrition of time, continue to resist narrative unity, whose meaning is endlessly deferred and therefore unavailable in any final or definitive form unless they are reconstituted by the narrator in "his" text.

In *Vertigo* Liverpool Street station is the entrance to "a vast system of catacombs" (259), whose "soot-stained brick walls" support a host of purple-flowering buddleias "which thrive in the most inauspicious conditions" (259–60), an image of resilience, literally flourishing against the inauspicious odds. The narrator recalls that on his last journey through the station on his way to Italy, the "sparse shrubs . . . just flowering," he had seen a "yellow brimstone butterfly . . . constantly moving" (260). Sebald's reference to butterflies may be construed as a reference to Nabokov (as Russell Kilbourn did in his paper, Davidson College, 2003), but here it is also the conjunction of "yellow" and "brimstone" which produces poetic connotations that are as interesting as the invocation of the Russian *émigré* writer with playful, postmodern tendencies. "Brimstone" catches the infernal and underworld notes in Sebald's earlier description in this text, and yellow is that resonant color that might suggest Proust's view of the exquisitely rendered patch of yellow in Vermeer's wall in *View of Delft* as the apogee of aesthetic accomplishment that he felt, through Bergotte and "Marcel," his own prose fell short of achieving (1954, 187), and the color which in van Valckenborch's painting of the view of Antwerp with the woman skating on the Schelde catches something of both the imminent and ultimate catastrophes for those whose wearing of yellow for quite other reasons would mark them for destruction. The disobedient reader might feel tempted to add that other association, at this underworld entrance, with the absent butterfly written about by the doomed children of Theresienstadt, on their own ghastly journey (De Silva xiv). This "butterfly memory" disappears too, "perhaps prompted only by a wishful thought" (*Vertigo* 260), itself subject to doubt and ambiguity, one of those Sebaldian textual moments when a memory or a thought, like Virginia Woolf's fish (*A Room of One's Own*), appears and disappears with a rapid series of movements, or as in Arthur Boyd's light-filled paintings of the Australian landscape, a raven darkens some tiny part of the canvas.

Sebald's textual topography maps the mental topology of the subjectivities of the text's twinned dyadic agencies: the author's and the narrator's, the narrator's and the reader's, as they go about their different textual journeys, blending the activities of memory, imagination, and contemplation. Virginia Woolf also does this, particularly in *Mrs Dalloway* (1925), where Clarissa's thoughts and their associations (not least the psychic damage done to Septimus Smith, traumatized by his experience of war) unfold as she walks contemplatively through the streets of London. This is something that Sebald seems to have drawn on, simply by cultural engagement and not least his readings of Virginia Woolf, in the encounters between Austerlitz and the narrator as they walk to and from Greenwich Park, meditating as one in their fused dialogical way, in Austerlitz's (or is it the narrator's?) monologue, on the nature of time, through the East End of London in the Borough of Tower Hamlets. This boundary is marked by the location of the Tower of London, its horrendous history a silent presence in the text, and the cemetery of Tower Hamlets, now in actuality a nature reserve, rich in the history of those who fled persecution earlier, the eighteenth-century Huguenot French silk weavers (shades of *The Rings of Saturn*) escaping religious persecution in Catholic France and one hundred years later, "Jews fleeing the pogroms in Eastern Europe" (The Borough of Tower Hamlets website).

What follows is that the often picaresque adventure of reading Sebald is a journey which takes us to real places but which exist in their discursive richness within the textual economy, framed as shimmering phantasms of actual experience that lodge in the reader's memory in a way that can be difficult to recall precisely, much like a dream. No journey to Paris, to the Cimitière Montparnasse, the Jardin des Plantes, the Maisons-Alfort, the Salpêtrière, the "half-deserted area between the tracks of the Gare d'Austerlitz and the Quai d'Austerlitz on the left bank of the Seine" (380), or the new Grande Bibliothèque Nationale, can be the same as the journey we take as readers to those textual spaces in passages of *Austerlitz* (360–62, 367–69, 370–75, 375–79, 380–84, and 384–403), just as we cannot, and do not expect to, find traces of Buck Mulligan's shaving lather in the

Martello tower on Sandymount Strand in Joyce's scrupulously rendered version of Dublin in *Ulysses*, or one of Emma Bovary's promissory notes in the Rouen archives office. We can catch the train from Vienna to Venice, take a ferry ride across the Venetian lagoon departing from the Riva degli Schiavoni, or arrive on foot at the alpine village of W in southwest Germany and stay in the Engelwirt Inn, but these are not the kinds of journeys we take with Jan Morris in the pages of *Trieste, or The Meaning of Nowhere*, or even with Bruce Chatwin in *In Patagonia*. The journeys which occur within the pages of Sebald's books occur in the mind of the reader in a double sense because these places are constructed as poetic spaces.

To visit Somerleyton or to stand in the park of Ditchingham Hall in Suffolk, once one has read *The Rings of Saturn*, is to visit and see them through the fictional lens that Sebald has created in his texts, that of the mind of his "writer"-narrator, his atavistic prose style and those strange manipulated images. The man who stands underneath the cedar in a photograph is no longer the same man who writes *The Rings of Saturn*, just as the document of a passport fixes the barest facts of a person's identity in a rudimentary and unsatisfactory rhetoric that has only a slight connection with the complex and enigmatic subject represented by the book in which both "appear." These are discursively constructed spaces, not the places we can visit and photograph for ourselves. The prism of the disobedient reader's mind affords productive disobedience; no plane or rail ticket will suffice.

The disobedient reader does not travel merely to geographical places, as one would in a travel narrative and as each text appears to invite the reader to do, but rather she travels to places that are palimpsests of cultural memories created by the associating, constructing consciousness or mind of the reflecting and remembering subject, the "dead" author's, the constructed narrator's (also the ghost of the author), and her own contingent one.

Austerlitz: Conversation Stations

> It was only by following the course time prescribed that we could hasten through the gigantic spaces separating us from each other. And indeed, said Austerlitz after a while, to this day there is something illusionistic and illusory about the relationship of time and space as we experience it in travelling. . . . (*Austerlitz* 14)

The narrator in *Austerlitz* has an unusually acute sense of place, possibly fostered by his thirty years' association with an architectural historian whose story he is telling. One of the best ways to keep track in this text of four hundred pages without paragraph divisions is to map the conversation-stations by indexing them to place. Within the conversations there are embedded narratives, itineraries which are interconnected, but the external or framing itinerary is the one that the reader needs to map to keep her own bearings. This is no easy task when Sebald has effaced any real distinction between the two voices in the text, each conversation segueing into the next with little demarcation. The dialogism of the text, as in those of Socrates and Phaedrus, of Jacques and his master, of Quixote and Sancho Panza, has a strangely fused quality about it that also in Sebald's case seems to abstract the definition of place so that it occupies a metaphysically suggestive plane, like Samuel Beckett's minimalist stage sets, rather than a realistically depicted spatial one. The Brasserie Le Havane, for instance, where three conversations take place, is merely a named space, with a television screen showing infernal scenes in Indonesia, within which Austerlitz's narrated memories are recorded by the deeply attentive narrator-writer.

The first six conversations between the narrator and Austerlitz take place in Belgium between June and December, in the late sixties, in the *salle des pas perdus* and the restaurant bar in the Centraal Station in Antwerp, on the promenade along the Schelde, in the *Café des Espérances* in Liège, on the steps of the Palace of Justice in Brussels, while waiting to catch the ferry traveling from Zeebrugge to England, and on the ferry itself. Several undocumented conversations take place in London, at the Courtauld Institute where Austerlitz works, until the narrator moves at the end of 1975 (and an absence of nine years) back to Germany without telling Austerlitz. After a year he returns to England. Twenty years later, in December 1996, he runs into Austerlitz in the bar of the Great Eastern Hotel next to Liverpool Street station. Their conversation, which is as usual a monologue from Austerlitz, lasts well into the night, so that the narrator takes a room at the hotel. They meet the next day by arrangement and take a walk together down to Whitechapel and Shoreditch, then from Wapping to Shadwell, and on to the Royal Observatory at Greenwich. They walk back down through Greenwich Park and catch a taxi to Liverpool Street station, where they continue and conclude the day's conversation. After three months, in March, Austerlitz sends the narrator a postcard inviting him to his house in Alderney Street near the Mile End junction in London's East End and after another very long conversation/monologue, the narrator stays overnight. An even longer "conversation" continues the next day, and then the two men take a walk to Tower Hamlets Cemetery and St Clement's Hospital. Their conversation continues during this walk, which concludes at Liverpool Street station, where the narrator catches a train. Six months later, in September, the narrator receives another postcard from Austerlitz, with his address in Paris in the thirteenth arrondissement. The narrator leaves for Paris and meets Austerlitz the following day in the Brasserie Le Havane near the Glacière Métro. Two long conversations take place in the Brasserie on consecutive days, and on the third the two men meet for morning coffee again on the

Boulevard Auguste Blanqui where the conversation resumes briefly for the last time. The narrator repeats the opening of the novel by visiting Antwerp, the Nocturama at the zoo and the fortress at Breendonk again.

The Centraal Railway Station in Antwerp shapes the first encounter between the narrator and the figure of Austerlitz: "that fantastical building" (4), the grandiloquent monument to King Leopold's exploitative colonizing greed, a silent memorial to the oppressed and persecuted Africans who served it. The narrator, having listened so carefully to Austerlitz's lesson about the history of European architecture, especially the built environment's manifestation of the rise of bourgeois capitalism in the nineteenth century, has appropriated into his own discourse Austerlitz's sense of place as architectural history voicing the lost presences of the past, memorializing them in both oblique and direct ways.

The station, which appears again at the end of the book, is a bizarre place, a site of dark shadows and odd corners where the experience of the passage of time is unusual, slowed down in a way that suggests sleep or dream, or perhaps a film sequence that memory runs in our heads. This diffused sense of space, the interiority of the narrator's mind and the external geometry or topography of place not entirely distinct from each other, is maintained throughout *Austerlitz* in the different places where the narrator's or Austerlitz's sensibility invests those coordinates of spatial geometry and topography with a temporal otherness. This encompasses places that are historically real, such as a bar in Antwerp or London or Paris, specific railway stations, a particular view from a train passing through the Rhine Valley, the space where the Grande Bibliothèque has been constructed on the Quai François Mauriac in Paris, the monumental shape of Breendonk, and the weird open and closed emptiness of Terezin, or which are fictionalized, such as a school in Oswestry in Shropshire named after a hotel in Norwich (Stower Grange) or a house with a monochrome, Beckett-stage-set interior in the East End of London in a barely fictionalized street. Here at the beginning the narrator, who sounds exactly like Austerlitz although we don't realize that until we read further (and perhaps it is Austerlitz who sounds like the narrator, for we can never be entirely certain) repeats the experience, as the text will repeat the description of the memory, of the train in Paris traveling over the viaduct into the dark upper concourse of the Gare d'Austerlitz, having come "from the Bastille" (406).

In real terms these are associations effected more by language than by the coordinates of a train itinerary. The Bastille no longer exists except as an empty site, the prison building demolished by the mob in Paris more than two hundred years ago, now only the suggestive name of a station in the Métro system. The name of the Gare d'Austerlitz commemorates the greatest of Napoleon's battles (1805) in which the French defeated the Russians and the Austrians through Napoleon's artful trickery, with

35,000 losses on both sides. As the surname of Jacques Austerlitz, born in Bohemia to Agata Austerlitz and Max Aychenwald (whose own surname is a play on "Oak Forest," no small arboreal compliment in a Sebaldian fiction in which he makes reference to the "lovely names" of Jews), named Jacques for his Russian and Austrian parents' love of all things French and carrying his unmarried mother's name, Austerlitz connotes both victory and defeat, triumph and disaster, his name a resolution of a knot of old tensions and a configuration of new ones. Sebald's enterprise sets the ineffable horror of Theresienstadt and Fort IX in Kaunas, the life-denying Calvinist bleakness of the manse at Bala, the systematized, institutionalized and Foucault-inflected horrors of asylums and prisons and hospitals, Denbigh, St Clement, Bedlam, Salpêtrière against the blissful interlude of the beauty of Andromeda Lodge in the Mawddach estuary near Barmouth in Wales, place of science (where Darwin wrote) and beauty (painted by Turner and written about by Wordsworth) and the transformed Paris wasteland between the Quai d'Austerlitz and the Gare d'Austerlitz where the Bastiani Traveling Circus pitched their shabby tent. In the following section I look at two of the places represented by the language of *Austerlitz*, the Gare d'Austerlitz and Andromeda Lodge, and I consider the textual space each offers its readers.

On the Far Side of Time

The reader's arrival at the Gare d'Austerlitz toward the end of *Austerlitz* has been prepared by her prior passage through several railway stations. The narrator has repeated Austerlitz's "obsession with railway stations" (45), Austerlitz's studies of railway architecture focusing what he calls "the agony of leave-taking and the fear of foreign places" (17), seeing stations as places which calibrate "the degree of our insecurity" (17). These are sites which signal departure and arrival, "places marked by both blissful happiness and profound misfortune" (45). Sebald catches at the ambivalence that Giuseppe di Lampedusa used in his metaphor for the death of the Prince of Salina in *The Leopard*, his dream imagining himself on a railway platform with an elegantly dressed woman walking toward him.

In *Austerlitz* railway stations speak metaphorically of the human condition, our mysterious coming and going, our traveling restlessness, our nomadic restlessness that Bruce Chatwin's writing represented for Sebald. They utter more particularly the terrible twentieth-century dislocations of children like Jacquot, the departures of the persecuted such as Austerlitz's mother, for whom there was no return, the mysterious disappearance of people like his father, to describe which horror Sebald employs Dantean images of hell and purgatory, empty perspectives. Paradise is elsewhere.

Railway stations are transit sites, borderless intersectional moments where the individual might be either departing or arriving, perhaps both, a pervasive dualism and ambiguity. They represent moments of stasis, literal stations in a traveler's journey, and in Sebald atemporal instantiations with uncanny spaces located within them, the *salle des pas perdus* in Antwerp, the disused Ladies' Waiting Room in London, difficult to "place" temporally or spatially. These are places which open up temporal perspectives like "those quiet courtyards in Paris" where time seems to have stopped altogether (359), where the past is still somehow available in a permanent present, if only we knew how to enter it, or to avoid it. In Paris the mysterious space is adjunct to the station, peripheral and liminal, site of arrest and transport.

The Centraal Railway Station in Antwerp is a place which conjures colonial exploitation and Joseph Conrad's poetic evocation of the evil, madness and folly within in *Heart of Darkness*. It is also a place whose architecture by Delacenserie is seen by the narrator to be "uniting past and future" (12), the fusion of medieval turrets on the viaduct, the Renaissance marble staircase, and the steel and glass roof of modernity. In the waiting room, the sonorous *salle des pas perdus*, where he first encounters Austerlitz photographing darkened mirrors, the narrator sees the few silent passengers as Lilliputians, dwarfed by the monstrous scale of the building, and Austerlitz as the archetypal German hero Siegfried from "Fritz Lang's *Nibelungen* film" (6), an ironic joke about Aryan types in German mythology, given Austerlitz's story and Sebald's own contempt for his first name (Winfried). Like the American painter Edward Hopper, Sebald can invoke a sense of disorientation in the viewer or reader, in which a place or setting that might otherwise be familiar is given a weird spin with strange perspectives, the quality of a Grimm fairy tale with dark undercurrents and silent shadows.

The restaurant in the railway station, like St Lucia in *Vertigo*, is also a curious place, painted in hyperreal terms: it is nearly midnight, and we see a room which is "the mirror image of the waiting room" off the "great domed hall" (8), a verbal joke about the reflection of mirrors which, like black holes, can swallow time with their infinite regression. There are two men, whom the reader knows as the narrator and the architectural historian, and a "solitary man drinking Fernet" who is also Sebald (Fernet was his preferred drink), a naughty authorial trinity, a three-in-one. The "barmaid, who sat enthroned on a stool behind the counter, legs crossed, filing her nails with complete devotion and concentration . . . whose peroxide-blonde hair was piled up into a sort of bird's nest" (8) is the "goddess of time past," a subject in a Hopper painting herself, sitting below a "mighty clock" whose measurement of time has slowed down to an extraordinary degree: "we both noticed what an endless length of time went by before another minute had passed" and the hand "like a sword of justice . . . slicing off the next one-sixtieth of an hour from the future" is transferred by Austerlitz to a different timeframe entirely as he begins, "Towards the end of the nineteenth century . . ." (9).

Time slows down, stops, and then runs backwards in the restaurant opposite the *salle des pas perdus* overseen by an unexpected goddess. Sebald's cross-hatching of time and place becomes a textual space, where time disappears altogether in an intensely contingent moment (as we read) and where place is a film-series of images, some running at the barest level of slow motion, some freeze-frames, where we hear the voice of the narrator painting (in a Baudelairean *correspondance*) a sense of place that exists purely in the discursive moment of the narrator's and the reader's consciousness. The restaurant disappears as Austerlitz tells the appalling story of the architectural history of the station, narrative threads leading from it to the Belgian Congo and the emerging paradigm of nineteenth-century industrialized, capitalist Europe. Austerlitz's own family story is inaugurated in this context, and in metaphor suggested by the Foucault-inflected Nocturama and the *salle des pas perdus*: imprisoned creatures whose world is an institutionalized travesty, manipulated by the powerful; disappearing people glimpsed in transit and never seen again, a handful of spectral, silent survivors whose stories, straining credibility, must be told.

Austerlitz was fascinated in Paris where he pursued his studies by "the idea of a network such as that of the entire railway system" (45). His daily visits to the Gare du Nord and the Gare de l'Est induce "dangerous and entirely incomprehensible currents of emotion" (45). This sense of the immanence of presence is the "only hint of his present life" (45) that Austerlitz reveals proleptically to the narrator, and it is expanded in the detailed account of Liverpool Street station that follows a little later, inaugurated not by Austerlitz this time but by the narrator, analeptically. By contrast with this expansiveness, the creation of the textual space that is the Gare d'Austerlitz at the end of the book has the compressed poetic intensity of a collapsed star.

The narrator feels "particularly apprehensive" every time he approaches Liverpool Street station, this time on his way to see Gregor, the Czech Harley Street ophthalmologist, the train having to "wind its way over several sets of points through a narrow defile, and where the brick walls rising above both sides of the tracks with their round arches, columns and niches, blackened with soot and diesel oil, put me in mind once again that morning of an underground columbarium" (49–50). For the reader this reversal, and the bizarrely named repository for ashes of the departed (in Latin, *columbarium* means a dovecote), recalls also the Nocturama, Breendonk and Theresienstadt, places of perpetual night. The tone is Kafkaesque and disturbing. The narrator's perception of this sinister quality appears to have been shaped by his Buberian encounter with Austerlitz.

Austerlitz later describes to the narrator his own experience of being drawn toward Liverpool Street station at the end of his restless night walks across London "together with all the other poor souls who flow from the suburbs towards the centre at that time of day. As I passed through the station, I thought several times that among the passengers coming towards me in the tiled passages, on the escalators plunging steeply into the depths, or behind the grey windows of a train just pulling out, I saw a face known to me from some much earlier part of my life, but I could never say whose it was" (179). These stations, offering uncanny glimpses, are also the "gigantic spaces" which make human encounter impossible (14), where passage — of time, space, and person — is a paradigm of perpetual movement and perpetual arrest, the one virtually indistinguishable from the other, like the actual movement and seeming stasis of celestial bodies, or the seeming arrest and perpetual motion of atomic particles.

Austerlitz describes Liverpool Street station as "one of the darkest and most sinister places in London" (180). Drawn there irresistibly, he describes it to the narrator, who tells the reader it is "a kind of entrance to the underworld" (180): "Even on sunny days only a faint greyness, scarcely illuminated at all by the globes of the station lights, came through the glass roof over the main hall . . ." (181). This "eternal dusk" (181) is the "objective correlative" (T. S. Eliot's term) of Austerlitz's lifelong despair (178), manifest in its various forms where vitality and color are leached away, replaced by a spectral grey monochrome. Austerlitz is reported as saying that "that constant wrenching inside me, [is] a kind of heartache which . . . was caused by the vortex of past time" (182).

At ugly Broad Street station, reflecting on the "starving paupers" who used to inhabit the bucolic parts of London, "the little river Wellbrook, the ditches and ponds, the crakes and snipes and herons, the elms and mulberry trees, Paul Pindar's deer park . . . Angel Alley, Peter Street, Sweet Apple Court and Swan Yard" (186), Austerlitz feels "as if the dead were returning from their exile and filling the twilight around me with their strangely slow but incessant to-ing and fro-ing" (188). This blurs temporal difference in the place of transit, between the living and the dead, and this observation, mediated by a despairing Austerlitz, seems to characterize the human as hopeless, a pathetic fallacy which the narrator corroborates. At the next station an unexpected encounter produces a surprising connectedness.

Following the porter in a snow-white turban on a whim, in one of those fairy-tale narratives with which Sebald paves the reader's way out of the banality of the modern world, Austerlitz comes to the entrance of the disused Ladies' Waiting Room due for demolition during the rebuilding of Liverpool Street station. Like the *salle des pas perdus*, this is a haunted space. Here "the icy grey light" (189) reveals a tiled floor, the pattern used by Dutch painters and by Tripp to create, and distort, perspective, which Austerlitz describes as the "board on which the endgame would be played"

(193), an overt allusion to Beckett's one-act play *Endgame* whose stage directions begin "Bare interior. Grey light," to the chess move in a game where the outcome is already determined, endgame. The certainty and inevitability of death stalk both Beckett and Sebald. In Sebald, waiting rooms in railway stations are both ominous and absurd, as we see in his extension of the black-and-white board which the floor in the Ladies' Waiting Room at Liverpool Street station represents for Austerlitz so that "it covered the entire plane of time" (193). This is a waiting game with appalling consequences.

Here in this half light and this empty space, Austerlitz "sees" a middle-aged couple and a small boy, that glimpse of his own past replayed in his imagination, possibly a fanciful reconstruction in its generic painterliness. In the details of the woman's light gabardine coat "with a hat at an angle on her head," the man's "dark suit and a dog-collar," the boy's white knee-length socks on legs that didn't reach the floor, and his small ruck-sack (193), memory's photograph, always potentially an *ersatz* one, freezes the sudden rush of time past into Austerlitz's mind more than fifty years after the event as he steps once more into the Ladies' Waiting Room, a revenant.

Both Eliases are dead, and in one sense so is the little boy with the rucksack, yet Austerlitz's presence in the room about to be demolished (195) is also that of the specter of the future haunting the place of the past, as though the oblivion of the future (the imminent demolition of the actual place and all that it represents to those who, like Austerlitz, waited within it) is perpetually arrested by the recording of Austerlitz's memory in the redemptive language of the narrator's text. In this way the waiting, the future, the past, the return of the dead and memory itself create the poetic space of the Ladies' Waiting Room at Liverpool Street station in the strangely timeless present of the text of *Austerlitz*.

Much later, Austerlitz is staring at "the pattern of the glass and steel roof above the platform" in the "labyrinthine" (308) Wilsonova station in Prague, an architectural feature it shares with Antwerp's Centraal Station and the Gare d'Austerlitz in Paris. A deep memory suggests that this is familiar to him. This, he learns, is where Austerlitz was farewelled by his mother (forever) and by Vera, now his *aide-mémoire*, on his departure for London. Austerlitz's memory is suggestive of a small boy catching sight of the roof's patterns, fascinated, but implying too a sense of enclosure in a dark, artificially lit place from which the only escape possible is the train's inevitable destination. In his case there will be a "station" at a manse in Bala, in his mother's the final one of Terezin.

In response to Austerlitz's card, the narrator travels to Paris by train, meeting Austerlitz in the Brasserie Le Havane near the Glacière Métro, a place now connected with Bishopsgate and the Schelde. The narrator retells Austerlitz's brasserie conversations, including his accounts of the walk between the tracks of the Gare d'Austerlitz and the Quai d'Austerlitz where Austerlitz and Marie de Verneuil see the Bastiani Travelling Circus, and his passage through the Gare d'Austerlitz.

The Gare d'Austerlitz is where Austerlitz, changing trains on the way back from the Bibliothèque Nationale, has a premonition "that he was coming closer to his father" (405). This should be a climactic moment in the book. It dissolves, however, into disappointment. In the silence induced by the partial railway strike, Austerlitz considers the idea that his father, living on the street named after the great French mime Jean-Louis Barrault, who the disobedient reader knows played the pierrot role in Marcel Carne's poetic realist film *Les Enfants du Paradis* (1945) written by Jacques Prévert, produced during the German occupation of Paris, may have left Paris from this station "after the Germans entered the city" (405). This is a curious and unfounded speculation, entwined with the suggestion of Carne'/Prévert's exquisitely poised subversion of Nazi suppression of French political disobedience in the picaresque story of the theater of Les Funambules, and Austerlitz's next sentence confirms that by beginning "I imagined . . ." (405). He observes, after imagining the memory of his father's departure in "white clouds of smoke" (406), that the Gare d'Austerlitz is "the most mysterious of all the railway terminals of Paris" (406). In that way it speaks the mystery of his father's disappearance, in perpetuity. This has wider poetic resonance.

Trains arrive from the Bastille, presenting a curious time slippage (see above) but suggesting a freight of invisible prisoners crossing the Seine, like the Styx, to "roll over the iron viaduct into the station's upper storey, quite as if the façade were swallowing them up" (406). This too is a con-juror's disappearing trick, recalling the dark-blue cloaked one with the col-orful cockerel in the Bastiani Travelling Circus (shades of Les Funambules) playing to the tiny audience in the patched tent with the false firmament, strung with orange light globes in the wasteland between the tracks of the Gare d'Austerlitz and the Quai d'Austerlitz (380–84). This magic intersti-tial place, like Carne/Prévert's 1840s allegory of Parisian street culture in 1945, occupied temporarily by an itinerant circus family with their strange seductive music transporting the listener to a state of bliss, is the counter-part to the bleakness of the sinister Gare d'Austerlitz with its disappearing prisoners, its "feeble light" (406), its emptiness, its rough platform fash-ioned out of "beams and boards" (406), its "scaffolding reminiscent of a gallows with all kinds of rusty iron hooks," its "plucked pigeon feathers lying all over the floorboards . . . the scene of an unexpiated crime" (407), like the Grande Bibliothèque built over the site of the warehouses filled with looted goods from Jewish homes (Cowan 2004).

The "grey pigeon feathers," the "dark patches, of leaked axle grease, perhaps, or carbolineum, or something altogether different," and the "dim light" (407) are surmounted by "two tiny figures" which move over the

iron work on the north façade "like black spiders in their web" (408),
funambulists. This is sinister and terrifying stuff, a place from where
Austerlitz determines, almost too quickly, that he must set off to seek his
father elsewhere. This is not just a Dickensian contrast between Sleary's
Circus and Gradgrind's institutionalized suppression of the imagination; it
is a contrast between the shabby small-scale provision of peace, beauty, and
blissful transport of delight into the music of the spheres afforded by the
marginalized nomads outside the station on the edge of its precinct and
the monumentally proportioned, systematized perversion, suppression,
and evil abuse of knowledge to unspeakable ends suggested within it. In
this decentered place with its anarchically poetic use of urban wasteland,
salvation of the soul lies; in the Gare d'Austerlitz, the state-sanctioned and
systematized *locus* of authorized passage, an "unexpiated crime" (407)
endures, haunting any disobedient observer with eyes to peer into the long
perspectives of the past.

The tiny scale and the powerfully memorable effect of this imaginative
little traveling circus, so affecting that Austerlitz could not have "said at
the time whether my heart was contracting in pain or expanding with happiness for the first time in my life" (383), produces "a mystery" which
Austerlitz imagines is "summed up in the image of the snow-white goose
standing motionless and steadfast . . . as if it knew its own future and the
fate of its present companions" (384). This strange fairy tale, like that of
the ancient caretaker and the Belgian sheepdog Billie in the Jewish cemetery in London, like the tales of Evan the Welsh cobbler, like Adela's
shadow play in the ballroom of Andromeda Lodge, are offset against the
historical horrors of Breendonk and Kaunas, of the social institutions of
prisons, hospitals, asylums, boarding schools, and railway stations, of the
dehumanizing bleakness of contemporary life. Beauty and imagination are
surprising, affirming threads in this dark text, the colorful Menippean carnival note of poetry, with its painted starry heaven, redeeming grey and
barren waste.

Andromeda Lodge — a Galaxy Apart

Austerlitz's bleak days in exile at Bala, in the marginal country of Wales, in
the cold and silent manse of the Eliases, the destination of his original rail
journey from Prague, are redeemed somewhat by the trips he makes with
Emyr into the beautiful Tanat valley on alternate Sundays, until a bomb
kills several villagers in "their Sunday best" (70), an event which strikes the
boy as a fearsome and inexplicable manifestation of Old Testament retri-
bution. This is associated in Austerlitz's memory with the story of the
drowning of Emyr's family home and the Vyrnwy reservoir in 1888, life in
Wales reflecting the bleak, life-denying religion of his Methodist foster

father. The spectral figure of the ironically home-burnishing Gwendolyn wastes away in this loveless, lifeless world of Calvinist Bala, and the widower Emyr goes mad, committed to the Denbigh asylum where he too dies. Only the mythological stories of the cobbler invest this bleak despair with an imaginative richness that offers Dafydd Elias "escape."

This living death is present too in Austerlitz's other Welsh "home," in Andromeda Lodge outside Barmouth, overlooking the Mawddach estuary. There have been two strands of Fitzpatricks living here for generations. The first is a dour Catholic one (unusual in Calvinist Wales), of whom great-uncle Evelyn is the current representative, characterized by duty and excessive asceticism, manifest in his pain-crazed, diminished life. He is bad tempered and cursed (a heavy irony for the disobedient reader) by rigidity, and by Bechterew's disease. The donor of 12 shillings a week to the Mission to the Congo for the salvation of black souls still languishing in unbelief, he is miserly and miserable, mocked by Austerlitz in retrospective telling which contrasts him with the other Fitzpatrick strand, its affirming representative great-uncle Alphonso. Alphonso is the natural scientist, whose path of enthusiasm and wonder Gerald will follow into astrophysics. These antithetical manifestations of a diminished institutionalized God and natural history/science (whose subject is the wonder of creation) are ironized, firstly by the reader's knowledge that Charles Darwin had been a neighbor further up the estuary near Dolgellau (119), and secondly by Sebald's depiction of the Mawddach estuary as a place whose great beauty attracted the poet William Wordsworth and the painter J. M. W. Turner. It is the world of imagination and contemplation that is privileged here; the beauty of nature and of art, and scientific curiosity, are valorized. Institutionalized religion is exposed as a perversion, a blasphemy against life. Sebald then connects this surprisingly associative Welsh landscape with an even more fearful perversion.

As Owen Chadwick points out, "the spread of Darwinianism in Germany . . . was to take greatest root (there), and bring its most potent consequences, including its nastiest" (1975, 175). Initially rejected by German intellectuals for its interdisciplinary approach, Darwin's writing was regarded as philosophical by "exact scientists" and "by philosophers as unphilosophical" (176). Darwin's presence in Sebald's text is both a historical presence (he did write *The Descent of Man* published in 1871 in that Welsh valley) but also a poetic one in the context of Sebald's fiction. The butterfly-lightness of the passing association made in Sebald's text draws the reader's attention to the science-religion debate of the nineteenth century, its profound effect on the history of the world in its manifestation of the appalling speciesism in its German application. Perhaps that is why great-uncle Alphonso is an artist as well as a natural scientist, and why dogs and fish and birds in Sebald are endowed with the possibility of sentience and memory: life itself in Sebald is always hallowed. Like the pro-Revolution

Romantic British poet, the British artist who changed the history of painting, and the British scientist who changed human perception, Sebald
"reads" art and science and literature from moral, social, and political perspectives as creatively salvationist — especially from this remote valley in
Wales, analogy for another. The ironic and dark gloss here is echoed in
Sebald's observation that, as a species, "we have evolved as some kind of
great error" (Zeeman 1998).

Austerlitz endures the bleakness of school in Oswestry in the marginal
Welsh Marches, where he is sent as Dafydd Elias, a Welsh Hebrew name
connoting Old Testament history and the patron saint of Wales, when
Gwendolyn falls ill. Sebald juxtaposes this "imprisonment" and intensified
exile with the invitations that Austerlitz's friend Gerald Fitzpatrick's
young, widowed mother Adela extends to him when she learns that he is
alone in the world. These afford Austerlitz an education of the imagination
and an introduction to a world of great natural beauty which help form
him, leading him toward his profession in art history, including architecture, which he interprets morally, as we see in his conversations with
Austerlitz. This is one train trip, at least, which leads to paradise, a textual
space invested with hope and affirmation.

The description of the journey from Oswestry up the Dee Valley and
into the Afon Mawwdach valley increases the expectation of arrival at
Barmouth as to a kind of promised land, the rich vitality of Andromeda
Lodge with its garden and natural history cabinets. Even with great-uncle
Evelyn's dreadful self-righteous piety, life here is enthused, a complete
contrast with the lifeless manse at treeless Bala, where the sermons of the
living God, visible all around, are diminished into tracts about man's
sinfulness.

What Austerlitz recalls in his conversation with the narrator in the bar
of the Great Eastern Hotel next to Liverpool Street station is the life of the
mind and the imagination that is awoken in him at Andromeda Lodge, the
great friendship with Gerald, the living presence of beauty, the expedition
to watch the moths on the hills at night, the breathtaking and changing
view from his room out to the Irish Sea. Alphonso's painting, the descriptions of which in their abstracted forms suggest Turner's watercolors
(126), becomes the trigger for a conversation about Alphonso's rather pessimistic view that "everything was fading before our eyes" (126), subverted perhaps by the comic suggestion of his wearing spectacles "with
grey silk tissue instead of lenses in the frames, so that landscape appeared
through a fine veil that muted its colours" (124). This is conveyed as a
rather endearing eccentricity, possibly Turner's habit, rather like the gentle vegetable world of Henry Selwyn in *The Emigrants*, but also as
Alphonso's enthusiasm for the rich variety and beauty and mystery of the
natural world, the Edmund Gosse world of the marine life found below
"the chalk cliffs of Devon and Cornwall" (126) and the "mysterious world

of moths" explored one night "on a promontory far above Andromeda Lodge" (127). The litany of beautiful names of these "night-winged creatures" (128), the exquisite details of their markings and colorings, their "keen hearing" (130), their flying in enormous numbers "that summer night . . . high above the estuary of the Mawddach" (131) when Alphonso talked of "the life and death of moths" (132), the boy Dafydd/Austerlitz wondering about "what kind of fear and pain they feel while they are lost" (133), connects with those bakelite tombs on the mantelpiece of the ghostly house in Alderney Street in London, the fear and pain felt during experiences of being lost, and the qualities of compassion and feeling that the narrator has responded to in his lonely friend Austerlitz's soliloquies.

For Austerlitz, who often felt as if he were "dreaming" (134) at Andromeda Lodge, that galactic place, a new world so far removed from life at Oswestry or Bala (but one subject to Voltaire's satirical reduction of utopian dream on Gerald's death and Austerlitz's discovery of what his own parents endured), the sheer changing beauty of light and color that he sees from "the room with the blue ceiling" becomes "the very evanescence of those visions that gave me, at the time, something like a sense of eternity" (135). The irony underpinning this is that the narrow, Bible-bound faith of Emyr Elias is light years away from this neo-Romantic engagement with the natural world, in the valley of the Mawddach River where the life-hallowing scientist, like Gosse on whom Sebald drew here (Bell 2003, 15), wrote up his theories challenging orthodoxy so profoundly, reinforcing, paradoxically, Voltaire's pessimistic view of man's nature in their subsequent misappropriation. Sebald's oblique satire here also appropriates Benjamin's short essay, "The Ring of Saturn" (2002, 885), which employs Grandville's cartoon of utopian fantasy satirizing the utopian socialism of Charles Fourier which envisaged a future in which humankind joined with the stars in cosmic harmony.

Gerald's observation about the swallows, that "they never slept on the earth" (136) but glided high up on the air, speaks the portent of his own death, in a flying accident in the lovely Savoy Alps after he becomes an astrophysicist. Natural beauty, as in *The Rings of Saturn*, is no magic charm against accidental death. This catches, intratextually, at the image of the swallows in *The Rings of Saturn* where the narrator recalls his childhood in W, watching the flight of the swallows and imagining that their ribboning flight paths somehow bound up the world for the evening. This is a beautiful illusion of safety or sanctuary, but an illusion that suggests "home" is only ever really temporary. As the Fitzpatrick dog Toby is curiously the same as the one with the little girl in the Vyrnwy photograph (136), before the flooding of the valley, in the same way that Sebald's friend Tripp appropriates the shoe from Van Eyck's *The Arnolfini Marriage* in one of his own paintings with a "board-game" floor (in *Logis in einem Landhaus*) as though the dog has traveled across a temporal plane, so Sebald suggests, our mapping of connection, of temporal and spatial itineraries, is a consoling illusion. Paradoxically this imaginative license does not respect boundaries, and makes new and unexpected associations, draws new patterns of connection that offer unexpected adventure. This is part of the rich poetic space in the Welsh section of *Austerlitz*.

In this beautiful rural place, a *Landhaus*, Adela Fitzpatrick has endured the loss of her husband "shot down over the Ardennes in the last winter of the war" (111). Compassion not bitterness is born out of her suffering. The precisely indexed journey from the railway at Barmouth, half an hour by pony trap to the gravel drive leading to "the two-storey house built of pale-grey brick, protected to the north and north-east by the Llawr Llech hills" (113), the panoramic view of the "full length of the estuary from Dolgellau to Barmouth" (113–14) with "the little village of Arthog" (114) and "the shadowy side of Cader Idris rising to a height of almost three thousand feet above the shimmering sea" (114) all make this a spot which the disobedient reader might mark very easily on a map, whether this house is there or not the real, ten-kilometer "Panoramic Walk" alongside the Mawddach up into the valley. There is a phenomenological and Proustian play of the distortion of space here, like Proust's twin spires of Martinville appearing in the same spatial plane as the third spire of Vieuxvicq in the viewer's perspective, the church at Vieuxvicq one hill behind Martinville. Sebald makes Austerlitz recall his own sense of Arthog seeming "in certain atmospheric conditions . . . an eternity away" (114), with the play of shadows in the sunset a pastiche of Plato's image of the shadows on the cave wall representing our occluded relationship with the real. Adela's palm trees and camel caravan across the wall, like the stars in Fitzgerald's *Rubaiyat of Omar Khayyam* in *The Rings of Saturn*, offer to Austerlitz Keats's magic window of the imagination in that strange interstitial time of day which is neither day nor night.

The natural history treasure-house of Andromeda Lodge, a paradise marred by the "schism in the Fitzpatrick clan" (119), is for Austerlitz an Edenic memory of a time that will come to an end with the double funeral of the great-uncles, a strangely blended shadow at Cutiau of a Turner watercolor of a funeral at Lausanne, the emigration of Adela to North Carolina (unsurprisingly with an entomologist), and the death of Gerald in an aeroplane accident, which causes Austerlitz such traumatic grief that he never recovers. The exquisite beauty of Andromeda Lodge in Wales becomes a site of melancholy and mourning as it recedes into the past. Only in its reconstruction, in Austerlitz's inaugural narration and the listening narrator's subsequent one, can the world of Andromeda Lodge be made resonant for a reader who consults maps, looks at photographs of the houses along the Mawddach, reads part of *The Descent of Man*, researches Turner's watercolors, consults Wordsworth's *Collected Poems*, but who might undertake in vain the ten-kilometer Mawddach Panoramic Walk.

Austerlitz's memory has transformed these experiences in the telling of them to his listener one night in the barely perceivable Great Eastern Hotel bar; for the narrator, as for the disobedient reader, the listening and retelling becomes a matter of poetry.

Place can represent our imprisonment in a material world which makes us mortal, but beauty, as with Marie de Verneuil's grandfather's beautifully printed little medical book of 1755 with its evocative language, Marie an "instrument[s] of divine mercy" (378), we can be delivered from our confinement in the world-hospital, as was the narrator from that hard place Salpêtrière, by "immersing" ourselves in a "better world" (379), through the redemptive power or the cure of reading ourselves into poetic space.

The Rings of Saturn: Pilgrimage Stations

The journey undertaken in *The Rings of Saturn* is circular, beginning in a hospital room in Norwich, and returning to the same city, this time as the place where the "beautiful black Mantua silk" (296) was woven for the mourning gown of the future Queen Consort, Mary, the German wife of George V, the "Duchess of Teck" (296), on the death of Queen Victoria. Norwich becomes a place where the finest connections are woven like silk, where death and mourning and the transmigration of the soul underpin the act of displacement that is the journey, the connection of threads woven by the narrator in "his" text. The book is a collection of memories in two senses. It recalls the actual journey that the narrator has made, and the other journeys he recalls while walking in Suffolk, an intricate braiding of different threads of itinerary and the places represented in them.

The traveling, thinking, imagining narrator lies in his hospital bed as an invalid for the duration of the text, much as Marlow and the other narrator of *Heart of Darkness* stay on board the yawl moored in the Thames for the duration of Marlow's tale, generating a remembered journey which the listeners undertake, as does the reader, following the narrative up the Congo into that heart of darkness. In Sebald's text the reader is taken on a journey whose stations are sites where traces of destruction can be discerned, as with the pilgrimage destination Orford Ness, the bleak wasteland from where Operation Gomorrah was launched, and where his narrator, as German pilgrim, can only wonder, wordlessly, at the awful mystery which haunts the place, and where the only response possible is some rite of exequy.

A Country House and a Seaside Resort

The train journey from Norwich to Lowestoft signals the analepsis to one year ago, when the narrator set off for the East Anglian coast. The reader has been taken to catch "the old diesel train" from which she and the narrator will alight at Somerleyton (31). Even the transportation is an anachronism. There has been a further time slip too, as the narrator has observed: the broken windmills and conical brick buildings seen from the train look like "the relics of an extinct civilisation" (29). Quixote has passed this way. As the train travels eastwards, the narrative seems to be traveling temporally backwards, through a landscape of ruin that suggests the past was civilized, where broken windmills code the abandonment of the practice of harnessing nature for productive rather than destructive ends. Place here is a temporalized site, where the narrator is ruminating about the desuetude he observes from the carriage window, the reader uncertain of the journey's purpose or destination but uneasy about this air of entropy, the ends of things.

Somerleyton Hall, the first station in the narrator's journey, is a remnant of time lost. "It takes just one awful second . . . and an entire epoch passes" (31). The original manor, dating from the Middle Ages, has been demolished and the present Somerleyton, rebuilt in the nineteenth century, has become a tourist attraction. Buildings are temporal palimpsests. This narrator is no idle tourist, but a sardonic observer, arriving as a transgressor, taking the reader with him through a hole in the fence. In his view Somerleyton has been prostituted to the commercial imperative of upkeep. His arch observations about the titled incumbent, "Her Majesty The Queen's Master of the Horse," driving a toy train around the park of his estate, a ticket satchel slung across his person (32), suggest a comic image of economic leveling in contemporary Britain, the country seats of the aristocracy reduced to amusement parks. What is the reader to make of this satire? Is this also a trace of "an extinct civilisation" (29)? Is civilization itself also at risk? Are there layers of change in the fortunes of Somerleyton Hall over time which suggest that "tradition" is a pattern which can run out in the fabric of society?

Great families may not last "three oaks" (24), and the builder of the extant Somerleyton was "a bricklayer's labourer" turned brilliant speculator and entrepreneur who built "prestigious construction projects in London" (32), but the history of the place the narrator describes takes on an oneiric quality in the telling which is at odds with its representation in the narrator's contingency. Its history was "an oriental palace in a fairy tale" (35), but to the eyes of some contemporary visitors, the narrator and his companion the reader, Somerleyton Hall has been degraded into a tawdry venture overseen by the "stuffed polar bear" in the entrance hall: "with its yellowish and moth-eaten fur, it resembles a ghost bowed by sorrows" (36). This displaced victim suggests that what was exotic has become in this disenchantment merely disposable.

The narrator observes, walking through the house, "there are indeed moments . . . when one is not quite sure whether one is in a country house in Suffolk or some kind of no-man's-land, on the shores of the Arctic Ocean or in the heart of the dark continent. Nor can one readily say which decade or century it is, for many ages are superimposed here and coexist" (36). The narrator surrenders to the disorienting effect that this indeterminate place induces in a suggestive visitor sensitive to ghosts, including the reference to Conrad's (and Casement's) indictment of colonial exploitation, here the building of urban ugliness that has provided the wealth from which the house was rebuilt, and cruel trophy hunting in the Arctic that the presence of the bear represents. The reader, by contrast, nudged by these intimations, is not in the thrall of spurs to imaginative historical transport here. On the contrary, she is goaded into this disobedience of interrogating the space created around the narrator's subject. As always in Sebald, the manifestations of the accumulation of capital and the exercise of power are to be scrutinized with a vigilance that a disobediently interrogatory reader brings to bear, following her own trajectories before returning to the narrator's side.

The imprisoned and exiled *émigré* Chinese quail, photographed from an empathetic position level with its own perspective, and the noble splendor of the park's trees grown to maturity, concern the narrator, not the accumulation of objects in the house. The narrator's view does not privilege the human. His attachment to the natural world, the emigrant Chinese quail (like the polar bear a forlorn victim) and the trees of the estate reflects his bias. Lebanese cedars, favored by Sebald as Old Testament symbols of sanctuary, appear in this text later at Ditchingham Park, and the yew maze at the "heart of this mysterious estate" (38) invokes a Borgesian labyrinth, compelling the narrator to escape his predicament of being lost by drawing lines in the sand to mark the dead ends, a joke which ironizes the fate of everything else at Somerleyton and implicates the narrator's and the reader's fates. Where is the clew of Ariadne's thread from which the narrator and the reader might make their escape from a maze of that funereal tree, the yew?

The narrator's encounter with the gardener, William Hazel, leads to an episode of embedded narrative which brings into view the Allied bombing raids on Germany from "the sixty-seven airfields that were established on East Anglia after 1940" (38), and the loss of more than fifty thousand men in the eighth airfleet alone. This appalling loss of life, like the loss of lives in the destroyed German cities, elicits a nonpartisan, supranational sense of almost incredulous horror in the reader, as the end of the journey is prefigured in this garden narrative, the horror at odds with the paradise-garden of the park where there is still another shadow.

Two American pilots staged a "dogfight," a game which ended in collision, the lake at Somerleyton swallowing them "without a sound" (40). This is sheer stupidity: two lives lost "playing at the game of war," the sexual innuendo of the names of each of the aircraft ironizing power, the Rhine mythology of travelers lured to their death, the appropriated European names of the hometowns (Versailles and Athens) of these American Flight Lieutenants satirizing the armistice of the Great War and the birthplace of reason and democracy. Progress in the New World? Their relics are buried in Somerleyton's earth, its garden their memorial. This threads another itinerary, connecting the Old and New Worlds — the hope of the Enlightenment dashed through folly as well as evil, as Voltaire predicted.

As the narrator continues his journey, walking now from Somerleyton to Lowestoft, he passes Blundeston prison with its capacity of 1200 inmates. This is a Dickensian site, David Copperfield's childhood home, but for the disobedient reader, who has registered this piece of literary and historical knowledge that the narrator does not gloss, it is a nineteenth-century anachronism, a "fortified town" where inmates, deprived of liberty as punishment, live as social ghosts. This too is a haunting mockery of "progress," increasing the bleakness of Suffolk. When the narrator arrives at Lowestoft, the reader is not surprised to discover that the town is deserted and run-down, and that a "feeling of wretchedness" overcomes the narrator as he walks through this landscape of despair, past its absurd "solution" to social ills like poverty. The disobedient reader, resisting the onward movement of the journey to nowhere in particular, for no destination has been given, might choose to stop, to exercise her own mind on this eloquent silence about what constitutes progress, what we have learned from history, how "cured" we might become, treating symptoms instead of causes.

As the narrator consults his "turn of the century guidebook" and reflects on the town's decline, the fact that it is deserted "at the height of the season — if one can speak of a season in Lowestoft" (42), becomes manifest at every turn. The empty lobby of the Albion Hotel (the mythological, here ironized, name for England) is presided over by another of those solitary figures reminiscent of Hopper's paintings. She "avoided eye contact; either her gaze remained fixed on the floor or she looked right through me as if I were not there" (43). The narrator has become a kind of specter himself, haunting the deserted hotel.

The meal the narrator is served is no ambrosia-and-nectar banquet: an appalling farce, it consists of "a fish that had doubtless lain entombed in the deep-freeze for years. The breadcrumb armour-plating . . . what eventually proved to be nothing but an empty shell . . . The tartare sauce which I had had to squeeze out of a plastic sachet . . . turned grey by the sooty breadcrumbs . . . the remains of soggy chips that gleamed with fat" (43). This travesty collapses the vaingloriousness of "Albion" into risible hyperbole, making even bleaker this place where there is neither beauty nor imaginative possibility, let alone any sense of England's glorious history, the poetry of Milton and Blake in which the name of "Albion" is inscribed as a promised land. Like Somerleyton, Lowestoft is a place whose representation in the narrator's telling codes entropy.

What is the disobedient reader to make of the Albion Hotel in Lowestoft, a seriously arrested place? The hotel window gives onto a view that is "somewhere between the darkness and the light" (43) where even the rolling waves are somehow "motionless" (43). The *coup de grâce* is the corpse in its coffin in the loading area at Lowestoft Central Station, on its way to its final journey. The disobedient reader, uncertain whether to laugh or not at this absurdist concatenation of hyperbolic stasis, must decide whether the narrator's ruminative melancholy, inflected by an intertwined humor, is serious social criticism or whether the invalid "writer's" melancholy is inflecting his prose, as his psychic affliction burdened his mood when he set out on that late August walk. The reader cannot be certain of the boundary between the narrator's subject and the places to which he is traveling, or the extent to which represented place has been displaced by the construction of a poetic space in which a meditation on last things is occurring.

The former glories of Lowestoft as a "most salubrious" resort, its historical prestige, have been communicated to the narrator by a Frederick Farrar, born in Lowestoft and brought up by three sisters — "Violet, Iris and Rose" — who endures the terrible pain of separation from them when he is sent to boarding school "near Flore in Northhamptonshire" (46). The bouquet of names and the coincidence of the name of the location of the school are sinisterly disguised clues to Frederick's frightful end, when he sets fire to his dressing gown and dies from severe burns in his exquisite garden filled with "rare roses and violets," and irises, "one of his favourites" (46–47). This voicing of Lowestoft's former glories by a gentle, cultivated individual who suffers a most appalling death, "one cloudless day in May," is inflected with the further irony of lying, dying, "in a cool, half-shaded place, where the tiny *viola labradorica* with its almost black leaves had spread" (47). Again the reader is uncertain how to reconcile the temptation to smile at the absurdly funereal leaves of this emigrant plant (a long way from Labrador to Lowestoft) and this ironically poetic place of death and the sense of horror and pity at the foolishness and fatefulness of Farrar's end. Just what, the disobedient reader wonders, is the nature of this thread of deaths in gardens, of paradise sullied by catastrophe, the agonizing death of a frail, gentle, elderly man, his mind filled with imagined dreams and memories of a single moment of great happiness seen "through flowing white veils" (48), of Albion's green and pleasant land turned grey? What place is this? The answer is quite possibly, given Sebald's narrator's saturnine view, the "World," that "Hospital" (Browne 83).

On the Cliff (Not with the Duke of Gloucester)

The curious sight of a set of tents containing solitary and uncommunicative fishermen, who have no hope of catching anything from the uneconomical and in any case fished-out sea beds off the East Anglian coast, is constructed as the next station, a waiting zone for men who "just want to be in a place where they have the world behind them, and before them nothing but emptiness" (52). Under the grey skies of East Anglia, a permanently melancholy skyscape, this stage-set of the bleak beach might recall Beckett or Lear, whose kingdom this was, to the disobedient reader, but to the narrator's mind it summons the herring, a fish "always a popular didactic model in primary school, the principal emblem, as it were, of the indestructibility of Nature" (53). "A species always threatened by disaster" (57), the herring is the victim of human predation in the narrator's meditation on the institution of a cycle of "endless destruction" (in 1770 the estimated haul was sixty billion) of a creature whose "intricate" (57) structure, its sentience, the beauty of its coloring when alive and the changes to its coloring in death, its emission of a glowing luminescence, enlarge the reader's sense of complicit guilt.

The juxtaposition in the text between this coastal scene and the effect of the liberation of the camp at Bergen Belsen on one Englishman is shocking, forcing the reader into forging a disobedient link of her own with that curious place of solitude the narrator observes on the shore "three or four miles south of Lowestoft" (51). "Gazing into eternity" (59) as he sits on the shore (recalling Joyce's Stephen Dedalus on the strand), a "grey shadow" (59) cast on the earth by the "great cumulus clouds" (59), the narrator recalls that solitary individual (nearly all the figures the narrator engages with in all the texts are solitary), the eccentric Major present at the liberation of Bergen Belsen, as permanently damaged by the sight of what human beings have been capable of doing to each other.

Living alone in a great stone house with a large neglected park in Henstead in Suffolk, except for his "simple" (62) housekeeper from Beccles, Le Strange's eccentricity, his madness even, like Gloucester's, are the product of his exposure to cruelty and betrayal (64). This pilgrimage, with its "stations" of reflection or recollection, send the narrator on a small side-trip before returning to the main itinerary, but for the disobedient reader, these alternative parallel paths call her seductively, potentially for longer.

Those other strange solitary individuals hunched in their tents on the pebbled beach staring out toward eternity are, like LeStrange, damaged in some mysterious way, their purposelessness, now that fishing is impossible, itself a kind of paralysis, stasis, even death. This is where the narrator sees a trace of the Ancient Mariner in the unmoving sailing boat (66), an image which recalls Coleridge's poem whose core considers the failure of love and the wanton destruction of living things. The coast between Lowestoft and Covehithe is a space of meditation and memory, a place of empty vistas, precarious cliff edges and despair.

Later in the text the narrator, meditating and lost on the (not so blasted) heath and then stumbling back onto the path, discovers one late summer afternoon at his friend the poet Michael Hamburger's house when he arrives "in the peaceful garden" (181) that "I felt . . . as if I was losing the ground from under my feet" (188). The reason for this threat of complete displacement is temporal, the perception of the "as yet unexplained phenomenon of apparent duplication" that he was somehow also living Michael Hamburger's life but just twenty years behind him on the road, is broken off but also reinforced when Michael's wife Anne appears and tells the fantastic story of Mr. Squirrel, an undertaker suffering from memory loss who aspires to act in *King Lear*. Dunwich Heath, where the narrator has just come from, is the blasted heath in *King Lear*, the play that Flaubert described as inducing madness in him (Steegmuller 211) by a writer whose work he likened to "the planetary system" (Steegmuller 210). Loss of memory and the absurd repetition of the line in Act 4, scene seven ("They say Edgar, his banish'd son, is with the Earl of Kent in Germany") give way to a dream retold by Anne which recalls Emily Dickinson's poem "Because I could not Stop for Death" and the images of paradise in the exotic dreamlike foliage of Leonardo's *The Annunciation* and his portrait of Ginevra de Benci (190). On this site the poetic space is so haunted as to be a threat to sanity.

These sequences, cinematic in their juxtaposition and displacement and destabilizing for the reader as well as the narrator, conclude in the garden later that evening with a Kafkaesque image of a beetle rowing across the dark water of the well, from "one dark shore to the other" (190), where the Hölderlin pump (bearing the year of his birth, 1770) signals an affinity between Hamburger, the narrator, and Friedrich Hölderlin, between whom vast spaces are mysteriously suggested. Hölderlin is the lyric poet, unsung in his own lifetime, born in southwest Germany and friend of Schelling and Hegel and mentored by Schiller, who was stricken with recurrent mental illness after the trauma of parting from his employer's wife with whom he had fallen in love, and who dreamed of restoring to Germany the cultural ideas of classical Greece. This common but displaced German tradition, and the other curious coincidences in that Suffolk garden, on that still summer's night waiting for a taxi, offer the disobedient reader a path which might disclose her discovery of, among other things, the deeply ironic fact that Hölderlin's poetry was celebrated during the years of the Third Reich, by Heidegger and others, as instilling a sense of patriotism and national pride because he sought to elevate the status of German as a language to the level of the ancient classical ones, Greek and Latin, in his own poetry, a private poetic ambition appropriated and perverted to tyrannous political ends. The strange poetic effect of the doomed but persevering Kafkan beetle rowing across the wine-dark well water is enigmatic but ominous, inducing a threat of madness in the narrator and offering the disobedient reader, in retreat from being drawn into that deep well of the past that speaks to the narrator, a space in which to consider the weird and uncanny effect of these happenstances now freighted with mysterious invitations to meaning.

Sebald's narrator's stories told here, not by a number of pilgrims to win a free dinner and to while away the time on the journey, but by one pilgrim to himself, show how the actual geographic journey is really a metonymy for the multiplicity of journeys that are occurring simultaneously to a rich diversity of places in the narrator's, and the reader's, mind, a proliferation of pilgrimages to places which the narrator has created as stations in the journey, where the actual journey fades away and the mind's journeying displaces it with its juxtaposed series of images.

The Emigrants: No One Home

Each of the four stories in this text is about displacement, as is the fifth embedded one. The narrator's own first experience of displacement is from the village of W in southwest Germany to the small town of S, "19 kilometres away," when he is eight, riding in the "cab of Alpenvogel's wine-red furniture van," "a voyage half-way round the world, though it will have lasted an hour at the very most" (29–30). The phenomenological shift which expands spatial distance (as it shrinks that separating the church steeples in Marcel's perception) is a child's perception here, and yet it also registers the significance of home as a place of belonging and everywhere else as alterity. This is the condition in which Selwyn, Bereyter, Adelwarth, Ferber, and the narrator can be found by the reader. For the narrator and his wife "Clara," Hingham and Prior's Gate offer a transit stop in their own journey into the future, a job, and a house of their own, but for Henry Selwyn it is the place where he waits for the end he accelerates. The narrator has left W behind him as he pursues the road ahead; for Paul Bereyter it is both the place that haunts him as the site of the ruined promise of happiness it once held for him and the place he consequently can never really leave, his choice of his own means of departure a terrible irony which recalls the fate of his beloved; for Ambros Adelwarth, grieving for Cosmo Solomon who became his life, returning to the sanatorium in Ithaca constructs that place of Cosmo's death as the wanderer's home, even when it is characterized by abjection; for Ferber home is the space in his studio where he displaces the memories of the past by painting seven days a week, before he is taken to hospital, that place "to dye in" (Browne 83).

In "anthracite-coloured Manchester" (156) the narrator takes a room at a tiny hotel, the Arosa, a "time when I felt a deep sense of isolation in which I might well have become completely submerged" (155). In this text isolation becomes a place, a place of such loneliness that it can lead to despair, and in three instances, death. These are individuals who have emigrated out of society into the deep vortex of their selves, their own loneliness.

Eccentric or marginalized, their fringe-dwelling, in flint hermitages in a garden, in the flats of friends, in a sanatorium, in a studio down by the docks, in a shabby hotel room or in someone else's house, internalizes these people so that they dwell increasingly in the privacy of their own subjectivity. Only Ferber's art and the narrator's text offer a way out, a point of the promise of contiguity or communication more substantial than brief encounters, conversations or dinners which afford temporal displacement of a short-lived kind, away from the burden of isolation. The spectator and the reader are themselves ghosts of the artist's imagination, the dialogical encounter between the artefact and the spectator/reader is an aspiration, making of the text a hopeful poetic space.

Ithaca

The place where both Cosmo Solomon and Ambros Adelwarth die, a private sanatorium, is visited by the narrator when he travels to Ithaca, New York in the summer of 1984 after visiting his emigrant American relatives in 1981 (71) and reading his great-uncle's travel diary given to him then. The drive to Ithaca from New York along Highway 17 "seems to be in the middle of nowhere . . . an outsize toyland where the place names [Deposit, Delhi, Neversink and Nineveh] had been picked at random by some invisible giant child, from the ruins of another world long since abandoned" (105). The narrator's sense of place in Sebald is often shaped by the distortions of the memory or of the imagination. Here, in what was the New World of America, from the perspective of the British-domiciled European relative of German immigrants, a world has somehow been "abandoned" and its names retrieved from desuetude and reallocated in a kind of game. This colonial appropriation of the names of the former world as a way of domesticating the strange is both an ironic part of Sebald's fiction and a means by which he destabilizes the reader's sense of place, uncoupling the connection between name and geographical location and reconnecting it in a new and unsettling way.

Observing and, as always, naming the trees in the landscape (the oaks and alders, spruces, birches, and aspens, pine, and larches), the narrator recalls his childhood fascination with American geography and the place names whose exotic quality — "Sabattis, Gabriels, Hawkeye, Amber Lake, Lake Lila, and Lake Tear-in-the-Clouds" (106–7) — he recites to himself like a litany, or the bracelet of names which designate a railway line, driving into the panoramic and beautiful sunset as he heads toward a place named after Odysseus' island home. Taking a room in a guest-house, the narrator mistakes the blossom on a shrub momentarily for snow, and from the window in his room smells the cypress in the garden and hears the rushing sound of the Ithaca Falls. The narrator, deeply sensitive to the

beauty of the natural environment, has researched the region before arriving, suggesting to the disobedient reader that the topography of this section of the journey is reliably "mapped" even though its names and its
features are disconcerting and suggest alternative itineraries to the reflectively disobedient reader.

The narrator's logical and systematic enquiries on arrival do not produce the information he is searching for, a confirmation to the reader that
all is not quite what it seems. In the Grimm fairy-tale modality that always
nibbles at the edge of Sebald's discourse, it is the "crooked" (108) porter
with the broom on the front path who provides what the narrator needs
and what more orthodox methods have failed to provide: the directions to
the sanatorium where no patients have been admitted for nearly twenty
years and where Professor Fahnstock's psychiatric successor, Dr. Abramsky,
still lives, having "become a beekeeper" (108), a curious change of occupation which the disobedient reader might construe as the retreat recom-
mended by Virgil's *Georgics*, albeit a pastoral idyll in which the beekeeper
Aristaeus kills Eurydice by hunting her in a forest, intending to violate her
(4.315–558).

On arrival the narrator immediately compares the decaying wooden
villa he finds in a hundred-acre park with a Russian dacha or an Austrian
hunting lodge, more historically resonant displacements. Observing again
by name the trees — "Lebanese cedars, mountain hemlocks, Douglas firs,
larches, Arolla and Monterey pines, and feathery swamp cypresses" (109)
— together with the "woodland meadows between the trees where blue-
bells, white cardamines and yellow goatsbeard grow side by side" (109),
and the ferns and maples growing in the shade, the narrator discovers, in
the middle of this paradise-garden concealing its original purpose, the
psychiatrist-turned-apiarist tending to his hives. The reader, more alarmed
than the narrator at this correction of position in Dr. Abramsky's career
in which he has made the sanatorium his own home, listens avidly to what
Abramsky has to say.

In this setting the narrator hears the story of Adelwarth's final period,
the "shock treatment, which in the early Fifties . . . really came close to
torture or martyrdom" (111). This replacement of the chemical induce-
ment of epileptic fits with shock treatment was regarded as great progress,
but in the telling of Dr. Abramsky, it becomes the reason he finally ceases
practice, confirming the reader's suspicion that he too is damaged in
some way. He explains: "I do not expect anyone can really imagine the
pain and wretchedness once stored up in this extravagant timber palace,
and I hope all this misfortune will gradually melt away now as it falls
apart" (110).

As is usual in Sebald, the weight of the living experience of dead
souls is still available in the places where that experience has occurred. The
souls of the dead haunt place, and place itself is constructed not just as

represented image, but as a space which affords perspective into the depths of the past. In Abramsky's telling these are horrific, making Ithaca's sanatorium into a hell, despite its exotic foreign building and its beautiful garden. Its otherworldiness presents like the witch's gingerbread house in *Hänsel und Gretel*, full of danger, fear, and death, where the wandering and the lost find not sanctuary but terror.

The "worst of the incidental injuries, such as dislocated shoulders or jaws, broken teeth or other fractures" were increased by Fahnstock's use of the "block" method, "more than a hundred electric shocks at intervals of only a very few days" (112). The gradual destruction of the minds of the patients, Adelwarth offering himself to the treatment willingly in a kind of appalling masochism induced by grief and loneliness, was, hideously, interpreted as "signs of successful therapy" (112), the kind of perversion of language that belongs to the deceit of tyranny, requiring a vigilant reader's interrogation.

Fahnstock's Austrian background and Abramsky's father's Viennese one suggest links with both Freud and Hitler. Fahnstock's "experimental mania" (114) taking over and Abramsky withdrawing more and more into his own disobedience, it is the description of the courtly, complicit behavior of the exquisitely dressed elderly man gradually being destroyed by his "treatment" that invades the mind of the reader as Abramsky and the narrator walk through the arboretum and up the drive, sending a deep chill of horror through the reader even though the walk up the drive is a virtual one.

Adelwarth's reference to the vision of "the butterfly man" (115) on the only day that he forgets to appear for his treatment, who appeared also before Aunt Fini on one of her visits as a "middle-aged man with a white net on a pole" (104), will appear again, eliding the boundaries of the discrete sections of *The Emigrants*, in the Max Ferber story when Ferber is in danger of leaping down from the top of Grammont in Switzerland, and is saved from doing so by the man with "a large white gauze butterfly net" who speaks "in an English voice that was refined but quite unplaceable" (174) and encourages him to descend for dinner in Montreux. This Nabokovian figure, recalling the narrator's picture in the first section, becomes the subject of a painting by Ferber in the last one, a faceless apparition which he spends over a year on, discouraged by his inability to catch "even the remotest impression of the strangeness of the apparition" (174). For the reader there appears to be some mysterious, inexplicable connection between the butterfly man and the "white goose wing" (116) with which Abramsky waves farewell, kept in his right-hand pocket. These mysteries, like parts of some terrible fairy tale, offer not coded meanings so much as the reader's experience of that strange uncanniness that suggests that she too may have wandered too far from home and be unable to find the way back.

A Suite at the Midland Hotel

At the beginning of the "Max Ferber" section of *The Emigrants*, the narrator makes his home for some months in a room on the third floor of Gracie Irlam's Arosa, a small but labyrinthine hotel in a laneway, a building "scarcely the width of two windows" (151) in Manchester. At the end he takes a room for one night at the Midland Hotel where his friend the artist Max Ferber has been living in a suite of rooms, before being taken to the Withington hospital, a former Victorian workhouse (231–32).

This marks the different turns that each of these emigrant lives has taken. Ferber's home is itinerant by definition, a hotel a transit point, much like a railway station, a place which suggests temporary rather than permanent dwelling, as the narrator makes clear. He describes the Midland as "a fantastic fortress" (232), built at the height of the industrial nineteenth century with its nine floors and six hundred rooms and "chestnut-coloured bricks and chocolate-coloured ceramic tiles" (232) suggesting permanence and solidity. This is ironized by the narrator's observation that the hitherto "luxurious plumbing," its "brass and copper pipes . . . highly polished," the capacious bathtubs and monsoonal showers (232), the palm courtyard with "its hothouse atmosphere" (233) are, like the rest of the hotel, "on the brink of ruin" (233). What the narrator described as "some tropical isle of the blessed, reserved for mill owners, where even the clouds in the sky were made of cotton" (233) has become the shabby, derelict home of the artist now consigned to hospital with pulmonary emphysema, a place the narrator likens to a hotel in Poland.

The target of his irony here is late twentieth-century Britain, particularly the economic legacy of the Thatcher years, but that this is the "home" of the exiled painter Ferber, with his terrible personal story of loss, makes it an eloquent site of elegy. The palmy days of prosperity in the city "from which industrialization had spread across the entire world" (156) have disappeared. The hotel staff prowl "like sleepwalkers" (233), the heating hardly works at all (the narrator keeps his coat on in his room), "fur flakes from out of the taps" (233), and the furnishing in his turret room on the fifth floor reminds the narrator of "the inside of a jewellery box or violin case" (234). All very well for a one-night stay, but for Ferber this seeming elevation in his living ("since his income permitted it" 232) represents "home." It seems to preserve him, too, like some *bibelot* or plangent instrument of a bygone age, the Europe of the nineteenth century perhaps.

The sounds of the rain and the wind and of the intermittent traffic below are bleak, confirming the desolation of this place and encouraging the narrator's reverie. He imagines he hears an orchestra tuning up, an opera singer singing arias from *Parsifal* in German. He sees and hears a music-hall scene, with prostitutes and barrels of Australian sherry, a woman in pink tulle playing the Wurlitzer. These are his memories of life in the sixties, not so very long ago, but an aeon given the bleakness of the present. He imagines stage flats and sees on them photographs of the Litzmannstadt ghetto in Lodz, so that Manchester (that nineteenth-century city of Germans and Jews 192) becomes "*polski Manczester*" (235–36), and the absence of the inmates of Lodz's ghetto and the absence of Ferber lying in Withington Hospital, contemplating the permanent cure of death (231), make the Midland Hotel, that halfway place to nowhere, even bleaker.

His mind filled with Ferber's mother's memoirs, Luisa Lanzberg/ Ferber is herself part of the narrator's experience of the absence in the Midland Hotel. Not because she was ever there, but because her son, the painter, has handed over all that remains of her life to the narrator, so that it is now invested in his presence. It is Ferber who describes the memoirs as "like one of those evil German fairy tales in which, once you are under the spell, you have to carry on to the finish, till your heart breaks, with whatever work you have begun — in this case, the remembering, writing and reading" (193). Now that Ferber is also perhaps on the point of disappearance in Withington Hospital, the narrator, who has traveled to Kissingen and Steinach where Luisa lived (218), and visited the Jewish cemetery there (222–25), observing the effect on himself of the German amnesia and "mental impoverishment" he sees everywhere (225), is also enchanted, "under the spell" of such an evil German fairy tale that he, writer and reader, is condemned to carry it everywhere with him, sitting alone in the haunted plush-lined interior of the turret room on the fifth floor of the Midland Hotel in Manchester, until his own "heart breaks" (193).

Vertigo: "Mind The Gap"

In Sebald's first fiction text the representation of place is consistently filtered through the narrator's psychic disorientation so that the reader cannot help but be mindful that she finds herself, in the textual journey, in a place that is configured by the disoriented mind of the narrator. There is no elsewhere outside that place except in the disobedient reader's interrogatory space which infiltrates itself into the gap where irony can, from time to time, be glimpsed as an authorial trace.

On the train traveling from London to the north of England at the end of the text, the narrator's dream conflates his own memory of a weirdly barren alpine scene with Pepys's eyewitness description of the Great Fire of London, suggesting a metaphoric layering of more recent conflagration. This is where the reader leaves the narrator's journey in *Vertigo*, a journey which began with an account of a transalpine expedition.

There is a symmetry about this journey, a circular one in two respects, actual and textual.

Sebald's narrator blends historical reality with memory and dream in "his" literary discourse, a vertiginous descent into a psychological destabilizing that induces disorientation in a reader expecting an historical account. The account of Beyle's Napoleonic crossing is indexed by doodles which serve as maps written by someone who also seems to be Henri Brulard. These "maps" produce a very imprecise sense of place that is less about geographical coordinates than it is about the experience of being somewhere foreign or new, the prelude to a journey which is also a sentimental education, and the sexual initiation of a young man never actually identified by the narrator as Stendhal. Literature and history are braided together in a way that suggests the representation of place itself is an arbitrary, ambiguous, unstable matter.

Milan is the place where opera and women initiate Beyle into experiences which shape his sense of himself, and also, like his military ones, afford him memories on which he will draw in the writing of his novels. These memories are part of fictional process, and the representation of Milan is less about place being represented than it is the site of a lesson to a young man. This lesson is that his first experience of Cimarosa's opera, in the provincial town of Ivrea, was filled with magic and enchantment, firing his imagination and his sensibility, and that the second time at La Scala, in the metropolis of Milan, is a disappointing echo of the earlier experience — something that entails melancholy and disappointment. This has an oblique suggestiveness about Beyle's other exploits, in the light of his life-long and obsessive pursuit of the chimaera of love, the focus of this first section.

This irony reflects on a traveler who underestimates or overestimates the significance of place, a disobedient reader who travels to actual places in pursuit of the imaginative resonance of their use in fiction, but also on the traveler-writer whose sense of place is shaped by the nature of his knowledgeable and contemplative engagement with it, "reading" it as a temporal palimpsest. When the narrator returns, in the words of Monteverdi's opera, "*Il Ritorno in Patria*," to W in the final section of *Vertigo*, the repetition of the pattern of the mythologized journey of Odysseus is ironized in the narrator's desire to "write" his own version of that story here in the final section, part of his literary itinerary, because the journey itself does not end here. W is no longer "home." After so long away, the narrator can only reconstruct W as a poetic space. This is also the way he presents Beyle's engagement with place to the reader, as a poetic space shaped by memory's recollection of it.

The transalpine expedition brings Beyle, in the narrator's account, belatedly to Marengo, a site which Beyle experiences already as historical because the great battle, Napoleon's first major victory, is over. All he sees are the results, the traces of slaughter rather than victory or defeat, even though he knows that the *Grande Armée* has been victorious. Marengo, like the appearance of General Marmont and like the painting of Ivrea a little later, is a site of slippage, a place which shows how quickly memories of events and people embedded in place become unreliable, even fictional. They mask what was real with a simulacrum which now represents reality, becoming that reality. This is how the painting of Ivrea displaces Beyle's actual memory of the place. What the narrator comes to W in search of is not so much the past, which he knows is unavailable, but the traces of it from which he can construct, in writing, his simulacrum of it, his verbal painting which will represent his memories of it.

This is disturbing and disorienting for a traveler who must keep a sense of her own bearings. Staying as a guest at the Engelwirt Inn in W in southwest Germany cannot be for her the experience of staying in the narrator's former home. She must take her own bearings in W, just as when she finds herself sitting on the Norwich–London train, she is able to get off the train, now that the narrator has fallen asleep, to consult her own copy of Pepys's Diary, to find out what really happened and where. A vigilant traveler, like a vigilant reader, takes responsibility for herself by questioning the authority of the guide, seeking her own "coign of vantage" if she wants a really good view of the surroundings.

At the Hotel Sandwirth

Dr. K. travels from Trieste to Venice across the Adriatic, fleeing the first city because he knows "there is an iron angel who kills travelers from the north" (145), a figure which "descends on great silk-white wings, swathed in bluish-violet vestments and bound with golden cords, the upraised arm with the sword pointing forwards" (146). Dr. K. sees this angel coming toward him from the ceiling as he lies on his hotel bed in Trieste, and just as he expects it to speak to him, when he looks at it again, he sees that it is "no longer a living angel but a garishly painted ship's figurehead, such as hang from the ceilings of sailors' taverns" (146).

In a state the narrator describes as "the waves [were] still breaking within him" (146), Dr. K. arrives in Venice. The disobedient reader has just been there with the narrator in the previous (second) section, "*All'estero*," for four days and three nights. The narrator walks the labyrinthine streets, reflects on the history of the Doge's Palace (called by Grillparzer an "enigma in stone" 54), including Giacomo Casanova's endurance of his inexplicable imprisonment there (the basis for Kafka's "fantasies" 148), and takes a mysterious midnight ferry ride across the Venetian lagoon, past the crematorium and the flour mill, with a Jewish Italian astrophysicist (named after an Old Testament prophet) who farewells him in Italian with

the Passover greeting ("Next year in Jerusalem!"). He descends, on a
foggy All Saints morning, into a reverie in which he transports himself to
W and images of mist, white flour, and baked rolls called "*Seelenwecken*,"
the New Testament admonition: "Sleepers, wake!" (Matthew 25:1–13)
commemorated in the still popular sixteenth-century German hymn (Philipp
Nicolai 1599), the music arranged by Bach (1685–1750) later. This is
Sebald's powerful juxtaposition of Jew and Christian within a European
context — the connectedness is deeply destabilizing. The narrator then
descends into a kind of cabin fever, a depressive paralysis like a kind of
death which prevents him from leaving his room (65).

What is a disobedient reader to make of the fact that Dr. K.'s four days
in Venice, retold here by the narrator, are a *lacuna* in this third section of
the text? Dr. K. too seems unable, "on the brink of disintegration" (147),
to leave his room in the Sandwirth Hotel, his "mounting despair" and the
stones of Venice "dissolving" (147) apparent in a letter he writes from the
lobby to his fiancée Felice Bauer. In effect the reader has been given those
four days already in the narrator's own version, re-experienced, re-imagined,
re-constructed in the previous section. The future of the text has been
determined by its past, in the reader's experience of it. Sebald has reversed
the past and the future in a destabilized present — an annunciatory lode
with its own angelic and prophetic manifestations. The disobedient reader
must contemplate, imagine, and reconnect for herself these terrible
threads, be roused from her own "sleep," to take action against the recurrent and endemic threat of madness, try to prevent the past determining
the future.

At the Engelwirt Inn

Returning to W after "a good thirty years" (185), on foot, the narrator
finds it "reassuring" that "everything was completely changed" (185). He
returns even more particularly to the place of his own past when he takes
a room at the Engelwirt Inn, on the first floor where his parents rented
accommodation for some years during his childhood.

He observes that the "village itself . . . was more remote from me than
any other place I could conceive of" (185), even though "localities" he
associates with it, "the Altachmoos, the parish woods, the tree-lined lane
that led to Haslach, the pumping station, Petersthal cemetery where the
plague dead lay, or the house in the Schray where Dopfer the hunchback
lived, had continually returned in my dreams and daydreams and had
become more real to me than they had been then" (185). For the reader,
arriving with the narrator "at that late hour" (185), the village is remote,
probably unknown, and very strange, seen in the "pale glow of the lamps"
(185). For what the reader "sees," guided by the narrator, is both what is

there in the contingent present and what the narrator conjures out of the past, just as Kafka's empty four days in Venice are supplemented by the reader's images gleaned from her time there with the narrator earlier and her own *bricolage*.

As the narrator "speaks," the reader "sees" both the holiday home and the head forester's "small shingled villa with a pair of antlers and the inscription '1913' above the front door" (185), together with its adjacent orchard. She sees too the ghost of the fire station with "its handsome slatted tower" and its "hoses hung in silent anticipation of the next conflagration" (185), reflecting at the same time on the terrible irony of the scale of this word in Sebald, and the inefficacy of the village hoses. The community represented by the small discrete buildings housing the parson and the curate, educating the children, officiated by the town hall clerk's punctuality, where cheese was made, where the poor were provided for, where people knew the grocer and haberdasher by name, has been "modernized" or has "disappeared" (186). This is a vanished world, conjured momentarily for the observing reader by the narrator's prose, a slow panning shot across a view hauled out of the vortex of the past, a specter glimpsed stepping out of a doorway or glancing through a window.

The Engelwirt Inn itself is almost unrecognisable to the narrator. Its "pseudo-Alpine" (186) vernacular architecture is an *ersatz* overlay, an ironic veneer over the authentic shabbiness. The tourist brochure appeal of the building gives way, in the narrator's prose, to its former disreputability, "the village peasants" drinking themselves "senseless" (186) deep into the night, the smoke-filled bar, the long, crooked stovepipe, the large function room with long tables for "weddings and funerals" (186), the newsreels and films shown there, and the production of Schiller's play *The Robbers*. These are the images of the past lodged as memories in the narrator's mind which his prose makes visible to the stranger, the companion-traveler who is the reader, at his side.

For the reader the Engelwirt Inn is not the sentimental or nostalgic place that was formerly the narrator's childhood home (192–93). The catalogue of furnishings which the narrator calls to mind, reflecting on the economic advantage to his parents of his father's enlistment in the "army of the One Hundred Thousand" (193), is made to strike the reader as ambitiously bourgeois, as though the Bavarian peasants were bought into the Reich's army. The resulting horror seems to have grown in the fear of poverty or need, out of the ambition for prosperity and security. The "ponderously ornate armoire" with its "tablecloths, napkins, silver cutlery, Christmas decorations" and unused "bone china tea service" (193) suddenly reappears in the expanded single room which the narrator takes, part of his parents' former living room, their rented accommodation eloquently at odds with their middle-class furnishings. The narrator mocks the "passing moment of aspiration to higher ideals" reflected in his father's purchase of cheap editions of the plays of "Shakespeare, Schiller, Hebel and Sudermann" (194), the curious list a withering, ironic indictment of his father's ignorance and the notion of purchasing cultural knowledge from a "passing salesman" (194).

Nonetheless the Engelwirt is also where the narrator encounters the exotic Sallaba, an agile Rhinelander with one leg and sartorial flair, and the postcard albums of Rosina Zobel, the wife of the invalid "old Engelwirt" (197), the stuff to feed a small boy's imagination. We "see" the ghost of this small boy sitting in Rosina Zobel's bed reciting prayers and "orisons" (198), Rosina's "head inclined against the bedstead, eyes closed, the glass and bottle of Kalterer wine on the marble top of the table beside her, expressions of pain and relief crossing her face in turn" (199). Her teaching the small boy to tie a bow is recalled in the same breath as his memory of her habit of blessing him every time he left, so strong a memory that the narrator fancies he can still "feel her thumb against my forehead" (199). There are strong Proustian echoes here, and a touch of Joyce's *Dubliners*. The child's memory of adult disappointment and despair, of kindness and love, is presented as it is summoned from the past by the narrator's presence in the Engelwirt Inn. It falls to the reader to construct these mediated glimpses of the past recalled in the narrative contingency of W, to slip into the gap between the memory of empirical reality and its representation in the narrator's verbal images, and catch there a disobedient glimpse of the authorial ghost.

Conclusion: A Farewell Note

> To set one's name to a work gives no one a title to be remembered, for who knows how many of the best of men have gone without a trace?
>
> — *The Rings of Saturn*

> From Chaucer to Marcel Proust, the novel's substance is the unrepeatable, the singular flavour of souls.
>
> — Jorge Luis Borges, "Personality and the Buddha," in *The Total Library*

> Sebald's originality is in his form.
>
> — Lilian Furst, Davidson College, 15 March 2003

> The negative form of the Greek word for truth, *aletheia*, which means something like "unforgetting," suggests that at a certain point searching for the unknown gives place to trying to remove the impediments to seeing what is there already.
>
> — Northrop Frye, *Words with Power*

I HAVE ARGUED THAT the prose fiction of W. G. Sebald, presenting to the reader as nonfiction, is fictional practice designed to engage the reader in a new way. This new way elicits or perhaps shapes the kind of reader I have called, after Umberto Eco's "model" or "obedient" reader (1995, 16), disobedient. This is a reader who is liberated from the tyranny of the text, from its authority, able to engage contemplatively and imaginatively in what Julia Kristeva described as *l'envol de la pensée* and *le vagabondage de l'imagination*, the flight of thought and the wandering imagination, which engages collaboratively in the construction of the textual imaginary.

Just as the historical or documentary claims of the opening of the Gospel of St Luke set up in the reader an expectation that what follows is the literal truth, because of Luke's use of a traditional rhetorical convention in his preface, only to be followed by mysterious stories in which metaphor appears to dominate in a literary or poetic practice soliciting a "leap of faith," so here in Sebald's textual practice what is presented as nonfiction, as historical or documentary writing, is subverted by Sebald's manipulation of the reading protocols. The reader, postmodern and skeptically impatient with illusion, myth-making, and imaginative fiction, desires engagement with the real and the true, which the old lie of mimetic realism accommodated through the use of tropes which represented a prior reality. In Sebald's "paradigmatically postmodern practice" (Atlas

1999) which rejects the tired trope of realism and the "grinding mechanism" of the conventional novel, a more playful engagement with the reader emerges, in which through a different kind of "swindle," that "questionable business of writing" (Sebald 1997, 230), Sebald engages a reader who is free to think and imagine as a result of the dialogical relationship established between that reader and the discourse of the text. No longer subject to the authoritarian sway of the writer — or of his constructed double, the writerly narrator — the disobedient reader can step backwards and forwards between the text and her own empirical otherness in a more "authentic" relationship between the discursively constructed subject which is also generating the text and her own. This is a Buberian transaction between "I" and "Thou," a Bakhtinian dialogism, a *rapprochement* which is a genuine, and therefore moral recognition of alterity, of the other, which in turn defines a sense of self. In Sebald this human dialogue is enriched by the resurrection of aspects of the collective past, a common culture of memory upon which our collective identity as human beings depends.

This emancipation of a reader designated disobedient is effected in Sebald's writing by his abandonment of the hegemony of the realist novel, what he calls that "tiresome *Realismusfrage*," its creaking artifice and grinding mechanisms, principally in his rejection of plot and character, pushing the fictional envelope out toward the new literary millennium that Italo Calvino sensed and Jonathan Culler called for, where the "literary" would prevail (Culler 289–90) and where the poetic values of imagination and language would be cherished (Calvino 92), where the postmodern condition (in Culler's sense of the contemporary moment and Calvino's forking path into the appropriation of used images in new contexts or a post-Beckett "world after the end of the world" 95) might be visible in new ways in the self-conscious discourse of the literary where the use of language is foregrounded.

Sebald's ironizing of his personal tendency to melancholia, that product of solitary practices like walking and reading and writing (Alvarez 2001), by turning the color "grey" into a sustained metaphor across all his books, can be reckoned in the spirit of Caroline Spurgeon and her study of Shakespearean metaphor, but it is perhaps better to leave it weirdly or uncannily present in the mind, like some vestige of a specter or phantom that can be banished by what Sebald called the glowing in the heart, or the wry smile that some embedded irony or joke elicits.

Mark R. McCulloh's observation that "The primary subject of Sebald's writing is, in the end, writing itself" (xxi), is a view reflected by others, including Sheppard and Williams and Summers-Bremner, who also see Sebald as centring the individual and the subjective consciousness of the reader in his texts. McCulloh construes Sebald's "blended" writing as "a modern pilgrim's progress" and suggests that he "creates a new kind of documentary fiction" that owes much to Borges, Kafka, Bernhard, Nabokov, and Stendhal (25). Sebald's "imaginative power" he describes as "postmodern" (although he doesn't say in what precise respect), coming "close on the heels of" Eco and Calvino (25). In McCulloh's estimate, Sebald's writing positions him in the broadest European tradition (paradoxically including the Argentinian Spanish-speaking Borges and the Russian-American immigrant Nabokov) among writers who, in very different ways, have practiced the art of fiction in a self-conscious or self-reflexive fashion and whose work has, again in very different ways, reinvigorated that art of fiction for an enthusiastic literary readership. McCulloh is insightful about the way Sebald's books "are inexpressible as anything less than the totalities of the books themselves . . . examples of their own syncretic genre . . . and meant to reflect the way consciousness acts" (24). Echoing Williams and Sheppard, this points up some of the complexity of Sebald's way of engaging the individual subject of the reader, and the resistance to inscription into particular discourses of meaning. "Consciousness is a theater" (25) reflects that Beckett influence, his portrait also included in *Unerzählt* (2003) together with Sebald's pastiche of Psalm 91 — a mysterious but eloquent and moving conjunction.

Stephen Spender offers an observation that reflects, and I thank my father for drawing to my attention to it, on Sebald's writing practice that is, in many ways, closer to poetry's scrupulous engagement with language and focuses something essential about Max Sebald:

> I began to realize how much audacity, patience and solitude are required to express one's experiences. For the imagination suggests to the poet the undefined sensation of a metaphor that explains to him the quality of some experience. But to feel his way beyond this vague sensation to the exact image of the metaphor, to pursue it through solitude to places where it is hidden from all that has been put into words before, and then to mould it within all the hazards of language, reconciled with grammar and form, is extremely difficult. Most writers allow their ideas to lead them back from terrifying solitude to the consolatory society of approximate and familiar phrases. An experience to them is the beginning of a journey where they soon arrive at already expressed ideas. The writer who clings to his own metaphor is facing his own loneliness: in fighting to distinguish a new idea from similar ideas which have already been expressed, he may find that his most hidden experience brings him in conflict with current ideas among people surrounding him, and face to face with the terrifying truth of his own isolated existence. For he is revealing a fragment of the ultimate truth of his loneliness. (*World within World*, [1951] 1991, 93)

Sebald's use of the color "grey," like his use of white mist or vapor and his use of silk, is an ashy metaphoric thread in his books which suggests, among a myriad things, the monochrome, even colorless despair of melancholy that is the life-denying inheritance of his temperament, the ghostly presence or trace of something that was formerly alive or present, a manifestation of an enigma or mystery, the finest natural threads of which (*nach der Natur*) can be woven into a frail but strong fabric of great beauty. In Sebald's textual weaving the hypotactic and paratactic syntax makes a net in which transient moments and impressions are caught by a melancholy man deeply aware of the terrible paradox of beauty and destruction, of the inevitability of death and the deep memory of our kind, and in which there is much new richness, a kind of hope for his surviving readers. In another image, the clouds he so often invokes can, occasionally, dissipate to reveal a moment of "claritas." In the *salle des pas perdus*, where we all move, and wait, from our arrival to our departure, Sebald encourages us to look up and around at the language with which he has shaped the textual space which speaks to him and which the reader occupies, perhaps in the spirit of Wren (*si monumentum requiris, circumspice*), to take our time, to walk more slowly, to think and imagine and perhaps to create, before our steps too are lost in the echoing air, the trajectories invisible in the now empty space.

Seamus Heaney wrote that what we want poetry to be is "a source of truth and at the same time a vehicle of harmony" (*The Redress of Poetry*, 1995, 193). This is something that doesn't seem so very far from Sebald's literary enterprise, with its sublimation of boundaries or borders and its exhortation to our common sense of compassion and humanity in a world weary of power, persecution, and posturing.

Some four years after Sebald's death, we are beginning to see his ghost in the writing of others in English. Jonathan Safran Foer's affecting novel, *Extremely Loud and Incredibly Close* (2005), weaves together the trauma of the effect of the Allied bombing of Dresden on Shrove Tuesday, 13 February 1945, and that of the 9/11 terrorist attack on New York in 2001 in a series of embedded narratives voiced in the first person of a gifted nine-year-old's perspective and of his German grandparents' letters, interspersed with black-and-white photographs. John Banville's very different novel, *The Sea*, won the 2005 Man Booker Prize and, while there are no photographs in Banville's book, the text is rich with painterly description which might remind us of Sebald's prose style, reflected also in the melancholic tenor of Banville's grieving narrator, the ironically named art historian Max Morden. Banville's scrupulous attention to detail in the nuanced descriptive writing recalls something of Sebald, the preoccupation with death and mourning, writing itself presented as a pathology of memory's redemptiveness.

The acclamation with which Sebald's writing has been met suggests that there is indeed an ongoing market, in Calvino's new millennium, for the patterns in which we shape truth and beauty, that literature can provide in this particular and mysterious transaction whereby the mind of one can pass into the mind of the other, leaving behind that suggestion of presence lodged in the images of memory.

Works Cited

Abbany, Zulfikar. "A Cure for Amnesia." *The Sunday Age*. 16 March 2003.

Aciman, André. "Out of Novemberland." *New York Review of Books*. 3 December 1998. Available: http://www.nybooks.com/articles/641. Accessed 19 May 2002.

Adorno, Theodor. *Minima Moralia*. 1951. Trans. E. F. N. Jephcott. London: Verso, 1978.

Ahearne, Jeremy. *Michel De Certeau: Interpretation and Its Other*. Cambridge: Polity Press, 1995.

Albaret, Celeste. *Monsieur Proust*. 1976. Trans. Barbara Bray. New York: New York Review of Books, 2003.

Albertson, David. "Wolfgang Iser." *Stanford Presidential Lectures in the Humanities and Arts*. 2000. http://prelectur.stanford.edu/lecturers/iser. Accessed 8 March 2006.

Almansi, Guido. *The Writer as Liar: Narrative Technique in the Decameron*. London & Boston: Routledge & Kegan Paul, 1975.

Alter, Robert. *Canon and Creativity*. New Haven and London: Yale University Press, 2000.

———. *Partial Magic: The Novel as a Selfconscious Genre*. University of California Press, 1975.

———. *The Pleasures of Reading in an Ideological Age*. New York & London: W. W. Norton & Co, 1996.

Alvarez, Maria. *The Significant Mr Sebald*. 24 September 2001. Available: http://www.arts.telegraph.co.uk/arts/main.jhtml?xml=/arts/2001/09/24/tlbase24.xml. Accessed 31 July 2004.

Annan, Gabriele. "Ghost Story." *The New York Review of Books* 48.17: 26.

Anonymous. *Die Wünschelrute in Der Tasche Eines Nibelungen*. Available: http://www.faz.net/IN/INtemplates/faznet/default.asp?tpl=book/printpage.asp&rub={9E7. Accessed 20 March 2001.

———. "Vertigo." *The Village Voice* 45.49: 102.

———. "Vertigo." *Virginia Quarterly Review* 77.3 (2001): 97–98.

Aristotle, Horace, and Longinus. *Classical Literary Criticism*. Trans. T. S. Dorsch. Harmondsworth: Penguin Books, 1969.

Atlas, James. "W. G. Sebald: A Profile." *The Paris Review* 41.151 (1999): 278–95.

Auden, W. H. "Musée des Beaux Arts." *Collected Poems*. Ed. Edward Mendelson. 1976 ed. London: Faber and Faber, 1994.

Baker, Kenneth. "W. G. Sebald: Up against Historical Amnesia." *San Francisco Chronicle*. 7 October 2001.

Bakhtin, Mikhail. *The Dialogic Imagination*. Trans. Caryl Emerson & Michael Holquist. Austin: University of Texas Press, 1981.

———. *Problems of Dostoevsky's Poetics*. Trans. Caryl Emerson. Minneapolis: University of Minnesota Press, 1994.

Baldick, Robert, ed. *Pages from the Goncourt Journal*. Trans. Robert Baldick. London: Penguin Books, 1984.

Bamforth, Iain. "Air War, Literature and Compassion." *Quadrant* XLVIII, Number 1–2. January–February (2004): 80–85.

Banville, John. "The Rubble Artist." *The New Republic* 225.22 (2001): 35.

———. *The Sea*. London: Pan Macmillan, 2005.

Barthes, Roland. *Camera Lucida*. Trans. Richard Howard. London: Fontana, 1990.

———. *Image–Music–Text*. Trans. Stephen Heath. London: Fontana, 1977.

———. *S/Z*. Trans. Richard Miller. London: Jonathan Cape, 1975.

Baudrillard, Jean. *Passwords*. Trans. Chris Turner. London & New York: Verso, 2003.

Beckett, Andy. *Long and Winding River*. September 29, 2001. Available: http://books.guardian.co.uk/Print/0,3858,4266247,00.html. Accessed 23 March 2002.

Beevor, Antony. *A Nation That Was Bombed into Silence*. 12 February 2003. Available: http://www.timesonline.co.uk/printFriendly/0,,1-1461-574095,00.html. Accessed 23 March 2003.

Bell, Anthea. "On Translating W. G. Sebald." *The Anatomist of Melancholy*. Ed. Rüdiger Görner. Munich: Iudicium Verlag, 2003. 11–18.

Benjamin, Walter. *The Arcades Project*. Trans. Howard Eiland and Kevin McLaughlin. Cambridge, MA & London: The Belknap Press of Harvard University Press, 2002.

Bere, C. "The Book of Memory: W. G. Sebald's the 'Emigrants' and 'Austerlitz.'" *Literary Review* 46.1 (2002): 184–92.

Berger, John. *Selected Essays and Articles*. London: Penguin Books, 1972.

———. *Ways of Seeing*. New York: Richard Seaver/Viking Press, 1973.

Berger, John, and Jean Mohr. *Another Way of Telling*. London: Writers and Readers Publishing Cooperative, 1982.

Bernhard, Thomas. *Correction*. Korrektur, 1975, Suhrkamp Verlag, Frankfurt. Trans. Sophie Wilkins. Chicago: The University of Chicago Press, 1990.

———. *The Loser*. Der Untergeher, 1983, Suhrkamp Verlag, Frankfurt. Trans. Jack Dawson. New York: Alfred A. Knopf, 1991.

———. *On the Mountain: Rescue Attempt, Nonsense*. 1st English language ed. Marlboro, Vt.: Marlboro Press, 1991.

Bersani, Leo. *The Culture of Redemption*. Cambridge, Mass.: Harvard University Press, 1990.

Bigsby, C. W. E. *Writers in Conversation with Christopher Bigsby.* Arthur Miller Centre for American Studies. Vol. Two. Norwich: EAS Publishing, 2001.

Blackford, S. D. "After Nature." *Virginia Quarterly Review* 79.1 (2003): A30–A31.

Blanton, Casey. *Travel Writing — the Self and the World.* New York & London: Routledge, 2002.

Bloom, Harold. *How to Read and Why.* 2000. London: Fourth Estate, 2001.

Böll, Heinrich. *The Silent Angel.* Trans. Breon Mitchell. London: André Deutsch, 1995.

Booth, Wayne C. *The Rhetoric of Fiction.* Chicago: University of Chicago Press, 1961.

Borges, Jorge Luis. *This Craft of Verse.* The Charles Eliot Norton Lectures 1967–1968. Cambridge and London: Harvard University Press, 2000.

———. *The Total Library — Non-Fiction, 1922–1986.* Trans. Esther Allen et al. Ed. Eliot Weinberger. London: Allen Lane, The Penguin Press, 2000.

Boyd, Brian. *Vladimir Nabokov: The Russian Years.* London: Chatto & Windus, 1990.

Brady, Philip. "Ghosts of the Present." *The Times Literary Supplement* (12 July 1996).

Britannica, Encyclopedia. "Sir Thomas Browne." 2004. Available: www.britannica.com/eb/article?tocId=9016716. Accessed 6 November 2004.

Brookner, Anita. "A Journey without Maps." *The Spectator* (6 October 2001): 64.

———. "Pursued across Europe by Ghosts and Unease." *The Spectator* (18–25 December 1999): 65.

Browne, Thomas. *The Religio Medici and Other Writings.* 1642. 1906 ed. London: J. M. Dent & Sons, 1947.

Buchanan, Ian. *Michel de Certeau — Cultural Theorist.* Theory, Culture, & Society. Ed. Mike Featherstone. London, Thousand Oaks, New Delhi: SAGE Publications, 2000.

Butler, Judith, et al. *What's Left of Theory? New Work on the Politics of Literary Theory.* Essays from the English Institute. New York and London: Routledge, 2000.

Butler, Michael. "The Human Cost of Exile." *The Times Literary Supplement* (2 October 1998).

Byatt, A. S. *On Histories and Stories.* 2000. London: Vintage, 2001.

———. "Only Connect." *New Statesman* (15 October 2001): 52.

Cadbury, Henry J. *The Making of Luke-Acts.* 1927. 2nd ed. Peabody, Massachusetts: Hendrickson Publishers, 1999.

Calvino, Italo. *Six Memos for the Next Millennium.* Trans. Patrick Creagh. Charles Eliot Norton Lectures 1985. London: Jonathan Cape, 1992.

Canfield, John V. *Wittgenstein — Language and World.* Amherst: The University of Massachusetts Press, 1981.

Carnley, Peter. *Reflections in Glass: Trends and Tensions in the Contemporary Anglican Church.* Pymble, N.S.W.: HarperCollins, 2004.

Cascardi, Antony. *The Subject of Modernity.* Cambridge: Cambridge University Press, 1992.

Castro, Brian. "Blue Max — W. G. Sebald: A Tribute." *Heat* 3.1 (2002): 119–29.

Catling, Jo. "Gratwanderung Bis an Den Rand Der Natur: W. G. Sebald's Landscapes of Memory." *The Anatomist of Melancholy.* Ed. Rüdiger Görner. Munich: Iudicium Verlag, 2003. 19–50.

———. *Silent Catastrophe — in Memoriam W. G. (Max) Sebald 1944–2001.* 2002. Available: http://www.new-books-in-german.com/features.html. Accessed 19 August 2003.

Chadwick, Owen. *The Secularization of the European Mind in the Nineteenth Century.* Cambridge: Cambridge University Press, 1975.

Chalmers, Martin. "Angels of History." *New Statesman* 9.411 (1996): 44.

Chambers, Ross. *Loiterature.* Nebraska: University of Nebraska Press, 1999.

———. *Story and Situation: Narrative Seduction and the Power of Fiction.* Manchester: Manchester University Press, 1984.

Chandler, J. "About Loss: W. G. Sebald's Romantic Art of Memory." *South Atlantic Quarterly* 102.1 (2003): 235–62.

Chatman, Seymour. *Story and Discourse.* 1978. Ithaca and London: Cornell University Press, 1980.

Chatwin, Bruce. *Anatomy of Restlessness.* New York: Viking Penguin, 1996.

———. *The Songlines.* London: Cape, 1987.

———. *The Viceroy of Ouidah.* London: Jonathan Cape, 1980.

Clark, T. J. et al. *A Symposium on W. G. Sebald.* Spring 2002. Available: http://www.threepennyreview.com/samples/sebaldsympos_sp02.html. Accessed 10 July 2002.

Coetzee, J. M. "Heir of a Dark History." *The New York Review of Books* 49.16 (2002): 25.

Cohen, Tom. *Ideology and Inscription — "Cultural Studies" after Benjamin, De Man, and Bakhtin.* Cambridge: Cambridge University Press, 1998.

Colebrook, Claire. *Irony.* The New Critical Idiom. Ed. John Drakakis. London and New York: Routledge, 2004.

Coleridge, Samuel Taylor. *The Poems of Samuel Taylor Coleridge.* 1912. Ed. Ernest Hartley Coleridge. London: Oxford University Press, 1951.

Conrad, Joseph. *Heart of Darkness and Other Tales.* 1902. Ed. Cedric Watts. Oxford: Oxford University Press, 2002.

Conrad, Peter. *At Home in Australia.* London: Thames and Hudson, 2003.

———. *Modern Times, Modern Places.* 1998. London: Thames & Hudson, 1999.

Cowan, James L. *Sebald's Austerlitz and the Great Library.* 2004. Available: http://www.davidson.edu/academic/german/denham/cowan.htm. Accessed 22 October 2004.

Craven, Peter. "Craven on the Classics." *The Age.* 12 May 1998.

———. "Out of the Shadows of Art." *The Age.* 23 November 1996.

———. "Shadows of Great Art." *The Age.* 7 May 2005.

———. "Towards Greater Art." 10 August 2002. Available: http://www.theage.com.au/articles/2002/08/09/1028158015260.html. Accessed 11 December 2002.

———. "W. G. Sebald: Anatomy of Faction." *Heat* 13 (1999): 212–24.

Crownshaw, Richard. "Reconsidering Postmemory: Photography, the Archive, and Post-Holocaust Memory in W. G. Sebald's *Austerlitz.*" *Mosaic* 37.4 (2004): 215–37.

Culler, Jonathan. "The Literary in Theory." *What's Left of Theory.* Ed. Judith Butler John Guillory, Kendall Thomas. New York & London: Routledge, 2000.

Cuomo, Joe. "The Meaning of Coincidence — an Interview with the Writer W. G. Sebald." *The New Yorker.* 3 September 2001. Available: http://www.newyorker.com/PRINTABLE/?online/010903on_onlineonly01. Accessed 5 February 2002.

Cupitt, Don. *The Long-Legged Fly.* London: SCM Press, 1987.

———. *The Revelation of Being.* London: SCM Press, 1998.

Czarny, N. "Austerlitz." *Quinzaine Littéraire* 843 (2002): 13–14.

Dagen, Philippe. "Bonnard, en grand et autrement." *Le Monde.* 2 February 2006, 26.

Dawsey, James M. *The Lukan Voice.* Macon: Mercer University Press, 1986.

De Botton, Alain. *The Art of Travel.* London: Penguin Books, 2002.

———. "W. G. Sebald." *City Pages* 20.994 (1999): 11.

De Certeau, Michel. *Heterologies: Discourse on the Other.* Theory and History of Literature; V. 17. Manchester: Manchester University Press, 1986.

———. *The Mystic Fable.* Religion and Postmodernism. Chicago: University of Chicago Press, 1992.

———. *The Practice of Everyday Life.* Berkeley: University of California Press, 1984.

De Silva, Carla, ed. *In Memory's Kitchen.* Trans. Bianca Steiner Brown. Northvale, NJ & London: Jason Aronson, 1996.

Deleuze, Gilles. *Essays Critical and Clinical.* Minneapolis: University of Minnesota Press, 1997.

Di Piero, W. S. "Another Country." *New York Times Book Review* (2000): 7.20.

Die Bibel oder die Ganze Heilige Schrift. Trans. Martin Luther. Stuttgart: Württembergische Bibelanstält, 1963.

Doerry, Martin, and Volker Hage. "Ich Fürchte Das Melodramatische." *Der Spiegel*. November 2001: 228–34.

Dotzauer, Gregor. "Tote Schreiben Keine Langen Sätze." 9 March 2003. *Der Tagesspiegel*. Available: http://archiv.tagesspiegel.de/archiv/09.03.2003/471104.asp. Accessed 27 April 2003.

Drennon, Bill. "The Roche Limit." 2003. Available: http://www.cvc.org/astronomy/roche_limit.htm. Accessed 12 August 2003.

Drury, John. "Luke." *The Literary Guide to the Bible*. Ed. Robert Alter & Frank Kermode. London: Collins, 1987. 418–39.

Dukes, Gerry. *Illustrated Lives: Samuel Beckett*. London: Penguin Books, 2001.

Eakin, Hugh. "War and Remembrance." *The Nation* 276.12: 31.

Easthope, Antony. *Literary into Cultural Studies*. London and New York: Routledge, 1991.

Eco, Umberto. *Six Walks in the Fictional Woods*. Cambridge, Massachusetts: Harvard University Press, 1995.

Eder, Richard. "Excavating a Life: The Title Character of W. G. Sebald's Novel Journeys into the Past in an Effort to Discover His Identity." *New York Times Book Review*. 28 October 2001: 10.

———. "Exploring a Present That Is Invaded by the Past." *New York Times*. 22 May 2000: E.8.

Eliot, T. S. *Collected Poems 1909–1962*. London: Faber and Faber, 1963.

———. *Four Quartets*. London: The Folio Society, 1968.

Evans, Richard J. *In Defence of History*. 1997. London: Granta, 2000.

———. *Max Sebald*. 2002. Available: www.nesta.org.uk/max_sebald.htm. Accessed 16 March 2002.

Falconer, Delia. "The Eloquence of Fragments." *Eureka Street*. December 2001 (2001a).

———. "A Unique View on the Stains of History." *The Age*. 22 December 2001 (2001b).

Ferguson, Harvie. *Modernity and Subjectivity: Body, Soul, Spirit*. Charlottesville and London: University Press of Virginia, 2000.

Fetz, Gerald A. *Review of Winfried G. Sebald, Luftkrieg Und Literatur*. 3 November 2003. H-German, H-Net Reviews. Available: http://www.h-net.msu.edu/reviews/showrev.cgi?path=277031069229918. Accessed 7 November 2004.

Fiddes, Paul. *Freedom and Limit*. Macon, Georgia: Mercer University Press, 1999.

Filkins, Peter. "The Labyrinth of Memory." *The World & I* 15.10: 223.

FitzGerald, Edward. *Rubaiyat of Omar Khayyam*. London and Glasgow: Collins, 1947.

Flaubert, Gustave. *Madame Bovary.* Paris: Le Livre de Poche Gallimard, 1961.

———. *Un Coeur Simple: Precédé des Mémoires d'un Fou, et de Novembre.* Grands et Petits Chefs-d'oeuvre. Ed. René Dumesnil. Monaco: Editions du Rocher, 1946.

Flusser, Vilem. *Towards a Philosophy of Photography.* Trans. Anthony Mathews. London: Reaktion Books, 2000.

Foer, Jonathan Safran. *Extremely Loud & Incredibly Close.* London: Hamish Hamilton, 2005.

Forster, E. M. *Aspects of the Novel.* 1927. London: Edward Arnold, 1953.

Foucault, Michel. *Discipline and Punish: The Birth of the Prison.* Peregrine Books. Harmondsworth, Middlesex: Penguin, 1979.

———. *The Order of Things: An Archaeology of the Human Sciences.* Routledge Classics. London: Routledge, 2002.

Fox, Matthew, and Rupert Sheldrake. *The Physics of Angels.* San Francisco: HarperSanFrancisco, 1996.

Franklin, Ruth. "Rings of Smoke." *The New Republic* 227.13 (2002): 32.

Frase, Brigitte. *"Vertigo" by W. G. Sebald.* 26 June 2000. Available: www.salon.com. Accessed 11 December 2001.

Freeman, John. "Another Stirring Account from Sebald." *Denver Post.* December 23, 2001 (2001): EE.01.

Freud, Sigmund. *Collected Papers.* Trans. Joan Riviere. Vol. 4. 4 vols. London: The Hogarth Press, 1948.

Fritzsche, Peter. "Sebald's Twentieth-Century Histories." W. G. Sebald: Works & Influences. The Third Occasional Davidson Symposium on German Studies. Davidson College, North Carolina, 2003.

Frye, Northrop. *Words with Power.* 1990. San Diego: Harcourt Brace Jovanovich, 1992.

Funder, Anna. *Stasiland.* Melbourne: Text Publishing, 2002.

Furst, Lilian. *All Is True.* Durham and London: Duke University Press, 1995.

———. "Realism, Photography, and Degrees of Uncertainty." W. G. Sebald: Works & Influences. The Third Occasional Davidson Symposium on German Studies. Davidson College, North Carolina, 2003.

Fusillo, Massimo. *Naissance du Roman.* Trans. Marielle Abrioux. Poétique. Ed. Gérard Genette. Paris: Editions du Seuil, 1991.

Gantcher, Benjamin. "Resurrecting the Essential: W. G. Sebald's *Austerlitz.*" *The Hyde Park Review of Books* 1. Fall (2002).

Gardner, Helen. *In Defence of the Imagination.* Oxford: OUP, 1982.

Gay, Peter. *Savage Reprisals.* New York: Norton, 2003.

Gellner, Ernest. *Language and Solitude.* Cambridge: Cambridge University Press, 1998.

Genette, Gérard. *Narrative Discourse.* 1972. Trans. Jane E. Lewin. Oxford: Basil Blackwell, 1980.

Gilmour, David. *The Last Leopard: A Life of Giuseppe Di Lampedusa.* London: Quartet Books, 1988.

Gimson, Andrew. "Looking — and Looking Away." *The Spectator* (15 February 2003): 37.

Glendinning, Victoria. *Jonathan Swift.* 1998. London: Pimlico, 1999.

Goldschmidt, G. A. "Les 'Anneaux De Saturne.'" *Quinzaine Littéraire* 770 (1999): (1999): 8.

———. "Les 'Emigrants.'" *Quinzaine Littéraire* 755 (1999): 6–7.

Görner, Rüdiger, ed. *The Anatomist of Melancholy — Essays in Memory of W. G. Sebald.* Munich: Iudicium Verlag, 2003.

Gorra, Michael. "*Austerlitz.*" *The Atlantic Monthly* 288.4 (2001): 146.

Gracia, Jorge J. E., Korsmeyer, Carolyn and Gasché, Rodolphe, eds. *Literary Philosophers.* New York & London: Routledge, 2002.

Grayling, A. C. "Age of Reckoning." *Financial Times.* 22 February 2003.

Green, Toby. *The Questionable Business of Writing.* 2000. Interview transcribed into print for amazon.co.uk. Available: http://www.amazon.co.uk/exec/obidos/tg/feature/-/21586/ref%3Ded%5Fart%5F121649%5Ftxt%5F1/026-2136764-0723615. Accessed 20 October 2004.

Greening, John. "Unforgotten Forests." *The Times Literary Supplement* (2 August 2002): 23.

Gussow, Mel. "W. G. Sebald, Elegiac German Novelist, Is Dead at 57." *New York Times.* 15 December 2001: C.16.

Gwynne, Philip. "Bookchat." *The Age.* 31 July 2004.

Hackett, Joyce. "Vertigo." *Boston Review* 25. Summer 2000: 34–35.

Hamburger, Michael. "W. G. Sebald." *The Anatomist of Melancholy.* Ed. Rüdiger Görner. Munich: Iudicium Verlag, 2003.

Hamilton, Edith, and Huntington Cairns, eds. *The Collected Dialogues of Plato.* Princeton, NJ: Princeton University Press, 1973.

Hardy, Thomas. *The Collected Poems of Thomas Hardy.* London: Macmillan, 1974.

Harman, Mark, ed. *Robert Walser Rediscovered.* Hanover and London: University Press of New England, 1985.

Harris, Stefanie. "The Return of the Dead: Memory and Photography in W. G. Sebald's *Die Ausgewanderten.*" *German Quarterly* 2001: 379–91.

Heaney, Seamus. *The Redress of Poetry.* London: Faber and Faber, 1995.

Hebel, Johann Peter. *Kannitverstan.* 1809. Available: http://www.hausen-im-wiesental.de/jphebel/geschichten/kannitverstan.htm. Accessed 22 October 2004.

Heidelberger-Leonard, I. "Melancholy as Resistance (W. G. Sebald)." *Akzente-Zeitschrift Fur Literatur* 48.2 (2001): 122–30.

Heinegg, Peter. "Memory's Martyr." *Cross Currents* 52.1 (2002): 126.

Hill, Barry. "Horror and Its Legacy." *The Age*. 29 March 2003.

Hitchens, Christopher. "The Wartime Toll on Germany." *The Atlantic Monthly* 291.1 (2003): 182.

Hoare, Philip. *Philip Hoare on W. G. Sebald*. 2002. Available: www.philiphoare.co.uk. Accessed 19 May 2002.

Hoesterey, Ingeborg. *Pastiche — Cultural Memory in Art, Film, Literature*. Bloomington and Indianapolis: Indiana University Press, 2001.

Holub, Miroslav. *The Dimension of the Present Moment: Essays*. Trans. David Young. London and Boston: Faber and Faber, 1990.

The Holy Bible — Authorized King James Version. London and New York: Collins, 1957.

Homberger, Eric. *W. G. Sebald*. 17 December 2001. Available: http://books.guardian.co.uk/news/articles/o,6109,619971,00.html. Accessed 19 May 2002.

Horn, Eva. "Narration and the Epistemology of the Human Sciences in Alfred Döblin." *MLN* 118.3 (2003): 719–39.

Howell-Jones, Gareth. "A Doubting Pilgrim's Happy Progress." *The Spectator* (30 May 1998): 34–35.

Hutcheon, Linda. *A Poetics of Postmodernism: History, Theory, Fiction*. New York: Routledge, 1988.

Huyssen, Andreas. "On Rewritings and New Beginnings: W. G. Sebald and the Literature About the Luftkrieg." *Lili-Zeitschrift Fur Literaturwissenschaft Und Linguistik* 31.124 (2001): 72–90.

———. *Present Pasts — Urban Palimpsests and the Politics of Memory*. Cultural Memory in the Present. Ed. Mieke Bal and Hent de Vries. Stanford, California: Stanford University Press, 2003.

Indyk, Ivor. "The Past in Present Writing." *Memory*. Ed. Ivor Indyk & Elizabeth Webby. North Ryde: Angus & Robertson, 1991. 238–51.

Iser, Wolfgang. *How to Do Theory*. Oxford & Carlton: Blackwell Publishing, 2006.

Iyer, Pico. "Dead Man Writing." *Harper's Magazine* 301.1805 (2000): 86.

Jacobson, Dan. *Heshel's Kingdom*. London: Hamish Hamilton, 1998.

Jaggi, Maya. "The Last Word." 21 December 2001 [edited version of interview, London, 24 September 2001]. Available: http://books.guardian.co.uk/departments/generalfictioin/story/0,6000,624750,00.html. Accessed 10 May 2002 (2001b).

———. "Recovered Memories." *The Guardian*. 22 September 2001 (2001a).

James, Henry. *The Art of Fiction and Other Essays. Partial Portraits* by Henry James 1888 London: Macmillan. New York: Oxford University Press, 1948.

James, William. *The Varieties of Religious Experience*. 1902. 1960 ed. London and Glasgow: Collins, 1971.

Jefferson, Margo. "Writing in the Shadows." *New York Times Book Review* (2001): 27.

The Jerusalem Bible. Trans. Joseph Alston et al. Ed. Alexander Jones. London: Darton, Longman & Todd, 1966.

Johnson, D. "The Natural History of Destruction." *The Times Literary Supplement* (2003): 7–8.

Juers, E. "W." *Heat* 3.1 (2002): 111–18.

Jury, Louise. *Heart Attack Could Have Caused Writer's Fatal Crash*. 16 May 2002. The Independent. Available: http://news.independent.co.uk/uk/this_britain/story.jsp?story=295567. Accessed 19 May 2002.

Kafka, Franz. *Metamorphosis and Other Stories*. Trans. Willa and Edwin Muir. London: Penguin Books, 1961.

Kaplan, Caren. *Questions of Travel — Postmodern Discourses of Displacement*. Durham and London: Duke University Press, 1996.

Keegan, Fin. *The Rings of Saturn by W. G. Sebald*. 2002. Available: http://www.thesecondcircle.com/fjk/seba.html. Accessed 19 May 2002.

Kennick, William E. *What They Are Reading*. Spring 2002. Available: www.amherst.edu/magazine/issues/02spring/authors/reading.html. Accessed 17 March 2004.

Kermode, Frank. *The Genesis of Secrecy*. Cambridge, MA: Harvard UP, 1979.

———. "On Being an Enemy of Humanity." *Raritan* 2.2 (1982): 87–102.

———. *The Sense of an Ending*. 1967. New York: Oxford University Press, 1977.

———. *Shakespeare's Language*. London: Penguin Books, 2000.

Kilbourn, Russell. "Kafka, Nabokov, Sebald: Intertextuality and Redemption in *Vertigo* and *the Emigrants*." W. G. Sebald: Works & Influences. The Third Occasional Davidson Symposium on German Studies. Davidson College, North Carolina, 2003.

King, Nicola. *Memory, Narrative, Identity: Remembering the Self*. Edinburgh: Edinburgh University Press, 2000.

Kinsella, John. "Silences That Speak a Thousand Words." *Observer*. 7 July 2002.

Konzett, Matthias, ed. *Encyclopedia of German Literature — Vols 1 and 2*. Chicago & London: Fitzroy Dearborn, 2000.

Korsmeyer, Carolyn, Rodolphe Gaschâe, and Jorge J. E. Gracia. *Literary Philosophers: Borges, Calvino, Eco*. New York: Routledge, 2002.

Koval, Ramona. *Interview with Colm Toibin*. 30 May 2004. Australian Broadcasting Commission. Available: http://www.abc.net.au/m/arts/bwriting/stories/s1115422.htm. Accessed 1 June 2004.

Krauss, Nicole. "Arabesques of Journeys." *Partisan Review* 68.4 (2001): 646.

Kristeva, Julia. *The Kristeva Reader*. Trans. Sean Hand and Léon Roudiez. Ed. Toril Moi. Oxford: Basil Blackwell, 1986.

———. *Visions Capitales*. Paris: Editions de la Réunion des Musées Nationaux, 1998.

Kunkel, Benjamin. "The Emigrant." *The Nation* 274.12 (2002): 42.

La Bible. 1988. Paris: Alliance Biblique Universelle — Editions du Cerf, 1990.

LaCapra, Dominick. *Soundings in Critical Theory*. Ithaca and London: Cornell University Press, 1989.

Lane, Anthony. "Higher Ground." *The New Yorker* 76.13: 128.

———. "The Talk of the Town: W. G. Sebald." *The New Yorker* 77.42: 22.

Langford, Michelle. *Alexander Kluge*. 2003. www.sensesofcinema.com/contents/directors/03/kluge.html. Accessed 12 January 2006.

Larkin, Philip. *Collected Poems*. London: The Marvell Press & Faber and Faber, 1988.

Levenson, Michael. *Modernism and the Fate of Individuality*. Cambridge: Cambridge University Press, 1991.

Levine, Suzanne Jill. "Notes to Borges's Notes on Joyce: Infinite Affinities." *Comparative Literature*. Fall 1997.

Lewis, Tess. "W. G. Sebald: The Past Is Another Country." *The New Criterion — on line*. December 2001 (2001).

Leyda, J., and Voynow, Z. *Eisenstein at Work*. London: Methuen, 1982.

Liddell, Henry George, and Robert Scott. *A Greek-English Lexicon*. Ed. Henry Stuart Jones. Ninth ed. London: Oxford University Press, 1966.

Liukkonen, Petri. *Alfred Döblin 1878–1957*. 2004. Available: http://www.biblion.com/litweb/biogs/doblin_alfred.html. Accessed 26 February 2004.

Lodge, David. *Consciousness and the Novel*. 2002. London: Penguin Books, 2003.

Loeser, P. "Of Names and Things. Studies on the Role of the I in Literature, as Exemplified by the Works of Ingeborg Bachmann, Peter Bichsel, Max Frisch, Gottfried Keller, Heinrich Von Kleist, Arthur Schnitzler, Frank Wedekind, Vladimir Nabokov and W. G. Sebald." *German Studies Review* 26.1 (2003): 128–30.

Long, J. J. "History, Narrative, and Photography in W. G. Sebald's Die Ausgewanderten." *Modern Language Review* 98 (2003): 117–39.

Long, J. J., and Anne Whitehead, eds. *W. G. Sebald — A Critical Companion*. Literary Conjugations. Ed. Richard T. Gray. Seattle: University of Washington Press, 2004.

Loquai, Franz. *Abschied Von Max — Zur Erinnerung an W. G. Sebald*. 2002. Available: http://www.literaturkritik.de/txt/2002-01/2002-01-0088.html. Accessed 7 August 2002.

———. *W. G. Sebald*. Eggingen: Isele, 1997.

Lowell, Robert. *Day by Day*. London: Faber, 1978.

Lubbock, Percy. *The Craft of Fiction*. 1921. London: Jonathan Cape, 1924.

Lubow, Arthur. "Preoccupied with Death, but Still Funny." *New York Times*. 11 December 2001: E.1.

Lucy, Niall. *Postmodern Literary Theory.* Oxford: Blackwell, 1997.

Luke. *The Gospel According to Luke.* Melbourne: Text Publishing, 1998.

Lyotard, Jean François. *The Postmodern Condition: A Report on Knowledge.* Theory and History of Literature; V. 10. Minneapolis: University of Minnesota Press, 1984.

Macfarlane, Robert. "W. G. Sebald." *Zembla* 1.2 (2003): 34–42.

Malin, Irving. "The Emigrants." *Review of Contemporary Fiction* 17.1 (1997): 173–74.

Malpas, J. E. "Holism, Realism, and Truth: How to Be an Anti-Relativist and Not Give up on Heidegger (or Davidson) — a Debate with Christopher Norris." *International Journal of Philosophical Studies* 12.3 (2004): 339–56.

———. *Place and Experience: A Philosophical Topography.* Cambridge, U.K.: Cambridge UP, 1999.

Mandeville, John, and Richard Pynson. *The Travels of Sir John Mandeville: Facsimile of Pynson's Edition of 1496.* Exeter Medieval Texts and Studies. Exeter: University of Exeter, 1980.

Martin, Terry. "Berlin: The Quiet German Author." *Europe* 416 (2002): 39.

Mason, W. "The 'Rings of Saturn.'" *American Book Review* 20.4 (1999): 19–20.

Masson, Georgina. *Italian Gardens.* London: Thames and Hudson, 1961.

McCrum, Robert. *Untimely Death Robs Writer of Recognition He Deserved.* 16 December 2001. Available: http://www.observer.co.uk/uk_news/story/0,6903,619710,00.html. Accessed 30 September 2002.

McCulloh, Mark R. "Allusions, Affinities, and Transcendence." W. G. Sebald: Works & Influences. The Third Occasional Davidson Symposium on German Studies. Davidson College, North Carolina, 2003.

———. *Understanding W. G. Sebald.* Understanding Modern European and Latin American Literature. Ed. James Hardin. Columbia: University of South Carolina Press, 2003.

McHale, Brian. *Constructing Postmodernism.* London & New York: Routledge, 1992.

———. *Postmodernist Fiction.* London & New York: Methuen, 1987.

McQuillan, Martin, ed. *The Narrative Reader.* London & New York: Routledge, 2000.

McQuire, Scott. *Visions of Modernity.* London: Sage Publications, 1998.

Mellor, Leo. *Austere Melancholia.* 6 February 2002. Available: http://www.buzzwords.org.uk/issue2/reviews_main.html. Accessed 29 March 2002.

Melnyczuk, Askold. *Shadowboxing the Future of Fiction: Toward a New Internationalism.* 2000. Available: www.bu.edu/agni/essays-reviews/print/2000/51-melnyczuk.html. Accessed 29 January 2004.

Merkin, Daphne. "Cordoning Off the Past." *New York Times Book Review* (2003): 13–14.

Minnis, A. J. *Medieval Theory of Authorship: Scholastic Literary Attitudes in the Later Middle Ages*. 2nd ed. Aldershot: Scolar Press, 1988.

Mitchelmore, Stephen. *A Thwarted Empathy*. 2001. Available: http://www.spikemagazine.com/1201sebald.htm. Accessed 16 February 2002.

Montesquieu, Charles de Secondat. *Lettres Persanes*. Paris: Garnier, 1963.

Morrison, Blake. "Suffolk through Death-Tinted Specs." *New Statesman* 11.507 (1998): 45–46.

Motion, Andrew. "After Nature and so on." *The Weekend Australian* June. 2002.

Muecke, Stephen. *No Road*. Fremantle: Fremantle Arts Centre Press, 1997.

Nabokov, Vladimir. *Lolita*. London: Weidenfeld and Nicolson, 1959.

———. *Speak, Memory*. 1967. London: Penguin, 1988.

Neubauer, Hans-Joachim. *Das Heilige Feld*. 2003. Rheinischer Merkur. Available: www.merkur.de/archiv/neu/rm_0351. Accessed 29 January 2004.

New Revised Standard Version Bible. Trans. Bruce M. Metzger et al. Glasgow: Collins, 1989.

Niehaus, Michael. "Without Support: The Role of the Institutional in the Work of W. G. Sebald." W. G. Sebald: Works & Influences. The Third Occasional Davidson Symposium on German Studies. Davidson College, North Carolina, 2003.

Nietzsche, Friedrich. *The Birth of Tragedy and the Genealogy of Morals*. 1872 & 1887. Trans. Francis Golffing. New York: Doubleday, 1956.

Novum Testamentum Graece. 2 vols. London: Alexander Macmillan for Clarendon Press, Oxford, 1863.

Ozick, Cynthia. "The Posthumous Sublime." *The New Republic* 215.25 (1996): 33–38.

Park, Ed. "The Precognitions." *The Village Voice* 47.41 (2002): 74–75.

Parks, Tim. "The Hunter." *The New York Review of Books* 47.10 (2000): 52.

Peake, Arthur S. Ed. *Peake's Commentary on the Bible*. London: Thomas Nelson, 1919.

Pensky, Max. *Melancholy Dialectics*. 1993. Amherst: University of Massachusetts Press, 2001.

Pettingell, Phoebe. "Old Masters of Suffering." *The New Leader* 85.4 (2002): 33.

Philips, Kevin. *Stares and Whispers*. 22 March 2003. Available: http://www.smh.com.au/cgi-bin/common/popupPrintArticle. pl?path=/articles/2003/03/21. Accessed 30 December 2003.

Plato. *The Collected Dialogues of Plato*. Trans. Lane Cooper et al. Ed. Edith Hamilton & Huntington Cairns. Princeton, New Jersey: Princeton University Press, 1973.

Poulet, Georges. "Criticism and the Experience of Interiority." *Reader-Response Criticism*. 1980. Ed. Jane P. Tompkins. Baltimore and London: The Johns Hopkins University Press, 1984.

Prince, Gerald. "Introduction to the Study of the Narratee." *Reader-Response Criticism*. 1980. Ed. Jane P. Tompkins. Baltimore and London: The Johns Hopkins University Press, 1984. 7–25.

Proust, Marcel. *A la recherche du temps perdu*. Ed. Pierre Clarac et André Ferré. Vol. III. Paris: Gallimard, 1954.

———. *Remembrance of Things Past*. 1913–1927. Trans. Andrea Mayor. Vol. 12 — *Time Regained*. London: Chatto and Windus, 1972.

Ray, Robert. "Mystery Trains." *Sight and Sound*. November 2000 (2000).

Riemer, Andrew. "On the Natural History of Destruction." *The Sydney Morning Herald*. 12 April 2003.

Rimbaud, Arthur. *Oeuvres de Rimbaud*. Paris: Editions Garnier Frères, 1960.

Roberson, Matthew. "The Rings of Saturn." *Review of Contemporary Fiction* 18.3 (1998): 241–42.

Robertson, Ritchie. "Introduction." *Kafka*. London: Haus Publishing, 2003.

Romer, Stephen. "Beyond Strangeways." *The Guardian*.

Roncevic, M. "Austerlitz." *Library Journal* 126.17 (2001): 110.

Ruskin, John. *Modern Painters*. 1873. Ed. David Barrie. London: André Deutsch, 1987.

Rutschky, Michael. *Das Geschenkte Vergessen — Besprechung aus der Frankfurter Rundschau*. 21 March 2003. Available: http://www.lyrikwelt. de/rezensionen/austerlitz-r.htm.

Sandywell, Barry, and Ian Heywood. *Interpreting Visual Culture: Explorations in the Hermeneutics of the Visual*. London and New York: Routledge, 1999.

Santner, Eric L. "Paratactic Composition in Hölderlin's 'Hälfte des Lebens.'" *German Quarterly* 58.2 (Spring 1985): 165–72.

Scammell, William. "In Pursuit of the Unspeakable." *The Spectator* 285.8981 (2000): 57.

Schlant, Ernestine. *The Language of Silence*. New York and London: Routledge, 1999.

Schlösser, Hermann. *Sebald: Logis in einem Landhaus*. 1998. Available: http://www.wienerzeitung.at/frameless/buch/buch.htm?ID=6573. Accessed 21 August 2003.

Schneider, Peter. "The Germans Are Breaking an Old Taboo." *New York Times* 18 January 2003: B.7.

Scholes, Robert. *The Crafty Reader*. New Haven and London: Yale University Press, 2001.

Schwarz, Robert. "Logis in Einem Landhaus." *World Literature Today* 73.3 (1999): 521.

Scott, Clive. *Remembering Max Remembering*. 2002. Available: http://www. appleonline.net/theaa/spiked10/max.htm. Accessed 19 May 2002.

———. *The Spoken Image: Photography and Language*. London: Reaktion, 1999.

Scott, Joanna. "Sebald Crawling." *Salmagundi* 135/136 (2002): 243 ff.

Scudieri, Magnolia. *Museum of San Marco*. Florence: Giunti, 1999.

Sebald, W. G. *After Nature*. Trans. Michael Hamburger. London: Hamish Hamilton, 2002.

———. *Die Ausgewanderten*. Frankfurt: Eichborn, 1993.

———. *Austerlitz*. Munich, Vienna: Carl Hanser Verlag, 2001 (2001a).

———. *Austerlitz*. Trans. Anthea Bell. London: Hamish Hamilton, 2001 (2001b).

———. *Die Beschreibung des Unglücks: Zur österreichischen Literatur von Stifter bis Handke*. Salzburg and Vienna: Residenz, 1985.

———. *Campo Santo*. Munich, Vienna: Hanser Verlag, 2003 (2003b).

———. *Campo Santo*. Trans. Anthea Bell. Ed. Sven Meyer. London: Hamish Hamilton, 2005.

———. *Carl Sternheim: Kritiker und Opfer der Wilhelmischen Ära*. Stuttgart: Kohlhammer, 1969.

———. *The Emigrants*. 1996. Trans. Michael Hulse. London: The Harvill Press, 1997.

———. *Logis in einem Landhaus*. Munich, Vienna: Hanser Verlag, 1998 (1998b).

———. *Luftkrieg und Literatur*. Munich, Vienna: Hanser Verlag, 1999 (1999b).

———. *Der Mythus der Zerstörung im Werk Alfred Döblins*. Stuttgart: Klett, 1980.

———. *Nach der Natur. Ein Elementargedicht*. Nördlingen: Greno, 1988.

———. *On the Natural History of Destruction*. Trans. Anthea Bell. New York: Random House, 2003 (2003a).

———, ed. *A Radical Stage: Theatre in Germany in the 1970s and 1980s*. Oxford, New York, Hamburg: Berg, 1988.

———. *Die Ringe des Saturn: Eine englische Wallfahrt*. Frankfurt: Eichborn, 1995.

———. *The Rings of Saturn*. Trans. Michael Hulse. London: The Harvill Press, 1998 (1998a).

———. *Schwindel. Gefühle*. Frankfurt: Eichborn, 1990.

———. *Unheimliche Heimat. Essays zur österreichischen Literatur*. Salzburg, Vienna: Residenz, 1991.

———. *Vertigo*. Trans. Michael Hulse. London: The Harvill Press, 1999 (1999a).

Sebald, W. G., and Tess Jaray. *For Years Now*. London: Hamish Hamilton, 2001.

Sebald, W. G., and Jan Peter Tripp. *Unerzählt*. Munich, Vienna: Hanser Verlag, 2003.

———. *Unrecounted*. London: Hamish Hamilton, 2004.

Seddon, Nicholas. "A World of Artifice." *The Tablet* (24 August 2002): 19–20.

Shakespeare, William. *Hamlet*. The Oxford Shakespeare. G. R. Hibbard ed. Oxford: Oxford University Press, 1994.

———. *King Lear*. The Arden Shakespeare. Ed. Richard Proudfoot. Kenneth Muir ed. London and New York: Routledge, 1990.

———. *Macbeth*. The Arden Shakespeare. Ed. Richard Proudfoot. Kenneth Muir ed. London: Methuen, 1987.

———. *Romeo and Juliet*. The Arden Shakespeare. Ed. Richard Proudfoot. Brian Gibbons ed. London and New York: Routledge, 1989.

———. *The Tempest*. The Oxford Shakespeare. Ed. Stanley Wells. 1987 ed. Oxford: Oxford University Press, 1998.

Sheldrake, Philip. *Spaces for the Sacred — Place, Memory and Identity*. The Hulsean Lectures 2000. London: SCM Press, 2001.

Sheppard, Richard. "Dexter-sinister." *Journal of European Studies*. 35(4): 419–63. London: Sage Publications. December 2005.

Sieburth, R. "Beggar at the Door (Reader's Response to Book-Review by Susan Sontag of W. G. Sebald's 'Vertigo')." *The Times Literary Supplement* (3 March 2000): 17.

Sill, Oliver. "Migration Als Gegenstand Der Literatur: W. G. Sebalds *Die Ausgewanderten*." *Nation, Ethnie, Minderheit: Beiträge Zur Aktualität Ethnischer Konflikte*. Ed. Armin Nassehi. Vienna: Böhlau, 1997.

Silman, Roberta. "In the Company of Ghosts." *New York Times Book Review* (1998): 5.

Silverblatt, Michael. *Bookworm*. 6 December 2001. KCRW FM. Archived recording. Available: http://kcrw.com/cgi-bin/db/kcrw.pl?show_code=bw&air_date=12/6/01&tmplt_type=show. Accessed 22 June 2002.

Simic, Charles. "Conspiracy of Silence." *The New York Review of Books*. 27 February 2003 (2003): 8–10.

Smith, A. "In Memory of W. G. Sebald." *Critical Quarterly* 44.2 (2002): 59–61.

Smith, Charles Saumarez. "Another Time, Another Place." *The Observer*. 30 September 2001.

Smith, William. *A Smaller Latin-English Dictionary*. 1855. Ed. J. F. Lockwood. Third ed. London: John Murray, 1968.

Sontag, Susan. "A Mind in Mourning." *The Times Literary Supplement* (25 February 2000): 3.

———. *On Photography*. London: Penguin Books, 1979.

———. *Where the Stress Falls*. 2002. London: Vintage, 2003.

Spender, Stephen. *World within World: The Autobiography of Stephen Spender*. 1951. London: Faber, 1991.

Spong, John Shelby. *Liberating the Gospels*. San Francisco: HarperCollins, 1996.

Spozio, Marianne. *Requiem Pour Un Passé Défunt*. 3 June 2003. Available: http://www.avoir-alire.com/spip/imprimersans.php3?id_article=2599. Accessed 17 March 2004.

Spurgeon, Caroline. *Shakespeare's Imagery: And What It Tells Us.* Cambridge: University Press, 1935.

Steegmuller, Francis, ed. *The Letters of Gustave Flaubert 1830–1857.* Cambridge, Massachusetts: The Belknap Press of Harvard University Press, 1981.

Steele, Peter. *Jonathan Swift: Preacher and Jester.* Oxford: Clarendon Press, 1978.

Stendhal. *Love.* 1822. Trans. Gilbert and Suzanne Sale. London: Penguin Books, 1975.

Sterne, Laurence. *The Life and Opinions of Tristram Shandy, Gentleman.* Ed. Graham Petrie. Harmondsworth: Penguin, 1967.

———. *A Sentimental Journey.* 1768. Oxford and New York: Oxford University Press, 1998.

Storr, Anthony. *Churchill's Black Dog.* 1989. Glasgow: William Collins Sons & Co, 1990.

Stow, R. "The Plangency of Ruins." *The Times Literary Supplement* (31 July 1998): 11.

Strawson, Galen. "'Elias' Alias Implausible: Galen Strawson Describes 'a Dangerously Available Source of Intensity.'" *Financial Times.* 6 October 2001: 04.

Summers-Bremner, Eluned. "Reading, Walking, Mourning: W. G. Sebald's Peripatetic Fictions." *Journal of Narrative Theory* 34.3 (2004) 304–34.

Swift, Jonathan. *Gulliver's Travels.* 1726. London: Oxford University Press, 1949.

Szabari, Antonia. "'Parler Seulement De Moy': The Disposition of the Subject in Montaigne's Essay 'De l'art de conférer.'" *MLN* 116.5 (2001): 1001–24.

Tabbart, Reinbert. "Max in Manchester." *Akzente-Zeitschrift Für Literatur* (February 2003): 21–30.

Tindall, Gillian. *Countries of the Mind.* Boston: Northeastern University Press, 1991.

———. "The Fortress of the Heart." *The Times Literary Supplement* (19 October 2001): 21.

Tonkin, Boyd. *Ghostly Trains of Thought.* 6 October 2001. Available: http://enjoyment.independent.co.uk/books/reviews/story.jsp?story= 97942. Accessed 30 December 2003.

Tucker, M. "The 'Emigrants.'" *Confrontation* 62–63 (1997): 369.

———. "Vertigo." *Confrontation* 72–73 (2001): 266–68.

Turner, Gordon. *Acceptance Speech.* [On behalf of Ute Sebald] 7 August 2002. Available: www.davidson.edu/academic/german/denham/Turner%20Independent.htm. Accessed 26 April 2003.

———. "Sebald in His Own Words." W. G. Sebald: Works & Influences. The Third Occasional Davidson Symposium on German Studies. Davidson College, North Carolina, 2003.

Van Oort, Richard. "The Use of Fiction in Literary and Generative Anthropology: An Interview with Wolfgang Iser." *Anthropoetics III.* No. 2. (Fall 1997/Winter 1998). www.anthropoetics.ucla.edu/ap0302/Iser_int.htm. Accessed 8 March 2006.

Veale, S. "After Nature." *New York Times Book Review* (2003): 20.

———. "The 'Rings of Saturn.'" *New York Times Book Review* (1999): 32.

Virgil. *Georgics 4.* Ed. J. L. Whiteley. 1956 ed. London: Macmillan & Co, 1967.

———. *Virgil Aeneid I.* Ed. John Jackson. Oxford: Clarendon Press, 1920.

Vollmann, Rolf. "Schwarzes Segel der Schwermut." *Die Zeit.* 19 December 2001: 36.

Voltaire. *Candide.* Ed. Lester G. Crocker. London: University of London Press, 1970.

Vourvoulias, Bill. "The Loss World." *The Village Voice* 42.2 (1997): 51, 53.

Wagenbach, Klaus. *Kafka.* 1964, 2002. Trans. Ewald Osers. London: Haus Publishing, 2003.

Walden, B. "On the Natural History of Destruction." *Library Journal* 128.1 (2003): 134.

Watt, Ian. *The Rise of the Novel: Studies in Defoe, Richardson and Fielding.* Pelican Book. Harmondsworth: Penguin, 1972.

Waugh, Patricia. *Metafiction: The Theory and Practice of Self-Conscious Fiction.* London: Routledge, 1988.

Weber, Markus R. "Bibliografie W. G. Sebald." *Text + Kritik* 158 (April 2003): 112–17.

Whitehead, Anne. *Trauma Fiction.* Edinburgh: Edinburgh University Press, 2004.

Williams, Arthur. "The Elusive First Person Plural: Real Absences in Reiner Kurze, Bernd-Dieter Hüge, and W. G. Sebald." *"Whose Story?" — Continuities in Contemporary German-Language Literature.* Ed. Arthur Williams. Bern: Peter Lang AG, 1998. 85–113.

———. "W. G. Sebald: A Holistic Approach to Borders, Texts and Perspectives." *German Language Literature Today: International and Popular?* Ed. Arthur Williams. Bern: Peter Lang AG, 2000: 99–118.

———. *W. G. Sebald. The Literary Encyclopedia.* 24 April 2002. The Literary Dictionary Company. 11 March 2006.

Wilson, Edmund. *The Triple Thinkers.* London: John Lehmann, 1952.

Winder, Robert. "The Unfortunate Traveller." *New Statesman* 16.745 (2003): 48–49.

Winston, Robert. "It's Right to Play God." *The Tablet* (31 January 2004): 14.

Wirtz, T. "Austerlitz." *Merkur-Deutsche Zeitschrift für Europäisches Denken* 55.6 (2001): 530–34.

Wolff, Larry. *"When Memory Speaks."* 30 March 1997. Available: http://www.nytimes.com/books/97/03/30/reviews/970330.30wolfft.html. Accessed 21 March 2004.

Wood, James. "An Interview with W. G. Sebald." *Brick* 69 [The 1997 interview originally published in 1998 and reissued with a tribute] (Spring 2002): 83–95.

———. "The Right Thread." *The New Republic* 219.1 (6 July 1998): 38–42.

———. "The Rings of Saturn." *The Guardian*. 30 May 1998.

Woodward, Christopher. *In Ruins*. 2001. London: Vintage, 2002.

Woolf, Virginia. *Mrs Dalloway*. London: The Hogarth Press, 1925.

Young, Robert, ed. *Untying the Text*. Boston & London: Routledge & Kegan Paul, 1981.

Zeeman, Michael (Interviewer) and Antoinette Grote Gansey (Director). *Kamer Met Uitzicht — Max Sebald, Peter Nadas*. Television program. 12 July 1998. VPRO, Holland, 1998.

Index